SYMBOLIC COMPUTATION

Managing Editors: J. Encarnação   P. Hayes

Computer Graphics
Editors: K. Bø   J.D. Foley   R. Guedj
J.W. ten Hagen   F.R.A. Hopgood   M. Hosaka
M. Lucas   A.G. Requicha

J. Encarnação   E.G. Schlechtendahl

Computer Aided Design

Fundamentals
and System Architectures

With 176 Figures
12 of them in Color

Springer-Verlag
Berlin Heidelberg New York Tokyo
1983

Prof. Dr. José Encarnação
Institut für Informationsverwaltung
und Interaktive Systeme
FB 20 – TH Darmstadt
Alexanderstraße 24
6100 Darmstadt

Dr. Ernst G. Schlechtendahl
Kernforschungszentrum Karlsruhe
Postfach 3640
7500 Karlsruhe

ISBN 3-540-11526-9
Springer-Verlag Berlin Heidelberg New York Tokyo
ISBN 0-387-11526-9
Springer-Verlag New York Heidelberg Berlin Tokyo

Library of Congress Cataloging in Publication Data.
Encarnação, José Luis.
Computer aided design.
(Symbolic computation. Computer graphics)
Includes bibliographies and indexes.
1. Engineering design – Data processing. I. Schlechtendahl, E.G. (Ernst G.), 1938–   .
II. Title. III. Series.
TA174.E47 1983   620′.00425′02854   83-528
ISBN 0-387-11526-9 (U.S.)

Typesetting, printing, binding: Universitätsdruckerei H. Stürtz AG, Würzburg

2145/3140-543210

Contents

1 Introduction

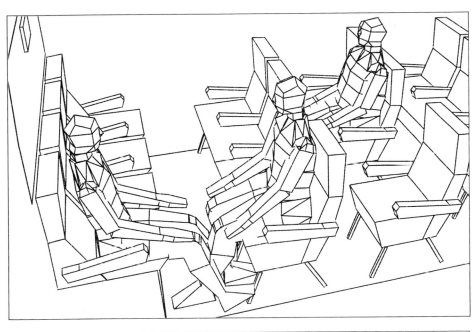

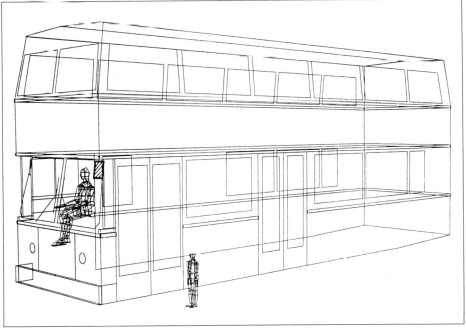

Vehicle design
(courtesy of Compeda Ltd., London, UK)

1.1 Purpose of This Book

The intention of this book is to describe principles, methods and tools that are common to computer applications for design tasks, independent of a particular product. It does not present cookbook recipes on how to select a commercially available CAD system for designing a particular product, or how to write a new CAD system for this purpose. When we consider CAD as a discipline lying somewhere between engineering and computer science, the tendency towards generalization inevitably leads us to emphasize the computer aspects. But the book is primarily for engineers who plan to work in CAD or who already do. They will recognize experiences they may have had, placed in a more general context. They should also find useful ideas which they can put into practice in their own environment. The book is also intended for students who want to give themselves a broader fundamental background in CAD.

1.2 Scope of CAD

The meaning of "computer-aided design" (CAD) has changed several times in its past twenty years or so of history. For some time, CAD was almost synonymous with finite element structural analysis. Later, the emphasis shifted to computer-aided drafting (most commercially available CAD systems are actually drafting systems). Handling smooth surfaces, as required in ship-building and the automobile industry, became another key issue. More recently, CAD has been associated with the design of three-dimensional objects, (this is typical in many branches of mechanical engineering). In this book, we consider CAD as a discipline that provides the required know-how in computer hardware and software, in systems analysis and in engineering methodology for specifying, designing, implementing, introducing and using computer based systems for design purposes.

Computer-aided design is often treated together with computer-aided manufacturing (CAM). We are not including CAM in this book, since CAM starts from data — preferably machine-readable data — that are produced in the design process, but CAM is not part of the design process itself. The same applies to computer-aided testing (CAT), computer-aided work planning (CAP), and computer-aided maintenance. Knowledge about the available manufacturing, testing, and maintenance capabilities certainly influences the design; but the methods applied in these other CA's are not the concern of this book.

Recently the term computer-aided engineering (CAE) has been used for summarizing all computer aids in design, while restricting CAD to computer-aided drafting. Here, however, we will continue to associate the term CAD with the wider meaning defined above.

Design is not only the more-or-less intuitively guided creation of new information by the designer. It also comprises analysis, presentation of results, simulation and optimization. These are essential constituents of the iterative process, leading to a feasible and, one hopes, optimal design.

1.3 Content of the Book

In Chapter 2 we present briefly the *history* of CAD. The main *components* of CAD systems are identified, and their principal functions described. Economical and interdisciplinary aspects are discussed.

Chapter 3 starts with a *systems analysis* of the *design process*. The notion of a process is introduced as a fundamental tool to describe activities like design as a whole, computer-aided design, program executions, terminal sessions etc. The *environment* and the *resources* which the environment must supply for the successful execution of any process are discussed. The problem of *modelling* the design objects in an abstract *schema* and the interrelation between the schema and the planning of the individual step in the design are analysed.

Chapter 4 concentrates on the *interfaces* among the components of a CAD system, including the human operator. The problem of *mapping* an abstract schema onto the capabilities of various programming, command, or data description languages is described in detail. Emphasis is laid upon the *resource* aspect and its influence on the design of CAD systems. The concept of a *CAD software machine* is introduced, and rules for designing such machines are given.

In Chapter 5 we deal with the most important computer science techniques and suitable types of software systems utilized in CAD. Specification techniques, data structures and *data base systems*, man-machine communication and *dialogue techniques*, *graphic kernels* and *system nuclei* are treated in some detail.

Chapter 6 presents selected engineering methods for CAD. Various numerical *analysis* methods (such as finite elements, simulation and optimization) are treated only to the extent that the reader may obtain select entry points into the extensive literature on these subjects. Not the methods themselves but rather their *embedding into CAD* lies within the scope of this book. Graphic techniques for *presentation* of numerical results are described in more detail.

Chapter 7 gives selected *examples* of CAD *applications* taken from industrial practice.

Chapter 8 summarizes the present *trends* in CAD, both with respect to computer hardware and software and with respect to the human and social aspects of CAD.

Color figures from all chapters are collected on pages 341 through 346.

1.4 Summary

The aim of this first chapter was to give the reader an impression of what he may expect to learn from this book. We have also explicitly indicated important areas which will not be covered at all, or will be touched on only briefly (computer-aided manufacturing or finite elements, for instance). Readers who prefer to study just one topic or another are invited to jump to the pertinent chapters immediately.

1.5 Acknowledgements

The authors gratefully acknowledge the support of their organizations, Technische Hochschule Darmstadt and Kernforschungszentrum Karlsruhe, which have made their facilities available for the preparation of this book. The laborious work of preparing the illustrations both manually and with computer aids was performed with great care by Frl. Stutz. We are much obliged to Mr. G. Becker who copy-edited the whole manuscript. Finally, we very much appreciate the ideal support we received from many experts in the field, both from Germany and other countries. Communication with them has been an invaluable help in collecting together the great variety of thoughts in the CAD world and presenting them here. We also wish to express our gratitude to our families, who had to spend many weekends without husband and father during the preparation of the manuscript.

1.6 List of Frequently-Used Abbreviations

AI	artificial intelligence
CAD	computer-aided design
CAE	computer-aided engineering
CAM	computer-aided manufacturing
CAP	computer-aided work planning
CAT	computer-aided testing
CODASYL	conference on data system languages
COM	computer output on microfilm or microfiche
DBMS	data base management system
DBTG	data base task group
DC	device coordinates
GKS	graphical kernel system
I/O	input and output
NDC	normalized device coordinates
2-D	two-dimensional
$2\frac{1}{2}$-D	two-and-a-half-dimensional
3-D	three-dimensional

2 History and Basic Components of CAD

Vehicle design
(courtesy of Versatec, Santa Clara, USA)

2.1 History

We will first give a brief review of the historical background of CAD. Knowledge about the history provides a better understanding of the present state of the art, and may even enhance the creativity of those planning to work in this field [1].

Up to 1978, this review is based on [2]. A more recent summary on the computer graphics part of the history of CAD is given in [3]. Early in the 1950s, the Servomechanisms Laboratory at the Massachusetts Institute of Technology (M.I.T.) developed the first automatically controlled milling machine using the Whirlwind computer [4]. This has led to the evolution of the Automatically Programmed Tool APT [5]. We note that computer-aided manufacturing is not a descendant of CAD, but has a distinct origin of its own. The step from APT to design programs including computer graphics functions was outlined by Coons [6]. Sutherland, one the first CAD pioneers, envisaged the designer sitting in front of a console using interactive graphics facilities developed at the Massachusetts Institute of Technology; he developed SKETCHPAD in 1963 [7]. The software principles of rubber band lines, circles of influence, magnification, rotation, and subframing were born in those days. In 1964, General Motors announced the DAC-1 (Design Augmented by Computer) system [8]. The hardware was built by IBM according to the specifications of General Motors Research Laboratories. DAC-1 was more concerned with producing hard-copies of drawings than with interactive graphical techniques. In 1965, Bell Telephone Laboratories announced the GRAPHIC 1 remote display system [9]. GRAPHIC 1 utilized a modified DEC 340 display and a PDP 5 control processor, connected to an IBM 7094. The system was used for geometrically arranging printed-circuit components and wirings, for the schematic design of circuits or block diagrams, for the composing and editing of text, and for the interactive placement of connective wiring. It was a very early implementation of the important idea of having the CAD processing power distributed among local interactive workstations and a central host computer.

In 1966, IBM Components Division described a system which was an aid to the design of hybrid integrated-circuit modules, as used in IBM's System 360 machines [10]. Freeman suggested, in 1967, an algorithm for the solution of hidden-line problems [11]. A system called GOLD was developed in 1972 at RCA for integrated circuit mask layout [12]. GOLD was implemented on a custom-made refresh display, driven by a small computer (Spectra 70/25) with a single disk, and was capable of interacting with a large time-shared computer. The first half of the '70s was a time of much enthusiasm among the early CAD scientists and system developers [13]. Much theoretical work was done, laying down the fundamentals of CAD as we know it today. The Integrated Civil Engineering System (ICES) was developed [14], followed by a number of systems [15] which implemented many principal ideas regarding a CAD methods base. The theory of finite elements and associated programs started a booming development [16]. At the same time, considerable research activity was going on in the area of hidden line/surface removal [17].

The University of Rochester started the Production Automation Project in 1972. As a result of this project, two geometric modelling systems PADL-1 and PADL-2 were developed [18].

In 1973, a Lockheed review demonstrated that computer graphics will not only be practicable in the design process, but also cost effective [19]. In 1975, Chasen from Lockheed Aircraft Corporation published an analysis of the financial benefits of computer graphics in CAD systems [20], and Eastman described a data base for CAD. As a specialty within CAD, computer-aided drafting began to appear. It soon had such an impact on the field that, more recently, the term CAD seems to have become associated with the drafting part of design alone, while CAE (computer-aided engineering) has been used to include the analysis and optimization aspects of design. In this book, however, CAD is considered as a supporting discipline for the whole design process, which includes synthesis, analysis, and evaluation. Hewlett-Packard announced in 1978 a microprocessor-based raster scan display terminal [21]. Several publications by General Motors [22] and Boeing [23] in 1978 confirmed the usefulness of CAD/CAM technology and described how to bridge the gap between CAD and CAM (computer-aided manufacturing). The late '70s may be characterized as the time of CAD's break-through from a scientific endeavor to an economically attractive and — in many areas — indispensible tool in industry. Governments became aware of this fact, provided fundings and initiated projects to promote the integration of CAD technology, particularly with respect to medium- and smaller-sized industries.

The beginning of the '80s sees CAD fully developed in the market place, and it is only a matter of time until CAD becomes a standard tool in all design offices, progressing in tandem with a steady adaptation of the work procedures there. Not only the industrial nations but also the developing countries are beginning to realize that CAD will be an essential constituent of practically all industrial enterprises in the near future [24].

2.2 Modules, Functions, Components

Computer-Aided Design (CAD) means the usage of computer hardware and software for the design of products that are needed by society [25]. Products, in the widest sense, are elements of some larger system: a transport system, a medical center, a state planning project, etc. CAD means the integration of computer science methods and engineering sciences in a computer-based system, providing a data base, a program library (sometimes called a program chain or methods bank), and a communication subsystem (Fig. 2.1). The program library contains both the modules used for the elementary system functions (data base, dialogue, data I/O, graphics) and the modules that represent the algorithms of the application area. Data I/O implies the functions of inputting data, performing tests to guarantee the integrity and consistency of the data in the base, and querying the data base for data. Some of these application

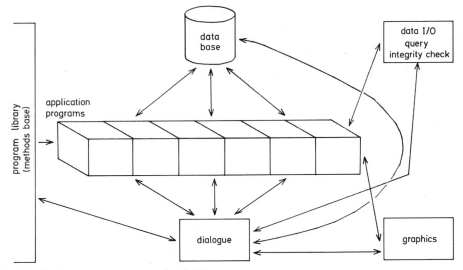

Fig. 2.1. The basic components of a CAD system

modules may be very large programs (for example, a module for finite elements). The communication subsystem includes modules for dialogue (commands addressed to the CAD system and messages returned to the designer), for input and output of data, and for graphical information processing.

The dialogue modules comprise the command language of the operating system to the extent that is required to set up the appropriate environment for its operation. The CAD system itself supports a special command language for dialogue with the user. The data acquisition, the integrity check and the query language are the modules for data I/O. The graphical I/O and the interactive graphic dialogue are processed in the graphical information processing module. It has become a generally accepted practice to distinguish between modelling functions and viewing functions. While modelling, the user is actually communicating with a part of the application program chain for the definition of the problem, its topology, its geometry, and other properties. For viewing, the user communicates with a set of functions for the display and manipulation of graphical data, independent of the particular application. Hence, viewing functions may be collected in an independent package, the "core" [26].

Fig. 2.2 illustrates the functional structure of a CAD system, with emphasis on the central role of the data base. From a system point of view, CAD systems can be classified in:

- Time-sharing.
  Several application programs are run on the same computer. They are independent from each other. The users only share the CPU usage.
- System-sharing.
  Several users work with one common application program using the same computer, the same data base, etc. The users share the CAD system resources.

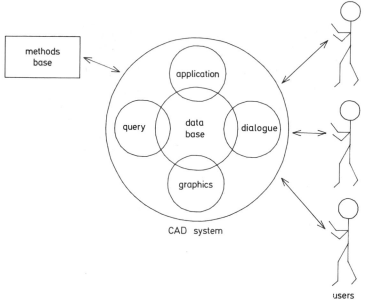

Fig. 2.2. The functional structure of a CAD system

From a hardware point of view there are two principal CAD system structures (Fig. 2.3, [27]):

– single programs; independent "stand-alone" systems;
– terminal systems linked to a host computer and its data base.

In addition, we find some special systems based on mini-computers. From a software point of view, one may distinguish between [28]:

– black-box (turn-key) systems with a predefined set of functions, generally operating only on specific hardware, with only limited capacity for being interfaced to other systems via data format conventions;
– freely programmable systems, usually transferable to a larger number of types of computers with a variety of terminals.

In CAD systems we find two types of languages: the command language and the programming language. The user uses the first one to control the system, while the second one is used to program the application modules. The programming language is in most cases FORTRAN. Some CAD systems (like ICES, IST, GENESYS, REGENT, DINAS; see Chapter 5.5.2) provide extensions of the normal programming languages [29]. These systems each have a nucleus to control the processing of the application programs, command interpretation, data handling, and the dynamic module loading. On the top of these nuclei, the systems support specialized tools enabling the CAD system developer to define new commands and new application modules.

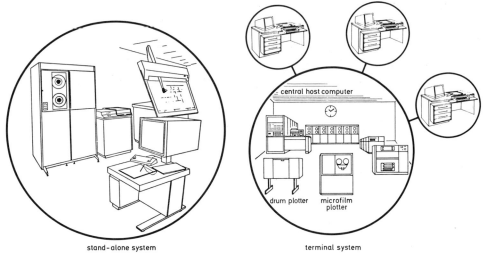

Fig. 2.3. Stand-alone and terminal systems

2.3 Interactive Graphic Interfaces

2.3.1 The Graphical Kernel System

Since interactive graphics is a prominent common feature of CAD systems, we will now deal with this aspect in more detail. As already mentioned, we generally distinguish between modelling and viewing.

1. Modelling.
   "Modelling" has a very broad and as yet ill-defined meaning. The term encompasses all sorts of problem domains and methodologies. It is used for defining three-dimensional solid objects, and for the construction of finite element meshes, as well as for more abstract modelling in simulation and optimization. In any case, the emphasis is on
   – definition of objects, their relations and their properties;
   – orientation within some suitable coordinate system chosen by the user;
   – particular application areas;
   – modules of the corresponding application program chain.
2. Viewing.
   The term "viewing" has a more generally applicable meaning. It is related to
   – the display of previously modelled objects
   – by mapping them onto a unified normalized coordinate system, and subsequently onto the display surface,
   – by means of standard functions of a graphic core system.

Modelling functions in different application areas will be discussed in more detail in Chapter 6. At this point, we will discuss viewing as provided, for instance, by the Graphical Kernel System GKS. GKS is the name for the graphics standard under development by the DIN-NI UA 5.9 and by the ISO TC97/SC5/WG2 Graphics [30]. The following brief introduction to GKS concepts is taken basically from ISO TC97/SC5/WG2 N117, the first official, international, functional description of GKS [31], as it evolved from earlier versions [32].

The Graphical Kernel System (GKS) provides a functional interface between an application program and a configuration of graphical input and output devices. The functional interface contains all the basic functions for interactive and non-interactive graphics on a wide variety of graphics equipment.

The interface is on such a level of abstraction that the hardware peculiarities are shielded from the application program. As a result, a simplified interface presenting uniform output primitives (POLYLINE, POLYMARKER, TEXT, FILL AREA, PIXEL ARRAY, GENERALIZED DRAWING PRIMITIVE) and uniform input classes (LOCATOR, VALUATOR, CHOICE, PICK, STRING) is obtained.

In [33, 34, 35] the concepts of basic output, input, and the organization of input and output sequences are outlined. A central issue both for structuring GKS and for realizing device independency is the so-called workstation concept [36]. A workstation is the addressee of all graphical output and the sender of all interactive input for an application program utilizing GKS. It is a parametric schema for practically all hardware facilities of today's graphical I/O devices. Facilities for picture manipulation and change are introduced via the segment facility, dynamic attributes, and transformations.

The concept of multiple workstations allows simultaneous output to and input from various display systems. Facilities for internal and external storage are provided by special workstations. Graphical information stored in these workstations may be copied or inserted into pictures produced for other workstations.

Not every GKS implementation has to support the full set of functions. Nine levels have been defined to meet the different requirements of graphics systems. These nine levels are defined by three orthogonal and upward compatible levels for both input and output. Any GKS implementation provides the functions of precisely one level.

GKS defines only the language-independent nucleus of a graphics system. For integration into a language, GKS must be embedded in a language-dependent layer providing the necessary language conventions (representation of data types, function names, calling sequences, etc.).

The layer model represented in Fig. 2.4 illustrates the role of GKS in a graphical system. Each layer may call upon the functions of the adjacent lower layers. In general the application program will utilize the application-oriented layer, the language-dependent layer, other application-dependent layers, and operating system resources. All workstation capabilities that can be addressed by GKS functions are used via GKS only.

The graphical output that is generated by GKS is built up from two groups

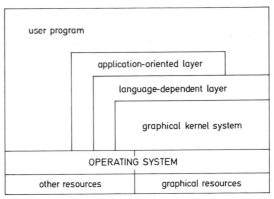

Fig. 2.4. Layer model of a graphical kernel system

of basic units of information called output primitives and primitive attributes. The output primitives are abstractions of the basic actions a device can perform, such as drawing lines and printing character strings. The attributes specify the visual appearance characteristics of the output primitives on a device, such as linestyle, color, or character size. Non-geometric attributes such as color and linestyle (but not character size) can be controlled individually in order for each workstation to make the best use of its hardware capabilities.

The graphical information consisting of input from a workstation as a result of operator actions is mapped by GKS onto five abstract classes of input (data types). One instance of such an input class is called a logical input device. The effect of input actions such as prompts and echoes on the display surface is controlled by GKS individually for each logical input device.

The two abstract concepts (abstract output and abstract input) are the building blocks of the workstation. A GKS workstation is a unit consisting of one display surfaces or none, and sometimes one or more input devices such as keyboard, tablet, and lightpen. The workstation presents these devices to the application program as a configuration of abstract devices thereby hiding the peculiarities of its hardware. The application program may (but does not need to) be aware of or take advantage of the actual hardware features associated with a workstation.

The geometrical information (coordinates) contained in output primitives, attributes, and logical input values (locators) can be subjected to transformations. These transformations perform mappings among three coordinate systems, namely:

a) World Coordinates (WC), used by the application programmer.
   Different world coordinate systems may be associated with different models.
   They need not have the same physical dimensions.
b) Normalized Device Coordinates (NDC).
   Normalized Device Coordinates define a unique coordinate system for graphical information in the span (0.,0.) to (1.,1.) of representable real numbers.

c) Device Coordinates (DC).
   One coordinate system for each workstation is based on the actual length
   dimensions of the display surface.

   Output primitives and attributes are mapped from WC to NDC by normalization transformations, from NDC to NDC by segment transformations (see
below), and from NDC to DC by workstation transformations. Locator input
is mapped from DC to NDC by an inverse workstation transformation, and
from NDC to WC by one of the inverse normalization transformations.
   Output primitives with their associated primitive attributes may be grouped
into segments. Segments are the units for manipulation and modification. Manipulation includes creation, deletion, copying and, insertion. Modification includes transforming a segment, making a segment visible or invisible, and high-
lighting a segment. Segments also form the basis for device independent storage
of pictures. Such storage capacity is provided by special workstations that have
neither input nor output facilities. Segments stored in this way can be manipulated, modified, and transferred to other workstations.
   The attributes which control the appearance of parts of the picture (output
primitives, segments, prompts and echoes of input devices) on the display surface
are organized in a uniform manner. Two groups of attributes apply to the
appearance of each output primitive. The first group called primitive attributes
is bound to the primitive upon creation. The primitive attributes include all
geometrical aspects, such as character size and spacing for text, and pattern
size for fill area. In addition, for each output primitive a representation is
selected by an index into a table of sets or "bundles" of attributes. The second
group of attributes is called workstation attributes. Upon creation of a primitive,
only an index defining an "attribute bundle" is bound to the primitive. This
index is an entry in a table — one for each workstation — that defines the
actual visual appearance (such as linetype, line-width scale factor, and color
index for polyline representation). Workstation attributes also specify the color
and pattern tables, and the control over the deferral of picture modification.
As the workstation attributes are bound at a later time, the application program
may actually modify them dynamically after having sent the picture to the
workstation (provided that the GKS level used and the particular workstation
support this feature).
   The appearance of segments is controlled by segment attributes, which
include segment transformation, visibility, highlighting, and detectability. These
may also be reset dynamically. Segment attributes can be a basis for feedback
during manipulations (such as highlighting).
   The attributes which control the operation of logical input devices can be
specified either upon initialization or as part of the input device setting, depending upon the attributes. Through initialization, an initial value, a prompt/echo
technique, and an area on the screen for echoing can be specified. A data
record may further provide device specific attributes. Through input device
setting, the operating mode may be selected and the echo may be switched
on or off. The operation modes of logical input devices specify who has the
initiative (operator or application program): SAMPLE input is acquired directly

by the application program; REQUEST input is produced by the operator in direct response to the application program; EVENT input is generated asynchronously by the operator and is collected in a queue for the application program.

At running time, GKS can be in any one of five different operating states. In Chapter 3.2.4. we will discuss the ideas upon which the stringent operating state concept is based, in greater detail. Associated with each state is a set of GKS functions allowed in this state, and a set of state variables called the state list. The operating state concept and the state variables allow for the formal specification of initializations (for example, at OPEN WORKSTATION) and the proper definition of the effect of various functions in a way that is independent from the hardware of the graphical devices, the operating system environment, and the programming language. A special set of inquiry functions is available to the application program for retrieving information from the GKS state lists. Upon occurrence of an error, GKS is put into the error state, in which the application program may inspect the GKS state to determine the possible cause of the error and take corrective action. When a new error develops during such inquiries, an error code is returned to the application program. This technique is able to handle errors arising in the error state properly. A subset of the inquiry functions permits access to formal descriptions of the capabilities of the individual workstations, to allow the application program to adapt its behavior accordingly.

GKS provides an interface to a system for filing graphical information for the purpose of external-long term storage and exchange with other computer installations supporting GKS. The interface consists of a GKS metafile workstation. A metafile output workstation produces a sequential file whose records reflect all the information that was directed to this workstation. In addition to the graphical output, the application program may imbed its own records with non graphical information in this file. Metafiles may be read from a metafile input workstation. The application program will treat the non-graphical records by itself, while it will pass the graphical records to GKS for interpretation. Thus, writing and reading a metafile will have the same effect as invoking the corresponding sequence of GKS functions directly from the application program.

2.3.2 The Graphical Dialogue System

An especially important aspect of interactive CAD systems is the implementation of an appropriate dialogue interface. In just the same way as it is possible to define a common set of graphical functions for viewing independently from their many different applications, it is also possible to establish a generally applicable core of dialogue capabilities. When discussing graphical dialogue systems in a CAD environment we usually distinguish between two classes of users: the author (system designer) and the operator. The latter handles his application problem in a dialogue process. He should be able to formulate his problem suitably for the system and to invoke solution methods as easily as possible. He should also be given guidance and advice by the system in a way which adjusts itself to his level of expertise. Only for simple problems, he should also be able to define and add new application functions to the system in an interactive way.

The task of the author is the design and implementation of problem-specific functions on top of the application-independent core of a dialogue system. In the end, the dialogue will exhibit all the necessary language constructs of the particular application, while still obeying the underlying rules of the dialogue kernel, its structure, interfaces, and concepts.

Generation of graphical dialogue-systems is best based on the existence of a graphical core system (such as the graphical kernel system GKS), which provides a standardized functional interface. As a tool for all problem-independent uses, GKS provides a good basis but is itself not suitable for immediate use as a dialogue system. On top of GKS, it is advisable to provide an envelope of standard dialogue functions, which may more easily be tailored for special problems.

GKS provides basic output and input functions. The data flow to output devices is controlled by the program which calls the respective GKS output functions. The GKS input functions are based on logical input devices. They perform primitive interactions with the operator by accepting input and generating echoes which — to some extent — can be controlled by the application program. However, there is no direct link from the input functions to the output functions. Whenever the application program wants to output information which was input by the operator, it has to accept the input via the GKS input functions, interpret it, and call upon the appropriate GKS output functions.

The only meaning of the operator's input on the functional level of GKS is related to the GKS input data types PICK, LOCATOR, VALUATOR, CHOICE, or KEYBOARD(STRING). The dialogue system must interpret these input data and attach to them a semantic meaning on the level of the application program by invoking appropriate application procedures. In addition, the dialogue system must pass messages from the application program to the operator as a sort of semantic echo to the input. GKS itself can provide echoes only on its own level, which in the light of the application may be understood as syntactical echoes.

A typical dialogue system is the command interpreter (KI) proposed by Borufka and Pfaff in [37]. Its main functions are to interpret the user commands and to initiate the execution of the corresponding application modules. Such a command interpreter should support the following tasks [39]:

- when a sequence of commands is to be executed with the same data, repeated input of these data should be avoided. This requirement implies that problems of storage, management and transfer of data have to be dealt with in the KI;
- on the other hand, when the same command or sequence of commands is to executed for different sets of data, repetition of the command input is to be avoided;
- information entered by the operator should be echoed immediately for even-

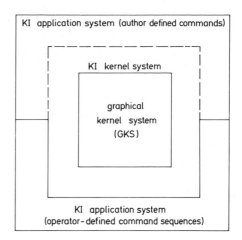

Fig. 2.5. Structure of a general purpose
dialogue system

tual correction. This requirement applies to both the syntactical echo via GKS (for instance, showing the actual state of the input device tracking ball as a system echo) and to the semantical echo. The production of a meaningful semantical echo may involve a considerable amount of processing, and imposes the necessity for efficient implementation techniques; operator guidance, help functions, and error messages should be adjustable to the level of expertise of the operator;
– it should be possible for the author to extend the system in a relatively simple way by adding new functions, while still remaining in the framework set forth by the dialogue core KI.

The command interpreter KI performs these functions. It is a dialogue module built on top of GKS (see Fig. 2.5). KI provides facilities for interpreting three types of operator commands:

– built-in commands of the KI kernel, which are predefined in every KI application;
– commands which were defined by the author of the CAD system when he embedded the KI dialogue module within his new application program;
– commands which are defined by the operator himself during an application session.

Using this KI system concept, the operator has the possibilities of:

– calling upon graphical and non-graphical functions by invoking KI commands;
– entering data for a previously activated command in a dialogue process (prompting);
– interactively defining macro-commands on the basis of a frequently-used sequence of previously defined commands.

The author has the possibility to define new commands in a batch process and link them to the system. The independence of functions from input and output devices is a characteristic which the KI system has inherited from GKS. Its kernel functions support a wide range of applications.

2.4 Data Bases for CAD

The use of large integrated data bases in the commercial world has been by now fully established. The need for similar data integration in engineering applications such as CAD/CAM systems has been recognized [39]. The question arises of whether data base management systems designed for commercial users can be incorporated in industrial systems, or whether some modifications are necessary. This problem has been given some attention in the past. Williams [40] has shown how design data (of graphical and non-graphical nature) can be stored using relational data description. Our contention is that to answer the above question three factors must be closely looked at: the structure and type of the information to be stored, the manipulation to be performed with this structure (the usage) and users themselves. We shall now analyze these three factors and derive some requirements for data management systems for CAD/CAM systems [41].

The advantages of having centralized control over data are [42]:

- application programmers can be relieved from all standard data management tasks;
- standards can be enforced more easily;
- performance aspects can be shifted away from the application programmer;
- the amount of data redundancy can be reduced;
- problems of inconsistency can be reduced;
- stored data can be shared;
- data integrity can be maintained;
- security restriction can be enforced.

Intuitively real world entities — and their graphical representations — can be modelled in terms of facts about things and or relationships between things [43] (see Fig. 2.6). For a more formal representation, the following concepts have been introduced [44]:

- an entity is anything that can be described by properties, some of which uniquely identify the entity;
- a property is an association of an attribute with an attribute value;
- an attribute is any characteristic (such as length or color) to which a value can be assigned;
- an attribute value is the state of an attribute.

By way of an illustration, let us look ahead to Fig. 3.24. This figure may be seen as representing three entities: a hammer, its shaft, and its head. The

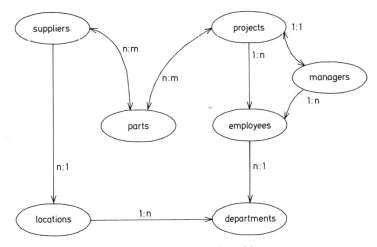

Fig. 2.6. Representation of facts and relationships in the real world

latter two entities each have a number of dimensional properties and one unique identifying property: the names "HEAD" or "SHAFT". The hammer seems not to have any properties at all, not even an identification. However, we can easily associate with it the identifying property "the only hammer on this figure". Implicitly, the figure shows the relation between these entities: the hammer "is assembled from" the two other parts. We note that this relation itself has an associated property: the only dimension in the assembly drawing whose value is 5 mm.

Information may be represented in terms of entities and relationships between them. Schematically, the entities can be represented by entity types. An entity type represents a set of entities having common attributes. Relationships between entities may be of type 1 to 1, 1 to many, many to 1, or many to many (Fig. 2.6).

The abstract information structure must somehow be modelled into the computer. Three fundamental models have been developed for commercial information modelling: hierarchical (as in IMS) [45], network [46] and relational [47]. Now some questions arise: Can the objects of engineering world be suitably modelled in terms of these models? If so, can one manipulate the resulting data structure in a simple way? Is it necessary to associate attributes with the relationships as well as with the entities? Is the representation of objects and relations in the form of data sufficiently powerful or do we need to include functions (algorithms) as entities or attributes? And finally, do CAD data bases require different performance considerations from data bases for commercial applications?

These questions have not yet been adequately answered. Several different approaches have been taken: the use of commercially available data base systems, the development of special CAD data base systems [48, 49], or the integration of data base management techniques with interactive graphical dialogue functions [50]. We will now discuss some of the more relevant aspects.

Many CAD systems handle pictures of three-dimensional solid objects. Conceptually, a solid can be visualized as an information hierarchy. A solid is assembled from parts; parts are defined by their faces; faces are bounded by edges between nodes. The relationship among these is obviously many to many. A simple example is an edge between two nodes that belongs to several faces. Other examples of many-to-many relationships might involve the same type of furniture situated in several rooms or, in modelling electrical circuits, a single component type (subcircuit) belonging to more than one circuit.

A predefined and fixed hierarchical structure is usually inadequate in design databases. Imagine a description of a ship in which compartments may be divided into smaller compartments [51]. Similar situations may be found in modelling electrical circuits built from more elementary ones, or in the field of building design, where rooms are divided by walls into smaller rooms. Even a simple curve may be constructed from several curve segments. In all of these instances an object of a certain type may be composed of other objects of the same type. Thus the possibility of defining homogeneous or recursive structures should be provided by the data model of CAD data bases.

In design, data usually cannot be adequately represented by a simple tree structure. Rather the information can be better modelled in the form of a network structure: this is because entities can have more than one functional property. For example, the pieces of a mechanical structure do not only provide strength, but may serve as heat sources or sinks as well; compartments can be associated with their surrounding surfaces [51]. Another example is the data structure for geometric modelling as given by Lillehagen [52] in Fig. 2.7.

The primary purpose of structuring the information in a certain way is to speed up processing of certain classes of operations (sometimes at the expense of slowing down other classes of operations). Hence, it is important to realize what kind of data management operations will most frequently be invoked by the the application algorithms. Some of the representative operations in applications related to graphics are:

- traversing an arbitrary number of levels in a hierarchical structure. This is needed for displaying pictures with an increasing level of detail;
- traversing hierarchical structures from bottom to top: as when searching for lines, planes, or objects which have a common set of points;
- traversing through an arbitrary number of intermediate levels to hide unnecessary details of structure from the user. This may result from a user's request to display, for instance, the furniture situated in each room of a building without displaying the intermediate building structure (which is immaterial to him at the moment);
- processing of a homogeneous structure, for example on a request to display all the compartments of a ship within a particular compartment. Since a compartment's position is relative with respect to the compartment containing it, the order of processing is important. An electrical circuit example would

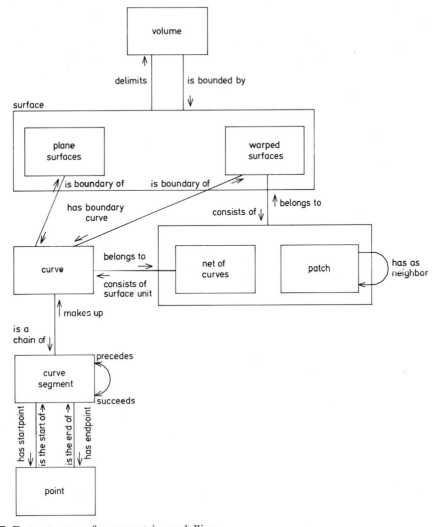

Fig. 2.7. Data structure for geometric modelling

be the task of displaying all gates (subcircuits) contained within a particular subcircuit;
– processing of a network structure. Again taking an example from the ship design, this might result from a request to display all the compartments which contain a particular piece of equipment.

Bandurski [51] analyzed some implementations in terms of DBTG and relational models and found that the programmer had to compose cumbersome algorithms to perform simple operations. Similar criticism was formulated in [50].

As mentioned before, we always have to consider two distinct kinds of persons involved in CAD systems: the application programmer (author) and the designer (the operator or the end user). The application programmer is most probably someone we can expect to have a certain level of abstraction capability, mathematical sophistication and familiarity with algorithms. He is probably capable of learning to navigate through complicated data structures, though he should avoid this activity as secondary to his task. His emphasis is more on the algorithmic processing of data, as perhaps opposed to commercial data processing, where only relatively simple processing takes place once the data have been located.

The engineer (designer) is involved in a creative process and tends to pose a large number of queries to the DBMS, any one of them rather infrequently. The user often requires various complex functions (such as the elimination of hidden lines) which demand fast access to a large number of interrelated data items. People of various skill are often involved in a design process. For instance, in building design, architects, draftsmen, mechanical engineers, electrical engineers, accountants and others are involved. Each group is interested only in information relevant to their work. Thus the DBMS must allow each user to define his personal view of the data, hiding all unnecessary detail from him.

Graphics systems are used in a number of applications. Here we shall focus on computer assisted interactive design environment. Design is a creative process. It differs from a process which merely extracts information by questioning from some data base, although it does involve querying the data base to a great extent. However, in contrast to most commercial applications, the number of different queries tends to be large, the number of items retrieved by a single query generally being small. The rate of modifications to the data base is very high, as the designer wants to construct interactively a data model representing his design in more and more detail as the design proceeds [53]. He wants to make use of standard components, or previously designed components. The programs processing retrieved data are usually complex. The designer works interactively at a terminal, and expects results to appear "instantly".

Ciampi and Nash [54] have pointed out that four types of data exist in a CAD data base. They studied circuit design in detail, but their findings apply to other CAD areas as well. In terms of circuit development, the different types of data in the data base are:

- data which constitue a primary circuit description as entered, say, at an interactive terminal by means of a light pen;
- data derived from the primary input — such as a printed circuit board diagram — which may be called a secondary circuit description;
- other data which are not a circuit description, such as manufacturing data.

The authors pointed out that derived data are generally not found in commercial data bases, where no other input data description exists but the primary type. The secondary (or derived) data create update consistency problems. If the primary data are changed, the secondary data must be invalidated. The programs that generated it must be rerun. Updates of the secondary description should not be allowed. It should be possible to prevent selective updating, and to define consistency rules to invalidate all derived data if the primary data have been changed. Problems of data dependency, which arise from storing derived data together with primary data, and their influence upon system architecture will be discussed in Chapters 3.3.5 and 4.2.1.

The problem of specifying data base requirements for CAD systems can be reduced to the following topics:

- what are the entities to be stored?
- what are the relationships between the entities?
- how can this information structure be modelled in terms of some data model?
- what are the operations to be performed on the data structure?
- are the resulting algorithms simple enough?
- who are the potential users?
- in what environment should the DBMS be embedded?
- how frequent will the different data management operations be?

Although it is significantly easier to pose these questions than to answer them, modelling of design objects for CAD system data bases cannot be achieved efficiently without their thorough consideration. We have briefly looked at these items from the point of view of engineering applications, and identified some requirements. We will return to some of these questions later (in Chapter 3.3) with emphasis on different aspects.

As a result of all these considerations, a DBMS for CAD applications should support the following features:

- relationships of type many to many;
- more flexibility than just fixed hierarchical structures;
- processing to start at any node, not necessarily at the root node;
- processing of the hierarchy from leaves to root (bottom up);
- modelling and processing of homogeneous or recursive structures;
- traversing from one level to another through an arbitrary number of intermediate levels;
- diverse users' views of data;
- logical data independency;
- a practical solution to the problem of data redundancy and data dependency;
- hiding of access paths from the user;
- hiding of performance aspects from the user (while still making it evident that complicated retrieval problems require greater expenditures of time and money).

2.5 Economical Aspects of CAD

Before introducing interactive CAD systems into any kind of R&D or production environment an economic justification is needed. We have to consider the following facts:

- A designer is only a few (2-4) hours a day concerned with interactive graphic work for a few (2-4) hours a day. As a result the system has to be used by several designers. The question is: how many?

Table 2.1. A sample for a profit analysis for CAD activities in an aeronautics industrial environment

Basic values	
Delay factor (hand washing, information gathering)	20%
Daily display usage	8 hours
Readiness demanded	90 %
Today's design price per hour	52.— DM
Reduction factor	5
Assumptions	
Number of designers today	48 persons
Percentage of draft work today	30%
Results	
Break-even point by number of displays (workstations)	4
Number of designers	27
Number of displays (workstations) needed	6
Daily work / display / man	0.67 h
Display (workstation) usage	68%
Production increase	40%
Operating time reduction	24%
Profit for each display (workstation) in DM/hour	170.— DM/h
Total gain/month	163.10 DM

– We must minimize the time a designer has to wait until the system (display) is available to him. The probability according to which a designer can find the system (display) available when he needs it is called the *readiness factor*.

If Z is the amount of daily design (drawing) time spent by each designer before the introduction of interactive computer graphics, and B is the daily time with interactive computer graphics, then $R = Z/B$ is the *reduction factor*. Westermann provides the Table 2.1 as a sample profit analysis based on these considerations [55].

Warman describes a more general method for cost justification of CAD systems in the USA [56]; Table 2.2 is an example. This example applies to a CAD system with four terminals, operated in two shifts. Installation costs are $430,000. The work of 32 draftsmen working without a CAD system may be done by 8 draftsmen with the CAD system in the same amount of time. Using these data, Warman finds a cost recovery time of only 1.1 years. Such calculations are performed in several steps, as shown in Fig. 2.8. Starting from a general schema for the economic evaluation of CAD systems, a special model is defined by applying the circumstances of a particular situation. Actual CAD system parameters are then introduced to obtain cost/performance results. It is vitally important that the analysis and evaluation should not only consider the design process itself, but also the consequences of using CAD for the minimization of costs in such areas as material savings, improved job planning, greater efficiency of experimental investigations, enhanced potential for product validation, shorter lead time, improved product quality, etc.

Table 2.2. Example of CAD cost justification in USA

Capital outlay (all monetary figures in US Dollars)		
Equipment	400,000	
Installation	30,000	
		430,000
Operating benefit		
4 terminals × 2 shifts × 3 drafts-men		
saved		
at $27.000 p.a. each		648,000
Less operation costs		
maintenance	48,000	
supervision	16,500	
power	10,000	
consumables	5,000	
	79,500	
Less depreciation (over 10 years)	43,000	
	122,500	

The first year *cash benefit* is calculated using the following assumption on efficiency of utilization:
    25 % for the first 3 months
    75 % for the next 3 months
    95 % after 6 months
This approximates 75 % for the whole first year

The first year benefit is therefore		486,000
Net cash benefit in the first year		
operating costs	− 79,500	406,500
depreciation	− 43,000	363,500
Net cash benefit in remaining years		648,000
operating costs	− 79.500	568.500
depreciation	− 43.000	525.500

Several other authors have investigated and proposed methods for the economic evaluation of CAD systems similar to those of Westermann [55] and Warman [56, 57], see, for instance, [58, 59, 60]. According to Chasen, we should distinguish between [61]:

direct cost benefits: cost reduction;
                            improved productivity ratio;

indirect cost benefits: increase of product quality;
                            shorter project development time;
                            better interfacing of programs;
                            better design;
                            rapid elimination of impractical approaches;
                            manpower augmentation.

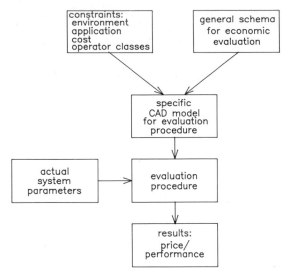

Fig. 2.8. The economic evaluation of CAD systems

The evaluation procedure proposed by Chasen is as follows:

1. $PR = \text{Productivity Ratio} = \dfrac{H_1 - H_2}{H_3}$

   H_1 = manhours prior to the introduction of CAD
   H_2 = manhours unaffected by CAD
   H_3 = manhours at the console

2. $CR = \text{Cost Reduction} = K + (H_1 - H_2)R_m - H_3 R_c - H_3 R_m$

   $$\frac{CR}{H_3 R_m} = \frac{K}{H_3 R_m} + \frac{H_1 - H_2}{H_3} + \frac{R_m + R_c}{R_m}$$

   R_m = average personnel cost (per hour)
   R_c = console rate (cost per hour)
   K = estimated indirect benefits (for worst-case evaluation, $K = 0$)

Equations (1) and (2), together with existing constraints, may be used as a basis for decision in introducing CAD to a company. Typical constraints imposed by the market and company policy are:

– allowable level of investment;
– priorities;
– organizational form;
– previous experience;
– competition;
– innovation pressure.

Table 2.3. Elements of the design process (from a CAD example in an aeronautics company) [55]

Drawing	25%
Information gathering	53%
Computation	2%
Other	20%

Utilizing the quantifiable decision aids of the cost-benefit analysis, management can come up with relatively reliable answers to these questions:

– How does has the economic situation of the company influence the decision?
– Where should CAD be mainly introduced?
– What will be the organizational consequences of introducing CAD?

As a further decision aid, it is helpful to know in what design areas CAD
is already being used to a significant extent. Grunau reports the following classes
of typical CAD applications in the USA [26]:

– electric circuit design and production (75% of the CAD installations in the
  USA);
– mapping (geometrical/graphical data processing; 5% of the CAD installations
  in the USA);
– construction of mechanical parts (20% of the CAD installations in the USA).

These applications demand not only a very high degree of interaction, of
data precision and of picture manipulation capabilities, but also the storage
of non-graphical data together with graphical data in one data base. In all
of these applications the design process includes as basic activities drawing,
information gathering, computations, and other tasks. The relative percentages
of these activities, taken from applications in an aeronautics company, are
shown in Table 2.3.

For drawing, values range from as low as 20% (for updates) to as high
as 40% (for new designs). 20% of the time — almost half of the time used
for information gathering (53% of all activities) — is accounted for by the
"info-walks" (absence from the place of work). The percentage for computation
depends very much on the application and the company.

Computation, although accounting for only a small percentage of the designers' activities, is the first area where computers have contributed significantly
to the design work. This is due to the fact that computational activities lend
themselves particularly well to the use of computers. The small percentage
should not mislead anyone to the conclusion that it will contribute no more
to the potential economic savings. Better computational capabilities (as provided
for instance by finite element structural analysis or optimization methods) can
drastically reduce the cost of production, thus resulting in an overall profit
despite the increased expense during design. Such effects are much more difficult
to evaluate than the benefits of introducing a mere drafting system.

2.6 Interdisciplinary Aspects of CAD

A basic characteristic of larger CAD systems is the diversity of the computer science and engineering science methods used in their implementation:

- design methodology;
- computational methods (for design, analysis and, optimization);
- data sorting and searching;
- interactive graphics;
- information handling and retrieval;
- numerous application-oriented algorithms.

Furthermore we have to consider at least three kinds of qualifications for various people concerned with the design, implementation and use of CAD systems:

- computer science specialists (both hardware and software):
  qualified to develop the fundamental methods, tools, and equipment of CAD systems;
- application programmers:
  highly qualified in the design methodology and algorithms of an application area and capable of composing problem-oriented or product-oriented CAD systems from the basic components;
- designers:
  highly qualified in their design work, and sufficiently well trained in utilizing the CAD systems' capabilities.

One of the most important aims for the coming years in this area will be to find widely accepted methods and concepts, and a common terminology. Then the effective education and training of CAD specialists will be possible in tall three of these domains.

2.7 Summary

CAD was defined as the creation, analysis and documentation of physical components, structures, or facilities. The concept and the precise form of the title CAD is due to the work of Coons early in 1958. CAD is firmly and profitably established in aerospace, ship design, chemical engineering, nuclear engineering, and electronics; in mechanical engineering, profitable applications have been mainly in the area of analysis, with a very rapid increase in the applications of Computer Aided Drafting.

The high percentage values for drawing and information gathering activities in design work indicate not only that there is a great need for interactive computer graphics in design, but also that CAD systems should be designed as information systems with adequate support for information retrieval. On the other hand, using computer-based methods for the computational part of the design process (which accounts for a small percentage only of the work) is more likely to increase than to decrease the cost of design, but with the potential of a respectable increase in overall production profits.

2.8 Bibliography

[1] J.J. Allan III: Foundations of the Many Manifestations of Computer Augmented Design. In: J. Vlietstra, R.F. Wielinga (eds.): Computer-Aided Design. Amsterdam (1973) North-Holland Publ. Co.

[2] I.D. Benest: A Review of Computer Graphics Publications. Computers & Graphics 4 (1979), pp. 95–136.

[3] S.H. Chasen: Historical Highlights of Interactive Computer Graphics. Mechanical Engineering 103 (1981) 11, pp. 32–41.

[4] W. Pease: An Automatic Machine Tool. Scientific American 187 (1952) 3, pp. 101–115.

[5] S. Brown, C. Drayton, B. Mittman: A Description of the APT-Language. CACM 6 (1963) 11, pp. 649–658.

[6] S. Coons: An Outline of the Requirements for a Computer-Aided Design System. AFIPS, SJCC 23 (1963), pp. 299–304.

[7] I. Sutherland: SKETCHPAD: A Man-Machine Graphical Communication System. AFIPS, SJCC 23 (1963), pp. 329–346.

[8] E. Jacks: A Laboratory for the Study of Man-Machine Communication. AFIPS, FJCC 26, Part 1 (1964), pp. 343–350.

[9] W. Ninke: GRAPHIC 1 — A Remote Graphical Display Console System. AFIPS, FJCC 22, Part 1 (1965), pp. 839–846.

[10] J. Koford, P. Strickland, G. Sporzynski, E. Hubacher: Using Graphic Data Processing System to Design Artwork for Manufacturing Hybrid Integrated Circuits. AFIPS, FJCC 29 (1966), pp. 229–246.

[11] H. Freeman: An Algorithm for the Solution of the Two-Dimensional "Hidden-Line" Problem. IEEE Trans. Electr. Comput. EC 16 (1967), 6, pp. 748–790.

[12] L.French, A.Teger: GOLD — A Graphical On-Line Design System. AFIPS, SJCC 40 (1970), pp. 461–470.

[13] U.Claussen: Konstruieren mit Rechnern. Konstruktionsbücher Band 29. Heidelberg (1971) Springer-Verlag.

[14] D.T. Ross: ICES System Design, Cambridge (1976) MIT Press.

[15] E.G. Schlechtendahl: Comparison of Integrated Systems for CAD, Int. Conf. Computer Aided Design, IEE Conf. Publ. 111, Southampton (1974), pp. 111–116.

[16] W. Pilkey, K. Saczalski, H. Schaeffer: Structural Mechanics Computer Programs, Surveys, Assessments, and Availability. Charlottesville (1974) Univ. Virginia Press.

[17] J. Encarnação, W. Giloi: PRADIS — An Advanced Programming System for 3D-Display. AFIPS, SJCC 40 (1972), pp. 985–998.

[18] A.A.G. Requicha, H.B. Voelcker: Solid Modeling: A Historical Summary and Contemporary Assessment. IEEE Computer Graphics and Applications 2 (1982) 2, pp. 9–24.

[19] R. Notestine: Graphics and Computer-Aided Design in Aerospace. AFIPS 42 (1973), pp. 629–633.

[20] S.H. Chasen: Economic Principles for Interactive Graphic Applications. AFIPS 44 (1973), pp. 613–620.

[21] P. Dickinson: Versatile Low-Cost Graphics Terminal 13 Designed for Each of Use. Hewlett-Packard J. (Jan. 1978), pp. 2–6.

[22] T. Reno: General Motors Network Station a Low Cost Graphics System for Body Tooling. AFIPS 47 (1978), pp. 337–341.

[23] B. Inman: The Boeing Electronic Computer Aided Design System. AFIPS 47 (1978), pp. 353–355.

[24] J. Encarnação, O. Torres, E. Warman (eds.): CAD/CAM as a Basis for the Development of Technology in Developing Nations. Amsterdam (1981) North-Holland Publ. Co.

[25] Diebold Deutschland GmbH: Rechnerunterstütztes Entwickeln und Konstruieren in den USA. Report KFK-CAD 7. Kernforschungszentrum Karlsruhe (1976).

[26] J. Encarnação: Interactive Computer Graphics — The Rich and Dynamic Man-Machine Environment. In: P.A. Samet (ed.): Proc EURO IFIP 79, London, 25–28 Sept. 1979. Amsterdam (1979) North-Holland Publ. Co., pp. 521–529.

[27] G. Nees: Struktur und Organisationsformen von CAD-Systemen aus der bisherigen Praxis. In: J. Encarnação (ed.): Proc. CAD-Fachgespräch bei der GI-Jahrestagung 1978, Berlin. Report GRIS 78-3. Darmstadt (1978) TH Darmstadt, FB Informatik, FG Graphisch-Interaktive Systeme.

[28] G. Spur, F.-L. Krause: Aufbau und Einordnung von CAD-Systemen. VDI-Berichte 413 (1981), pp. 1–18.

[29] J. Encarnação, E.G. Schlechtendahl: Konzepte, Probleme und Möglichkeiten von CAD-Systemen in der industriellen Praxis. Informatik Fachberichte 16. Heidelberg (1978) Springer-Verlag, pp. 308–325.

[30] G. Enderle, K. Kansy, G. Pfaff, F.-J. Prester: Die Funktionen des Graphischen Kernsystems. Informatik-Spektrum 6 (1983) 2, pp. 55–75.

[31] ISO TC97/SC5/WG2 N117; Draft International Standard ISO/DP 7942; Information Processing, Graphical Kernel System (GKS). 1982.

[32] R. Eckert, G. Enderle, K. Kansy, F.J. Prester: GKS '79 — Proposal of a standard for a graphical kernel system. Eurographics 79, Conference Proceedings Bologna (1979), pp. 2–17.

[33] G. Enderle, K. Kansy, G. Pfaff: GKS — The Graphics Standard. Heidelberg (1982/83) Springer-Verlag.

[34] P. Bono, J. Encarnação, F.R.A. Hopgood, P. ten Hagen: GKS — The First Graphics Standard. IEEE Computer Graphics and Applications 2 (1982) 5, pp. 9–23.

[35] R. Kessener, J. Michener, G. Pfaff, D. Rosenthal, M. Sabin: The Detailed Semantics of Graphics Input Devices. IEEE Computer Graphics and Applications 2 (1982) 4.

[36] J. Encarnação, G. Enderle, K. Kansy, G. Nees, E.G. Schlechtendahl, J. Weiß, P. Wißkirchen: The Workstation Concept of GKS and the Resulting Conceptual Differences to the GSPC Proposal. Proc. SIGGRAPH '80, Computer Graphics 14 (1980) 3, pp. 226–230.

[37] H.G. Borufka, J. Encarnação, G. Pfaff: A Graphical Command Interpreter Concept to be Built on the Top of a Graphical Kernel System (GKS). Proceedings of the Crest-Course "New Trends on Man-Machine-Communication." April 1979, Orsay, France.

[38] H.G. Borufka, G. Pfaff: Ueberlegungen zum Kommandointerpreter (KI). Report GRIS 79-3. Darmstadt (1979) TH Darmstadt, FB Informatik, FG Graphisch-Interaktive Systeme.

[39] F.M. Lillehagen, J. Oian: Focusing on the Internal Model in CAD/CAM Systems. In: B. Gilchrist (ed.): Information Processing 77. Amsterdam (1977) North-Holland Publ. Co., pp. 273–278.

[40] T. Williams, G.M. Giddings: A Picture-Building System. IEEE Trans. on SE, Vol.SE-2 (1976) 1, pp. 62–66.

[41] J. Encarnação, T. Neumann: A Survey of DB Requirements for Graphical Applications in Engineering. Proceedings of the Int.Conf.on "DB for pictoral applications." Florence, Italy (June 1979).

[42] C.J. Date: An Introduction to Database Systems. Reading, Mass. (1976) Addison-Wesley Publ. Co.

[43] M.E. Senko, E. Altman, M. Astrahan, P. Fehder: Data Structures and Accessing in Data Base Systems. IBM System Journal Vol.12 (1973) 1, pp. 45–63.

[44] A. Blaser, U. Schauer: Aspects of Data Base Systems for Computer-Aided Design. In: R. Gnatz, K. Samelson (eds.): Methoden der Informatik für Rechneruntersütztes Entwerfen und Konstruieren. Informatik Fachberichte 11. Heidelberg (1977) Springer-Verlag, pp. 78–119.

[45] IBM: Information Management System/360, Version 2 General Information Manual. IBM Form GH20-0765.

[46] T.W. Olle: The CODASYL Approach to Data Base Management. Chichester (1978) John Wiley.

[47] E.F. Codd: A Relational Model of Data for Large Shared Data Banks. CACM 13 (1970), pp. 377–387.

[48] P. Blume, W.E. Fischer: Datenbanksystem für CAD-Anwendungen. Report KfK-CAD 111. Kernforschungszentrum Karlsruhe (1978).

[49] S. Ulfsby, S. Meen, J. Oian: TORNADO: A DBMS for CAD/CAM Systems. Computer Aided Design 13 (1981) 4, pp. 193–197.

[50] K. Leinemann: Ein System zum funktionellen Modellieren unter Verwendung von Datenbanktechniken und interaktiven graphischen Arbeitsmethoden. Report KfK 3217. Kernforschungszentrum Karlsruhe (1981).

[51] A.E. Bandurski, D.K. Jefferson: Data Description for Computer-Aided Design. Proceedings of the ACM SIGMOD Int. Conference on Management of Data. San Jose (Cal.) (1975), pp. 193–202.

[52] F.M. Lillehagen: Modelling in CAD Systems. CAD Tutorial, ACM-SIGGRAPH Conference Atlanta (Georgia) (1978).

[53] C. Eastman, J. Liudini, D. Stoker: A Database for Designing Large Physical Systems. AFIPS 44 (1975), pp. 603–611.

[54] P.L. Ciampi, J.D. Nash: Concepts on CAD Data Base Structures. Proceedings of the 13th Design Automation Conference. San Francisco (Cal.), June 28–30, 1974, pp. 249–364.

[55] A. Westermann: Graphische Datenverarbeitung im Konstruktionsbüro. IBM-Nachrichten 30 (1980) 248, pp. 61–67.

[56] E.A. Warman: CAD/CAM Management and Economics. Lecture Notes from a Tutorial during ACM SIGGRAPH '78, August 21–25, 1978.

[57] E.A. Warman: Investment Strategy and Choice of System. In: J. Encarnação, O. Torres and E. Warman (eds.): CAD/CAM as a Basis for the Development of Technology in Developing Nations. Amsterdam (1981) North-Holland Publ. Co.

[58] D. Scott: Computer Aided Graphics: Determining System Size, Estimating Costs and Savings. Computers in Industry 2. Amsterdam (1981) North-Holland Publ. Co., p. 23.

[59] G. Neipp: Methodisches Vorgehen zur Auswahl und zum Einsatz von CAD-Systemen. VDI-Berichte 413 (1981), pp. 19–31.

[60] H. Grabowski: Verfahren zur Beurteilung der Wirtschaftlichkeit von CAD-Systemen. VDI-Berichte 413 (1981), pp. 119–136.

[61] S.H. Chasen, J. Dow: The Guide for the Evaluation and Implementation of CAD Systems. CAD Decisions, Box 76042, Atlanta, GA 30328, USA (1979).

3 The Process Aspect of CAD

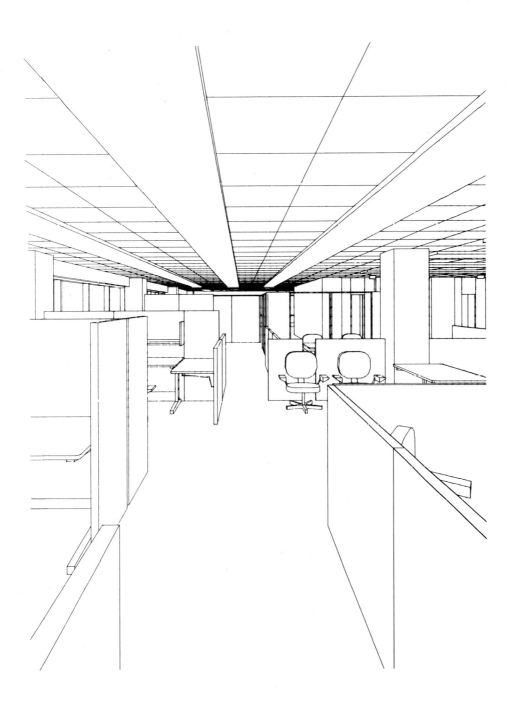

Architectural CAD application
(courtesy of GMW Computers, Hertshoreshire, UK)

3.1 Modelling of the Design Process

3.1.1 A Crude Model of the Design Process

CAD provides computer support for the design process. Hence, if we want
to talk about CAD, we must first talk about the process of design; that is,
we must construct at least a crude model of the design process. The problem,
however, is that design processes are quite different from one another, depending
on the product (a bicycle versus a nuclear power plant), on the company's
size ,and organization (a large architectural engineering firm versus a specialized
engineering bureau), and on the type of design (the restatement of a basically
fixed design versus the completely original design of a new product). The purpose of establishing modelling concepts for the design process is to provide
the system analyst with means of describing the global system into which a
CAD system must fit (and to set forth a basis for the terminology used in
the subsequent chapters). Both the designer of a CAD system and its potential
user must be able to agree on a description of the interfaces of the computer-
aided part of the design process with the remaining part of the process. Such
interfaces will be easy to describe if the design process can be adequately represented by a sequence or chain of actions where each action passes its results
on to its successor. We will see, however, that the design process is far more
complex, and that neither a chain nor a tree is sufficient to represent its essential
characteristics, even though it may sometimes look like a chain or a tree in
certain respects. In view of the complexity of the design process, it is perhaps
not very surprising that there have been many attempts to establish a systematic
description of design, resulting in a number of proposals, which are similar,
but without complete agreement in detail (see [1], for example). The complex
structure of the design process will have to be reflected in the structure of
CAD systems, if such systems are to support the design process as a whole
and not only isolated parts of it.

At this time we will set up a very general (and hence rather simple) model
of a "typical" design process. Using the terminology of Grotenhius and van
den Broek [2], this is an intuitive conceptual model. Fig. 3.1 is a first attempt
for such a model. The basic assumptions of this model are:

- the design goal is fixed (at least temporarily),
- a certain kind of know-how is required to construct the design,
- the design process produces information (the "design"), which in one way
  or another can be documented and used for production.

What is labelled "design" in Fig. 3.1 is not yet the product itself. It is
a model of the product which allows us to talk about the product before it
exists.

Using Nijssens approach [3], such a model may be deduced from the real
world by a sequence of two operations: perception and selection (see Fig. 3.2).
We perceive only a subset of reality: the perceptible reality. The subjectivity

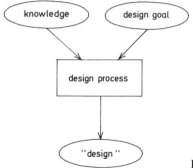

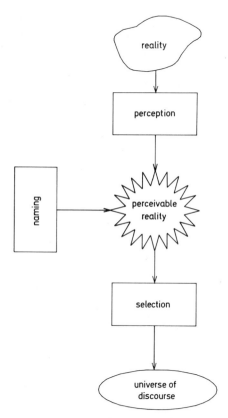

Fig. 3.1. A crude model of the design process

Fig. 3.2. Modelling of the real world

of this step in modelling is emphasized by the definition of a "system", which we quote from [4]:

> "A *system* is a part of the world, which a *person* (or group of persons) — during some time and for some reason — chooses to regard as the whole consisting of *components*, each component characterized by *properties* which are selected as being relevant and by *actions* which relate to these properties and to other components."

We can talk about perceptible reality by assigning names to its entities and the attributes of the entities. One of these entities is the anticipated product. In general, however, we are not interested in all aspects of perceptible reality; we select those aspects which are relevant in some pragmatic way. This process of selection generates what Nijssen calls the "universe of discourse". It is not a formal model but an "intuitive conceptual model" in the sense of Grotenhuis and van den Broek.

3.1.2 A More Refined Model of the Design Process

Our first crude model of the design process, however, does not yet reflect important characteristics of many design processes. We will modify the model to account for the following points:

- The design process is not self-contained. The design process is always embedded in another process (called its environment), and is initiated and controlled by a higher level process (the "company" process or "world" process). This aspect has been pointed out in particular in [5].
  When the design process is started, it will be accompanied by the submission of a design specification to the designer. This specification is not identical with the final goal, but is rather a formulation of the goal. It is possible that due to misinterpretations, or to incomplete or incorrect formulation in the design specification, the goal cannot be reached. For long-running and large-scale design projects the specification cannot be assumed to remain constant. The specification may not only be developed in more detail, but may actually be changed. As an example new environmental protection laws becoming effective during the design period of a chemical plant will affect the specification. The design process must involve precautions to accommodate such specification changes (at least to a certain extent). The design specification may be influenced not only by such external forces. In the course of the design it may turn out that certain aspects of the specification are undesirable with respect to the design goal. For instance, tight tolerances may cause very high costs. A reevaluation at a higher level might lead to less stringent specification requirements and thus to a better design. In order to allow for such corrective measures, the model of the design process should include the presentation of preliminary design achievements to the higher-level stages of the overall process.
- The design process is most often iterative. Decisions on certain product characteristics are made in a heuristic way at an early design stage on the basis of incomplete knowledge about their consequences with respect to the design goal. We call this the "synthesis" part of the design process. As a result, the "design" must be analysed and evaluated in the light of the design specification. In the software oriented world these activities are associated with the terms "validation" or "verification". If the goal is not met, the design decisions must be appropriately corrected.

Fig. 3.3 reflects these points. It shows that the design process is of a control loop type. The inner loop operates on a fixed design specification and consists

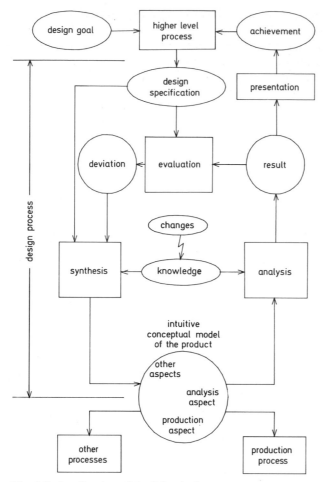

Fig. 3.3. A refined model of the design process

mainly of the operations "synthesis", "analysis", and "evaluation ". The deviation of the preliminary design from the specification is fed into the synthesis
operation. A second loop is closed not within the design process itself but
rather in the higher-level process. Thus, the design specification is (or at least
may be) a moving target. For the sake of economy in the design process it
is essential that appropriate specification methods are used to minimize the
rate of change of the target.

    Fig. 3.3 illustrates additional important aspects. The design process does
not only generate the information needed for production of the product. The
conceptual model must also represent all the information necessary for the
analysis part of the design process, and for all the other processes which may
follow. Testing, marketing, and maintenance, for instance, require information
produced in the design process. The conceptual model, which is generated by

the synthesis and checked against the specification via analysis and evaluation, thus becomes the central point of all subsequent operations. It is for this reason that literature on CAD emphasizes the importance of the data base and the particular requirements posed by CAD applications [6].

Another point reflected in Fig. 3.3 is the fact that the available knowledge is not necessarily fixed. As with the potential changes in the specification this is particularly true for long and large projects, such as a chemical or nuclear plant, and for anything which is being designed for the first time. Design and production schedules for large projects would be intolerable if the start of the design process had to be delayed until all the required knowledge was collected. The knowledge used for the design of a particular product — like the design specification — is the result of another process. This other process is necessary to provide the resources for successful execution of the design process; knowledge is one of these resources. Continuous improvement of design methods is especially important for CAD, and provisions must be made to incorporate such improvements in the design process.

Not only the set point (the specification) of the design process control loop, but also the resources (the knowledge) may vary during the process. Using this analogy, it is obvious that the lifetime of the specifications and of the knowledge should be large compared to the cycle time in the loop from synthesis via analysis and evaluation back into synthesis; otherwise a lot of spurious and costly transients will occur before the design reaches a new stable situation. With respect to the knowledge we will need to consider this point in connection with the problems of introducing CAD in industry. The introduction of such innovative techniques is restricted by the requirement that it must be gradual enough not to conflict with the current design processes.

There are some aspects of the design process which are not shown in Fig. 3.3:

- Every process has not only a functional aspect (which is illustrated) but also a resource aspect. The process can be executed only if the required resources are available and in a suitable state. We will deal with this aspect in more detail in Chapter 3.2.4. Resources in this context may include the designer, paper, slide rules, computers, time, money, etc. In addition, also knowledge about facts and methods may be interpreted as one of the resources.
- The design process may itself create other (dependent) design processes by specifying the design for a component of the whole product (the design of the control system of a power plant may serve as an example). Synchronization of these dependent processes and allocation of resources to them are part of the original design process. The interaction between two environment processes and the corresponding design processes is schematically shown in Fig. 3.4.
- Furthermore, the design process for a particular product does not stand alone. It is executed in the environment of other design processes (for similar or completely different products) within the organization. All these individual design processes are embedded in a "company" process which coordinates design with manufacturing, marketing, etc. to achieve the company goals.

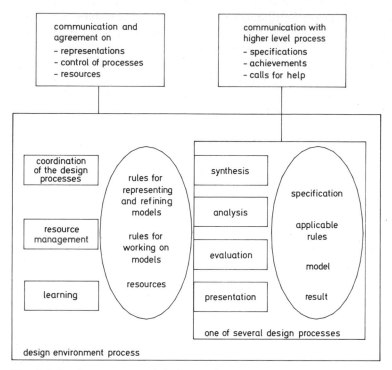

Fig. 3.4. Design process and design environment

The different processes must be synchronized and supplied with resources by the "company process".

We will now take a closer look at the knowledge. Knowledge is mostly a set of rules such as

when you recognize situation a ⟶ try a certain refinement of the model;
when you recognize situation b ⟶ analyze and evaluate
                                                             a property of the model;
when you recognize situation c ⟶ correct part of the model.

These types of rules may be associated with the main parts of the design process: synthesis, evaluation, and analysis. This distinction is clearly pointed out by Sussmann [7]. Synthesis and analysis are not merely inversions of each other. Synthesis is an attempt to refine the model in such a way that the subsequent analysis will be likely to produce a satisfactory result. Such attempts may fail, which will become evident in the evaluation phase of the process. Upon failure, part of the model refinement will have to be redone. Backtracking will be necessary to find out which refinement steps were responsible for the mismatch between specification and result. If no satisfactory solution is found within the limits of the available resources (time, money etc.) the process will have to call upon the higher-level process for help. It is interesting to note that in computer science the concept of "refinement" has become a key issue. This reflects the fact that designing a program and designing any other product are quite similar tasks on a basic level. The notion of refinement might also be expressed as a selection of a subset of all known rules, to be added to the set of those rules which are already being considered applicable. Analysis, as opposed to synthesis, is the application of previously selected rules. Thus we may associate synthesis, analysis, and evaluation with the following rules:

- *Synthesis:*
  when you recognize a certain situation —>
    include a certain subset of all known rules to the set of applicable rules;
- *Analysis:*
  apply the set of applicable rules;
- *Evaluation:*
  if result satisfies specification then finish; otherwise remove from the set of applicable rules those which are the probable reason for mismatch or call for help.

Note that the rules in the various phases obviously belong to different levels or types of rules. The objects to which the analysis rules apply may be considered as the primitives, while the synthesis and evaluation rules operate on sets of rules. It is probably this multilevel sense of rules (pointed out in [8]) which makes it so difficult to introduce formal methods not only into analysis but into the other parts of design as well. Synthesis, in particular, requires "intelligence". We quote Hofstadter [8] in order to illustrate what we mean by this term:
"... essential abilities for intelligence are certainly:
- to respond to situations very flexibly;
- to take advantage of fortuitous circumstances;
- to make sense out of ambiguous or contradictory messages;
- to recognize the relative importance of different elements of a situation;
- to find similarities between situations despite differences which may separate them;
- to draw distinctions between situations despite similarities which may link them;
- to synthesize new concepts by taking old concepts and putting them together in new ways;
- to come up with ideas which are novel."

With the separation we have now introduced between the set of applicable rules and the set of known rules, we can easily express what is meant by *changes in the knowledge* (which we call "learning" in accordance with [5]) and by *specification*:

- *Learning:*
  add new rules to the set of known rules;
- *Specification:*
  specify the rules which have to be applied in any given case.

We have seen that the whole design process can indeed be formulated in terms of rules. Such a unified approach to design, and computer-aided design in particular, is taken if artificial intelligence and pattern recognition methods are applied [9]. A human, as an information processor, can work with rules immediately. He is particularly suited for "recognition of situations", which is generally a tough job for computers. Attempts have been made to provide systems with the capability to recognize situations and to choose properly among a potentially applicable set of rules. Such systems are called "expert systems" [10]. However, they are still in an experimental stage.

3.1.3 Design Processes and Design Environments

The aspects of learning and environment introduced in the previous paragraph lead to a further refinement of our design process model, which is represented in Fig. 3.4. Here we do not show the control loop relationships between the various tasks (which were the key aspect in Fig. 3.3). We simply show that synthesis, analysis, evaluation, and representation all operate on the same set of information which we call the "knowledge" associated with the design process for a given product. Several such design processes potentially using the same basic knowledge may be going on in parallel within a particular design environment. The design environment is again considered as a process with the following tasks:

– it is the recipient of requests (coming from other processes) for doing some design work, or in other words for the creation of a new design task of the particular type it can perform;
– it must agree with these other processes about the methods for representing design specifications and achievements, and for the creation, control and termination of the newly created design tasks;
– it creates and coordinates design tasks;
– it manages resources in order to make the necessary resources available for the tasks. It attempts to avoid resource allocation conflicts, and to improve the efficiency of resource usage;
– it is responsible for providing, maintaining, and improving the knowledge (which is a particular resource).

The design environment is generally taken for granted, simply because it exists in all organizations doing design work. Moreover, the above-mentioned functions of the design environment seem to be trivial enough that one need not talk about them. The situation, however, is quite different if we consider the computer as part of the design process. In fact, using the computer one has to define the representation of specification, achievement, and so forth, very explicitly. Such agreements aready exist in human-based design due to a long development and learning process.

Fig. 3.5 illustrates the hierarchical cooperation of a design process (for a product) with one or more subordinate processes (for various parts of the product).

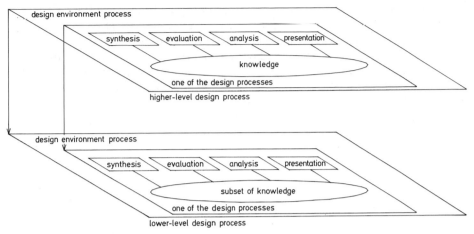

Fig. 3.5. Cooperation between design processes and environment processes

3.1.4 Differences Between Conventional Design and CAD

Information processing by a human does not require a formal representation, while computers can process information only if it is represented in some formal way. The question of whether all information (design specification and knowledge) can be completely formalized is perhaps a philosophically interesting speculation. But in any case the development of a formal language for representing the information is a task which in itself consumes resources. People, time, and money are needed for this task. For this reason, in the typical case, only part of the design goal and only part of the knowledge will be represented in a formal way.

We must be aware of the essential difference between science and engineering. In science, the question of "cost" in the general sense is of secondary interest. In engineering, however, economy is a priority. Therefore, in CAD we must consider economy as important as any other aspect.

As a consequence, complete design by computer will be possible only in exceptional cases. Computer-aided design, however, will be most successful if a good synergetic cooperation between the designer (or more often, designers) and the computer (or sometimes computers) is achieved.

Another important difference between conventional design and CAD (besides the need for formal representations) has been mentioned earlier: the need to establish the environment in which the design process can work. Limitations in computer capacity (memory, disks, graphic display units, as well as the commonly used programming languages) are part of the environment. Even if we could conceive an "ideal" CAD system for certain design processes in terms of functional aspects, we cannot realize it because we have to cope with the environment. The most critical computer limitations appear to be:

- the inability of computers (or their programs) to "recognize situations";
- their inability to work with rules. Instead, computer programs require rules to be cast into an *algorithmic* form which is most often yet to be developed;
- their unsatisfactory efficiency in handling model changes within the synthesis task (as compared with the excellent computer's capabilities for working on fixed models within the analysis task).

These deficiencies may become less important if artificial intelligence methods are more widely introduced into CAD [11]. Nowadays, however, CAD methods generally call for the operation of the two main design activities with

- synthesis preferably associated with human designers;
- analysis preferably associated with the computer.

3.1.5 A Network Model of the Design Process

In the previous paragraphs we discussed a hierarchical structure of design environment processes; a design process could generate subordinate processes only in an environment subordinate to its own. This, however, is only a special case of the more general situation. Any design process may contact any design environment process and request the creation of a new subordinate process. In order to represent these more general situations in a graphical representation, we replace the schema of Fig. 3.4 by Fig. 3.6. The line connecting the environment process to the individual design process indicates the same "belongs to" relation as the embedding used in Figs. 3.4 and 3.5. With this graphical schema we are able to represent a network of processes within a structure of levels as illustrated in Fig. 3.7. This schema has been influenced by proposals for the architecture of so-called "open systems" [12]. Open systems are systems which permit processes to establish communications with other processes on the same level, while using facilities of a lower level. Networks of processes are also discussed in [13].

In Fig. 3.7 the design process DP_{i-1}^{N+1} (e.g. design of a vehicle) has created two subprocesses DP_{i-1}^{N} and DP_{i}^{N}, which now do work for DP_{i-1}^{N+1}. These two subprocesses are of a different type, as indicated by their respective environment processes (one perhaps being the overall design and the other being the shape design of the vehicle, for example). Parallel to process DP_{i-1}^{N+1} another design process DP_{N+1}^{i} is being executed in the same universal environment. Note that in this particular example both (N + 1)-level processes require subprocesses at the (N − 1)-level of the same type (namely of the type provided by the environment process EP_{k-1}^{N}). Thus, while on the N-level process DP_{i-1}^{N} does not (necessarily) know of the existence of the other process DP_{i}^{N}, their subprocesses may create conflicts in the use of the resources required on the (N-1)-level, which have to be resolved by the environment process EP_{k-1}^{N}.

So far we have not dealt with the problem of the creation of subprocesses: how can process DP_{i+1}^{N} create its subprocess DP_{i+2}^{N-1}, for instance? A strict interpretation of the schematic representation in Fig. 3.7 would mean that pro-

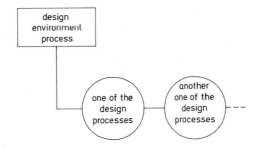

Fig. 3.6. An alternative representation of environment and design processes

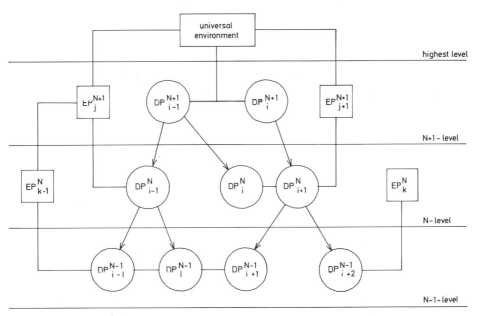

Fig. 3.7. A network model of the design process

cess DP^N_{i+1} would have to send a corresponding request either to DP^i_{N+1} or to its environment EP^{N+1}_{j+1}. If these processes cannot satisfy the request because they do not know of the existence of the environment EP^N_k, the request would first have to be passed upwards in the hierarchy of process levels until a process is reached to which both EP^N_k and the requesting process DP^N_{i+1} belong. This, however, may reduce the efficiency of all processes considerably. For this reason, the individual design processes usually have access to knowledge about environment processes on the same level. In our example, DP^N_{i+1} would probably know about the existence of the environment process EP^N_k and its capabilities in order to request the creation of subprocess DP^{N-1}_{i+2} directly. Such knowledge was passed to the processes when they were created. Part of this knowledge is

– knowledge about the capabilities of the environment processes;

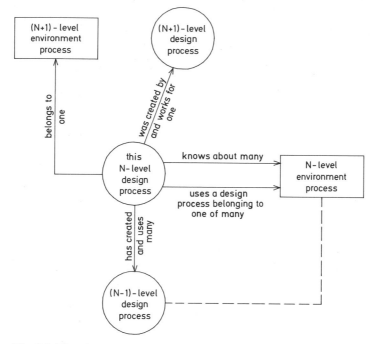

Fig. 3.8. The elementary building block of design processes

– knowledge of how to address these environment processes, and how to communicate with them.

Thus DP_{i+1}^N may know directly about EP_k^N. It would then request directly from EP_k^N the creation of a subordinate process DP_{m+2}^{N-1}, without the need for communication up and down the hierarchy.

This concept allows us to model a design process and its interfaces without considering the totality of all processes. We may simply look at one process and its interface to other processes. The schema illustrated in Fig. 3.8 may be considered as a model building block for constructing small or large networks of design processes.

3.2 CAD Processes

3.2.1 Design Process and CAD Process

Using the constructs derived in the preceding paragraphs, we are now able to introduce CAD into the model. A design process, having identified and specified a certain subtask, may want to create a subordinate design process.

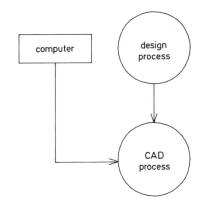

Fig. 3.9. A primitive CAD process model

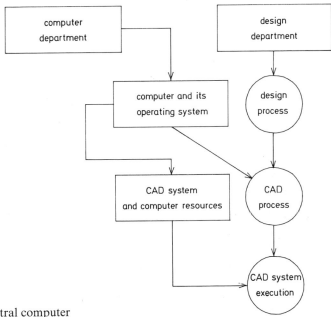

Fig. 3.10. CAD on a central computer

If this subordinate design process operates in a computer environment, we call it a *CAD process*.

The general schema as sketched in Fig. 3.9 is, however, far too abstract to be useful. Let us consider two extreme cases which occur quite often in practice:

– the application of CAD systems on a large central computer in batch mode;
– the use of a dedicated CAD system in the environment of the design office in an interactive mode.

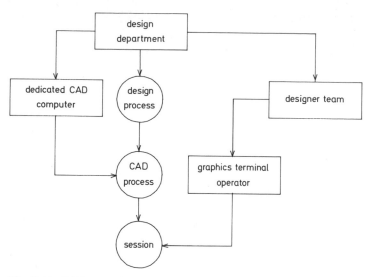

Fig. 3.11. CAD on a dedicated computer

In the first case, as illustrated in Fig. 3.10, the computer environment is not immediately suitable for CAD application. Instead, the general purpose computer (or, more precisely, its operating system) must first be addressed in the language of the operating system, and requested to establish the appropriate environment: this means to make available the necessary programs, data files, and communication facilities which, all together, we call a CAD system. Each CAD application requires not only knowledge about the CAD system itself — its capabilities and its means of communication — but also requires a purely computer-oriented job training; this fact is a particular burden of this type of CAD environment.

A much easier way to establish a CAD process is shown in Fig. 3.11. A specially programmed or "dedicated" computer within the design environment presents the CAD system in usable form to the designer, immediately or with only a few general commands required. The designer can then execute his CAD task without the problems imposed by the many other processes running on a large general-purpose computer. This system is more readily available and can be tuned more specifically to a small group of designers and design tasks. On the other hand, it may be lacking the flexibility, the computing power, and the large data bases of a big computer. Fig. 3.11 illustrates in particular the interactive mode. The CAD execution process itself addresses a human operator via a terminal (usually a graphics terminal), and thus creates a new subprocess which we call a session. It is important to distinguish among the various levels of processes, and not to confuse the design process itself with the process of a session, even though both processes may be driven by the same person.

3.2.2 Design Process Characteristics and Their Influence upon the CAD Process

According to Hatvany [14], the main components of a CAD system are

- a person;
- computer hardware;
- software;
- a certain type of problem.

The type of problem is a characteristic which the CAD process has inherited from its superordinate design process. Here, we will discuss the type of problem in a very general sense. We will basically follow the classification schema used in [15] and illustrated in Fig. 3.12. Much work regarding the classification of individual phases of the design process was done at the University of Aachen (e.g. [16]). A survey of several attempts to classify the design activities in a systematic manner is given by Pahl and Beitz [1]. We might also refer to the work of Roth [17], Hansen [18], Koller [19], Rodenacker [20], Baumann and Looschelders [21].

In the context of the previous chapters, however, it seems more appropriate to use the classifications indicated in Fig. 3.13.

The development of a product is the response to a certain request which is to be satisfied. As an example of such a request let us use J.F. Kennedy's well-known statement (on May 25, 1961) of the goal to land a man on the moon and bring him back safely before the end of the 1970's. This is not a specification of a vehicle which would be suitable to do the job! As a first step, the functional requirements of the product have to be worked out. For this task, the environmental conditions in which the product will have to operate need to be considered. This leads to a functional structuring of the anticipated product, and results in a functional specification. This process, which we call functional design, is informal, and highly intuitive. This does not mean that computer support is completely precluded at this stage. Though the process itself is informal, representations of the elements in this process (the requests, the environmental conditions, and the resulting specifications) may be formalized. Certain systems which we will discuss later have been constructed to support this part of the product development.

Design, however, in the more strict sense used in this book, does not start until after the functional specification exists (see Fig. 3.13). The functional specification determines part of the conceptual schema of the product to be designed. The selection of working principles (such as welding versus screwing to hold two pieces together) and the gross shape and dimensional design, along with the selection of basic manufacturing methods, is part of the schematic design. As a result of the schematic design, the conceptual schema of the product is complete. This means that we know which constituent parts (entities) make up the product and which properties (attributes) of these constituents must be determined. The relationships among the entities are now fixed.

The final part ("detail design") deals with the assignment of specific values for all the attributes of an instance of this schema. For example, while the

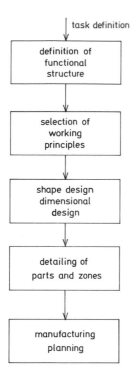

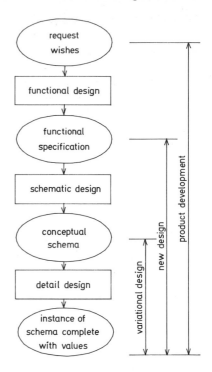

Fig. 3.12. Classification of design activities

Fig. 3.13. Relationship between design activities and conceptual schema

schematic design has determined the fact that certain edges of an object must be rounded and that the material is an essential property, the detail design will assign a value to the rounding radius and a material name to the material attribute.

The difference between schematic design and detail design will show up in the appropriate CAD systems used in these areas. In the detail design, theoretically at least, one could conceive an algorithm which would produce the unknown attribute values of the conceptual schema from the representation of the specification within this schema. This algorithm may not be straightforward but may require a lot of iterations. However, the result (or at least one result if one exists) is totally predetermined. In schematic design the situation is different. Under what conditions a schema can be derived in algorithmic form from functional requirements — or whether this is at all possible — is a question we will not discuss here. In any practical case, the design of a schema has a pronounced heuristic and pragmatic character. Human judgement is the principal decision mechanism. Thus CAD systems in this area must be interactive from the basic principles, while in detail design CAD systems may or may not be interactive.

3.2.3 The Environment of CAD

3.2.3.1 The Organization

Considerable variety may be found with respect to the organizational embedding of CAD. This depends not only on the size and organization of the company, but even reflects differences in attitude towards CAD (as for example between the U.S. and Europe). As Allan [22] pointed out, American companies have a tendency to use CAD as a technical service whenever the need arises. The responsibility for CAD is more directly associated with the design departments themselves. In Europe, CAD (or CAD/CAM) is regarded as "an extension of management". Responsibility for the introduction and use of CAD methods and systems is preferably associated with higher-level management. This latter attitude may reflect the fact that the application of CAD is often accompanied by an increasing trend towards formalization and standardization, both in the products and in manufacturing. Full benefit will only be gained from CAD (and from these side effects) if not just the design aspect but also work planning and manufacturing are involved.

3.2.3.2 The Human Environment

The human factor is dominant in the early phases of introduction of CAD in an organization. The spectrum of skills required to perform a certain design task will generally change when computer support is introduced. The most obvious change is that a certain amount of knowledge about computers and how to deal with them will be required. Exactly how much computer knowledge is necessary in the design environment will depend mainly on the following factors:

- access to a central data processing department versus the installation of one or more computers in the design department;
- use of black-box ("turn-key") CAD systems versus the development or modification of CAD systems;
- complexity and amount of knowledge required to perform the design task.

Another change in skill requirements, however, is of much greater concern with respect to the people working in the design office. Since computer based systems are so well suited to performing analytical work along prescribed algorithms (programs) but so ill-suited for the actual "design" work (which is basically decision making), the introduction of CAD will cause a change in job content, as pointed out in [23]. High-level designers will be able to increase productivity and product quality by using CAD; however, they may be subject to more stress during their work because they may miss certain periods of relaxation which had been caused by the more-or-less routine work prior to the introduction of CAD. On the other hand, low-level designers whose capabilities are limited to routine work may no longer be needed.

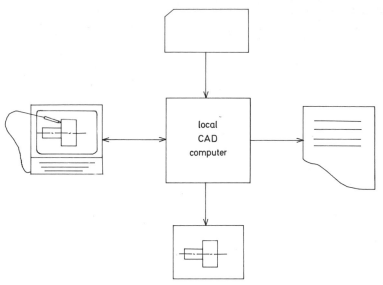

Fig. 3.14. Configuration of a local computer

Besides skills, a necessary condition for the successful introduction of CAD in a company is the motivation of the design personnel to use the new CAD tools and methods instead of the familiar conventional ones.

The introduction of CAD in general requires

– higher-level skills (planning and decision making rather than execution and analysis);
– motivation.

3.2.3.3 Computer Resources

In a CAD environment, three computer configurations are mainly found:

– the local computer;
– the remote computer;
– the local satellite of a remote host computer.

Any one of these configurations may be found in different operational modes:

– batch mode only;
– interactive mode only;
– both batch and interactive mode.

Three of the many variations of CAD computer configurations are shown in Fig. 3.14 through Fig. 3.16. Fig. 3.14 indicates the most primitive case:

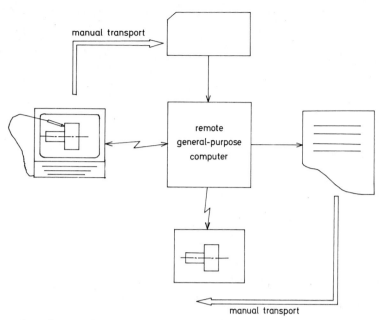

Fig. 3.15. Configuration of a remote computer

a local CAD computer. It is used in batch mode, with some means of program and data input (the punched card version is just one of the many possibilities), and with text output on a printer and plot output on a plotter. Fig. 3.15 shows a configuration with a local terminal (both alphanumeric and graphic) attached to a remote computer center. Fig. 3.16 shows what is generally considered the most powerful configuration: a local computer with all alphanumeric and graphic input and output capabilities, backed up by a powerful remote computer.

The decision, as to which configuration and which operational mode is "best" depends very much on the individual situation. This is particularly true for the first five years or so after the introduction of CAD into a company. Organizations which make significant use of a large general-purpose computer for non-CAD applications will in all likelihood start using CAD batch programs, and proceed by attaching remote terminals to the central computer. Organizations with less computer background will probably increase the computer capacity of the design office from desk calculators to one or more special-purpose CAD computers until they find it advantageous to connect some of these individual CAD computers to a bigger background computer. The final configuration in a large organization will quite often have the structure shown in Fig. 3.16. (Note that the background computer may in fact be a network of computers, not necessarily a single machine.)

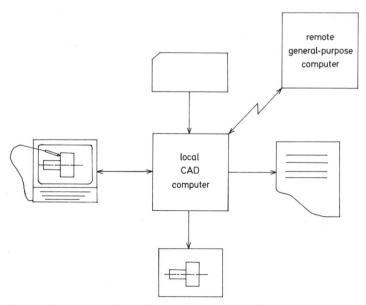

Fig. 3.16. Configuration of a local computer with remote support

3.2.3.4 The Interaction Phases of the CAD Process

In the cooperation between a design process and a subordinate CAD process we may often distinguish various degrees of interaction in different phases. These phases are illustrated in Fig. 3.17. The first phase consists of the transmission of a prepared task specification to the CAD process. This "primary input" often includes a considerable amount of information which has to be checked for completeness and correctness before it is processed any further. The next step is usually a highly interactive communication between the two partners, involving adjustments and modifications of the specification until both can agree. The next step is the actual execution of the task. Interaction should be less prominant in this phase. Finally, the presentation of results often requires a high degree of communication when it emerges that more details are wanted than were included in the first presentation, or the way of representing the results should be modified for a better visualization of the essential aspects.

These phases may be more or less pronounced in a particular environment, so that they do not always show up in the architecture of CAD systems; but this principal structure is always useful to compare real CAD systems against. Besides the two highly interactive phases of a CAD process mentioned above there are two more situations which are associated with a high degree of interactive communication:

– information retrieval;
– synergetic cooperation of human and computer
  (as is typical for computer-aided drafting).

amount of information exchanged	interaction phases in CAD	interaction rate
high	task specification primary input	low
low	input validation	high
high for synthesis low for analysis	execution	high for synthesis low for analysis
high or low	presentation of results	high or low

Fig. 3.17. The interaction phases in CAD

3.2.4 The State of CAD Processes

3.2.4.1 The Lifetime of Processes

In the previous chapters we have not explicitly dealt with the aspect of time. Time, however, is an essential aspect of processes. Each process has a beginning and an end: we call this the lifetime of a process. The process exists only during its lifetime. At any moment during its lifetime, the process is in a certain state. The lifetime of a process is not independent of the lifetime of other processes. Note that the lifetime of a process includes both its "active" and its "dormant" phases (see Chapter 3.2.4.3.). As Fig. 3.4 suggests, a process can exist only during the lifetime of its environment. Furthermore, a process which was created by another process as a subtask should (in most cases) return a result and terminate before the original process is terminated. In certain cases, however, a process may create another process without the need for a result; in such a case the creating process may well terminate before the created process. The basic requirement of process lifetime is illustrated in Fig. 3.18 for three examples.

First the general situation is illustrated. The second example shows the environment process which makes a look-up table available (a book in the office or a data base on a computer). Although there is only one administration process which creates, maintains and deletes from the table, several independent look-up processes may be executed. The third example is related to the design environment. Independent of a particular design process, the need for a CAD

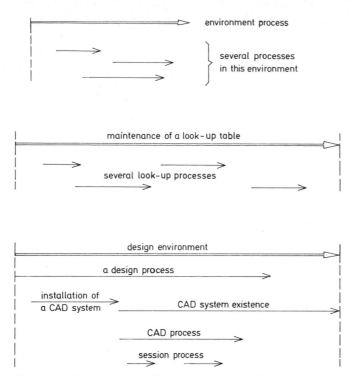

Fig. 3.18. Three examples illustrating process lifetime

system has been realized and a process for the installation of a CAD system created. As a result, the CAD system has become available in the design environment. Some design process may now create a CAD process utilizing the system, during which process several sessions will be held. Several other design processes may easily utilize the same CAD system in parallel with the design process shown in the figure, provided that no conflicts arise.

3.2.4.2 The Representation of the Process State

At any point during its lifetime, a process is either active or inactive. To call a process active means that the process is changing its own state, or that the process is communicating with another process. We will have to deal with this concept of the state of a process in more detail. A designer can usually formulate the state of the design process he is working on. Certain design goals may have been achieved,while others are still to be reached; certain documents may have been produced but only in a "preliminary" version; inconsistencies may exist in the design itself due to incomplete updating of documents according to the most recent design changes, or there may be inconsistencies between the achieved solution and the design goals as a consequence of inadequate choices made in an earlier phase of design; even the knowledge about such

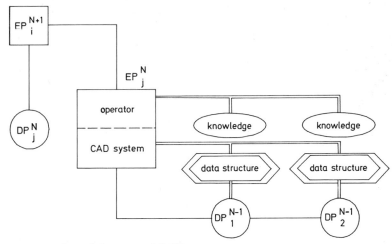

Fig. 3.19. The representation of the state of CAD processes

inconsistencies is part of the changing state of the design process as analysis proceeds.

In general, one will be able to express the state of the design process in terms of the state of certain "things" (such as design drawings, written documents, know-how in human brains) which constitute the specific resources of the design process:

– The resources which represent the state of the process must be reserved for exclusive use by this process alone.

The same situation exists for a CAD process, except that the resources which represent the state of the CAD process are restricted to

– machine-readable storage media and
– the knowledge of the "computer-aided designers", usually called operators in the CAD process.

We will deal with the knowledge of the operators in more detail when we discuss the communication aspect of interactive CAD systems. The state representation of a CAD process is related closely to the discussion of data structures and their representation. At this point it is sufficient to note that machine-readable storage media may be of very different types and may be looked at on different levels. The lowest level is represented by hardware, like holes in punch cards, for instance, or bits in computer primary memory and on external storage devices. This aspect is of minor interest to the CAD user. However, only in rare cases can he avoid dealing with the state representation on the level of a computer operating system, data base, or file management system, or on a programming language level. On these levels, the objects in a data base, the sequence of values in a file, or the values of variables in a program together with the corresponding underlying schema represent one part of the state of the CAD process at any instant. The second part of the

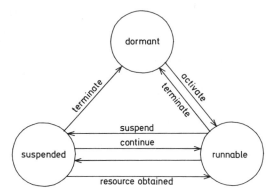

Fig. 3.20. The operating states of an environment process

CAD process state representation is the associated knowledge in the brain of the "computer-aided designer". Consequently, a major task in CAD is

– to communicate the schema of the CAD process state to the computer in machine readable form and
– to fill an instance of this schema with values in a particular CAD process.

Fig. 3.19 is a more detailed representation of the schema shown in Fig. 3.6. It distinguishes more precisely between the CAD processes themselves and their states. Furthermore, the CAD environment is separated into its two main components: "operator" and "CAD system". The state of process DP_{N-1}^1 is defined as the combination of the data structure of the CAD system and the associated knowledge of the operator. While the schema is the same for all CAD processes DP_{N-1}^i, the content is different for each of them. The machine-readable resources representing the state of the processes are associated with the overall CAD system (that is, the environment process), while the values belong to the individual processes.

3.2.4.3 The Operating State

It is advantageous to define the various situations of a process in terms of an "operating state". This is common practice in process control, and we will use a simplified version of the state diagram used in the definition of the PEARL language [24, 25]. Other programming languages which support the concept of a process might be used as a reference as well [26, 27]. The correspondence between PEARL and the notions used here is as follows:

PEARL	*this book*
task	environment process
activity of a task	CAD process

Fig. 3.20 shows the operating states of the environment process (we have omitted the scheduling feature of PEARL). The environment process EP(N)

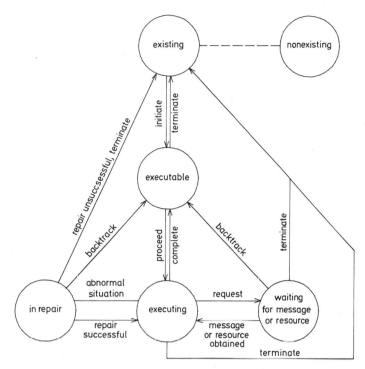

Fig. 3.21. The operating states of a CAD process

(in Fig. 3.19) is said to be dormant if no CAD processes exist in this environment. It is runnable if at least one process exists and is executable or being executed; it is suspended if at least one process exists, but none of them wants to proceed. In addition it is useful to introduce the state "unknown", which actually is not a state of the environment itself, but is rather associated with the relation between this environment and some other (environment or CAD) process. An environment is unknown to some other process if the latter does not know about its existence, or at least does not know how to communicate with it. The operating state of an environment is thus closely related to the operating states of the CAD processes which belong to it (Fig. 3.21). Every CAD process must pass the operating state "existing". It is in this state immediately after it has been created in the environment upon the request of some other process. In order to become executable, the CAD process must be initialized. For initialization, values which are meaningful and consistent with the operations to be performed are assigned to certain objects in the corresponding data structure. This corresponds to the communication of the design goal to a subordinate design process, as discussed in Chapter 3.1.2. If there are any steps to be taken, the process will pass to operating state "executing", from which it will return when the task is completed. In the executing state, the need for support by other processes may occur. Resources may be needed; new subprocesses may have to be created and their responses awaited; "help" may be needed from a higher-level process or the environment process. In such cases, the CAD process will pass to the operating state "waiting". The operating state "in repair" is reached if abnormal conditions arise. It might be emphasized that this operating state should be investigated much more intensively than has been done in the past. Computer-based systems often become complicated not because their normal tasks are complicated, but rather because abnormal situations and repair mechanisms have not been taken into account in sufficient detail.

From both the "waiting" and "in repair" states the process can normally return to "executing". However, if the message cannot be received, or the resource cannot be obtained, or the repair is not successful, the process will have to return to either "executable" or "existing". The first is certainly preferable, because it leaves the process in a consistent state from which it can proceed (for instance, by repeating the step which has just failed).

3.2.5 The Problem of Resources

3.2.5.1 Resource Availability and Conflicts of Resource Requirements

In the previous paragraphs we have mentioned "resources" several times as something indispensable for a process. Examples of such resources are

– time, money, manpower, storage capacity, a processor;
– a certain piece of hardware, a certain file, a certain compiler, a name.

The difference between the two groups of resources mentioned above is their ability to be substituted by other resources. This will later cause differences in how these two groups of resources have to be treated. At this time we will deal with their common aspect: we consider as a resource

anything needed which may have limitations of availability
in the environment considered [28].

The resource problem is less evident if only one process exists (or can exist) within the environment. In this simple case, practically all the resources of the environment are available to the process. However, when several processes exist in parallel, conflicts may arise already due to the fact that the state representation of each process requires resources which cannot be shared. Serious conflicts are even more likely if several of the processes are in the executable operating state (including the "executing", "waiting", and "in repair" states). Computer science has developed several constructs, like semaphores [29] and others, which deal with the problem of resolving conflicts [30]. Furthermore, Petri nets (or P-nets) may provide the necessary tools to handle the problems of coordinating the individual parallel tasks in a design process [31]. However, to the authors' knowledge these techniques have not yet been introduced into CAD systems. The reason why CAD has disregarded this problem thus far is probably that CAD systems which support several CAD processes in parallel and in real time are uncommon. Furthermore, the notion of a "process" is usually associated with a "job" or a "run" on a computer, not with the longer-lasting design task. Finally, constructs for the coordination of concurrent processes have found their representation in programming languages [32, 24] which are as yet unfamiliar to the CAD community, while in data base systems these problems tend to be hidden from the user. In Chapter 4.3 we will have to deal with the problems of resource management in an environment which does not provide semaphores or similar constructs for resource management.

Names are a special kind of resource. Names are used in processes as substitutes for objects, while the objects themselves are each represented by some lower-level process. The action of replacing the name by the actual object is called binding [33]. Resource problems may arise in two ways:

– the use of identical names for different objects may cause an inconsistency; during binding (replacement of the name by the object itself) it may turn out that the required resources are not available.

Examples of binding actions are:

– the inclusion of subprograms from a library into a program module in a process. The words "binding", "mapping", or "linkage editing" are common, depending on the computer manufacturer's terminology;
– the establishment of a connection from a terminal to the main computer (by telephone dialing for instance);
– the opening of an actual data file by a CAD program; the substitution of a computer memory address for a programming language variable name during compilation.

The aspect of resource availability is important with respect to CAD systems. CAD systems which are designed to operate on a large central computer may not be applicable in an environment which does not provide sufficient memory capacity. On the other hand, an interactive CAD system which is used successfully on a small computer may be unacceptable when operated from a remote terminal on a large central computer where it has to share resources (central processor time, communication channels) with other processes. Software such as compilers for certain programming languages, or specific data base systems or subroutine packages may as well constitute resource requirements which restrict the applicability of CAD systems. The same even applies to human resources when a certain kind of know-how for operating the CAD system is required. As a consequence, a CAD system is fully described only if its resource requirements are spelled out in addition to its functional capabilities. It is not surprising that several CAD systems exist which are quite similar in functional respects but differ in their resource requirements.

3.2.5.2 The Efficiency Aspect of Resources

Besides the functional aspect of availability of resources, efficiency of their utilization is also an important consideration in CAD systems. Efficiency is related to cost, and hence introduces a commercial aspect. CAD systems which operate efficiently in one environment may operate less efficiently in another. In the early years of CAD the size of primary computer memory was limited because of high costs. For this reason, CAD systems were developed which could operate with a minimum of primary memory by storing all but the most immediate data on peripheral devices. The tremendous decrease in primary memory cost [34] has caused a shift towards larger memories for the optimal use of resources, while on the other hand time is becoming more valuable. Thus recently a trend may be noticed to utilize more primary storage while minimizing time-consuming accesses to secondary storage. It should be noted that the economic factors related to resources may have a considerable influence upon CAD systems.

3.2.5.3 CAD Machines and CAD Tools

Engineers are used to thinking of machines. By analogy, a CAD system may be compared to a machine. In CAD the product is design information, and the resource representing the product is paper or a certain region in a data base (rather than a piece of hardware). The resources which this "machine" uses in the production process are mainly computer hardware and software (instead of hydraulic forces and lubrication oil). Both the CAD system and the conventional production machine need control or at least supervision by a human.

The analogy goes further. Machines may be designed for "stand-alone" use. This is the common situation when so-called "turn-key" CAD systems are used [35]. But machines are quite often used in a larger environment where a transfer system stores the intermediate product and transports it from one machine to the other, while in the meantime some checking may be performed and the piece of work may have to be oriented in a different way before it is inserted into the next machine. The transfer system finds its analogy in CAD in a data base system, the intermediate human checking being done with a suitable query language, while the different orientations of the same pieces of work correspond to the different "views" of the same objects in the data base according to different subschemas (see Chapter 3.3.2). As in conventional engineering, the CAD machines must themselves be produced. For the production of machines, other machines (machine tools) or at least some manual tools are required. Again we find a correspondence in CAD, where special software systems (often called "integrated systems" [36]) and specialized tools (software packages) have been developed for the sole purpose of facilitating the design and development of CAD systems. A particular aspect of these integrated systems (or system nuclei, as they are also called) is the adaptability of the generated CAD systems to the resources of the environments in which they are to operate (see Chapter 5.1.2.4).

3.3 Modelling in CAD

3.3.1 Developing a Schema

3.3.1.1 Basic Considerations

In the previous paragraphs, we have tried to develop a conceptual model of the design process. The model is far from being formal, — since that was not the intent. But it provides a suitable basis for talking about CAD, for developing more formal models of CAD, and for designing CAD systems. The task of developing a model recurs in every design task (see Fig. 3.22 and Chapter 3.1.2). Because computer systems are lacking in the ability to do synthesis, the development of a model — or more precisely: the set of models that belongs to the scope of a CAD system — is generally a task to be performed by the designer of a CAD system. The user of the CAD system can develop product models only within the restrictions imposed by the designer of the CAD systems. The description of the whole set of possible models that can be developed by the designer when using a CAD system is called the conceptual schema. The design of the schema, however, does not only depend on the objects to be designed, but also on the anticipated actions to be taken. In conventional design the actions to be taken are all related to human information processing. Over many years a suitable schema for a very large class of objects has been developed: the standards for design drawings. Note that the standards for design drawings are not identical all over the world. Fig. 3.23 shows the same object

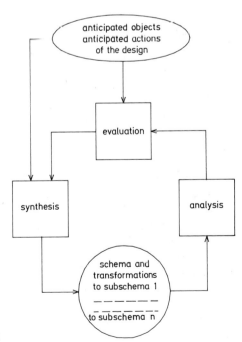

Fig. 3.22. The CAD process and its schema

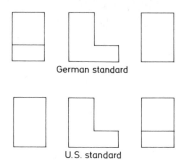

German standard

U.S. standard   **Fig. 3.23.** Design drawing standards

according to German [37] and American [38] standards. These two standards serve the same purpose equally well, yet they are different. They illustrate that "correctness" is not an applicable criterion for evaluating a conceptual schema. "Suitability" is more appropriate. We quote from [39]:

"The categories in terms of which we group the events of the world around us are constructions or inventions. The class of prime numbers, animal species, the huge range of colors dumped into the category "blue", squares and circles: all of these are inventions and not "discoveries". They do not "exist" in the environment. The objects of the environment provide the cues or features on which our groupings may be based, but they provide cues that could serve for many groupings other than the ones we make. We select and utilize certain cues rather than others."

The essential question to be answered by analysis and evaluation of a conceptual schema is:

– Is the schema suitable for efficient transformation to and from the various subschemas required by the different design steps anticipated?

The examples in the subsequent chapters will illustrate these considerations.

3.3.1.2 A Sample Problem

This sample problem may appear to be too trivial. Yet it exhibits all the essential features of schema planning in CAD applications. Fig. 3.24 represents an object which has some similarity with a hammer (although we do not claim that it is a good hammer). It would not be too difficult to manufacture this hammer in a workshop with the information given in the figure. Let us take a closer look at this information. It contains

– structural information:
  the object consists of two subobjects (head and shaft);
– geometrical information:
  the geometrical shape of head and shaft, and
  the geometrical position of these two pieces after assembly;

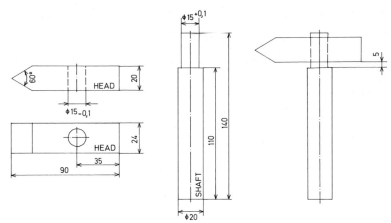

Fig. 3.24. The graphical representation of an object

– information regarding manufacturing:
  the material information (presumably together with the geometrical data) will influence the selection of the raw material for both pieces. The tolerance data will influence the quality control.

Note that the drawing itself is not a complete description of the hammer. It is complete only in a certain environment. In order to complete the geometrical information, one must additionally apply the rules for representation of bodies in design drawings. Only with this additional knowledge can one conclude that the shaft is basically a circular cylinder with flat ends which are perpendicular to the center line of the cylinder. Furthermore, one must know that the standard length unit is mm. If we neglect the implied rules, we find tremendous difficulties in describing the geometry. A verbal description without any graphic support would be quite lengthy if at all feasible. A particular problem of CAD is that computers do not know about the rules of design drawings and cannot read a design drawing as a human does. Hence a different schema is required to represent the information.

3.3.1.3 Naming of Objects and Attributes

A fundamental difference between a design drawing and a schema suitable for computer application is the naming requirement. While on the design drawing entities may be pointed at ("this length is 140 mm"), the entities in a schema and their attributes must have names assigned to them [33]. We obtain one possible schema of the hammer by simply replacing each number by a respective name. We have many choices in doing this, the first choice being the set of allowable names. In Fig. 3.25 we choose as names identifiers built from an arbitrary number of capital letters and numbers. However, we might as well have chosen another naming system, such as assigning a positive integer value to each of the entities. In a more general sense, even a position may be taken as the name ("the lowest line of the HEAD representation"). Since information processing with computers is generally based on information representation in the form of character strings and numbers, names of this form are most common. In the context of graphic data processing, we will discuss the use of graphic representation of names in more detail. In this chapter we will restrict ourselves to the usual form of names, namely character strings.

In any case, names must be unique in the environment where they are used. In Fig. 3.25 we select D0 and L for two entities each. Nevertheless the names are unique if we prefix (or qualify) them with the name of the object to which they belong: HEAD.D0 and SHAFT.D0 are two unique names. The same principle applies if we consider the possibility of two different processes in the same environment using the same name for independent entities. Again the technique of qualifying the name (in this case with the name of the appropriate process) will make the name unique. Problems will arise only if we restrict the rules for naming so that qualification is not possible. In this case conflicts are likely to occur.

3.3.1.4 Alternatives for a First Schema

A logical next step would be to transform Fig. 3.25 into a machine readable representation. We choose a Pascal-like notation:

```
TYPE    MEASURE = RECORD
            VALUE, TOLERANCE : REAL
                END;

TYPE    HEAD_SCHEMA=RECORD
        ANGLE, H, W, OFFSET, L : REAL;
                    D0          : MEASURE
                END;

TYPE    SHAFT_SCHEMA= RECORD
                    D1, L1, L : REAL;
                    D0          : MEASURE
                END;

TYPE    HAMMER_SCHEMA=RECORD
                    GAP         : REAL;
                    HEADPART    : -> HEAD_SCHEMA;
                    SHAFTPART   : -> SHAFT_SCHEMA;
                END;
```

We now ask ourselves: Is this a suitable schema? As mentioned before this question can be answered only if we consider the actions to be taken. Consideration of the objects alone is insufficient. First of all, we note that

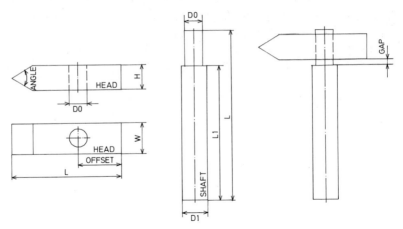

Fig. 3.25. The graphical representation of a schema

we are able to identify objects of the types defined above by combining the name of each object with the name of a schema:

```
VAR  HAMMER : HAMMER_SCHEMA;
     SHAFT  : SHAFT_SCHEMA;
     HEAD   : HEAD_SCHEMA;
```

We call HAMMER an "object" of type HAMMER_SCHEMA in order to distinguish between a schema and an instance of this schema. We use "object" as a synonym for "data structure", whenever the representation of a real world object in terms of data is concerned. In the literature, we can also find "data structure" being used instead of "schema", i.e. for a whole class of objects. Since we generally allow several processes to exist in one environment, each of them being characterized by its appropriate state, we must distinguish between the abstract schema and its individual instances, which are associated one with each process (see Chapter 3.2.4.3).

We can also assign values to certain quantities:

```
HAMMER.GAP      := 0.0005;
SHAFT.DO.VALUE  := 0.015;
HEAD.DO.VALUE   := 0.015;
```

Here implicitly we have introduced the convention of using the ISO standard for physical units (i.e., m for length) instead of the mm unit which was the design drawing standard. At this point we could use a data structure built according to the above schema as a memory. All we need is a query language which allows us to retrieve data from the storage and to represent them in a form readable to man or program. This is in fact a fundamental function of data banks. Note, however, that we do not use the "pointers" of the schema hammer. Indeed, we have not needed them so far. It would

be more appropriate to include the HEAD_SCHEMA and SHAFT_SCHEMA
in the HAMMER_SCHEMA as follows:

```
TYPE COMBINED_SCHEMA=RECORD
                GAP : REAL ;
                 DO : REAL ;
             SHAFT : RECORD
                DO_TOLERANCE : REAL;
                   D1, L1, L : REAL
                         END;
              HEAD : RECORD
                DO_TOLERANCE : REAL;
         ANGLE, H, W, OFFSET, L : REAL
                         END
          END;
```

Note that the COMBINED_SCHEMA differs from a simple combination
of the three previous schemas: the nominal value of diameter D0 has been
removed from both the SHAFT_SCHEMA and the HEAD_SCHEMA and
is now given only once. This reflects the functional requirement that the two
parts must have the same nominal value for this diameter in order to fit together.
This is a consistency condition of the original data structure, which results
from a redundancy in D0 in just the same way as in the design drawing (Fig.
3.24). While the COMBINED_SCHEMA implicitly guarantees consistency, the
first solution with separate HEAD_SCHEMA and SHAFT_SCHEMA requires
an explicit check of the consistency, whenever HEAD and SHAFT are combined
into HAMMER.

3.3.2 Influence of the Operations upon Schema Planning

We will use the example HAMMER from the previous section to illustrate
the type of considerations necessary during schema planning. Let us plan for
the following actions:

- we wish to deal with hammers with different values of D0;
- we wish to combine heads and shafts having different length dimensions
  but the same value of D0. We do not expect any changes in the angle value
  of 60 degrees assigned ANGLE;
- we want to produce design drawings similar to Fig. 3.24 from the data base;
- we want to compute the weight of shaft and head for each hammer;
- we want to query the data base;
- we will apply these actions one at a time to one hammer at a time

Before we continue we must make some additional assumptions:

- The algorithm (the program) for producing the design drawing must know
  all the lines and texts to be displayed. It must know where to place these
  lines and in what line-width.

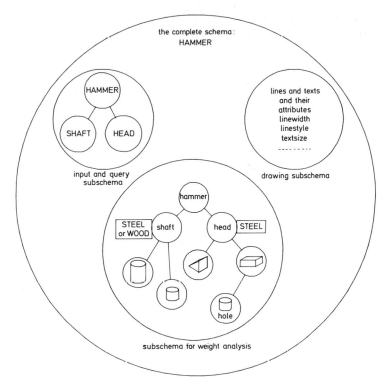

Fig. 3.26. Refinement of a schema by the definition of subschemas

-   The algorithm for calculating the weight must know the material density. It will work only for simple volume shapes such as cylinders, quadrilaterals, and prisms. The head material will always be steel, shafts may be made from steel or wood.
-   The query action is satisfied by a schema like the one described in the previous chapter. The same applies to the action of assigning values to the quantities in the data structure.

    A graphical representation of the situation is given in Fig. 3.26. Within the overall schema we distinguish the input and query subschema (which is identical to the original schema for HAMMER, SHAFT, and HEAD derived in the previous chapter but including the WEIGHT in order to facilitate queries for the weight after it has been determined by the weight analysis algorithm). The drawing subschema contains all the graphical data, the weight analysis subschema all data relevant for this action. Each subschema presents the data in the form which is suitable for the respective action. Comparing this schema with the previous one and with the planned actions, we note:

-   the original schema has become a subschema for input and query, but the weight has been included as an additional attribute;
-   it has become advantageous to use the more complicated triple of HAMMER,

HEAD, and SHAFT, rather than the COMBINED_SCHEMA, since we want to combine different shafts and heads to build all sorts of hammers;
- two additional subschemas have been developed, one representing all data required for the weight analysis algorithm based on elementary geometrical shapes plus material information, the other one representing all data required to produce a design drawing;

The situation, however, is as yet unsatisfactory because

- we cannot derive the data required to fill the drawing and the weight analysis subschema from the input subschema;
- we may calculate the weight, but the value cannot yet be returned to the input and query schema;
- no provisions have been made to avoid the construction of a hammer with a shaft of 15 mm D0 and head of 12 mm D0; the important query schema contains ANGLE and WEIGHT, although ANGLE should always be 60 degrees, and WEIGHT can never be a legal input value.

The two attributes weight and material may be considered as examples, illustrating the freedom that we have in schema planning. Instead of the solution illustrated in Fig. 3.26, we might have included the weight in the weight analysis subschema and/or the material information in the input and query subschema. Depending on our choice, either the input or the query action has to access one or both of these subschemas. Efficiency considerations, based on the estimated number of occurrences of the various actions, must generally be applied to decide which of these solutions is to be preferred.

3.3.3 Subschema Transformations

3.3.3.1 Subschema Transformations as Part of the Schema

How can we produce the data required to fill the drawing schema? These data are necessary for the plotting operation. Two extreme positions may be taken:

- we generate all drawing data from scratch;
- we generate all drawing data from the data in the input and query schema.

The first approach (as shown in Fig. 3.27) is certainly feasible. In fact, it was the standard approach taken in the early stages of CAD. However, two drawbacks are quite evident: the expected economical advantage of introducing CAD is lost if the user has to handle basically the same information many times and cast it into a different subschema once for every action; furthermore, the problem of inconsistency arises since it may easily happen that the drawing displays a length value of 200 mm for the shaft while the corresponding value in the SHAFT subschema is 140 mm.

The second approach (shown in Fig. 3.28) corresponds to the CAD user's paradise. But this paradise is almost nonexistent. How could we possibly derive the size of the drawing text from the input and query subschema? We might,

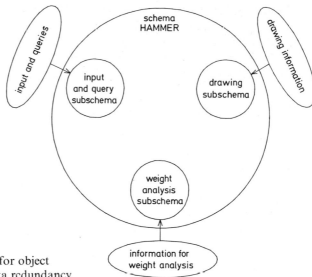

Fig. 3.27. Information flow for object
definition with complete data redundancy

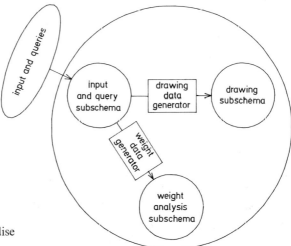

Fig. 3.28. The CAD user's paradise
(which does not exist)

of course, build this knowledge into the "drawing data generator". But this
eliminates the flexibility which is needed whenever the outcome of this built-in
procedure is unacceptable to the user (in the context of Chapter 3.1.2, we would
say that the achievement presented to the higher level process is unsatisfactory).

It will be necessary to guide the drawing data generator when it produces
the drawing by adding the information on how the object should be displayed
while all information about what to display may be taken from the input and

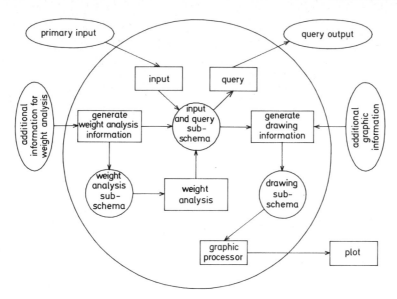

Fig. 3.29. The relationship between subschemas and operations

query subschema. In general, we find that transformation of information from one subschema to another requires additional information. The transformers which take data from one subschema and generate data of another subschema (with additional information) obviously must know two subschemas rather than one. For the sample case discussed so far the situation is shown in Fig. 3.29.

3.3.3.2 The n-square Problem of Subschema Transformations

In CAD system design, one often tries to minimize the number of subschemas in one schema. The reason for this tendency is evident if one assumes that information may have to flow from any subschema to any other subschema. In this case, with n being the number of subschemas, a total of n*(n-1) transformations would be necessary. Because of the quadratic increase in the number of necessary transformations (which would roughly result in a quadratic work increase for the implementation of the CAD system), the CAD system designer will often attempt one of two solutions:

– use only one subschema even if this is unnecessarily complicated and wastes resources in many instances;
– use one preferred subschema, from which and to which all transformations are done.

The first solution is the basis of many successful CAD systems. Finite element programs are typical representatives of this class. The great advantage of the finite element approach lies in the use of a single subschema (or very few) for even the most complicated problems (triangles and rectangles, for in-

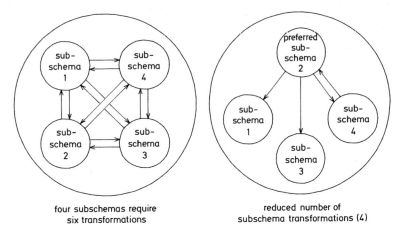

four subschemas require
six transformations

reduced number of
subschema transformations (4)

Fig. 3.30. The n-square problem of data transformation

stance, in the two-dimensional case). The same approach is taken in a number of line drawing systems which are based entirely on polylines for storing geometrical information, even for such regular objects as circles and rectangles.

The second solution corresponds to the preferred mental model of today's data base systems [40]. This preferred model is a flexible schema on which all other subschemas are based. In many realizations, however, only a one way transformation is implemented. In line drawing systems, for instance, the polyline is most often the preferred subschema for graphical information. Circles, arcs and texts may easily be transformed into polylines. But one does usually not bother about the reverse.

In a general case, subschema transformations may have to use data from more than just one subschema in order to produce data for an additional subschema. For four different subschemas the situation is illustrated in Fig. 3.30. The subschema transformations must of course be part of the environment in which the schema exists. In fact, it is advantageous to consider the subschema transformation as part of the total schema itself.

3.3.4 Flexibility — A Measure of Prudence — Versus Efficiency

CAD experts are quite familiar with a very serious problem: after some effort has been put into the planning of a CAD system (or maybe even after implementation) suddenly the goal changes. There may be many reasons for such changes:

- technical development calls for a design change of the objects;
- economical development sets different priorities;
- increased insight into the effect of introducing the CAD system opens a door to new wishes.

It is therefore good policy of CAD system developers to anticipate such new wishes, and to clarify possible problems beforehand. It is often prudent

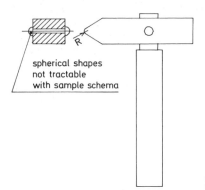

spherical shapes
not tractable
with sample schema

Fig. 3.31. Modification of an existing schema

to plan for goals which are somewhat beyond what is actually requested. This will allow the classification of future wishes into:

- options which should immediately be included in the plan, even if they are not actually required;
- options which may be added later at low cost, provided that such future modification is taken into account in early planning;
- options which would require a more or less new approach.

In the example of the hammer used above, we have already mentioned the first type of these options: although the angle at the front edge of the hammer should always be 60 degrees, it is good strategy to include this information in the schema instead of building this knowledge into all the algorithms (for drawing and weight analysis). Storing the angle value without using it for computation would be dangerously redundant, as both the data structure and the algorithms would know the same information. If the angle value is made part of the schema, the algorithms should use it even if it always the same constant value. Efficiency of execution may be increased in one case, while the algorithms would require an extra look at the data structure in the other case. But the gain in efficiency is probably less important than the increased flexibility. The safety is not reduced by this approach, since the input subschema can easily be restricted so that the value of "angle" can never be input but is rather initialized with the desired 60 degree value. The second type of options may result from the consideration that the front edge of the hammer should perhaps be rounded in more advanced versions. This could be achieved by a slight modification of the schema and somewhat more sophisticated algorithms. The designers of the CAD system might choose to provide the schema for this more advanced goal, but still implement the algorithm for the primitive version only. This approach would make a steady enhancement easier than if the old schema had to be replaced by a new one. The third class of options may be illustrated by the consideration that head and shaft of the hammer might be pinned together as shown in Fig. 3.31 in some later version. Since the pin would involve spherically shaped bodies for which (according to our assumptions) the algorithms for weight analysis are not available, and hence the corresponding subschema is yet undetermined, this option should not be included in the planning of the schema. The purpose of this example is to illustrate the arguments which should be considered in planning a schema. However, the appropriate decisions must be taken in each individual case. There are no general rules, with one exception:

– mistakes in the planning of the schema of a CAD system will drastically limit the success of design processes using the system.

3.3.5 Schema Planning and Design Process Planning

3.3.5.1 Subprocess Planning and Data Validity

Thus far, in the discussion of schema planning we have not adequately considered the process aspect. Schema planning is strongly influenced by the planning of the design process. We can say

CAD modelling = schema planning + design process planning

We will again use the example of the hammer in order to illustrate this point. The basis of our considerations is the schema illustrated in Fig. 3.29. Let us assume that the task to be solved is the design of a hammer with properties which

– (class A) in some parts can be represented by certain values of quantities in the input subschema (such as geometrical data);
– (class B) in other parts can be formally represented as restrictions, with respect to values which are associated with the query schema but not found in the input schema (such as the weight, which should never be input);
– (class C) in certain other parts can not be represented in a formal way within the schema (the design drawing "doesn't look good").

Most design goals include all these three aspects. Class A properties can be specified directly in the input. Class B properties may be obtained only by an interactive process, but this process may potentially be formalized. Thus the successful design process may or may not include a human. Class C properties require that a human be included in the process to perform the task of evaluation (see Fig. 3.3). In this example, we ignore the possibility of automatic iteration of the weight and leave the evaluation task altogether to a human. Process planning consists mainly of combining the elementary operations available in an environment into subprocess units. It is obvious that certain primitive operations must precede others: without prior input no other operation would be meaningful; without prior generation of weight data, the weight analysis would not be useful. The necessary sequence of precedence is illustrated in Fig. 3.32.

One extreme alternative would be to combine all operations into a single process. In this most simple case the process would pass from the operating state "existing" immediately after creation through "executable" to "executing", and would return to "existing" after completion. Finally the process would become "nonexisting". The individual operations would be scheduled within

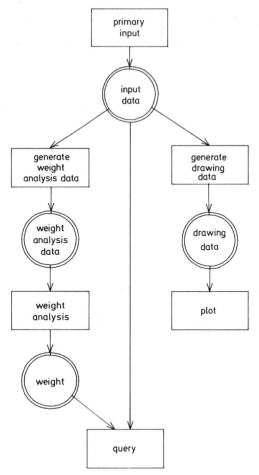

Fig. 3.32. The precedence of operations required for data validity

the process in a predetermined way consistent with the precedence requirements to guarantee that each operation uses only valid data. The data validity problem is thus completely resolved once the internal scheduling is fixed in accordance with the needs. This approach is the basis of many batch-oriented CAD systems. The great advantage of this approach is that the validity problem can be solved once for all processes in the environment. A second easy way to solve the problem is to redo all dependent operations after modification of the data from which they depend. This approach would lead to a subprocess structure as follows:

subprocess 1: primary input, immediately after creation of the process, generate weight analysis data, weight analysis;
subprocess 2: generate drawing data, plot;
subprocess 3: query.

With this partitioning of the operations into subprocesses, no validity problems arise since both subprocesses 2 and 3 can start only with valid data.
However, this approach is far too restrictive in many cases. It may even be
unacceptable: it may well happen that the weight is totally irrelevant in a particular case. No designer would readily accept the necessity to provide additional
information for weight analysis if he is not interested in weight. Furthermore,
the weight analysis may be costly, and should not be carried out unless wanted.
Thus we may prefer the following subprocesses.

Subprocess 1 : primary input immediately after creation of the process;
Subprocess 2 : generate weight analysis data;
Subprocess 3 : weight analysis;
Subprocess 4 : generate drawing data, plot;
Subprocess 5 : query (with options for weight or no weight data).

In the subschemas this approach would be reflected in the following way

```
TYPE   HAMMER_SCHEMA = RECORD
               GAP : REAL;
         HEAD_PART : ->HEAD_SCHEMA;
        SHAFT_PART : ->SHAFT_SCHEMA;
      WEIGHT_VALID : BOOLEAN  INITIAL (FALSE);
            WEIGHT : REAL
                 END;
```

or perhaps

```
TYPE   HAMMER_SCHEMA = RECORD
               GAP : REAL;
         HEAD_PART : ->HEAD_SCHEMA;
        SHAFT_PART : ->SHAFT_SCHEMA;
CASE  WEIGHT_VALID : BOOLEAN  INITIAL (FALSE) OF
             FALSE : ( );
              TRUE : (WEIGHT : REAL)
                 END;
```

The query operation would first have to check WEIGHT_VALID and then
present either the value or an error message. Furthermore, the operation of
adding weight information to the schema would have to be modified to set
the "weight analysis data validity" value to true. This value would then have
to be initialized with false upon creation of the data structure. A request for
weight analysis would first check whether the data to be used are valid. This
approach eliminates the possibility of algorithms using invalid data. However,
it introduces the less obvious but (for that reason) possibly more serious problem
of inconsistency. Let us assume that weight analysis has been performed once
(hence the weight in the query subschema is valid); and let us assume that
a new set of weight analysis data is input afterwards. As a consequence (except
for some rare cases), the weight value in the query subschema is inconsistent
with the weight analysis data; it still reflects an outdated situation.

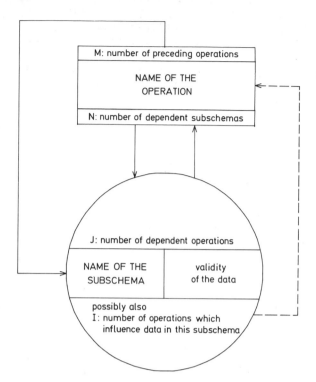

Fig. 3.33. A schema representing the precedence of operations

The question whether results of intermediate operations (such as the weight analysis) should be stored in a system or regenerated whenever needed is fundamental. Storing intermediate results introduces a redundancy which helps to improve efficiency, as it saves the unnecessary repetion of operations. However, the same measure introduces the danger of using invalidated information if the origin of the intermediate results undergoes a change.

There are several methods to insure the correct precedence of operations:

– *Method A*: Leave it to the user.
  In this case no security measure is taken to prevent the user from requesting a weight analysis without valid data, or to query for the weight value before it has been computed. The results of such requests are unpredictable. Nevertheless, in many cases this solution is acceptable. The user will probably be surprised by the result of an invalid request, and will recognize the mistake. Chances are often very small that the result would be so close to what the user expects that he does not recognize the problem. Obviously, this approach should be taken only when the user is experienced enough to judge correctly. In a more complicated situation this probably can not be justified.
– *Method B*: Modify the schema by adding a validity value, and add a validity initiation operation.

This approach influences the subschemas for "input and query" and for "weight analysis data". Both subschemas would have to be enhanced as illustrated for HAMMER below.

- *Method C*: Method C: Add a "validity check" subprocess and a validity subschema.

The validity subschema might have the form

```
TYPE VALIDITY=RECORD
     INPUT_DATA, WEIGHT_ANALYSIS_DATA,
     WEIGHT, DRAWING_DATA          : BOOLEAN INITIAL(FALSE)
          END;
```

The subprocess responsible for the validity of the data would be called upon at the beginning and end of other operations. At the beginning of an operation the validity subprocess would be asked whether all data to be used are valid; at the end the subprocess would be requested to set the validity of the new data to true and the validity of all dependent data to false. In this case, the knowledge of precedence would have to be built into the validity check algorithm. In a more complicated situation this knowledge would preferably be built into a data structure, which may have a schema as represented in Fig. 3.33.

3.3.5.2 The Information Packages

The ideas in the previous chapter lead us to consider another aspect of information in CAD systems: How should we group the information which is to be exchanged among the various subprocesses? In particular, how should we group the information which flows between user and system? Information is always transported in certain packages (for input, output, and storage). In the implementation, these packages may appear as statements, commands, or records. In the example used in this chapter it is not possible to modify the material properties for the hammer shaft without repeating the whole weight analysis — even for the head piece which remains unchanged. Similarly, the additional drawing information must be input as a complete set of data. It would not be possible to change the width of an individual line without regenerating the complete drawing data structure.

The aspect of how information should be grouped has been given much attention recently in the area of artificial intelligence. In particular, investigations related to chess playing by humans and computers [41] have shown that a human stores and handles information not always in the most obvious way, but rather on various levels of abstraction in so-called information chunks. In chess play, for example, certain situations are not memorized as a set of pieces located on certain fields of the two-dimensional array on the chess board, but as a single chunk that represents the whole strategic situation. Communication between a human and a CAD system would probably be optimal if information packages corresponding to such chunks in the design task could be exchanged. On output, graphical representation of information comes very much closer to this ideal than lists of figures do.

Large information packages are quite adequate for batch processing, which is characterized by much work in the preparation of a complete and correct set of input data. In interactive processes, however, the information packages must be reduced to a size which is easily tractable by the user without great risk of mistakes during input, or misunderstanding or frustration during output. Thus, in interactive CAD systems, one is forced to break the information packages and hence the individual subprocesses down to small sizes. As a consequence, the number of subschemas and of subprocesses becomes large, and the problem of data validity and consistency becomes more important than in batch-oriented systems.

The information packages which are exchanged between the user of a CAD system and the system itself are not merely groups of information units. They must be formulated subject to certain rules. On input (to the system) they must be transformed into a machine-readable representation, on output (from the system) they must be transformed into a form which is perceptible by the operator (in most cases a visible form). The set of rules for the formulation and representation of the information packages and constitutes the operator language of the CAD system.

One particular question in the design of the communication language is whether it should have a descriptive or more of a command character. For interactive communication, the general trend is to split the user input into a large number of commands containing relatively few descriptive data. The advantage of this approach is that it makes echoing and correcting input a relatively simple task. The commands may often be classified into the following groups:

- commands for building a model;
- commands for starting significant processing;
- commands for display of results;
- commands for addressing system utility functions (such as "help").

A more descriptive type of language would tend to eliminate the commands for initialization of processing steps. A system based upon this approach would have to determine itself what processing steps ought to be taken, on the basis of the types of results that are asked for. A precedence schema, as illustrated in Fig. 3.33, could be used in a CAD system to derive such information. An example of this kind of approach to CAD has been proposed by Pomberger [42].

Modelling in CAD is a task which consists of the following main subtasks, which must be performed in a parallel and coordinated way:

- planning of the schema:
    * identification of the objects to be treated,
    * specification of the relations between the objects,
    * specification of the attributes of objects and relations,

* specification of the allowable range of values for the attributes,
* refinement of the schema, introduction of subschemas;

– planning of the process:
  * identification of the subprocesses,
  * specification of the subschemas required for the subprocesses, including the efficiency aspect,
  * specification of precedences among the subprocesses,
  * specification of the data validity requirements for each subprocess;

– planning of the language:
  * specification of the information packages for communication between man and machine,
  * specification of the rules for formulating and representing these information packages.

3.3.6 Resulting Data Base Management System Requirements

The close interrelationship between the operations in a design process and the schema poses special problems which do not arise (for instance) in commercial applications to the same extent. When computer methods are to be applied, the conceptual schema of the design process, or at least a subschema of it, will have to be represented on two levels:

– in the programs;
– on external storage media.

In the programs, a subschema representation takes the form of the set of declarations of records, arrays, and variables (specifying names and attributes) which represent the entities in the schema. For external storage, we find two solutions: files or data base management systems (DBMS). Files contain records which represent the individual entities and relations, while the associated subschema is implicitly defined by the corresponding declaration of records in all programs which access the file. In a DBMS, however, the schema is explicitly stored as an integral part of the data base itself.

When we discuss the exchange of data between programs, we have to consider filling systems and DBMS's as alternatives. The DBMS provides several well-known advantages (see also Chapter 2.4):

– relief of the application program from details of data and storage space administration;
– relief of the application program from access efficiency considerations;
– reduced data redundancy;
– reduced redundancy of the schema representations;
– improved consistency;
– shared access by separate parallel processes;
– improved data security.

These advantages do not imply that filing systems are completely outdated. They are still superior to a DBMS for rapidly accessing large amounts of data.

DBMS's have a wide-spread application in commercial data processing, while they are as yet less frequently found in a CAD environment. The reasons are mainly the following:

- In commercial applications, the number of entities of a single type is generally large, but the number of entity types is limited. In design, however, the situation is opposite. The number of entity types is extremely large (how many different parts are in a car?!) while there are usually just a few instances of each entity type;
- the relationships between entities are generally much more complex in a CAD schema (functional relationships, topological relationships, geometric relationships) as compared to commercial data processing. In short, CAD requires that significantly more complex schemas be handled;
- as described in Chapter 2.2.2 and illustrated by Fig. 3.13, design consists largely of the development of a schema. Only in detail design (variational design) can the schema be considered as fixed. Otherwise, the schema is subject to continuous development, while in most DBMS's the schema is assumed to have a relatively long lifetime without modification. As a consequence, DBMS's which are suited for commercial data processing applications may be expected to satisfy the requirements of CAD for variational design, but not necessarily for the whole design process.

Hence, a data base management system for CAD application must provide facilities for

- handling very complex schemas with up to a thousand different types of entities, or even more;
- allow for frequent modification of the schema, with the associated necessary transformation of the previously defined data base content into the new schema

3.4 Summary

This chapter had two main purposes. First, we introduced a concept (or a model) of the design process which can be used as a basis for describing CAD processes. Secondly, we introduced a terminology which will be used for describing design processes, CAD processes, and CAD systems. A key issue was the structuring of the design process into the activities of specification, synthesis, analysis, evaluation, and presentation. These activities are centered around a conceptual model of the objects to be designed. However, when the design process starts, the conceptual model is only partly determined (namely by the specification). It will be developed, refined, and possibly modified as the design proceeds in the synthesis activity. Analysis does not change the conceptual model, but rather determines values for object attributes in the model. Evaluation compares the results with the specified goals, and influences the synthesis activity. The achievement of the design is presented to the higher-level process from which the specification was issued.

The important concept of the environment was introduced. The environment is considered as a process in which the design process is embedded. The environment provides the required resources for the design process and coordinates resource requests if more than one process is executed in parallel. Learning was identified as an activity of the environment.

The fundamental difference between a human-based design process and CAD processes is the need for formal representation. While man can work on an informal basis, CAD is possible only if the conceptual schema and the rules to be applied in synthesis and analysis have been formalized. This requirement applies both to conventional CAD systems and to systems based on artificial intelligence (AI) methods. While in conventional CAD the synthesis is mainly the task of a human operator, AI methods offer the chance to transfer this task to the CAD system. The reason for this difference stems from the fact that conventional CAD systems are based on the common programming languages and the algorithmic approach to problem-solving that underlies them. Furthermore, conventional data base systems and programming languages generally consider the determination of a schema as a task which has to be completed before any other operation using the schema. In synthesis, however, we apply rules which are not in algorithmic form and we should be able to manipulate schemas freely. For this reason, AI methods have a potential for progress in the synthesis area of CAD, but more research is needed before such methods are ready for production.

Finally, we investigated modelling in CAD. Modelling, or developing a schema, is a task which cannot be performed by simply studying the anticipated properties of the objects to be designed (although this is one prerequisite). The schema and its various subschemas are significantly influenced by the operations. Along with functional aspects, the consideration of efficient utilization of the available resources (manpower being the most precious) will influence schema planning. As a third constituent (besides schema and operations), we have identified the CAD system language. CAD system design requires the development of these three constituents in parallel.

3.5 Bibliography

[1] G. Pahl, W. Beitz: Konstruktionslehre. Handbuch für Studium und Praxis. Heidelberg (1977) Springer-Verlag.
[2] G. Grotenhuis, J. van den Broek: A Conceptual Model for Information Processing. In: G.M. Nijssen: Modelling in Data Base Management Systems. Amsterdam (1976) North-Holland Publ. Co., pp. 149–180.
[3] G.M. Nijssen: A Gross Architecture for the next Generation Database Management. In: G.M. Nijssen: Modelling in Data Base Management Systems. Amsterdam (1976) North-Holland Publ. Co., pp. 1–24.
[4] K. Nygaard, P. Nåndlykken: The System Development Process. In: K. Hünke: Software Engineering Environments. Amsterdam (1980) North-Holland Publ. Co., pp. 157–172.

[5] R. Wächtler: Die Dynamik des Entwickelns (Konstruierens). Feinwerktechnik 73 (1969), pp. 329–333.

[6] H. Grabowski, M. Eigner: Anforderungen an CAD-Datenbanksysteme. VDI-Z 121 (1979) 12 pp. 621–633.

[7] G.J. Sussman: SLICES : At the Boundary between Analysis and Synthesis. In: J.C. Latombe: Artificial Intelligence and Pattern Recognition in Computer Aided Design. Amsterdam (1978) North-Holland Publ. Co., pp. 261–299.

[8] D.R. Hofstadter: Gödel, Escher, Bach: An Eternal Golden Braid. New York (1980) Vintage Books, pp. 24–27.

[9] J.-C. Latombe: Artificial Intelligence and Pattern Recognition in Computer Aided Design. Amsterdam (1978) North-Holland Publ. Co.

[10] J. Lumley: Expert Systems. Systems International. June 1982, pp. 53–56. n.

[11] E. Warman: Computer Aided Design: An Intersection of Ideas. In: J.C. Latombe: Artificial Intelligence and Pattern Recognition in Computer Aided Design. Amsterdam (1978) North-Holland Publ. Co., pp. 1–18.

[12] Reference Model of Open Systems Interconnection (Version 4 as of June 1979). Report ISO/TC97/SC16 N227, Paris (1978) Association Francaise de Normalisation.

[13] J. Misra, K. Mani Chandy: Proofs of Networks of Processes. IEEE Trans. Softw. Eng., Vol.SE-7, (1981) 4, pp. 417–426.

[14] J. Hatvany: The Engineer's Creative Activity in a CAD Environment. In: J. Vlietstra, R.F. Wielinga (eds.): Computer-Aided Design. Amsterdam (1973) North-Holland Publ. Co., pp. 113–126.

[15] F.-L.Krause, V.Vassilakopoulos: A Way to Computer Supported Systems for Integrated Design and Production Process Planning. In: J.J. Allan III: CAD Systems. Amsterdam (1977) North-Holland Publ. Co., pp. 5–34.

[16] R. Simon: Rechnergestütztes Konstruieren. Dissertation Techn. Hochschule, Aachen (1968) Amsterdam (1977) North-Holland Publ. Co., pp. 5–34.

[17] K. Roth, H.J. Franke, R. Simonek: Algorithmisches Auswahlverfahren zur Konstruktion mit Katalogen. Feinwerktechnik 75 (1971), pp. 337–345.

[18] F. Hansen: Konstruktionswissenschaft — Grundlagen und Methoden. München (1974) Hanser-Verlag.

[19] R. Koller: Konstruktionsmethode für den Maschinen-, Geräte- und Apparatebau. Heidelberg (1976) Springer-Verlag.

[20] W.G. Rodenacker: Methodisches Konstruieren. Konstruktionsbücher Bd. 27, 2. Aufl. Heidelberg (1976) Springer-Verlag.

[21] H.G. Baumann, K.-H. Looscheelders: Rechnerunterstütztes Projektieren und Konstruieren. Heidelberg (1982) Springer-Verlag.

[22] J.J. Allan III: CAD in the U.S. and in Europe. In: Report GRIS 78-3, Fachgebiet Graphisch-Interaktive Systeme. Darmstadt (1978) Techn.Hochschule.

[23] J. Hatvany, W.M. Newman, M.A. Sabin: World Survey of Computer-Aided Design. Computer Aided Design 9 (1977) 2, pp. 79–98.

[24] "PEARL": Full PEARL Language Description. Report KfK-PDV 130, Kernforschungszentrum Karlsruhe (1977).

[25] "DIN 66253 Teil 1": Programmiersprache PEARL. Basic PEARL. Vornorm. Berlin (1981) Beuth.

[26] J.F.H. Winkler: Das Prozeßkonzept in Betriebssystemen und Programmiersprachen I. Informatik Spektrum 2 (1979) 4, pp. 219–229.

[27] J.F.H. Winkler: Das Prozeßkonzept in Betriebssystemen und Programmiersprachen II. Informatik Spektrum 3 (1980) 1, pp. 31–40.

[28] E.G. Schlechtendahl: Rules for Designing CAD Software Machines. Proceedings of the International Conference "Interactive Techniques in Computer Aided Design". Bologna, Italy (1978).

[29] E.W. Dijkstra: Cooperating Sequential Processes. In: F.Genuys: Programming Languages. New York (1968) Academic Press.

[30] P. Brinch Hansen: Distributed Processes: A Concurrent Programming Concept. Computing Surveys 5 (1973) 4, pp. 223–245.

[31] K. Zuse: Petri-Netze aus der Sicht des Ingenieurs. Braunschweig (1980) Vieweg & Sohn.

[32] P. Brinch Hansen: The Programming Language Concurrent Pascal. IEEE Trans. Softw. Eng. 1 (1975) 2, pp. 199–207.

[33] J.H. Saltzer: Naming and Binding of Objects. In: G. Goos, J. Hartmanis (eds.): Operating Systems. Lecture Notes in Computer Science, Vol. 60. Berlin (1978) Springer-Verlag, pp. 99–208.

[34] C. Schuenemann: Speicherhierarchie-Aufbau und Betriebsweise, Informatik-Spektrum 1 (1978) 1, pp. 25–36.

[35] J.J. Allan III, K. Bø: A Survey of Commercial Turnkey CAD/CAM Systems. Dallas (1978) Productivity Int. Corp.

[36] E.G. Schlechtendahl: Comparison of Integrated Systems for CAD., Int. Conf. Computer Aided Design, IEE Conf. Publ. 111, Southampton (1974), pp. 111–116.

[37] "DIN 6": Darstellungen in Zeichnungen. Berlin (1968) Beuth.

[38] "ANSI Y14.3-1975": Multi and Sectional View Drawings. New York (1975) Americ. Soc. Mech. Eng.

[39] J.S. Bruner: A Study of Thinking. New York (1956) John Wiley & Sons, pp. 232.

[40] K. Ecker: Organisation von parallelen Prozessen — Theorie deterministischer Schedules. Reihe Informatik 23, Bibliographisches Institut Mannheim (1977) B.I.-Wissenschaftsverlag.

[41] P.W. Frey: Chess Skill in Man and Machine. Heidelberg (1978) Springer-Verlag.

[42] G. Pomberger: Ein Modell zur Simulation von Konstruktionsprozessen. Angewandte Informatik (1982) 1, pp. 26–34.

4 The Architecture of CAD Systems

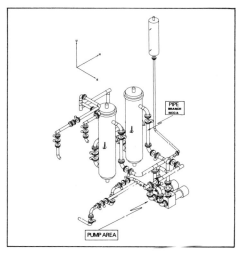

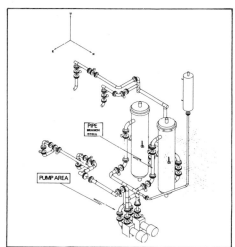

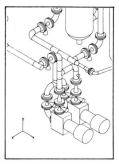

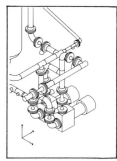

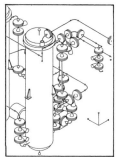

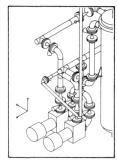

Plant layout in 3-D
(courtesy of Compeda Ltd., London, UK)

4.1 The Gross Architecture

4.1.1 Components

Just as it would be difficult to define "the typical program" or "the typical house", there is no such thing as "the typical CAD system". The architecture of a particular CAD system will certainly depend on

- the task to be solved by the system;
- the computer resources available for its implementation (both hardware and software);
- the experience of the CAD system designer;
- rules established within the company or on a wider scale, which restrict the freedom of the system designer.

Graphical representations of CAD systems depend very much upon the aspects which their authors wished to emphasize. Fig. 2.1 is a representation which illustrates the major functional components. The individual components may be more or less pronounced in a given CAD system, and may be implemented with more or less sophistication depending on the particular needs. In one case the "data base" is realized as a commercially available data base system with all its functions, in another case the "data base" may be a set of files handled by the user by means of the computer's operating system. A different representation of the same functional concept is given in Fig. 4.1, based on [1]. This representation emphasizes the time sequence of the execution of several CAD programs as the design process proceeds through its various phases. The

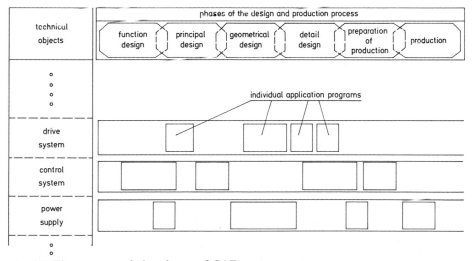

Fig. 4.1. The program chain schema of CAD systems

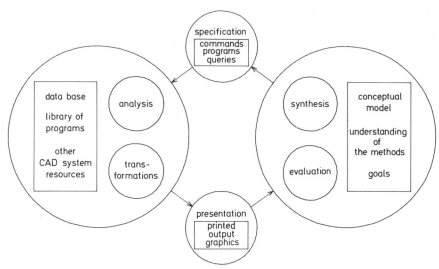

Fig. 4.2. CAD activities and CAD system components

representation shown in Fig. 4.2 relates the main system components to the major activities in a design process as described in Chapter 3:

– specification;
– synthesis;
– analysis;
– transformation;
– presentation;
– evaluation.

    The specifications are passed from the system user (the operator) to the CAD system as commands, queries, or programs, expressed in a language that is understood by both partners (man and machine). Within the CAD system, analyses and transformations are performed accordingly. The state of the process is represented in the data base, while the program libraries and other system resources are used during execution. Results are presented in graphical or printed form to the operator who performs the evaluation by comparing the results with the goal. The operator (usually) performs the synthesis task as well. For this purpose he must have a conceptual model of the objects handled by the CAD system, and of the state of the CAD system process. He must also have a conceptual understanding of the methods that are implemented in the system as programs, and he must know how these methods affect the objects. With this knowledge, he can formulate the specification of the next steps to be taken and send this request to the CAD system. In certain cases, however, the synthesis task is at least partially located within the CAD system. For special products in a special environment, it may be possible to formulate a synthesis algorithm which can be programmed. Furthermore, systems based upon artificial intelli-

Table 4.1. Correspondence between functional, hardware, and software aspects

Functional	Hardware	Software
knowledge, memory	peripheral storage devices: disks, drums, tapes, etc.	program libraries data files, data base systems
state represen- tation of process	same as above	data files, data base systems
analysis	central processor and primary memory	programs, modules, program packages
man → machine communication		
control and data	punched card keyboard (terminal)	card image files, text editors; character string records, commands;
control	function keys	case constructs
identification	light-pen	case constructs
machine → man communication		
inquiries, messages	printer (terminal) or display (alphanumeric) indicator lights, graphics display	character string records menu technique, prompting; graphical representation of objects and commands
presentation: of text	printer, terminal, COM	sufficiently supported in most programming languages
of pictures	plotter, graphics display, COM	graphics packages
mixed text and pictures	plotter, graphics display, COM	graphics packages
information transport	mail local computer periphery, networks (telephone, computer, etc.)	mail software packages which are usually hidden in the computer environment (except for their time and money aspects)
evaluation, synthesis	man man	man man

gence methods attempt to support synthesis in a wider range of problems [2]. But the standard case corresponds to the situation shown in Fig. 4.2.

The components of a CAD system may be viewed in various aspects. The functional aspect relates the system components to the model of the design process, the hardware aspect concentrates on pieces of equipment, while the software aspect deals with programs and data. There is typically (but not neces-

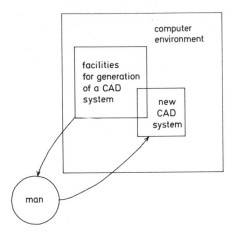

Fig. 4.3. The implementation of a new CAD system in an environment

sarily) a correspondence between the functions and the hardware/software components which perform them. Table 4.1 summarizes this correspondence.

4.1.2 Interfaces

4.1.2.1 Development and Installation of a CAD System

Before a CAD system can be used it must be developed and installed. In the case of turn-key systems [3], these activities are reduced to the analysis of commercially available systems, and the evaluation of how well they will suit the actual needs. In other cases, especially with the so-called "integrated systems" [4], the implementation of a CAD system uses components of the environment — and sometimes components of the system itself — in what is known as "bootstrap" technique (Fig. 4.3). In designing and implementing new CAD systems, such techniques very effectively reduce the time and cost of system development.

4.1.2.2 The Invocation of a CAD System

Let us assume that a CAD system has been installed in a computer environment. Before he can operate with the CAD system on a given project (new or old), the designer must invoke the CAD system: he must bring it to execution. In order to do this, the designer (whom we call the operator while he is using the CAD system) must deal with a number of obstacles before he can address the CAD system itself. There may be organizational barriers (the access to the CAD system may require him to move physically to another room or another building), but in any case there will be barriers due to the computer environment.

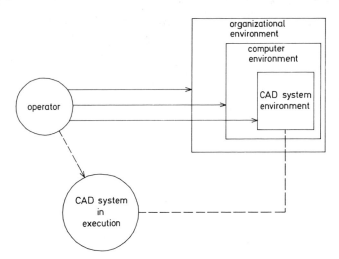

Fig. 4.4. Interfaces during invocation of a CAD system

If he uses a central computer, both the CAD system and the data structure representing the state of his CAD process may be on resident storage devices, and the obstacle is merely a language barrier: he must use a limited subset of the computer's operating system control language to hook the CAD system both to the data (files) of the process and to the communication channels (terminals) he wants to use. If he uses a dedicated CAD computer in his office, he may even have to deal with hardware: he may need to load a couple of floppy disks (one for the CAD system, one for his data) and perform some manipulations to start the computer. Compared to the large central computer, he may find that the operating system of his dedicated computer is much easier to use. In any case the communication interface of the computer environment always constitutes a part of the interface between the operator and the CAD system (see Fig. 4.3). Only after the invocation of his CAD system can the operator address the system itself (Fig. 4.4).

4.1.2.3 Functional Interfaces in a CAD System

Fig. 4.2 is an overview of the main functional components of a CAD process during execution. The representation, however, is not very helpful with respect to the interfaces between system components. Either the interface is not shown, or it is represented simply by a solid line. But a solid line between two circles can mean almost anything. We will now investigate in more detail the interfaces between some CAD system components, although such a detailed analysis complicates the picture considerably (even if we concentrate on a just few components). A graphical representation of the interfaces among all components would become unreadable. When investigating an interface between components, we will apply the following consideration:

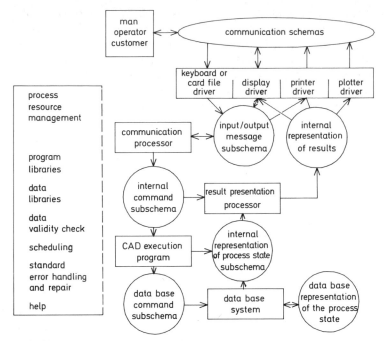

Fig. 4.5. Interfaces between main CAD system components

| An interface between two components represents the use of a
| shared resource according to one or more agreed-upon
| schemas.

Thus, in order to discuss an interface between two components, we must say something about this common resource and about the related schema. Note that the two components do not necessarily have to use the same schema. In a general situation, particularly in open systems configurations [5], the interface resource may provide a schema transformation alowing each of the interfacing components to use a different schema to represent the same information. The situation occurs quite frequently when data are exchanged between computers of different manufacturers, which use different coding for data representation (see Chapter 4.3.4). Except for the extra schema transformation, which may require some additional information for correct operation, there is no basic difference from the situation where both partners use the same schema. For this reason, we will discuss only the simple case where one schema is used by both communicating partners.

We can use Fig. 4.5 as a model for discussing the execution of a CAD system. The figure concentrates on the interfaces between the main functional components. For the moment, let us ignore the box on the left-hand side of the figure. As in Fig. 3.29, the CAD system programs (which perform the analytical work) and the subschema transformations play a central role. They operate on an internal representation of the process state by using primary memory (with computer words as the resource), according to a certain sub-schema. This subschema is defined by the declaration of some global data structure in the programs. For long-term saving of the process state, a data base system is used. The rules for transformation of the schema into the data base's internal representation are carried out within the data base system; the data definition language of the system has been used to define this transformation. All CAD execution programs and the communication processor use the command subschema of the data base to access data in the data base system.

Transformation of process state data from the data base into an internal representation takes place in a similar way.

The internal state representation is also the interface between the CAD programs and a result presentation processor (one or several), which produces an internal representation of results suitable for output on a number of devices. The output device processors (printer, plotter, display) will then transform the results into optically perceptible information in a schema as required by the operator or other persons (a customer, for instance).

Communication from the operator to the CAD system is mainly in the form of a conversation between the operator and a communication processor (interpreter, compiler) within the CAD system. The purpose of this communication is to build up or to change the internal state representation (the "model"), and to inquire about the actual model state [6]. If more than one input device is to be used, it is advisable to have a common interface for representing messages (in either direction) between the drivers of the input device and the actual communication processor. Often a character string representation is used as a common command schema for all input devices. Input originating from any input device is first converted to the character string representation, and can then be processed by the command interpreter in just the same way as if it had come from the keyboard. Part of the conversation will take place in a local way (errors in basic input syntax can be detected by the device drivers, and correction will be requested so that only "legal" commands are passed to the communication processor). The communication processor controls the execution of the CAD programs by passing information from the input to them in a special interface.

The schematic described so far represents what might be called the "abstract CAD machine". Only the main functions are considered here. All processes within the executing CAD system, however, need to be supported by a number of utility functions which designers of CAD systems tend to hide from the users. The resource management in the CAD system provides the necessary environmental conditions for the successful operation of the "concrete CAD machine".

4.1.2.4 Man-Machine Communication Channels

From Fig. 4.5 it is evident that several communication processes will occur between the operator and the CAD system at any given time. Problems may arise if these communication processes share the same resource for visualization.

Table 4.2. Use of available hardware for man-machine communication

Available hard-ware	Used for message visualization	Used for result presentation
printer	printer	new page before and after blocks of results
printer + plotter	printer	plotter
teletype + display	teletype	display surface
storage display	display surface, possibly limited to a certain area	(erase display surface before presenting a block of results)
refresh display	restricted area on display surface (message viewport)	remaining area of display surface
two displays	one display for alpha-numeric	one display for graphics

In the extreme case where there is only a single display available, the input echo and computer operating system messages — among others — compete with each other for the limited display space (in printer output all these processes may share the same paper, but at least they do not have to compete with each other for the lines). In order to avoid severe problems, it has become a good practice to use at least two separate visualization surfaces, one for the presentation of results and one for the messages of the communication processes, including the input echo. Examples of solutions to this problem of conflict are listed in Table 4.2.

4.1.3 CAD Tools and CAD Machines

In an established CAD environment, one is unlikely to find a CAD system being developed from scratch. Generally one finds certain components in other systems which (at least in principle) could be used beneficially in the new CAD system. Considerable economic savings are possible if, for a new CAD task, either an existing CAD system can be used (possibly with some adaptation) or — if some amount of new development cannot be avoided — the work of development can be reduced by utilizing available tools. The necessity for and the benefits of such tools were pointed out by Hatvany [7]. Two categories of such tools may be distinguished:

– tools which become part of the CAD system and will be used during its operation. We will call these tools "machines";
– tools which are used only during the CAD system development.

4.1.3.1 Tools Used in CAD System Application

Typical low-level components which one would choose from the rack to combine them into an operable CAD system are:

- a data base system;
- a file management system;
- a program package for handling common data structures in primary memory;
- a command interpreter for character-string-type commands and for interactive graphic communication;
- a graphics package;
- mathematical subroutine packages.

One would also like to select from an available set of higher-level tools for such tasks as:

- finite element analysis;
- two-dimensional geometry handling;
- computer-supported drafting;
- three-dimensional geometry handling;
- smooth surface design;
- hidden line removal.

It is a well-known problem in the world of CAD that even if such machines are available (and quite often they are), it is a major task to put them together into a satisfactory or even barely functional system. They just do not fit together. This is one reason for the continual rewriting of programs all over the world. The question is obvious: Is it possible to design such software machines so that they can be put together into an operational system, in any arbitrary combination, more easily than the present state of the art allows? We will devote Chapter 4.3.2 specifically to this question.

Many of the points to be discussed are not new and may be found in other areas. In particular a technically oriented reader should note the similarity between the software machine concept developed here and real machines in an industrial process.

4.1.3.2 Tools Used in CAD System Development

In an environment where the development of CAD systems is a routine job, one is likely to find special software systems for this work. These tools include:

- specification aids;
- testing aids;
- documentation aids;
- precompilers and
- program generators.

Although the specification is (or should be) completed before the development of a CAD system is started, while the documentation is performed in parallel with the development, specification aids are often suited for documentation purposes as well. This applies particularly to relatively informal methods like SADT [8] (see also Chapter 5.1.) or PSL/PSA [9]. Such systems are already being used for production purposes. Formal specification methods based on abstract data types [10] or on "traces" [11] are still undergoing rapid development. For a survey of specification and planning methods, see [12, 13, 14, 15]. Special tools for testing have been developed, too [16].

Precompilers usually serve two purposes. They may guarantee the consistency of data declarations in different programs which are intended to operate on the same objects. For this purpose, data declarations are retrieved from a data base and inserted into the programs (in the most simple case, by including a piece of declarations text or by expanding macros). The second purpose is to permit the algorithms to be written in a language that is better suited to express the operations, or simply shorter than the available programming language. The higher-level program text is then compiled into a language for which standard compilers are available (e.g. FORTRAN, PL/1, etc.).

One example of a collection of software tools is the National Bureau of Standards Software Tools Database [17]. Recent developments in this area are reported in [18].

4.2 Data Models

4.2.1 Mapping

4.2.1.1 The Ideal Situation

We will assume that a conceptual model of the objects to be handled in a CAD system has been derived. We will further assume that this model satisfies all functional requirements, that is, it is suitable for all operations to be performed on a conceptual level. Finally, we have defined which information the system should receive from the user and supply to the user, and how this information is to be packed into information packages (see Chapter 2.3.5.2). We are now faced with the problem that a computer does not operate in the abstract space of the abstract data types [19]. The objects of abstract data types must somehow be mapped onto the hardware of the computer. The same statement applies to the operations to be performed with the objects, and to the information packages. In practice, the mapping from abstract space to hardware is not done in a single step. An intermediate mapping level (at least one) is introduced. The intermediate level is the level of a language which can be understood by both man and machine. The closer this language is to the concepts used in the abstract space, the more easily man can use it. This is the level of "high level languages" or "problem oriented languages". Of course, it would be advantageous if only one intermediate mapping is required. Fig. 4.6 illustrates this situation.

In the ideal situation, man would only have to deal with the mapping between the conceptual level and that of the high-level language. The mapping from this level to the hardware level would be hidden in the language compilers and the operating system. In reality, the ideal situation is rarely found. This

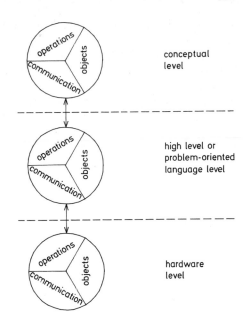

Fig. 4.6. The ideal two-step mapping between the conceptual world and hardware

is particularly true when FORTRAN is considered as the main (or perhaps the only) available high-level language. Since FORTRAN is by far the most common programming language for CAD, we cannot simply ignore the deviations from the ideal. We have to identify such deviations in order the make them evident.

4.2.1.2 Reasons for Non-Ideal Mapping

There are two basic reasons for deviations from the ideal situation: inadequate functional capabilities of the high-level language, and loss of efficiency of the system execution process. The following examples will illustrate these cases.

(1) SCALAR TYPES IN FORTRAN. Let us assume that we wish to express a calendar date on the language level. With PASCAL this could be done as follows [20]:

```
type DATE= record
DAY   :     1:  31;
MONTH:  (JAN,FEB,MAR,APR,MAY,JUN,JUL,AUG,SEP,OCT,NOV,DEC);
YEAR  : 1900:2200
            end;
```

Thus all calendar dates from Jan. 1, 1900 through Dec. 31, 2200 are mapped from the conceptual model space into the language level. The reverse mapping,

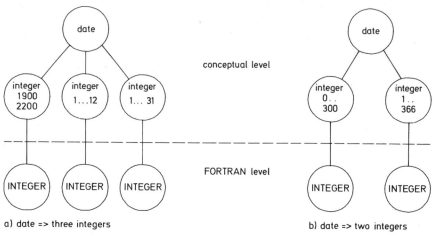

a) date => three integers   b) date => two integers

Fig. 4.7. The mapping of calender dates (as an example) onto integers

however, might produce some illegal calendar dates such as Feb. 30, 1930, which makes the above record definition somewhat unsatisfactory and indicates the limitation of even advanced programming languages like PASCAL.

In FORTRAN, however, the situation is worse, since only a very limited number of data types is available (basically INTEGER and REAL). Hence we must map all abstract data types onto these few data types. A common way of doing this is to introduce an intermediate mapping between the abstract level and the language level. Two possibilities are shown in Fig. 4.7a and 4.7b using the data type "date" as an example. In the case of Fig. 4.7a, we map day, month, and year onto one integer each. In Fig. 4.7b, we define the year 1900 as a reference (mapped onto the integer value 0) and count the days from 1 through 366. Thus all calendar dates between Jan. 1, 1900 and Dec. 31, 2200 find their mapping on the language level, but the reverse mapping is really inadequate. A rather complicated algorithm is required to retrieve from the single integer value the separate information of day and month. The inverse mapping may not even be unique: other objects of the conceptual space may also have been mapped onto integers. Considerable confusion and significant economic losses for program debugging arise from this deficiency in FOR-TRAN. Due to a programming error, it may easily happen that "green" (mapped onto integer 3, say) is added to the "third of February" (mapped onto integer 34) with unforeseeable consequences.

(2) STORAGE SPACE CONSIDERATIONS. We are still using the above example, but will now introduce the resource aspect of storage space. Mapping a calendar date onto two integers (as in Fig. 4.7b) instead of three immediately saves one-third of the storage space. This statement may be derived from even a rough understanding of compilers, which tells us that every integer quantity needs one computer word for storage. The same line of argument may be carried further; mapping of the calendar date onto a single integer (as indicated in

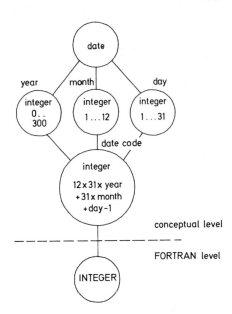

Fig. 4.8. The mapping of calender dates onto
a single integer

Fig. 4.8) will save two-thirds of the storage space, as compared to Fig. 4.7a. The saving in storage space must, however, be paid for with extra processing cost whenever the normal calendar representation (month, day, year) has to be retrieved from the single integer.

4.2.1.3 Mapping Around the Language

A most peculiar situation arises if the high-level language is totally unsuited for mapping certain objects, while adequate support could be provided on a lower level (assembler language and hardware). The system designer is then tempted to map around the language level in order to achieve what he needs *despite* the properties of the high-level language. We will use a version of FORTRAN which does not support character handling to illustrate such attempts. Let us write a program which reads characters, one at a time, and checks for the occurrence of A, E, I, O, or U. We assume that the computer has a byte structured memory and that INTEGERs are stored in two bytes, LOGICAL∗1 data in one byte.

Most FORTRAN programmers know how the compiler will map arrays of integers and logicals onto a sequence of computer storage words by bytes. They also know that reading a character will result in setting certain bits in a storage byte of the computer, and that this sequence of bits might be interpreted as an integer. Using this knowledge, the program designer can now map the character of the conceptual level onto computer storage bytes (see Fig. 4.9): he maps the bytes onto a two-dimensional array of logicals (CHAR)

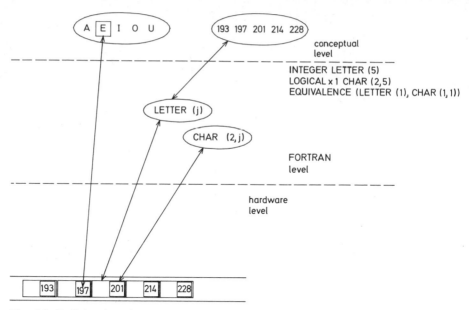

Fig. 4.9. Deficiencies of programming languages cause mapping around the language

which — using an EQUIVALENCE — is imbedded in an array of INTEGERs. The INTEGER array corresponds to a sequence of integers in the conceptual world. Instead of testing for 'E', which is not possible in our assumed FORTRAN, the program might test for 197. Note: the fact that we have included this example does not imply that we recommend the procedure described. However, the technique of mapping around the language level is common practice especially in FORTRAN programming, and in fact is sometimes unavoidable. Experienced FORTRAN programmers can do almost everything in this language, particularly if a couple of FORTRAN callable Assembler routines are added. Of course, it would be much better to use a language which provides the necessary features without requiring techniques — such as EQUIVALENCE — which are known to be a frequent source of error.

4.2.1.4 Mapping Between Aspects

We will use a plane truss to illustrate the mapping between the aspects of operation, representation and communication. On the conceptual level, we characterize the geometry of a plane truss by

- the set of nodes (node name and location for each node);
- the set of frame members (member name, names of starting node and end node for each member, cross sectional area).

    The location is always assumed to be given by X and Y coordinates in a unique Cartesian coordinate system. The corresponding schema is graphically

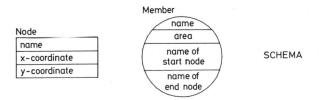

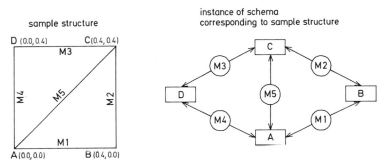

a) Graphical representation of the schema

sample structure

instance of schema
corresponding to sample structure

b) Two representations of a sample structure

Fig. 4.10. Sample schema: plane truss

represented in Fig. 4.10a. together with a sample truss structure (Fig. 4.10b). We assume that a DBTG data base system as described in [21] is to be used for implementation purposes. In the DBTG data definition language, the schema definition would be as follows:

```
RECORD NAME IS NODE;
LOCATION MODE IS SYSTEM;
WITHIN MODEL;
02 NAME; TYPE IS CHAR 20;
02 X; TYPE IS REAL;
02 Y; TYPE IS REAL;

RECORD NAME IS MEMBER;
LOCATION MODE IS SYSTEM;
WITHIN MODEL;
02 STARTNODE; TYPE IS CHAR 20;
02 ENDNODE; TYPE IS CHAR 20;
02 AREA; TYPE IS REAL;
```

The program which will perform the design calculations for the truss structure is assumed to be written in PASCAL. Although PASCAL supports sets, we prefer to map the two sets (of nodes and members) onto a list structure (a simple queue in this case). In the program, the names are mapped onto pointers, while the original character string names appear as additional attributes, and the coordinates are real values. The schema representation in the PASCAL program would read as follows:

```
type NODE   = record
        NEXT_NODE  :  ->NODE;
        NAME        :  array((20)) of char;
        (X,Y)       :  real
                 end;

type MEMBER= record
     NEXT_MEMBER  :  ->MEMBER;
        NAME        :  array((20)) of char;
     (START_NODE,
        END_NODE)  :  ->NODE;
        AREA        :  real
                 end;

    type SET_OF_NODES    :  ->NODE;
    type SET_OF_MEMBERS  :  ->NODE;
```

With respect to communication, we distinguish between input and output. For input, each node can be mapped onto an 80 character record beginning with NODE, followed by the node name and the two coordinate values. A member is mapped onto a similar record beginning with MEMB and followed by the two node names. The input for a structure as shown in Fig. 4.10b would be as follows:

```
NODE   A   0.   0.
NODE   B   0.4 0.
NODE   C   0.4 0.4
NODE   D   0.   0.4
MEMB   M1    A    B
MEMB   M2    B    C
MEMB   M3    C    D
MEMB   M4    D    A
MEMB   M5    A    C
```

In addition we may use the interactive input of the data base system. If we intend to use interactive graphic input, we have to define how the communication should be performed in terms of actions with light-pen, keyboard and function keys. For output we will be likely to use a graphical mapping. The schema is mapped onto labelled points placed in a geometrically correct way (with some viewing transformation) on a sheet of paper or a display screen. The members are mapped onto straight lines between the starting and end nodes. It is worthwhile to remember that the transformation functions which convert the object representation from one of these subschemas to another must know both subschemas (see Chapter 3.3.3).

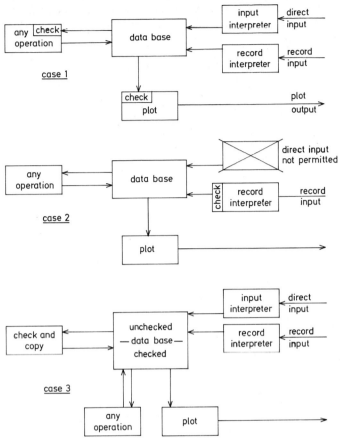

Fig. 4.11. Three different CAD system architectures with respect to data validation

Note that the mapping from the DBTG schema to the declarations in the PASCAL programs is not a complete one-to-one mapping. The PASCAL declarations of the records NODE and MEMBER guarantee that each member can refer only to nodes (not to other members) and, in particular, to exactly two nodes. These properties of the abstract model are not adequately reflected in the DBTG schema. Here, a limitation of DBTG-oriented data base systems with respect to their application in CAD becomes evident (see Chapter 2). Thus we are forced to include in our system a checking (validation) routine which determines whether an instance of the DBTG schema is consistent with this restriction or not.

Due to this discrepancy, we have now a choice between various architectures, as shown in Fig. 4.11. They differ in how the validation process cooperates with the other processes (input, output, data storage and other operations). In Case 1, direct input to the data base is permitted. Thus the above-mentioned restrictions may be violated and must be checked before a program uses the data. In Case 2, we allow input to the data base only via an interpreter, which uses the PASCAL record declarations to represent the objects. In this case we can guarantee that the DBTG data base content is consistent with the restrictions. Both of these architectures have their pros and cons. In Case 1, the user may be confronted with an error message at a late stage in the problem solution process and may lose time in having to go back to input (not to mention the fact that the repeated checking consumes unnecessary computer resources when applied again and again to unmodified data). In Case 2, we lose the option of direct input to the data base, and we may be unnecessarily constrained to provide the input in a form that is consistent not only at the end of all the input but also at all intermediate steps.

A third way of structuring the system is shown as Case 3 of Fig. 4.11. Here the consistency check is used as a significant intermediate step between input and all subsequent operations, which thus guarantees that all operations act on valid data only. This advantage is achieved at the expense of imposing more restrictions on the user of the system. He can no longer switch back and forth between input and analysis; but he must realize that there is a fundamental difference between the raw input data and the validated data, and that data validation is an important intermediate step.

4.2.2 Binding

According to [22] the term binding stands for the replacement of a name by the object it actually represents. Thus binding occurs when the variable name PI in a program is replaced by its value 3.14159, binding also occurs at a lower level when the decimal value 3.14159 is substituted by its bit representation in computer storage. Other examples of binding are: the substitution for a subprogram name (in CALL SUB(...), for instance) of the subprogram itself; the association of a file that is addressable in a piece of program with an actual data set on a specific peripheral storage medium; or the assignment of the address of a data structure to the corresponding pointer variable.

In the design of a CAD system it is essential to pay attention to the time at which such binding occurs (the "binding time"). The following times, at least, should be distinguished:

– *Case 1*: Binding at programming time (the time when the program is written in a programming language);
– *Case 2*: Binding at module binding time (the time when the program and all its subroutines are bound together to form an executable module);
– *Case 3*: Binding at job preparation time (the time when a job is prepared for execution);
– *Case 4*: Binding at job execution time (the time when a process is executed).

These different times are often not identified as being separate. For instance, if we write a simple FORTRAN program which reads some data, performs certain calculations, and prints results, only the programming time and the run time are obvious. But let us take a more common case for illustrative purposes. Consider a program which needs an "equation of state" for a material (e.g., the pressure as a function of density and temperature for water) for performing calculations. The following approaches correspond to different binding times of the equation of state to the program.

– *Case 1*: Binding at programming time.
  The equation of state is explicitly coded into the program as an internal procedure or simply as inline code. This corresponds to binding at programming time. The equation of state (and, hence, the material to be treated by the program) cannot be modified at a later time. The possibility of including a case option to select among a number of predefined equations of state does not alter the basic situation, as it merely replaces one material by a limited and predetermined number of choices.

– *Case 2*: Binding at module binding time.
  The equation of state is declared as an external procedure in the program. Different procedures corresponding to different materials are loaded in different subprogram libraries. During the binding of all subprograms to an executable module ("linkage editing"), only one of these libraries is used. Thus, the function which computes the equation of state for the desired material may be selected shortly before the program is submitted to execution. Here we have no limitation at all with respect to the material. The only condition is that a unique pressure must be computable from any given density and temperature values.

– *Case 3*: Binding at job preparation time.
  For the moment let us assume that all the equations of state that might be used are of a parametric type: they involve the same mathematical expression, with only some parametric values to be adjusted for each material. In this case we can delay the binding of the actual equation of state until after the module binding time. For instance, we could let the program read the parameters from a file which is not associated with an actual data set until immediately before running the job. We have used the parametric version of an equation of state here since most programming languages allow for the delayed binding of data, but not of routines. In some systems (see Chapter 5.1.2.4), however, it is possible to delay the binding of routines as well.

– *Case 4*: Binding at job execution time.
  Let us now assume that the material to be used or the equation of state is not known until part of the program has been executed (possibly because the program selects a mixture of other materials depending upon certain design criteria, and the equation of state is not determined until the mixture is defined). Again, as in Case 3 above, most programming languages would allow a delay of binding if a parametric representation of the equation of state is used. In this case, the parameter values would have to be computed in the program, or obtained from a data base and assigned to the variables which map the parameters. Certain systems, like REGENT [23], would allow us to treat routines in just the same way as data, in that they would allow us to generate, compile, bind, and execute a complete subprogram in a single program step.

The following example shows the binding of an equation of state which computes pressure p as a function of density rho and temperature T for various materials (using PL/1 as a programming language);

– *Case 1*: Binding at programming time combined with a selection between predefined options at execution time.

```
DECLARE P ENTRY(DECIMAL,DECIMAL) RETURNS(DECIMAL) VARIABLE;
P1: PROCEDURE(rho,T) RETURNS(DECIMAL);
   /* code for material 1 */
   RETURN( p );
   END P1;
P2: PROCEDURE(rho,T) RETURNS(DECIMAL);
   /* code for material 2 */
   RETURN( p );
   END P2;
P3: PROCEDURE(rho,T) RETURNS(DECIMAL);
   /* code for material 3 */
   RETURN( p );
   END P3;
      . . . . . . . . . . . . . .
SELECT (material) ;
   WHEN (mat1) P=P1;
   WHEN (mat2) P=P2;
   WHEN (mat3) P=P3;
   END;
any statement using P(rho,T);
```

– *Case 2*: Binding at module binding time.

```
DECLARE P ENTRY(DECIMAL,DECIMAL) RETURNS(DECIMAL) EXTERNAL;
```

any statement using P(rho,T);
/* the operating system language is used to assure that the desired version of the function P (corresponding to the desired material) is bound into the load module */

– *Case 4*: Binding at job execution time.
/* the following programming language is an extension of PL/1 provided by the CAD system REGENT [24];
the attribute DYNAMIC indicates that binding is to be performed at execution time */

```
DECLARE MATERIAL_NAME CHAR(4);
MATERIAL_NAME= any_expression_defining_the_material_name;
BEGIN;
   DECLARE P ENTRY(DECIMAL,DECIMAL) RETURNS(DECIMAL)
      DYNAMIC MODULE(MATERIAL_NAME);
   any statement using P(rho,T);
END;
```

The next example shows how the value of 3.14159 may be bound to a variable PI at different times, again using PL/1 as the programming language:

— *Case 1*: Binding at programming time.

```
DCL PI DECIMAL STATIC INTERNAL INITIAL(3.14159);
```

— *Case 3*: Binding at job preparation time

```
DCL PI INTERNAL;
DCL INPUT FILE STREAM;
GET FILE(INPUT) LIST(PI);
```

/* operating system language is used to allocate file INPUT to an existing data set containing the value of PI */

— *Case 4*: Binding at job execution time.

```
DCL PI INTERNAL;
DCL TERMINAL FILE STREAM;
GET FILE(TERMINAL) LIST (PI);
/* the value of PI is input by the user at the terminal */
```

It is obvious that Case 1 is the preferred solution, because we know at programming time that PI should always have this value. Delaying the binding introduces a flexibility which in this case can only produce errors. In other cases we might be willing to sacrifice the safety and efficiency of early binding for increased flexibility. The designer of a CAD system will always have to choose between the criteria of

— flexibility (enhanced by late binding) and
— safety (enhanced by early binding) as well as
— efficiency (enhanced by early binding).

It is important to realize that this decision has a very great influence upon the architecture of a CAD system. Two CAD systems may look quite different even if they perform the same fundamental tasks, depending on the choices made with respect to binding time. Also packages like the graphical kernel system GKS are influenced very much by the decisions taken with respect to binding. An essential characteristic of GKS is the way how graphic representation attributes are bound to primitives and segments [25].

4.2.3 The Block Structure Dilemma

As shown in Fig. 4.1, CAD implies the execution of a sequence of programs with appropriate interfaces. Each program will produce more data which are to be added to the data base. Much of this data will be used by some other program later in the program chain without the need for consultation or modification by man. It is generally accepted as good practice that such sequences of actions should be contained in an enclosing block which receives the first input and returns the final result (block structure approach in system design). We will see, however, that this approach is not always feasible or useful.

First let us note that for transferring data from one program (or process or block) P1 to another program P2, the interface must be declared in the containing block. We will call this interface P1 _ TO _ P2 with the schema P1 _ TO _ P2 _ SCHEMA. Similarly, all other interfaces have to be declared in the containing block. The following is a PASCAL-type formalization:

```
procedure CAD_PROCESS(INPUT, RESULT);
     type INPUT_SCHEMA      =record.......end;
     type P1_TO_P2_SCHEMA =record.......end;
     type P2_TO_P3_SCHEMA =record.. ....end;
     ..........................................
     type PN_TO_PLAST_SCHEMA=record.......end;
     type RESULT_SCHEMA      =record.......end;
        var P1_TO_P2 : P1_TO_P2_SCHEMA;
        var P2_TO_P3 : P2_TO_P3_SCHEMA;
        ......................................
        var PN_TO_PLAST : PN_TO_PLAST_SCHEMA;
        var  INPUT        : INPUT_SCHEMA;
        var  RESULT       : RESULT_SCHEMA;
           call P1(INPUT   ,P1_TO_P2);
           call P2(P1_TO_P2,P2_TO_P3);
           ...................................
           call PLAST(PN_TO_PLAST,RESULT);
end CAD_PROCESS;
```

A solution of this type, however, is not satisfactory for several reasons:

– When we realize that a CAD process may take many months or even years for completion, it is evident that we cannot wait until the schema of the data to be transferred from PN to PLAST is defined before we start executing P1 and P2. At the beginning of the activities, we do not even know how PLAST will look.
– There is no good reason why CAD_PROCESS should know the schema of any of the transferred data unless it has to request or modify part of that data. On the contrary, details of the transport data schemas should be hidden from the enclosing process in order to avoid inadvertent modification.
– Associated with the declaration of the data in the above example is the allocation of resources for the representation of these data (storage space in the case of programming languages). Thus, in the above example, resources would be allocated to all interface data throughout the whole time, even though such a need exists only from some point within the producing program to some point within the consuming program. This is a waste of resources.

The problems associated with block structures have been investigated in [26, 27, 28] and others. From a system designer's point of view, one would

like to define an "envelope" for data. Such envelopes should be able to accomo-
date data of different schemas (Letters enclosed in envelopes are transported
by mail regardless of their contents, provided that the exterior of each envelope
follows certain standards). The possibility of allocating such envelopes and dis-
posing of them at any suitable time would be desirable. Envelopes could be
used to transfer data from one block to the other. With two envelopes, the
above example might read as follows:

```
procedure CAD_PROCESS(INPUT, RESULT);
var   INPUT_SCHEMA      =record.......end;
var   RESULT_SCHEMA     =record.......end;
var   P_ODD_TO_P_EVEN : envelope;
var   P_EVEN_TO_P_ODD : envelope;
var   INPUT             : INPUT_SCHEMA;
var   RESULT            : RESULT_SCHEMA;
call P1(INPUT              ,P_ODD_TO_P_EVEN);
call P2(P_ODD_TO_P_EVEN,P_EVEN_TO_P_ODD);
.......................................
call PLAST(P_ODD_TO_P_EVEN,RESULT);
/* or perhaps
call PLAST(P_EVEN_TO_P_ODD,RESULT);
depending upon whether the number of processes
is even or odd  */
end CAD_PROCESS;
```

Let us take a look at various programming languages under this aspect.
In fact, the envelope technique is being used extensively in systems which are
based on FORTRAN or PL/1. In FORTRAN, envelopes may be mapped onto
arrays of real and/or INTEGER data of a COMMON block or a parameter
with the EQUIVALENCE technique. In PL/1, based variables offer a great
variety of options to implement envelopes. In both FORTRAN and PL/1, files
may serve as implementations of an envelope. In the more restrictive languages
of the ALGOL and PASCAL families, it is much more difficult (if at all feasible)
to violate the block structure principles and to implement envelopes for data
of unknown schemas. We do not want to underestimate the dangers associated
with the misuse of EQUIVALENCE in FORTRAN or based variables in PL/1
(or files in both); but the judicious use of these features offers possibilities
which are urgently needed in practical CAD system implementation, and which
do not find adequate support in more restrictive programming languages. The
package concept in the programming language ADA [29, 30] provides a step
towards a solution of this problem. It allows us to hide the internal interface
data structures safely within the package, so that they cannot be accessed by
the containing block. However, it does not resolve the problems of wasted
storage space, or the problem of the yet unknown schema for interfaces between
future activities.

Let us now consider data base systems under the same aspects. Obviously
data base systems are well suited to transport data from one program to another,

since this is one of their fundamental tasks. To some extent, they offer sufficient flexibility to allow us to augment and modify the schema at later times without the loss of already existing data. Thus one might be tempted to leave all data transfer tasks to a data base system. However, there are drawbacks to this approach. If solely used for interfacing programs, data base systems require a considerable amount of overhead due to the necessary transformations from the external schema (used in the programs) to the internal schema (used for data storage) and in the return. It is unlikely that a user would want the stiffness matrix of a finite element program to be stored in a data base, where it is stored less efficiently than on a simple file. The advantage of being able to query or possibly modify individual data elements does not apply to stiffness matrices, which are more or less meaningless except to the analysis program for which each matrix has been assembled.

After the general trend towards restrictive block-structure-oriented programming techniques and languages in the 1970's, from the CAD standpoint it is desirable to see the development of efficient and practicable techniques for passing data between programs (modules, processes) which are safer and theoretically better founded than the constructs that are now available in FORTRAN and PL/1. A typical situation which calls for the violation of block structure is the interactive definition of graphical information at a terminal, where the information is to be moved upwards in the process hierarchy in order to be stored somewhere for future use in other programs. During the process of defining this information in an interactive way, we must be able to deal with information chunks [26], which are created and deleted in a random way and not in a block structure.

4.2.4 Algorithmic Modelling

So far we have dealt with models which could be mapped relatively easily onto a data schema. The representation of an object was always considered to exist, though it might be undefined or defined at a given time. Such a data representation of objects consumes resources; and in many cases these resources are too valuable to be spent. As an example: when graphic information is displayed at a remote terminal, the transport of the information across the connecting line consumes both transmission cost and manpower (the time of the operator who has to wait until the transport is complete). In order to save part of the resource, it would be preferable to condense the information. For graphic text, for instance, a data representation of the letter strokes consumes more storage space and transport time than a character string along with the information on how the character string should be expanded into line strokes (see [31]). In general, a data model may be replaced by

– the identification of an algorithm;
– a set of (condensed) data which will be used by the algorithm to generate the complete data model.

Table 4.3. The choice between data models and algorithmic models.

Aspect	The preferred modelling is:	
	data model	algorithmic model
storage capacity	high	low
processing costs	high	low
usage rate of data	high	low
processing rate	low	high
time to retrieve and transport data	low	high
change rate of data	low	high

We call such a condensation an "algorithmic model". The prerequisites, of course, are that the algorithm is properly implemented and that the mapping from the condensed data to the expanded form has been agreed upon by all users of this "shorthand" model. Similar algorithmic models are implemented in conventional programming languages. Arithmetic functions like SIN or COS are not supplied as tables of data, but rather as algorithms. A graphical system for two- and three-dimensional objects, which is completely based on algorithmic modelling, is described in [32]. In an algorithmic model, data are not stored, but they are evaluated whenever they are needed. The questions arise:

– When should a model be represented as data?
– When should algorithmic modelling be used?

The answer cannot be given on the basis of abstract operations which the system is to perform. A particular operation may be implemented with either approach. The answer must be derived from resource considerations, as indicated in Table 4.3.

In the extreme cases the preferred solution is obvious:

– A data model is preferred when storage capacity, processing costs, and usage rates are high.
– An algorithmic model is preferred when the computer has a fast processor, when the retrieval costs or transport times for data are high, and when the model is rapidly changing.

In the wide range of practical situations, the choice is a matter of judgment based on experience more often than on objective criteria. A particular problem is posed by the fact that the "best" solution is a function of how the system is used. In the early design phase of a three-dimensional body, the rate of change of the model is usually so high that perspective views (and dependent data such as weight) are used only once before the next change is made. Thus it is preferable to use an algorithmic model for the projection of the body (and other data). When a display is requested, the projection lines may be evaluated and displayed on a plotter or a storage tube, line by line, with a minimum of storage requirements. At a later stage in the design process, modifications of the body become rare, but editing of the two-dimensional pictures of the body may be required. Now it is advantageous to store the projection of the body as data, in order to avoid unnecessary repetition of the projection operation.

The opportunity to choose between algorithmic modelling and data modelling of the same object, depending upon the type of work to be done, may have a significant influence on the usefulness of a CAD system in the different phases of the design process. This aspect will require much more attention in the future.

4.3 The Resource Aspect

4.3.1 Software Machine Design

When we investigate software machines which are potential candidates for incorporation into larger systems, we generally note that they obey special rules for using certain resources. Examples of such standardized use of resources are: a filing system (rules for naming and structuring external data storage, most often used in program chains, see Fig. 4.1), the COMMON-block technique (probably the most widely used CAD system basis of the FORTRAN-oriented world, with rules for naming and structuring sharable internal memory), and subroutine packages (based on rules for naming the procedures and structuring their argument lists).

Such systems work fine as long as they are just used by themselves. However, when put together into a bigger system, conflicts usually arise either because some of the "subsystems" do not allow the sharing of certain resources with others, or because they use shared resources according to conflicting rules. Let us illustrate this point by a few examples:

– Obviously one cannot use two independent subroutine packages in one program if both together demand more memory capacity than is available.
– Even if each of the packages has its own dynamic memory allocation facility (as some FORTRAN packages provide by means of Assembler extensions) they may not be useable in combination anyway. Each of them must be limited to a maximum amount of memory: the authorization to use a resource must explicitly or implicitly be passed from some higher level or organization.
– The same is true if the resource to be used is not of a quantitative nature (such as memory space), but of a qualitative nature. Software machines cannot be used in parallel if they make independent use of certain global names such as program names, file names, common block names. This conflict becomes evident if one thinks of using two graphics packages in a single program, one for data presentation and one for geometrical design. The chances that both of them use different subroutines with identical names — like OPEN, CLOSE, or PLOT — are rather high.

It is not sufficient that the required resources are available: some of these resources, namely those which represent the state of a process, must be reserved for exclusive use by this process. Other processes must be inhibited from modifying such resources. The design of software machines for general use in a large number of CAD systems will have to deal with the following questions:

- What is the function of the software machine?
- Which resources does it require?
- How are these resources to be supplied? How must they be initialized (set up in a proper state prior to their actual use)?
- How do we guarantee that certain parts of these resources will remain unchanged as long as they are needed?

4.3.2 Designing Against Resource Conflicts

4.3.2.1 The Abstract Machine

Let us consider the execution of a CAD application program as a running process. During this process certain other processes are created, executed, and terminated (such as the looking up of design rules from a library, or the display of graphical information on a display screen, see Chapter 3.2.4.1). Some of these processes last only as long as a "call" to a subroutine, as is often the case for mathematical algorithms. Other processes live longer; for example, the looking up of design rules in a data base is usually implemented in the following way: Make the design rules available ("open"), look up as often as needed ("search"), terminate the availability ("close"). In such a case many short-lived look-up processes exist parallel to a long living process which we may call "maintenance of the environment for the look-up table process" (see Fig. 3.18). Similarly the communication process between the application program and a graphics terminal lasts much longer than the display process for some picture.

Let us take a look at implementations of such processes in today's CAD systems (which in most cases means FORTRAN). Short-lived processes are usually found as calls to subprograms which require all information to be passed as arguments (or possibly in a COMMON block which is filled prior to the call). Long-living processes may be found in the form of a sequence of calls to a subroutine package. Graphics packages designed on the basis of GKS [31] or GSPC [33] may serve as examples. All the values of the variables in the COMMON block for such a package represent the actual state of the corresponding process. It is essential for correct operation that these variables will be used exclusively by this particular package. Note that there is a functional difference between the uses of COMMON in these two examples: in the first case it is merely a shorthand writing for arguments; in the second case it is the realization of the state of the process. Confusing these two functions inevitably leads to problems (and one of the drawbacks of FORTRAN is that it supports this confusion).

However, the situation is even more complicated. Quite often several processes of the same type exist parallel to each other. A typical example is the

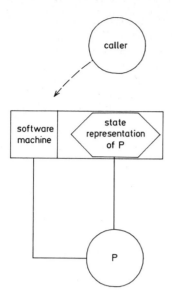

Fig. 4.12. A software machine for a single process

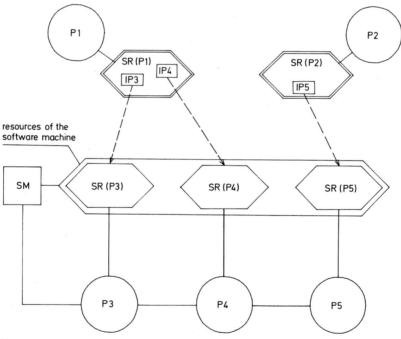

Pn   = process n
SR (Pn) = state representation of process n
IPn   = identification of process n

Fig. 4.13. A software machine for many parallel processes

use of several graphic displays for different purposes in the same program: some are used for close-up views, diagrams, and communication, while others are used for design drawings and overall representations. It is obvious that whenever a software machine is to continue such a process, it must be made clear which one of the particular processes should now be continued. While in the first case (only one process executing) there is no apparent need to distinguish between the process and the machine, this need becomes evident whenever a machine can operate parallel processes. In the first case the resources which represent the state of the process may or may not be included in the software machine (the COMMON technique includes them in the machine; see Fig. 4.12) while in the second case the software machine must be able to manage a varying number of process state representations (Fig. 4.13). The management of resources and the management of the different processes become clearly separated tasks [34, p.49].

The various functions of an abstract machine either change the state of the process or provide to the "father process" information as a function of certain input parameters and the present state [35]. In a symbolic way one might write

abstract machine function: $= (O, V, \text{state})$

where O is a set of operating functions o;
which change the state

state $:= o(\text{state}, \text{input})$

while V is a set of value delivering functions v;
such that

output $:= v(\text{state}, \text{input})$

As noted above, whenever the software tool is to be used for parallel processes P_i, a reference to the state of one particular process P_k must be passed among the input. Hence

input $:= (\text{identification of process } P_k, \text{other input})$

A user can use a software tool intelligently only if he has a clear understanding of its functional capabilities. For this reason we formulate the first rule

(R1) The functional documentation of a software machine must give a precise definition of the type of process which is driven by this machine. This means
   – a complete description of the state in terms of objects of the abstract object type, corresponding to the underlying conceptual schema;
   – a complete description of all operating functions in terms of their effect on the state;
   – a complete description of the value-delivering functions.

This rule should require no special explanation. However, it is violated quite often with respect to completeness.

The second rule applies to software machines which are to be used to drive similar processes in parallel:

(R2) Whenever a software machine may conceivably drive more than one process in parallel, caller and software machine should agree upon a unique identification of each newly-created process in order to be able to communicate about this process at a later time.

There are many ways an agreement about the identification of the new process (its name) can be achieved. The caller may pass a name to the software machine, or the software machine may determine the name. In the first case, conflicts may arise if more than one caller wants to use the same name; this conflict may be removed if the name is prefixed by the caller's name. In the second case, it may happen that a process is created and later terminated and another process is then given the same name by the software machine. If the caller erroneously refers to the name of the already terminated process, a misunderstanding would result without the possibility of detection. The caller would think that operations are being performed on the old process, while the callee is performing the actions on the new process. This problem may be removed if the creation time (date and time) is made part of the process name. In either case, at least one of the partners (the caller or the software machine) must maintain a table which associates the name which was fixed in the other's environment with a private name within its own environment (a name is valid only within a given environment, see Chapter 3.3.1.3). A very efficient means of communication between caller and software machine may be achieved when both agree to use a combination of their respective private names. An illustration of this technique will be given in Chapter 4.2.4.2.

4.3.2.2 Process State Representation

In Chapter 3.2.4.2, we characterized a process by the fact that its state is modified only by the process itself. The process state is represented by the situation of certain resources (values of variables, position of a magnetic tape on its unit, existing connection to a certain terminal, etc.). If we have more than one parallel process, then the problem may arise that one process modifies the state representation of other processes. In order to avoid this, we formulate the rule:

(R3) A software machine should be designed and implemented so that the state representations of processes which it creates cannot be modified by other software machines.

It is not always easy to implement this rule in a strict sense. If a software machine is used for one process only, the state representation of this process may be integrated with the software machine itself as shown in Fig. 4.12. In FORTRAN a common technique is to include a COMMON block which contains declarations representing the process state in all subroutines and functions which constitute the machine. This method efficiently protects the process state

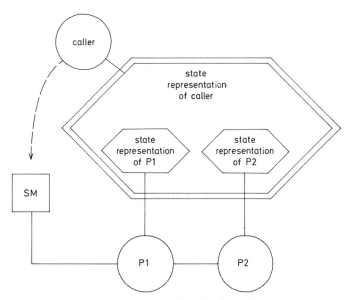

Fig. 4.14. Allocation of the resources for state representation by the caller

against modification by other processes *provided* that no other program uses the same name for a COMMON block. Safer and much more powerful techniques are provided by the package concept in the programming language ADA.

If, however, a number of independent processes are to be driven by the software machine, the machine should have the capability to maintain a variable table of process state representations as illustrated in Fig. 4.13. Here the two processes P1 and P2 use the same software machine SM. P1 has created the processes P3 and P4, P2 has created P5. The software machine (following rule (R2)) has agreed with the "callers" about the identification of the processes. The identifications of the subprocesses are stored within the state representation of the higher-level processes (IP3 for process P3, for instance). The state representations of P3 through P5 are accessible only to the software machine SM, and are thus effectively protected (an example is given in Chapter 4.3.3.). When a caller calls the software machine, it supplies the identification of the process to be continued. The corresponding state representation is then bound to the software machine (the name is replaced by what it means), and the process continues.

Another approach is shown in Fig. 4.14. This solution is feasible even in FORTRAN, where the above method is difficult to implement because of the inability of FORTRAN to perform dynamic storage management for allocating and deleting the data structures which represent the process states. Here the state representations of all subprocesses (created by the software machine SM under control of a "caller" process) are embedded in the state representation of the caller itself. In a FORTRAN implementation, one would implement this as an array of REAL or INTEGER data which are not used at all by the calling program, but passed to every routine of the software machine upon the request of a software machine function. It is a matter of discipline *not* to use this array of data for any other purpose. Some programming languages (PL/1 for instance) provide limited capabilities for the higher-level process to treat the data structure representations simply as resources (or as "envelopes" of the data structures which they contain) without being able to access the contained data structures (see Chapter 4.3.3.2).

4.3.2.3 The Concrete Machine

Software machines do not only use resources for representing the state of a process. They also use resources for operational purposes. Examples of such resources are: primary memory, working files, names of files in communication with the operating system, names of subroutines. Some of these resources are merely a certain quantity out of a larger pool (memory is an example). Other resources, however, are well identified and must be reserved for exclusive use (such as the names of the subroutines). In either case, problems may arise whenever more than one software machine is used in a CAD system.

With respect to quantitative resources, conflicts may arise if one process monopolizes a resource. (Certain systems such as ICES tend to make optimal use of primary memory by using as much as possible. This will cause failure if combined with another package which itself provides a dynamic storage management facility.) Hence, we state the rule:

(R4) If a software tool is able to obtain certain quantities of a resource for its operational purposes, the father process should authorize it to allocate up to a certain amount of that resource. Otherwise, the necessary resources should be supplied by the father process. In any case, the documentation must include a list of the resources from which the software tool needs a certain quantity.

With respect to qualitative resources (those which can be identified as individuals, such as all names), we state the following rule:

(R5) Qualitative resources should be obtained from the father process. If this is not possible (as for the names of subroutines), the description of the software machine must identify which qualitative resources are used and how the software machine might be modified to permit the replacement of qualitative resources with others, if necessary.

It is worth noting that the potential of name conflicts has been recognized in the proposal of the graphical kernel system GKS [31]. This proposal of a standard for graphic systems suggests that GKS implementations should provide a "name converter", which allows for the replacement of any global name in the package during the process of installation in a computer environment where name conflicts would otherwise arise.

4.3.2.4 Resource Management Strategies

Sometimes the number of quantitative resources needed by a process depends heavily on certain process parameters. The buffer area for a graphic display file is a familiar example. The particular requirements may also grow and shrink considerably with time. The design of software tools depends heavily on the resource management strategy followed:

Case A) During the whole process a maximum amount of resource is allocated to the process, no matter whether it is really needed. (This is typical for local FORTRAN working arrays in subroutines). If many processes follow this strategy the resource may soon be exhausted.

Case B) The process obtains resources when needed and returns them when they are no longer needed. Although this strategy makes "optimum" use of the resource, it may cause considerable overhead and may also lead to the so-called "fragmentation problem" unless the sequence of allocate and free requests is issued on a last-in-first-out basis [36]. As noted in Chapter 4.2.3, block structuring of the individual processes with respect to their resource allocations is not always a satisfactory solution.

Case C) The process provides a resource estimate algorithm. The father process usually has sufficient information available to produce good estimates of the relevant process parameters for a certain period of time. With these parameters, an estimate of the amount of resource needed may be generated so that the father process can supply this resource to the process. Problems similar to those in Case B above may arise, but their probability is significantly reduced.

Each of these strategies has its advantages and disadvantages and we do not pretend to recommend one as being superior in all cases. It is not surprising that software machines which perform the same function may appear totally different in their implementation, depending on the resource management strategy. Hence, we formulate the rules:

(R6) The documentation of the software machine must contain a complete list of the resources which are needed for successful operation.

(R7) The documentation of a software machine must include a description of the resource management strategy of this machine in particular for
(Case A) the limitations on the relevant process parameters and the amount of resources needed at all times;
(Case B) an estimate of the amount of a resource needed as a function of relevant process parameters;
(Case C) same as for Case B. In addition, information should be given about the consequence of providing more or less than the estimated amount of a resource.

It is suggested that the resource estimate algorithms should not only be documented in the user's manual, but should also be provided as callable subroutines within the software machine itself.

In some cases a certain amount of one resource may be replaced by another. As an example: external storage may be used instead of primary storage. In such a case, the software machine itself is unable to determine the optimal global balance between these resources, because it does not know how an attempt to improve its own performance would influence other processes. Hence, if the software machine has the capability to adapt itself to different resource configurations, strategy C is the only one which allows for a global optimum.

In any case, the software machine should provide information about the amount of resources actually used for a particular process, so that the user is able to learn from previous applications and use the machine more efficiently in the future.

4.3.2.5 The Components of a Software Machine

Let us combine the functional aspect of a software machine with its resource aspect in the following schema, which is illustrated by Fig. 4.15.

software machine := (abstract machine function,
                     resource management machine,
                     documentation);

The abstract machine function has been described in Chapter 4.3.2.1. The resource management machine must be explained in more detail:

resource management machine := (management state,
                                management functions);

The resource management state includes a list of the authorizations (or limitations) obtained from a higher-level resource management process, and a list of the resources which have actually been allocated by the various processes of the "abstract machine" part of this software machine. The resource management functions are operational functions which authorize or limit the use of resources by the software machine, or which deliver information about resource requirements (estimated or actual).

Note that while the abstract machine part may drive several processes in parallel, there is only one resource management process associated with a software machine.

The machine is completed by its documentation:

documentation := (documentation of the abstract machine,
                  documentation of qualitative resource requirements,
                  documentation of resource management strategy);

With respect to requirements and standard formats for software documentation see [37].

In the previous pages (Chapters 4.3.1 and 4.3.2), we have emphasized that the design of software machines should try to avoid potential conflicts in the assembly of such software machines into larger units. This means that we have emphasized the bottom-up approach to system development, as opposed to

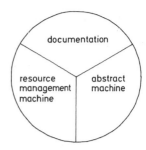

Fig. 4.15. The components of a software machine

the top-down or "step-wise refinement" approach which is often advertised, particularly in computer-science-oriented literature. However, top-down design may imply that the system is broken down into components at an early stage, when the knowledge about the consequences of such a decision is yet too sparse [38]. Furthermore, the practical problems in designing and implementing large systems for CAD and CAM are very often too great. A top-down approach might easily result in the final system being available at a time when it is no longer needed. Hence, one often has to be satisfied with partial solutions that are feasible in the required time scale. If time and the judicious design of the partial solution permit, they may later be combined into larger systems [39].

4.3.3 A Sample Software Machine: The Stack Machine

4.3.3.1 The Task and a Simple Solution

Many operations in CAD require a set of objects as operand. As an example, we might mention the problem of hidden line removal from a drawing of a three-dimensional body, where all the surfaces of the body have to be considered simultaneously. This example further illustrates that the objects in such a set may have different representations (a cylinder will have a different representation from a plane). Only very few programming languages (PASCAL for instance) provide a limited set facility. In general, sets are mapped onto list structures [36], which are available in a much greater number of programming languages. In order to minimize the amount of work involved for this example we will use the most simple list structure: a stack. The idea of the following paragraphs can easily be extended to more complicated structures. The basic operations of a stack are:

```
o-functions: push(item);  /* puts an item on top of the stack */
             pop(item);    /* removes the item from the top of the stack and
                              delivers it */
v-function : empty();      /* true if stack is empty false otherwise */
```

The implementation of these functions in various programming languages is straightforward and may be found in a number of textbooks. Here we will

Sample Listing 4.1. A stack machine for a single item type. The ADA version.

```
package STACK_MANAGER is

    type ITEM is
        record
            .....record declaration....
        end record;

    NULL_ITEM : constant ITEM := ....value of an ITEM which will be
                                     recognized as NULL_ITEM .....;
    procedure PUSH ( NEW_ITEM : in  ITEM );
    procedure POP  ( TOP_ITEM :out  ITEM );
    STACK_FULL : exception; - may be raised by push
    end;

package body STACK_MANAGER is
    SIZE  : constant INTEGER :=2000;
    subtype INDEX is INTEGER range 0..SIZE;
    type INTERNAL_ITEM is
            record
                CONTENT : ITEM ;
                SUCC    : INDEX;
                PRED    : INDEX;
            end record;

    STACK : array (INDEX'FIRST..INDEX'LAST) of INTERNAL_ITEM;
    FIRST_BUSY_ITEM : INDEX :=0;
    FIRST_FREE_ITEM : INDEX :=1;

    function BUSY_LIST_EMPTY return BOOLEAN is .... end;
    function FREE_LIST_EMPTY return BOOLEAN is .... end;
    procedure EXCHANGE (FROM : in INDEX; TO : in INDEX ) is .... en
    procedure PUSH (NEW_ITEM : in ITEM) is
        begin
            if FREE_LIST_EMPTY then raise TABLE_FULL; end if;
            .....
            - remaining code for PUSH
            .....
        end PUSH;
    procedure POP   (TOP_ITEM : in ITEM) is .... end POP;
        begin
            .....
            - code for initialization of stack linkages
            .....
    end STACK_MANAGER;
```

use the programming language ADA [29], whose "package" concept can be interpreted as a formal way of describing software machines.

The ADA program in Sample Listing 4.1 deals with the abstract machine only. The resource aspect is completely hidden. Only the compiler has to care about the memory resources, but not the programmer. The resource aspect becomes apparent, however, if we specify the task as follows:

Sample Listing 4.2. A stack machine for a single item type. The PL/1 version.

```
PROCEDURE STACKM;
 DECLARE 1 ITEM BASED,
              2 ....
              .....STRUCTURE declaration....;
 DECLARE 1 NULL_ITEM STATIC,
              2 ....  INITIAL( ... value of NULL_ITEM ...)
              .....repeat declaration of ITEM with initial values;
   /* PUSH : ENTRY   ( NEW_ITEM : IN  LIKE ITEM )
      POP  : ENTRY   ( TOP_ITEM : OUT LIKE ITEM )
      STACK_FULL : CONDITION  , MAY BE RAISED BY PUSH   */
   /* PL/1 MACRO PROCESSOR CAPABILITY IS USED TO REPLACE
      "SIZE" BY "2000" AND "INDEX" BY "BINARY FIXED(15)
      IN THE FOLLOWING PROGRAM TEXT                      */
   % DECLARE SIZE FIXED;
   % SIZE=2000;
   % DECLARE INDEX CHARACTER;
   % INDEX='BINARY FIXED(15)';
   /* WHEREVER A VARIABLE OF TYPE INDEX IS MODIFIED CHECK
      THAT IT REMAINES WITHIN 0..SIZE                    */
   DECLARE 1 INTERNAL_ITEM BASED,
              2 CONTENT LIKE ITEM,
              2 SUCC    INDEX,
              2 PRED    INDEX;
   DECLARE 1 STACK STATIC
              2 INTERNAL_ITEM ( 0 : 2000 ) LIKE ITEM,
              2 FIRST_BUSY_ITEM INDEX INIT(0),
              2 FIRST_FREE_ITEM INDEX INIT(1);

   BUSY_LIST_EMPTY:PROCEDURE RETURNS(BIT); ..... RETURN;END;
   FREE_LIST_EMPTY:PROCEDURE RETURNS(BIT); ..... RETURN;END;
   EXCHANGE:PROCEDURE (FROM , TO ) ;
      DECLARE (FROM,TO) INDEX;
      ......
   RETURN;END EXCHANGE;
   PUSH:ENTRY    (NEW_ITEM );
      DECLARE NEW_ITEM LIKE ITEM;
          IF FREE_LIST_EMPTY THEN SIGNAL TABLE_FULL;
          .....
          /* remaining code for PUSH */
          .....
   RETURN;END PUSH;
   POP :ENTRY    (TOP_ITEM );
      DECLARE NEW_ITEM LIKE ITEM;
      .....
   RETURN;END PUSH;
          .....
          /* code for initialization of stack linkages */
          .....
   RETURN;END STACKM;
```

- the software machine should be able to manage several stacks;
- the software machine should not make any assumptions whatsoever regarding the structure of the items. The ADA module of Sample Listing 4.1 is applicable for one ITEM schema only. Using a case construct, one could easily expand the applicability to a finite number of *predefined* schemas (see Chapter 4.2.2). But *all* schemas which should ever be stored in the stack would have to be bound to the package at *programming* time by including their declaration. Hence, ADA does not readily provide answers to our problem;
- the resource (storage space) allocated to each stack should be restricted. One reason for this restriction is to avoid storage overflow and uncontrolled program failure in a case of incorrect use (in an external loop of push operations, for instance). If the limit is too restrictive, the machine should be able to call for help;
- the possibility to save whole stacks and to restore them at a later time should be provided.

Before we plan the "stack machine" in more detail, let us rewrite the above ADA module in PL/1 in order to be able to compare the purely functional program with the final software package more easily. We choose PL/1 rather than ADA for comparison purposes because in PL/1 it is much easier to implement features which are *not* readily available in the language. ADA (just like as PASCAL) is less permissive, and allows us only to express objects and operations which the designers of the language wanted to allow. For this reason, these languages are much more suitable for teaching purposes than PL/1 or FORTRAN. PL/1 may appear too powerful to be a "good" language, but often this extra power is quite helpful in systems programming. (See Sample Listing 4.2).

4.3.3.2 Planning of the Stack Machine

The fundamental operations which we want to provide are:

- management functions:
  initiate–stack–machine(/* no resource restrictions*/,
  file for messages, help)
  terminate–stack–machine(final report, help)
  estimate–resource–requirement(stack characteristics, help)
  create–stack(resource allowance, stack name, help)
  save–stack(stack name, resource for saving, help)
  restore–stack(stack name, resources for saved stack, help)
- o-functions:
  push(stack name, item, help)
  pop(stack name, item, help)
- v-functions:
  empty(stack name, help)

We will now deal with the problem of mapping the abtract object types mentioned in the above functions onto PL/1. We have to make decisions on the following issues:

– What are the items which we want to push on the stacks?
  In our ADA example (and in practically all examples which may be found
  in literature), the stack machine knows the schema of the items to be handled.
  At best, the machine knows a small number of schemas such that objects
  of various structure may be handled. But there is actually no reason why
  the stack machine should have this knowledge. In fact, this knowledge is
  bad knowledge. The stack machine is not allowed to perform any action
  with the objects in the stack items, so why should it know the names and
  structures of these objects? What is worse, if at a later time we decide to
  utilize the stack machine for stacking items with a different schema, we will
  be forced to include the new schema in the stack machine and recompile.
  The solution to this problem is to use a very general schema onto which
  most items may be mapped in an efficient way: the contiguous storage space.
  We allow the user to push and pop all items which may be mapped onto
  a contiguous storage space or "envelope", as introduced in Chapter 4.2.3.
  This generalization requires a "mapping-around-the-language" (see Chapter
  4.2.1.3) and will be difficult (if at all possible) to perform in restrictive programming languages of the Algol or PASCAL type. Other languages like
  PL/1 and even FORTRAN are much more permissive and make it relatively
  easy to perform such mappings. The stack machine should actually not deal
  with the objects pushed on the stack, but rather with the resources (storage
  space) that represent these objects. In Pl/1, two possibilities offer themselves
  for the mapping of items to a contiguous area of storage space: CHARAC-
  TER strings and AREA data. The mapping around the language level for
  a byte-oriented computer according to Fig. 4.9 would be as follows:

```
abstract   |
level      |        storage space
.......... | ...........| .......................................................................
language   |           |              CHARACTER(*)          AREA(*)
level      |           |                    |                   |
.......... | ..........|....................|...................|..........
machine    |  a set of           _____|_____|
level      |  contiguous bytes ∫
```

The caller of the stack machine would have to perform this mapping, and
would pass to the stack machine the length of the storage area (the PL/1
built-in function CURRENTSTORAGE may be used to determine this value
in terms of bytes, corresponding to CHARACTERS on the language level)
and the address of the first byte of the aggregate (which may be obtained
by the PL/1 built-in function ADDR).

– How do we represent saved stacks?
  The problem here is similar to the problem of representing items with a
  yet unknown structure. In this case, the representation of the stack is to
  be handed over to a higher level process (the caller) who should not do
  anything to the content of the stack. Hence, the caller should not know
  the schema of the stack. In a way similar to the treatment of the stack

items, we map the representation of a stack onto a contiguous storage space (a Pl/1-STRUCTURE) which contains the stack representation and additional information (size, identification, producer and consumer). We call this an "envelope", by analogy to the envelope in which someone may send a letter (information in a certain schema) to someone else (or to himself) without the post office having to know the contents of the letter.

– How do we represent a stack?

The stack is the representation of a stack process. We choose to use list structure. An array would be an alternative; but for storing items with varying storage space requirements, a list structure is more economical with respect to storage usage. The question arises whether the stack implementation should take into consideration right at the outset that stacks might have to be saved in form of an envelope. This would mean that not only would the stack have to be enveloped for saving and restoring, but every stack would be implemented within an envelope, whether saving is requested or not. The decision cannot be derived from functional aspects. A consideration of the resources (here, effort involved in planning the data structure, processing and storage requirements) must give the answer. In order to reduce the planning effort, we decide to use only one representation of stacks for both saved and nonsaved stacks. In a real-world case, the decision might come out differently.

– How do we represent the state of the stack management machine?

The state of the resource management machine is characterized by the actual stacks, the storage allowance for each stack, and the actual storage use. In order to keep track of its state, the machine itself needs some storage space for a stack table. We do not decide at this point how the stack table should be implemented; we leave this decision until after further refinement of the schema and the algorithm. With respect to the operating states of the stack machine (see Chapter 3.2.4.3), the distinction of three different states appears to be necessary:

* "existing" prior to initialization of the stack machine, and after termination;
* "in repair" during a call to a help procedure;
* "executable" otherwise.

– How do we represent names?

The options among we may choose in PL/1 are: integers, character strings with fixed or variable length, pointers, and offsets. The most efficient solution with respect to execution is the use of pointers. Pointers may be used both for naming and for accessing objects. Their use as names avoids the need for an address table. The disadvantage of using pointers as names is the reduced security of data: every process that knows the pointer to data can potentially access these data. With respect to the names of the stack items this is not a point of concern, since these items belong to the calling process anyway. With respect to the stack names, we use a combination of names corresponding to the two environments involved: The caller supplies a character string (limited to 32 characters), while the stack machine adds a pointer and the generation time of the stack.

– How do we represent the help functions?
The possibilities available in Pl/1 are
* to return a record (a PL/1-STRUCTURE) which is to be interpreted by the calling program. The information in this record (error code) will tell the caller whether the stack machine has detected an abnormal situation, and which of the predefined possible actions it has taken. The caller may then react appropriately;
* to call a help procedure which was passed to the stack machine as an argument, either in the present or in an earlier call. The help procedure itself is supplied by the caller.

Referring to our example, we decide to use the first option in most cases. The stack machine will then return an integer error code, which is set to 0 for a normal case and will be set to specific integer values if abnormal situations are detected. In such cases the state of the stack machine will not be changed. A full-stack-exception, however, will cause a help procedure to be called. The stack machine will supply to this procedure the stackname, the present storage size of the stack, and the size of the item to be pushed on top of the stack; and it will expect from the help procedure the information of whether the storage allowance for the stack is to be raised and to what value.

4.3.3.3 Implementation of the Stack Machine

First we will summarize all declarations which are needed for representing the stack machine and the stacks. Part of the schema is still to be refined and mapped onto the possibilities of the PL/1 language. The declarations shown in Sample Listing 4.3 must be included in all modules of the stack machine. Communication between the modules is achieved by declaring the basis of the data structure (STACKB) as EXTERNAL; this attribute assures that all modules of the stack machine operate on the same data structure (provided that they are bound into a single load module before execution).

Two tests which should be performed in almost all entries to the stack machine are represented as macros in Sample Listing 4.4. These lines of codes have to be inserted wherever they are referenced.

We must choose a module structure for the different operations of the stack machine. In the sense of Parnas [28] or in the programming language ADA, all the operations together would form a "module". The term module, however, is associated with different meanings. A module is sometimes used for the portion of code which is treated by the compiler as one unit. Sometimes the term module is used for the loadable and executable unit of machine code that is produced by the linkage editor (or binder) from various separately compiled programs and additional subprograms retrieved from a library. At this point, we are associating "module" with the program unit to be submitted to the compiler. Such modules would also usually represent the units which would be documented and listed separately.

Sample Listing 4.3. The PL/1 stack machine. The declarations of the state representation.

```
/* the following declarations are to be included in all modules      */
      DECLARE 1 STACKB EXTERNAL,
                2 MESSAGE_FILE FILE,
                2 OPERATING_STATE CHAR(32) VARYING INITIAL('EXISTING'),
                2 STACK_MACHINE_NAME CHAR(32) VARYING
                                    INITIAL('STACK_MACHINE'),
                2 stack_table INITIAL(empty);
      DECLARE ERROR_CODE BINARY FIXED(15);
      DECLARE 1 NAME_OF_STACK,
                2 EXTERNAL_NAME CHAR(32) VARYING,
                2 INTERNAL_NAME POINTER /* to stack_entry */
                2 GENERATION_TIME CHAR(16);
      DECLARE ACTUAL_STACK_ENTRY POINTER;
      DECLARE 1 STACK_ENTRY BASED(ACTUAL_STACK_ENTRY),
                2 INTERNAL_NAME POINTER,
                2 linkages_in_stack_table,
                2 ACTUAL_STACK POINTER;
      DECLARE 1 ENVELOPE BASED(ACTUAL_STACK),
                2 LENGTH BINARY FIXED(31),
                2 EXTERNAL_NAME CHAR(32) VARYING INIT(EXT_NAME),
                2 PRODUCER CHAR(32) VARYING INITIAL(STACK_MACHINE_NAME),
                2 CONSUMER CHAR(32) VARYING INITIAL(STACK_MACHINE_NAME),
                2 BASE OFFSET(ENVELOPE.STACK) INITIAL(NULL()),
                2 STACK AREA(ALLOWANCE REFER(ENVELOPE.LENGTH));
      DECLARE 1 STACK_HEADER BASED(BASE),
                2 GENERATION_TIME CHAR(16) VARYING INITIAL(DATE()||TIME())
                2 TOP OFFSET(STACK);
```

Sample Listing 4.4. The PL/1 stack machine. The test macros.

```
/* the following macros are to be included where they are referenced */

  /* test whether stack machine is initialized                      */
     IF OPERATING_STATE¬='EXECUTABLE' THEN DO;
                        /* set ERROR_CODE */   RETURN;END;

  /* test for existence of stack with NAME_OF_STACK in stack table  */
  ACTUAL_STACK_ENTRY=NAME_OF_STACK.INTERNAL_NAME;
  IF NAME_OF_STACK.EXTERNAL_NAME¬=ENVELOPE.EXTERNAL_NAME |
     NAME_OF_STACK.GENERATION_TIME¬=STACK_HEADER.GENERATION_TIME
       THEN DO;   /* set ERROR_CODE */   RETURN;END;
```

The first module represents the operations which are related to stack machine management. Initialization and termination make the stack machine available as an operable resource in the environment. These two functions would bracket any other utilization of the stack machine. The second module is related to the lifetime of the stacks (see Sample Listing 4.5). Creation and deletion of a stack (Sample Listing 4.6) would bracket all other operations with the stack. The third module is related to the saving and restoring of stacks (Sample Listing 4.7). Note that although a stack is no longer accessible to the stack machine

Sample Listing 4.5. The PL/1 stack machine. The module for initialization and termination of the machine itself.

```
INITST:PROC(FILE_FOR_MESSAGES,ERROR_CODE);
/* INITIATE STACK MACHINE  */
MESSAGE_FILE=FILE_FOR_MESSAGES;
OPERATING_STATE='EXECUTABLE';
/* set ERROR_CODE */  RETURN;

TERMST:ENTRY(NUMBER_OF_ACT4E_STACK_PROCESSES,ERROR_CODE);
/* TERMINATE STACK MACHINE */
/* test whether stack machine is initialized             */
/* delete all remaining envelopes and stack */
/* write message on MESSAGE_FILE;                         */
OPERATING_STATE='EXISTING';
/* set ERROR_CODE */  RETURN;
END  INITST;
```

Sample Listing 4.6. The PL/1 stack machine. The module for creating and deleting stacks.

```
CREAST:PROC(ALLOWANCE,EXT_NAME,NAME_OF_STACK);
/* CREATE STACK */
/* test whether stack machine is initialized             */
   DECLARE EXT_NAME CHAR(32) VARYING;
   ALLOCATE STACK_ENTRY;ALLOCATE ENVELOPE;
/*  insert stack entry into stack table;                 */
   STACK_ENTRY.INTERNAL_NAME=ACTUAL_STACK_ENTRY;
   NAME_OF_STACK.EXTERNAL_NAME  =STACK.EXTERNAL_NAME;
   NAME_OF_STACK.INTERNAL_NAME  =STACK_ENTRY.INTERNAL_NAME;
   NAME_OF_STACK.GENERATION_TIME=STACK_HEADER.GENERATION_TIME;
/* set ERROR_CODE */  RETURN;

DELEST:ENTRY(NAME_OF_STACK,NORMAL_END);
/* DELETE STACK */
/* test whether stack machine is initialized             */
/* test for existence of stack with NAME_OF_STACK in stack table */
/* delete envelope and remove stack entry from stack table       */
/* set ERROR_CODE */  RETURN;

ESTIST:ENTRY(ESTIMATED_SIZE,ESTIMATED_NUMBER,GUESS,ERROR_CODE);
/* ESTIMATE STORAGE REQUIREMENT */
   DECLARE (GUESS,ESTIMATED_SIZE,ESTIMATED_NUMBER)BINARY FIXED(31);
   GUESS=(ESTIMATED_SIZE+4)*ESTIMATED_NUMBER)+20;
/* set ERROR_CODE */  RETURN;
END  CREAST;
```

after saving (until it is restored), the stack process is considered to continue. The saved stack carries with itself the identification given by the program that created it. In a hidden way, the saved stack also contains within itself the unique identification given to it by the stack machine (the creation date and time). Thus saved, stacks maintain their identity on whatever storage medium they may reside, and they can be deleted legally only by the stack machine. Due to the method of implementation, however, we cannot guarantee that a

Sample Listing 4.7. The PL/1 stack machine. The module for saving and restoring stacks.

```
SAVEST:PROC(NAME_OF_STACK,ENVELOPE_ADDRESS,ERROR_CODE);
/* SAVE    STACK */
/* test whether stack machine is initialized                    */
/* test for existence of stack with NAME_OF_STACK in stack table */
            ENVELOPE_ADDRESS=ACTUAL_STACK;
        /* remove stack entry from stack table and delete it;    */
/* set ERROR_CODE */  RETURN;

RESTST:PROC(NAME_OF_STACK,ENVELOPE_ADDRESS,ERROR_CODE);
/* RESTORE STACK */
/* test whether stack machine is initialized                    */
   ACTUAL_STACK=ENVELOPE_ADDRESS;
   IF ACTUAL_STACK->OWNER¬=STACK_MACHINE_NAME THEN DO;
       /* set ERROR_CODE */  RETURN;END;
/* test for non-existence of stack with NAME_OF_STACK           */
       /*allocate stack entry and insert stack with stack entry */
       /*into stack table;                                      */
   STACK_ENTRY.INTERNAL_NAME=ACTUAL_STACK_ENTRY;
   NAME_OF_STACK.EXTERNAL_NAME  =STACK.EXTERNAL_NAME;
   NAME_OF_STACK.INTERNAL_NAME  =STACK_ENTRY.INTERNAL_NAME;
   NAME_OF_STACK.GENERATION_TIME=STACK_HEADER.GENERATION_TIME;
/* set ERROR_CODE */  RETURN;
END   SAVEST;
```

saved stack will not be "killed" illegally by another process which has access to its representation (the program which issued the save call, or a human operator using utility programs of the operating system to delete a data set which represents a saved stack). The last module (Sample Listing 4.8) is related to the proper stack functions of an abstract stack machine: push, pop and empty.

4.3.4 Distributed Systems

Much attention has been devoted recently to the concepts of distributed CAD systems. The basic idea is simple. We have a small local computer (in the design office) for doing that part of the work which has to be done fast and can be done with the limited resources of the local computer. (Note that we use the terms "local" and "remote" with respect to the user — the local computer being in the design office, and the remote computer at some other place. In other literature these terms are often used with respect to the central computer, which is then considered as local while the attached satellites are remote.) If we need more computer power, we connect to the big computer in the computer center and submit the task for processing on "big brother". This central computer may in turn be backed up by a network of computers. However, the realization of this concept turns out to be not quite so simple. Even if there were no problems in connecting two computers (generally of different manufacturers) to each other in such a way that they can exchange messages, essential problems on the user level have to be resolved:

Sample Listing 4.8. The PL/1 stack machine. The module for the abstract stack functions.

```
PUSHST:PROC(NAME_OF_STACK,OBJECT_SIZE,OBJECT_ADDRESS
                          ,HELP,ERROR_CODE);
/* test whether stack machine is initialized                */
/* test for existence of stack with NAME_OF_STACK in stack table */
/* PUSH ITEM ON STACK */
   DECLARE 1 OBJECT BASED(OBJECT_ADDRESS),
             2 SIZE BINARY FIXED(31),
             2 CONTENT CHARACTER(OBJECT_SIZE REFER(OBJECT.SIZE));
   DECLARE ITEM_SIZE BINARY FIXED(31);
   DECLARE 1 ITEM OFFSET(TOP),
             2 IS_BELOW OFFSET(STACK),
             2 SIZE BINARY FIXED(31),
             2 CONTENT CHARACTER(ITEM_SIZE REFER(ITEM.SIZE));
       DECLARE NUMBER_OF_ATTEMPTS BINARY FIXED(15) INIT(0);
/* test whether stack machine is initialized                */
/* test for existence of stack with NAME_OF_STACK in stack table */
       ON AREA(STACK) BEGIN;
           IF NUMBER_OF_ATTEMPTS=0 THEN DO;
               NUMBER_OF_ATTEMPTS=1;
               /*try to compress stack by allocating a new envelope */
               /*with the same storage size; copy the old envelope  */
               /*into the new envelope, update the stack entry in    */
               /*stack table and delete the old envelope that caused*/
               /*the area overflow;*/ END;
           ELSE BEGIN;
               DECLARE ALLOWANCE BINARY FIXED(31);
               OPERATING_STATE='IN REPAIR';
               CALL HELP(STACK.SIZE,OBJECT_SIZE,ALLOWANCE);
               OPERATING_STATE='EXECUTABLE';
               IF STACK.SIZE>=ALLOWANCE THEN DO;
               /*set ERROR_CODE and RETURN;*/ END;
               ELSE DO;
               /*try to resolve problem by allocating a new envelope*/
               /*with new ALLOWANCE; copy the old envelope into the */
               /*new envelope; update the stack entry in the        */
               /*stack table and delete the old envelope that caused*/
               /*the area overflow;*/ END;
       END /* of AREA exception handling */;
       ALLOCATE ITEM IN(STACK);
/* set ERROR_CODE */   RETURN;
POPST:ENTRY(NAME_OF_STACK,OBJECT_SIZE,OBJECT_ADDRESS,HELP);
/* POP ITEM FROM STACK */
/* test whether stack machine is initialized                */
/* test for existence of stack with NAME_OF_STACK in stack table */
DECLARE NULL_OBJECT_SIZE BINARY FIXED(31) STATIC INIT(0);
/* if stack is empty set OBJECT_SIZE=NULL_OBJECT_SIZE;       */
/* otherwise set OBJECT_SIZE=ITEM.SIZE, allocate object, copy */
/* ITEM.CONTENT into OBJECT.CONTENT, delete ITEM and readjust TOP;*/
/* set ERROR_CODE */   RETURN;
EMPTST:ENTRY(NAME_OF_STACK,YES,ERROR_CODE);
/* IS STACK EMPTY ?    */
DCL YES BIT;
/* test whether stack machine is initialized                */
/* test for existence of stack with NAME_OF_STACK in stack table */
/* YES=true if found; otherwise yes=false                   */
/* set ERROR_CODE */   RETURN;
END   PUSHST;
```

− Which tasks should be executed on the local computer? Which ones remotely?
− Should there be a choice of executing a specific task either locally or remotely? If so, the corresponding functions would have to be available on both machines (redundancy of functions).
− How do we split the data base? Which parts of the data base should be kept as copies on both computers (redundancy of data)?

In most cases the dominant criterion is the response time. In order to decide the above questions, an estimate of the response time for the individual functions (as a function of the characteristic data supplied to the functions) would be required. Even for a dedicated local computer (with no other users competing) this is difficult, and more so in the time-sharing environment of a computer center. The processing time (for rotation of a three-dimensional object or for searches in a data base) depends very much on the amount and complexity of the data. On the remote central computer, the work load coming from many users is a highly varying function and is hardly predictable in a response time estimate. Thus, a suitable split of the tasks between local and remote computers is often based on practical experience rather than objective criteria. Recently, Cullmann [40] has proposed an interface architecture between a host and a satellite computer, which principally allows for run-time adjustment of the work. Cullmann proposes to implement the respective functions on *both* the satellite and the host and to call upon the particular version of the function which may be expected to give better performance. Some parameters which characterize the actual work load on both processors could be used by the interface system to decide autonomously (that is without being helped by the operator) whether the host-side or the satellite-side version of a function should be used.

The design of distributed systems requires much pre-planning of the distribution of processes among the participating computers [41, 42]. Hence it is not surprising that the architectures of distributed CAD systems show more variety than CAD systems based on a single computer. However, the three types shown in Fig. 4.16 through Fig. 4.18 may serve as a reference.

Fig. 4.16 represents a local computer with remote backup. The local computer is the master, the remote computer a slave. Data base and program base are concentrated on the local computer. For the activities which require large computational resources, programs and data are sent to the remote computer (as an alternative, the programs may have previously been implemented on the remote computer's library). A typical application of this sort is the finite element analysis of a structure which has been designed interactively on the local computer. The remote computer is operated in batch mode. Large amounts of information are exchanged between the two computers before the start and after the termination of the remote task. The response time of the programs ("number crunching" like finite element or finite difference analyses, hidden line removal, or operations on large data bases) generally forbids interactive operation. The advantages of this arrangement are simplicity and fast response to the user for many activities. The problems which are often encountered are:

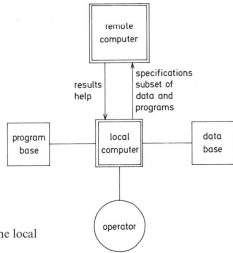

Fig. 4.16. A distributed CAD system with the local computer as a master

- the methods for maintaining a growing data and program base may turn out to be less powerful on the small local computer than on the large remote one. Either the user approaches the limits of his small computer before he can satisfy his needs, or (if possible) the small computer soon grows and becomes a big one itself. In this latter case the "small" dedicated local computer loses its desired simplicity, and requires more money and computer expertise for its operation and maintenance than had originally been anticipated.
- If more than one user at different locations should want to work with the same program and data base, this arrangement is inadequate.

The concept shown in Fig. 4.17 does not produce the problem of limited computing power and storage capacity. Similar to time-shared usage of a CAD system on a big central computer directly from a terminal (without an intermediate local computer), this concept is well suited for a greater number of users at different locations. Compared to the centralized approach, however, it has the advantage that prior to a sequence of activities all (or most) of the related programs and data may be transmitted to the local computer. Thus we avoid the need for exchanges of information across the connection line for even the most primitive operations. The gain in response can be significant. This benefit has to be paid for:

- Since the transmitted part of the data base is no longer under the control of the central data base system, the problem of consistency arises. Different users may work on different copies of the same part of the data base and make changes which are not consistent with each other. Features (possibly of an organizational nature) must be added to the system to deal with this problem, thus increasing the level of complexity.

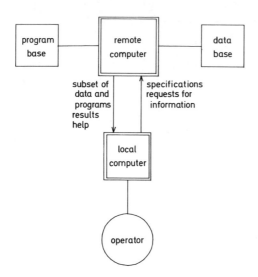

Fig. 4.17. A distributed CAD system with the remote computer as a master

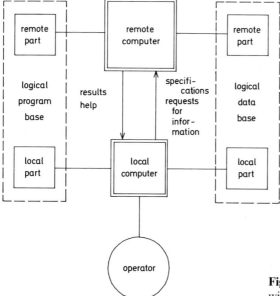

Fig. 4.18. A distributed CAD system with split program and data bases

– More preplanning is required. The user cannot freely follow his intuition when working at the local computer. He can work (efficiently) only with the subset which has previously been copied from the remote computer. Thus the possibility of switching between activities (such as information retrieval, drafting, and calculation), which is typical for design work, is reduced.

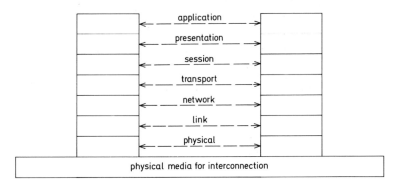

Fig. 4.19. The seven-layer model for connecting two systems

Fig. 4.18 shows what appears to be the solution of the dilemma. The logical program and data bases have been split into a local and a remote part according to the resource requirements (response time, processing, and storage capabilities). The problem with this concept, however, is that it does not find adequate support in reality. It is still a subject of much research work going on [43]. If despite the undeveloped methodology an attempt is made to implement such a system, one will likely be confronted with the fact that data base support, programming languages, and other tools are not compatible on the two computers. Methods that have been developed in the area of process control systems may possibly be borrowed to the advantage of distributed CAD system development [44]. In this case, a once-defined separation is likely to be fixed forever because otherwise much programming would have to be redone (consider two different data base systems on the two computers, PASCAL on the big computer, FORTRAN on the small one). Portability of system functions from local to remote and vice versa is important because, as experience with the implemented system grows, the need to adapt the response behavior to changing user attitudes and changing computer loads will arise. A system which is split among two computers is probably much less portable to other installations than a system based on one computer only (at least in the general case of two different computer manufacturers).

Nevertheless, the potential benefits of a distributed CAD system require more consideration and research. The architecture developed in [5] (see Fig. 4.19) is promising. Seven levels (or layers) of processes have been identified. The highest layer would correspond to one or more CAD processes; the lowest level represents the hardware which connects the computers. The need for subschema transformations (see Chapter 3.3.3) is recognized in the proposal. Fig. 4.20 indicates that subschema transformations may take place:

– not at all, if the same subschema is used on both computers;
– on one computer or the other;
– on both computers, if the interconnection between the components requires a different subschema for the transport itself.

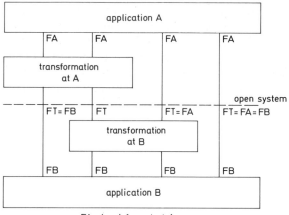

FA: local format at A
FB: local format at B
FT: format for transport

Fig. 4.20. Transformations in connected systems

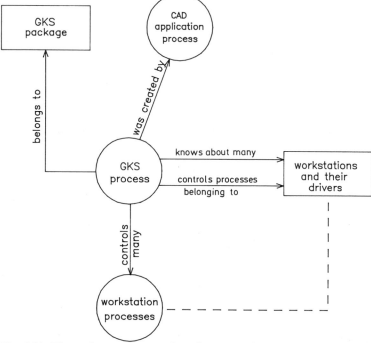

Fig. 4.21. The main processes and environments in a GKS application

There is a remarkable agreement between the Open Systems proposal and the CAD process model as derived in Chapter 3 (Figs. 3.7 and 3.8) with respect to the importance assigned to management functions. A layer in the Open Systems proposal is characterized by a varying number of "application-process-entities" (say, abstract processes) and a single "management-entity" (say, the environment process). The "application-process-entities" have direct relations to corresponding entities on higher and lower levels; the "management-entity" is linked to a "system-management-entity" (Fig. 4.21). The similarity between the ISO Open Systems proposal and the concepts of CAD processes and CAD software machines (see Chapter 4.3.1) suggests that this proposal will suitably support distributed CAD processes (once it becomes available). At present, however, designers of distributed CAD systems have to deal with incompatibilities of computer systems on all levels (even down to the hardware), and either must refrain from utilizing the benefits of distributed processes or must themselves provide interfaces at low levels instead of concentrating on their actual problem: the optimal split of the process functions on the user level.

4.3.5 The Graphical Kernel System GKS as a Software Machine

4.3.5.1 The Process Aspect in GKS

The design of the Graphical Kernel System GKS has been influenced considerably by the ideas described in Chapter 3 with respect to processes, and by the concepts developed in this chapter regarding software machine design. GKS is indeed a typical software machine. It has been specified functionally in the GKS standard [31] for a wide range of applications (not only CAD) on an abstract level, independent from any particular programming language — though the GKS designers (more precisely, the designers of the specification) always kept in mind that it should be implementable in a FORTRAN environment. During its development, nobody could foresee the possible resource conflicts which might arise in future application programs, when GKS would start to compete with other software components for resources. Hence, it was necessary to consider the resource aspect as an essential part of the GKS functional specification.

The application program using GKS obviously has to know about the existence of the GKS package in its environment. This condition is achieved by appropriate programming (like the use of the correct names of GKS functions) on the programming level, and by binding the corresponding GKS subroutines into the executable application module. In the sense of Chapter 2 (see Fig. 3.8) the GKS package is an environment that is known to the application process. The application program may request the creation of a GKS process from the package (called OPEN GKS in the GKS terminology); it may modify the state of this process by calling upon the different GKS functions, and it may finally terminate the process by CLOSE GKS. As part of the GKS process state, several subprocesses may be created, each one corresponding to an individual workstation. These subprocesses have names (the workstation identifiers), while the GKS process itself does not need an explicit name: only one GKS process may exist in an application program. Via GKS and a workstation process, the application program may address the drivers of graphical hardware. Both the graphical hardware and the associated drivers constitute part of the computer environment in which the application is executed. The knowledge

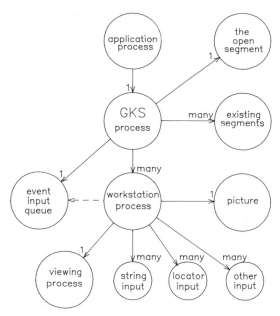

Fig.4.22. The subprocesses under GKS control

about the capabilities of the various types of workstations in a computer environment is passed to the application program via GKS as the "workstation description table". Fig. 4.21. illustrates this situation; it is a special case of the more general schema shown in Fig. 3.8.

In Chapter 2.2.4.3 (Fig. 3.19), we stated that each process has a certain state representation. We will now refer to Fig. 4.22 for the discussion of the subprocesses in GKS. The environment aspect has not been included in this figure in order not to make it overly complicated. In the GKS standard, the state representation of the *GKS process* is defined as the "GKS state list", and each workstation process has a "workstation state list". Among other information, the workstation state list contains the definitions for the visualization of the graphical primitives.

A subtask of the GKS process is the management of segments. A particular segment is the *open segment*. The lifetime of the *open segment process* is bracketed by OPEN SEGMENT and CLOSE SEGMENT. This latter statement transfers the newly created segment process into the set of the *existing segments*, where it continues to exist until it is deleted. A second way to create segment processes under GKS control is to read segments which were created in previous GKS applications from a GKS metafile.

Another task of GKS is the maintenance of the "list of associated workstations" for each segment. This list may be interpreted as an inversion of a *picture* definition. The notion of a picture is not available in GKS. We regard a *picture* as a collection of segments, and represent the correspondence between a picture and a workstation by considering the picture as a subprocess to a workstation process. It would be desirable to have the concept of a picture in a graphical kernel system in order to be able to treat such pictures as entities (for copying, deleting, etc.). However, very early in the GKS specification work it was decided to use only a single level of naming for identifying graphical entities. The introduction of named "pictures" would have created a second such level. The state of a picture is modified by creating new segments or by reading segments from a metafile while the corresponding workstation is "active", or by copying existing segments from one picture into another.

Each workstation process has (potentially) a number of *input subprocesses*. The input processes are associated with input devices of various types. Each one of the input processes may be uniquely identified by a qualified name consisting of workstation identification, device class, and device number. The state of each input process is characterized by an input class mode (REQUEST, SAMPLE or EVENT). The GKS standard defines "measure" processes and "trigger" processes in order to describe the state of the input processes in more detail. For the REQUEST and SAMPLE input modes, the input processes are synchronized by GKS. For EVENT input, the input processes operate asynchronously and communicate their event reports through the workstation processes to the *input queue* (see dashed line in Fig. 4.22), from which these reports may be retrieved by the application process via GKS.

One *viewing process* is associated with each workstation. It presents an image of the workstation picture (that is, of the set of segments associated with the workstation) to the operator. The viewing process lifetime equals the lifetime of the workstation process. The state of the viewing process is what the operator can visually perceive on a display screen or a sheet of paper. This image is not necessarily identical with the visual representation of the corresponding picture according to the actual state of the workstation state list. Due to deferred updating there may be a delay, which we interpret as a difference between the states of the workstation process and its viewing subprocess.

4.3.5.2 The Resource Aspect in GKS

As is common in functional specifications, the GKS standard concentrates on abstract functions and does not elaborate on the resource aspect in great detail. Nevertheless, the necessity of dealing with this aspect has been realized to the extent that a whole annex has been devoted to it under the title "interfaces". A number of rules, roughly corresponding to rules (R1) through (R7) of Chapter 4.3.2, are documented as a means of minimizing the potential for resource conflicts in future applications. For instance, every GKS implementation is requested to supply a renaming facility. This feature should eliminate conflicts between GKS names and names, used by other parts of the application program. It concerns both programming time conflicts (names of GKS functions that are visible to the application program) and binding time conflicts (global names of SUBROUTINES or COMMON in GKS, which are not visible to the application program). Another rule calls for the description of all additional files (for buffer overflow or GKS module libraries, for instance) as resources that have to be provided by the application process in order to make GKS operable.

But beyond that, it should be noted that the concept of workstations [45] has resulted from resource considerations. It was found essential to provide both GKS itself and the application process with knowledge about the capabilities of the various types of graphics workstations that are available in their computer environment. The quantification of the graphical resources was intentionally not hidden in the drivers, but made apparent so as to allow the higher-level processes (GKS and application) to adjust their behavior in line with whatever the drivers and the hardware can or cannot perform. The workstation description table is a special case of a quantified resource description, and should be considered a powerful tool in the implemention of portable software machines.

One point where more consideration of resource aspects would have been appropriate in GKS is the need for storage capacity for the graphical information. It would be a significant help for designers of CAD systems that using GKS for their graphics part if GKS provided a storage estimate inquiry function, which would tell the estimated storage capacity needed for a segment of given complexity (number and type of graphical primitives in the segment). As it is, GKS will respond with an error message like "storage overflow" if the resources are insufficient; the application program may then take corrective actions. Instead of correcting and redoing previous work, one would probably prefer to have an estimate of the resource requirements in advance in order to prevent the error condition from occurring at all.

4.4 Summary

In the first paragraphs of this chapter, we concentrated on the components and interfaces of CAD systems. The components were considered under various aspects (hardware, software, functional). The functional aspect was related to the main design activities:

- specification;
- synthesis;
- analysis;
- transformation;
- presentation;
- evaluation.

The interface between the components has been identified as an important characteristic of CAD system architectures. Different interfaces exist during the development, invocation and application of a CAD system. The development and use of a CAD system is greatly improved if suitable CAD tools (or CAD machines) are available. CAD tools are "black box" components which perform certain tasks in whatever environment they are used. Thus, CAD systems can conceptually be built by assembling a number of suitable tools.

While in conventional design the conceptual model of real-world objects may be described informally, in CAD the conceptual model must be mapped in a formal way onto the computer hardware. This mapping is done in (at least) two steps:

1) conceptual model $\longrightarrow$ language level
2) language level $\longrightarrow$ hardware

Many languages may be used for this mapping process (programming languages as well as data-definition languages of data base systems). Different languages may offer different capacities for expressing important properties of objects relating to the conceptual model. Not all will be languages equally suitable. Often it is necessary to introduce intermediate mappings (as when calendar dates are mapped onto integers). In extreme cases, the desired mapping can be achieved only by "mapping around the language", and the language becomes more of an obstacle than a help.

Binding was identified as an important step between the definition of an object and its use. The binding process replaces a reference to a name by the reference to the object denoted by the name. Binding may occur at different times: programming, module binding, job preparation, execution. Flexibility and efficiency are competing criteria which influence the decision of whether early or late binding is preferable.

Besides the representation of objects by data, objects may be represented in algorithmic form. Data modelling and algorithmic modelling both have their pros and cons. The "best" model depends very much on how the model is to be used in practice.

As a key issue of CAD system architectures the resource aspect was described in some detail. The abstract function of a CAD system is essential, but the question of resource management may equally well determine the usefulness of a system in a given environment. Questions like

– which resources are needed?
– how does the system try to optimize resource usage?

should *not* be hidden from the user, but should rather be made evident. CAD tools (or CAD machines) can be freely combined to new CAD systems only when the design of the CAD machines avoids potential conflicts. A set of rules, significantly reducing the conflict problem, has been formulated. A sample problem (a stack machine) illustrates the difference in the amount of work required for the writing of an algorithm in programming language and for the realization of a powerful CAD machine for the same task.

Distributed CAD systems offer a promising compromise between the use of a dedicated (usually small) CAD computer and the time-shared use of a large central computer system. The benefits of a distributed system (fast response to small problems, back-up by a powerful computer for big problems) must be paid for: distributed systems are much more complex, and portable solution concepts are still in the development stage.

Finally, the Graphical Kernel System (GKS) was discussed under the aspects of processes and software machine design, which had been developed in Chapters 3 and 4.

4.5 Bibliography

[1] R. Noppen: Technische Datenverarbeitung bei der Planung und Fertigung industrieller Erzeugnisse. Informatik Fachberichte 11, Heidelberg (1977) Springer-Verlag, pp. 1–19.

[2] J.-C. Latombe: Artificial Intelligence and Pattern Recognition in Computer Aided Design. Amsterdam (1978) North-Holland.

[3] J.J. Allan III, K. Bø: A Survey of Commercial Turn-key CAD/CAM Systems. Dallas (1978) Productivity Int. Corp.

[4] Integrierte Programmsysteme. Report KfK-CAD 2, Kernforschungszentrum Karlsruhe (1975).

[5] Reference Model of Open Systems Interconnection (Version 4 as of June 1979). Report ISO/TC97/SC16 N227 Paris (1978) Association Francaise de Normalisation.

[6] F.M. Lillehagen: CAD/CAM Workstations for Man/Model Communication. IEEE Computer Graphics 1 (1981) 3, pp. 17–27.

[7] J. Hatvany: Trends and Developments in Computer-Aided Design. In: B. Gilchrist (ed.): Information Processing 1977. Amsterdam (1977) North-Holland, p. 267–271.

[8] D.T. Ross, K.E. Schoman: Structured Analysis for Requirements Definition. Proc. IEEE/ACM 2nd Int. Conference on Software Engineering, San Francisco (1976).

[9] D. Teichrov, E.A. Hershey III: PSL/PSA: A Computer-Aided Technique for Structured Documentation and Analysis of Information Processing Systems. IEEE Transactions on Software Engineering, Vol. SE-3 (1977) 1, pp. 41–48.

[10] J.V. Guttag: Abstract Data Types and the Development of Data Structures. Comm. ACM 20 (1977), pp. 396–404.

[11] W. Bartussek, D.L. Parnas: Using Assertions about Traces to Write Abstract Specifications for Software Modules. In: G.G. Bracchi, P.C. Lockemann: Proc. Information Systems Methodology. Heidelberg (1978) Springer-Verlag.

[12] J. Ludewig, W. Streng: Überblick und Vergleich verschiedener Mittel für die Spezifikation und den Entwurf von Software. Report KfK 2509, Kernforschungszentrum Karlsruhe (1978).

[13] H. Balzert: Methoden, Sprachen und Werkzeuge zur Definition, Dokumentation und Analyse von Anforderungen an Software-Produkte. Teil I. Informatik-Spektrum 4 (1981) 3, pp. 145–163.

[14] H. Balzert: Methoden, Sprachen und Werkzeuge zur Definition, Dokumentation und Analyse von Anforderungen an Software-Produkte. Teil II. Informatik-Spektrum 4 (1981) 4, pp. 246–260.

[15] W. Hesse: Methoden und Werkzeuge zur Software-Entwicklung. Informatik-Spektrum 4 (1981) 4, pp. 229–245.

[16] U. Voges, L. Gmeiner, A. Amschler von Mayrhauser: SADAT — An Automated Testing Tool. IEEE Transactions on Software Engineering, Vol. SE-5 (1980) 6, pp. 286–290.

[17] R.C. Houghten Jr., K.A. Oakley: NBS Software Tools Database, NBSIR 80-2159, Washington (1980) National Bureau of Standards.

[18] K. Hünke: Software Engineering Environments. Amsterdam (1980) North-Holland.

[19] B.H. Liskov, S.N. Zilles: Specification Techniques for Data Abstractions. IEEE Trans. on Software Engineering 1 (1975), pp. 7–19.

[20] K. Jensen, N. Wirth: PASCAL User Manual and Report. Second Corrected Reprint of the Second Edition. New York (1978) Springer-Verlag.

[21] T.W. Olle: The CODASYL Approach to Data Base Management. Chichester (1978) John Wiley.

[22] J.H. Saltzer: Naming and Binding of Objects. In: G. Goos, J. Hartmanis (eds.): Lecture Notes in Computer Science 60: Operating Systems. Heidelberg (1978) Springer-Verlag, pp. 99–208.

[23] K. Leinemann, E.G. Schlechtendahl: The REGENT System for CAD. In: J.J. Allan III: CAD Systems. Amsterdam (1977) North-Holland, pp. 143–168.

[24] E.G. Schlechtendahl, K.H. Bechler, G. Enderle, K. Leinemann, W. Olbrich: RE-GENT-Handbuch. Report KfK 2666 (KfK-CAD 71), Kernforschungszentrum Karlsruhe (1978).

[25] P. Bono, J. Encarnação, F.R.A. Hopgood, P. ten Hagen: GKS — The First Graphics Standard. IEEE Computer Graphics and Applications 2 (1982) 5, pp.9–23.

[26] E. Towster: A Convention for Explicit Declaration of Environments and TOP-Down Refinement of Data. IEEE Transactions on Software Engineering, Vol. SE-5 (1979) 4, pp. 374–386.

[27] W. Wulf, M. Shaw: Global Variable Considered Harmful. Sigplan Notices 8 (1973), pp. 18–29.

[28] P.L. Parnas: A Technique for Software Module Specification with Examples. Communications of the ACM 15 (1972) 5, pp. 330–336.

[29] J. Ichbiah et al.: Preliminary ADA Reference Manual. SIGPLAN Notices 14 (1979) 6.

[30] J. Ichbiah: Reference Manual for the ADA Programming Language. United States Department of Defense, July 1980, Proposed Standard Document. LNCS 106. New York (1982) Springer-Verlag.

[31] ISO TC97/SC5/WG2 N117; Draft International Standard; Information Processing, GRAPHICAL KERNEL SYSTEM (GKS), 1982.

[32] R. Schuster: System und Sprache zur Behandlung graphischer Information im rechnergestuetzten Entwurf. Report KfK 2305, Kernforschungszentrum Karlsruhe (1976).

[33] ACM-SIGGRAPH Graphics Standards Planning Committee, Special Issue on GSPC 79. Computer Graphics 13 (1979) 3.

[34] P. Schnupp: Rechnernetze; Entwurf und Realisierung. Berlin (1978) de Gruyter.

[35] D.L. Parnas: On the Need for Fewer Restrictions in Changing Compile-Time Environments. SIGPLAN Notices 10 (1975), pp. 29–36.

[36] D.E. Knuth: The Art of Computer Programming. Vol 1: Fundamental Algorithms (2nd ed.) Reading, Mass. (1969) Addison-Wesley Publ.

[37] Informationsverarbeitung; Programmdokumentation; DIN 66230, Ausg. 1.81. In: DIN Taschenbuch 166, Informationsverarbeitung 4. Berlin (1981) Beuth.

[38] M.A. Jackson: Software Development as an Engineering Problem. Angewandte Informatik (1982) 2, pp. 96–103.

[39] W. Lincke: Zukünftige CAD-Anwendungen; Forderungen und Perspektiven. VDI-Berichte 413 (1981), pp. 137–142.

[40] N. Cullmann: Optimized Software Distribution in Satellite Graphics Systems. In: C.E. Vandoni (ed.): Proc. Eurographics 80 Int. Conf. & Exhibition Geneva, 3-5. Sept. 1980. Amsterdam (1980) North-Holland.

[41] P. Brinch Hansen: Distributed Processes: A Concurrent Programming Concept. Computing Surveys 5 (1973) 4, pp. 223–245.

[42] S.S. Yau, C.-C. Yang, S.M. Shatz: An Approach to Distributed Computing System Software Design. IEEE Trans. Softw. Eng., Vol. SE-7 (1981) 4, pp. 427–447.

[43] S. Schindler, J.C.W. Schröder (eds.): Kommunikation in verteilten Systemen. Informatik Fachberichte 22, Heidelberg (1979) Springer-Verlag.

[44] C.V. Ramamoorthy, Y.R. Mok, F.B. Bastani, G.H. Chin, K. Suzuki: Application of a Methodology for the Development and Validation of Reliable Process Control Software. IEEE Trans. Software Eng., Vol. SE-7 (1981) 6, pp. 537–555.

[45] J. Encarnação, G. Enderle, K. Kansy, G. Nees, E.G. Schlechtendahl, J. Weiß, P. Wißkirchen: The Workstation Concept of GKS and the Resulting Conceptual Differences to the GSPC Proposal. Proc. SIGGRAPH '80, Computer Graphics 14 (1980) 3, pp. 226–230.

5 Implementation Methodology

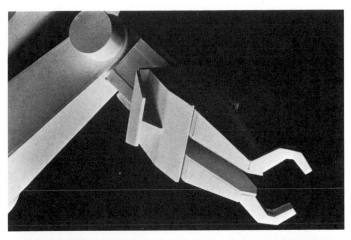

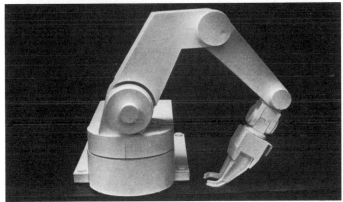

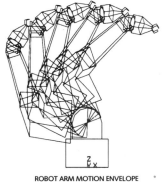

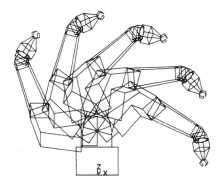

ROBOT ARM MOTION ENVELOPE

Simulation of a robot model
(courtesy of DEC, Maltorough, USA)

5.1 Techniques and Tools for CAD System Development

Program development may be considered as the sequence of the following activities:

- definition of requirements;
- specification;
- logic design;
- programming;
- testing;
- completion of documentation.

The first two activities are basically of an analytical nature on a level which is above the level of the design and realization of the new system (see Chapter 3 and Fig. 3.5 in particular). The result of this analysis is a functional specification (see Fig. 5.1). In the subsequent design phase the system architecture is defined. The design has to be evaluated with respect to the specification and the goals to be achieved. Programming and testing are the activities that build the operational system. Documentation accompanies all of these activities. The lifetime of a program is comprises the following additional phases:

- installation and adaptation;
- maintenance, correction of errors, adjustment to changing needs, performance tuning;
- user training.

We will discuss the first steps briefly in a general way, and will then address our attention to some aspects which relate specifically to CAD, leaving a more detailed treatment of all the many aspects of program development to the literature on software engineering (e.g. [1]).

The specification, logic design, and implementation of CAD systems are very often begun before all the real needs, boundary conditions, and system functions are known. However, even the best programmer cannot write a good program if he does not understand the problem precisely. And an optimally structured program cannot produce meaningful results if the problem was not stated properly. The remedy is a complete and comprehensible *definition of requirements* which the program will have to meet [2, 3].

The definition of requirements involves problem analysis, and leads to a functional specification. Basically, the following three questions have to be answered (see Fig. 5.2):

- *Why* is the system needed?
  Analysis of the larger context into which the system is to be embedded is required.
- *What* should the system do?
  The essential capabilities must be spelled out in a functional specification.
- *How* can the system be realized?
  This question refers to the resources that can be made available for the design implementation and operation of the system, and to the constraints imposed

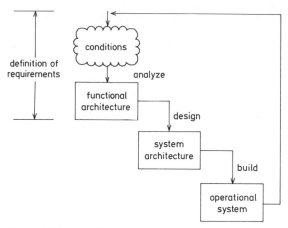

Fig. 5.1. Phases of system development

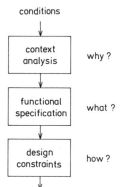

Fig. 5.2. Questions related to system development

by the environment. The question of which steps will have to be taken for implementation will be posed later in the system development process.

Together, the answers should completely define the requirements that need to be met by the system. Descriptions of this sort provide a framework for the problem, but do not solve it. The definition of requirements gives only the boundary conditions needed for the subsequent specification, logic design, and implementation. The systems analysis process that produces the functional architecture should be carried out on a level of detail that will precisely determine:

- the system's functionality (the set of functions and the constraints imposed by the environment);
- the type of description (whether it should be formal or in ordinary language);
- the optimization criteria (which are needed for finding adequate compromises between contradictory requirements).

Each of the three subjects — context analysis, functional specification, and logic design constraints — must be considered under at least three aspects: technical, operational, and economic.

The SADT system is a typical example of a software tool that may be helpful throughout a CAD system's development (see also Chapter 4.1.3.2). SADT can already be used during the definition of requirements for the whole system. It may also aid in the subsequent specification phase, and in the refinement steps that follow. In these steps, a close interaction exists between the level of logic design, where a suitable structuring into components has to be worked out, and the specification of these components. Here we encounter the level structure that was discussed in Chapter 3 with respect to design processes in general. SADT is based upon a conceptual distinction between functional architecture and system architecture [4]. The functional architecture accurately reflects the activities performed by the system and the things with which they interact. Typical examples are:

Things	Activities
Objects	Operations
Information	Processing
Passive	Active

Conceiving things and activities on different levels of abstraction, and then connecting them by appropriate relations into a functional architecture, is the object of systems analysis. The result of this analysis is best represented not in ordinary language alone, but also in graphical schemas. The graphical representations in SADT allow us to distinguish clearly between things which interact by means of some activities, and other things which actually perform these activities. (For example, two persons communicating by writing letters to each other would belong to the first category; the postman carrying the letter would belong to the second one.) Thus, a principal aspect of SADT is the use of graphic techniques. The graphic language of SADT offers a limited number of basic elements which can be used by analysts and designers to compose ordered structures of any required size (Fig. 5.3). These basic elements are blocks and arrows. A block represents a part of a whole, while an arrow represents an interface between parts. Block diagrams represent a whole (unit) consisting of blocks, arrows, names in ordinary language and other descriptions. A model in SADT is a sequence of diagrams with associated text on the same level. On the next higher level, an entire substructure is represented by a brief summary (shown as a single box in Fig. 5.3). A model in SADT is a graphic representation of the hierarchical structure of a system decomposed into any desired degree of detail. Substructuring may be done under different aspects corresponding to the different kinds of people who will have different views of the same system. Consequently, SADT provides the means to specify various human roles with respect to a system: the author of the specification, a technical reviewer, the project manager and so forth. All the people involved in the development and later use of the system have to contribute in some way to its specification. SADT anticipates this requirement by allocating names and functions to appropriate human roles. *Specification* means the precise definition

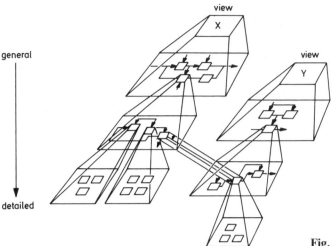

Fig. 5.3. The SADT structure

of the given programming problem. The principal rules in logic and writing the specification are:

– a specification should contain only statements concerning "what" (requirements to be met by the programmed product) and none concerning "how" (realization as program);
– a specification should represent a complete and precise description of the problem which the program is to solve;
– various classes of readers of a specification should be able to locate easily the information of interest to them. The information should be given in a comprehensible form;
– since the majority of readers of a specification are not data processing specialists, the use of data processing terminology should be avoided as far as possible. Formal representations should be confined to an appendix, and examples should be provided for illustration purposes;
– all specifications should be constructed in modular form. All subsequent documention describing the finished product should be developed from parts of the specification without the need for restructuring (basically by some additional text editing);
– a specification should be easy to maintain and should be written in such a way that additions, alterations, and deletions will require no great effort.

In the *design phase*, the system is broken down into components, each of which has to perform a certain function. The goal of the design activity is to *transform the specification into a system of components that can be implemented* either directly or after repetition of the design process on the next lower level. CAD system design, like any other design (see Chapter 3), is an inherently recursive process [5]. As a result of design, specifications for the system components are developed, which will then pass through their own design phase.

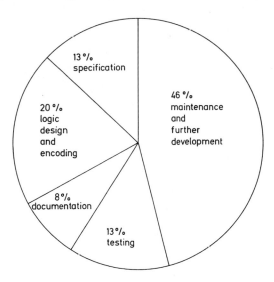

Fig. 5.4. Software development costs

This is typical of the recursive character of design. The following points are specified for each module contributing to the implementation:

- the interface (procedure or macro statements, input data and output data);
- the process environment (state of the process that may be taken for granted or that has to be checked);
- the programming environment (programming language, resources, etc.);
- the desired action of the module.

As pointed out by Jackson [6], software development is distinguished from conventional development by the fact that there is no clear-cut boundary between design and production. The result of program design is the program itself, possibly not yet in the desired programming language for compiling but ready to be converted into compilable form by rather formal steps. Programming and testing are essential parts of program implementation. Testing, being a non-productive activity, should be kept at a minimum. The cost of testing programs can easily reach between 20% and 40% of the cost of program development [7]. [Program development costs do not include the cost of later maintenance or further development after installation (Fig. 5.4).] Hence, a fundamental goal of "software engineering" applied to CAD system development is to *avoid errors instead of detecting them*. According to Altmann and Weber, we have to consider two basic types of errors [8]:

- Execution errors: Constructional errors, specification errors, design errors, and errors in requesting resources.
- Logic errors: Omitted control flow segments, wrong conditions, wrong or omitted actions.

Errors will always sneak in, despite all efforts to avoid them. Unfortunately, errors generally show up at a point in space and time that is far away from their origin. Hence, errors must not only be found but also located. This must be done selectively and not by random sampling. Including pieces of protective code at critical points in the program, to serve for checking and tracing errors whithout contributing at all to the "normal" problem solution, may well return the additional cost in planning and execution effort by saving debugging time.

Programming is the application of many techniques developed in the software engineering field to make the production of programs easier and more reliable. Once the requirements are fixed and the specification of a module is given, a transformation into a suitable programming language is the next step. Various programming techniques have been developed in recent years; they share the following common objectives [8]:

– reduction of problem complexity;
– implementation of programs from standardized modules;
– problem-oriented formulation;
– assurance of correctness;
– comprehensibility of logic design to allow proper communication.

The most widely used programming techniques are:

– standardized programming;
– structured programming;
– modular programming;
– precompilers and program generators for the transformation of compact and descriptive languages (such as decision tables) into compilable languages.

A fundamental idea is the use of previously developed software machines to implement new systems (see Chapter 4.3). This technique avoids the need of "re-inventing the wheel" by coding from scratch algorithms that have already been developed and implemented by others. All available software machines (in most cases subroutine packages) — which may serve, for instance, to guide all kinds of operators, to support physical and logical devices, to construct application-specific models or to monitor an interactive dialogue — should be used and adapted to build a new system for a special task. Thus, an optimized configuration may be formed with a minimum of new development. A configuration may be considered as optimal, if

– only those functions are realized which are actually needed by an application or an application class (minimality), and
– the software structures of the available functions are reproduced by processor structures for optimized performance, applying the "best fit" mapping.

Such an approach of selective reconfiguration and adaptation of available software on the source level provides, among other advantages, the possibility to install systems on small machines equipped with inexpensive workstations, or to satisfy high-performance requirements by suitably structuring processor systems to specific software structures, or to adapt systems to specific user (operator) requirements by tailoring dialogue components.

A notion often used in CAD system development is the orthogonality of user characteristics and application characteristics. This notion means that an

Fig. 5.5. The CAD system interfaces to humans

adjustment of the communication interface and a modification of the methods provided for solving application problems should be feasible independent from each other. In this context of orthogonality, the following factors have to be considered:

- User characteristics:
  1. required user knowledge about the system;
  2. help functions and error messages;
  3. interactive tutorial for user guidance;
  4. need for explicit support (documentation and training);
  5. expected response time for interactions of various complexity.
- Application characteristics:
  1. data model of the application (complexity and size);
  2. data flow characteristics;
  3. functionality (the set of functions that operates on the data model);
  4. control mechanisms.

When designing a CAD system, design conflicts will generally arise from conflicting wishes and requirements. Fig. 5.5 illustrates the most important human interfaces that will give rise to conflicts in CAD system design:

- the acceptance conflict:
  A CAD workstation fulfilling the desired ergonomic characteristics may simply not be available on the market.
- the dialogue conflict:
  For the system programmer a language like PASCAL may be suitable, but the workstation may not have the corresponding compiler. Or perhaps the dialogue has been designed for English-speaking operators, with no provision for conversion to a French or Chinese environment.
- the operation conflict:
  A workstation providing the desired functionality and dialogue characteristics may not have the ruggedness needed for operation in the design office.
- the price conflict:
  Last but not least, the "perfect" system may be identified, yet turn out to be far beyond the budget limits.

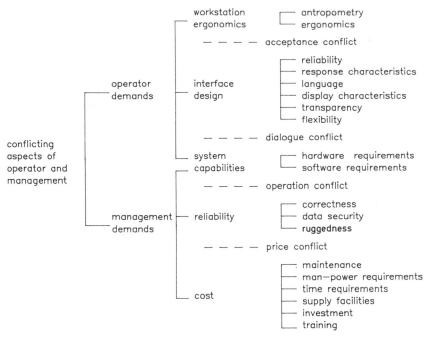

Fig. 5.6. Potential conflicts between the operator and the purchaser of a CAD system

An evaluation of these interfaces based on user characteristics and application requirements is the basis for the definition of the application-oriented CAD system environment. These interfaces are interrelated in the sense that they influence each other; for instance, the dialogue interface influences the system performance, and is influenced by the workstation ergonomics (Fig. 5.6).

Today's efforts in the area of interactive man-machine communication aim at the development of systems capable of adjusting their dialogue behavior to the user characteristics. A prerequisite is a good dialogue structure and a well-defined interface description, strictly separated from the application (orthogonality). The interactive part of the system is designed by a dialogue author. He has to "describe" the information packages that constitute the individual "sentences" of the interaction with respect to their semantics and syntax. It is advisable to order them in a hierarchical structure representing the interaction flow. This "description" will then be interpreted by a dialogue processor at run-time.

No matter how thoroughly the design analysis is made, the system designer has to anticipate that the system will not immediately satisfy the user after implementation. Moreover, the user's needs will change, as well as his expertise in using the system. Hence, it is good practice to design components into the system which will facilitate later adaptation and performance tuning. Recently [9], a technique has been proposed for tuning the interface between operator and system on the basis of quantitative information, which the system itself collects during execution (Fig. 5.7). The technique provides a monitor as a

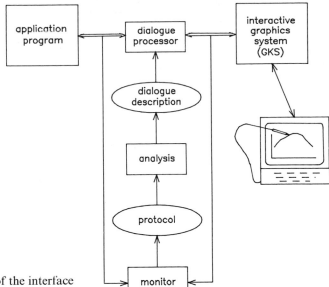

Fig. 5.7. The evaluation of the interface
between the operator and the CAD system

software machine within the CAD system, to sample such data as user and
system response time, types and occurrence rates of errors, times and rates
of transfer of data. By applying statistical analysis to these data, the dialogue
monitor evaluates user and system behavior, setting up a protocol of the progress
of interaction. From this protocol, the monitor extracts a profile of user characteristics and system performance. This information may be provided as feedback
to the dialogue processor; thus, adaptive interactive dialogues can be achieved.

However, there is also the potential of applying this approach during system
design by means of simulating later system applications [10]. Interpretation
of the simulated system performance will reveal criteria for suitably structuring
a dedicated interactive system:

– user characteristics and CAD system architecture;
– user characteristics and dialogue type;
– application characteristics and CAD system architecture;
– application characteristics and dialogue type.

Such correlations (see Fig. 5.8) may be used to resolve some of the above-
mentioned design conflicts by finding suitable compromises. They may also
be used as a starting point for price, performance, and acceptance evaluations.
These, in turn, may suggest that new compromises ought to be found in the
correlation tables of Fig. 5.8 (type of dialogue and CAD system architecture).
The final result is a CAD system design with transparent information about
the implications of the design decisions for the costs, the system integration,
the organizational embedding, etc.

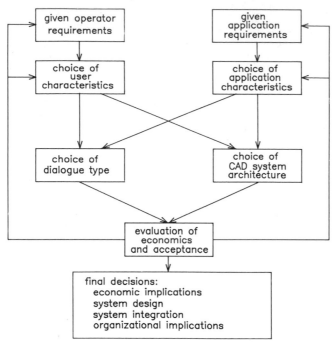

Fig. 5.8. A general procedure for CAD system design evaluation

The *documentation* of a system evolves (or at least should evolve) during the whole development process. The definition of requirements contributes to the documentation just like all the other steps (specification, logic design, implementation, testing). Documentation must provide lucid information on the following points [1]:

1. purpose of program
2. handling of program by user and system operator;
3. required hardware configuration, operating system, programming language, and other details relating to system environment;
4. concept and structure of logical system design;
5. modular structure, function and interfaces of modules;
6. information on the realization of the various modules that is not given in the program text (name of author, version codes, expiration dates, algorithms and techniques, prerequisites and limitations for use);
7. details of the technical solution that are not immediately comprehensible;
8. tests that have been executed.

Parts 1, 2, and 3 of the documentation are obtained from the specification phase, parts 4 and 5 from the design phase. There is also the documentation obtained from the design evaluation, some of which may be of special interest for 6 and 7. The documentation for 8 is generally represented as protocol files of the input and output of test runs (Fig. 5.9). As a standard for documentation layout, we refer to [11].

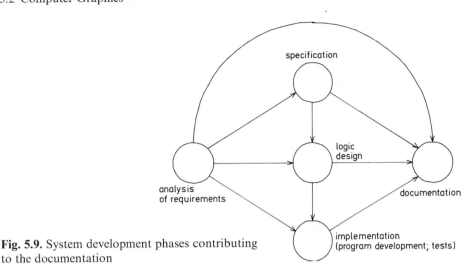

specification

logic
design

analysis
of requirements

documentation

Fig. 5.9. System development phases contributing
to the documentation

implementation
(program development; tests)

5.2 Computer Graphics

5.2.1 Introduction

A CAD system has to present data to the operator, and to provide means
for manipulating them by means of a computer graphics system. A distinguished
compilation of the many titles which have been published in the area of computer graphics is given by Machover [12, 13]. The efficiency of the computer-aided
design process — and the acceptance of the system by the user — depend
very much on how easily the operator can communicate with the system [14].
The man-machine interface (see Fig. 5.10) is implemented by having the man
control the communication (user commands) in order to get some alphanumeric
data and pictures as a system reaction. If *graphical* displays and *input devices
connected to them* are used for this process, combined when necessary with
some local intelligence, then we are in the domain of *interactive computer
graphics*.

Systems implementing this communication process are *interactive graphic
systems*. We call them interactive when user's demands to the system are answered quickly enough that he can wait for the answers without dealing with
other tasks in the meantime. The degree of interaction is dependent on the
size of the information packages exchanged in the communication, and on the
speed with which a choice is made among the various possible activities.

5.2.2 Interactive Graphics Systems

A classification of interactive graphics systems according to the distribution
of functional capabilities is proposed by Lindner [15, 16]. Basically, two types

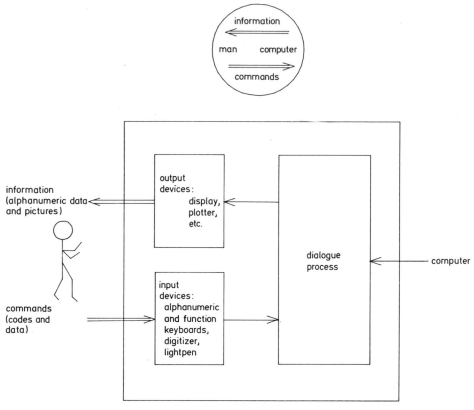

Fig. 5.10. The communication interface of CAD systems

of systems are distinguished, the second type being somewhat arbitrarily split once more into three subtypes (though the distinction among these subtypes may not always be easy to make). This subtyping is done to maintain the two standard terms "intelligent terminal" and "intelligent satellite":

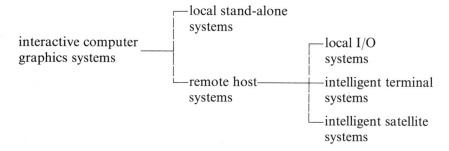

Separation of the three subtypes of the remote host system type may be done by describing the extent of local facilities, starting with the simplest case

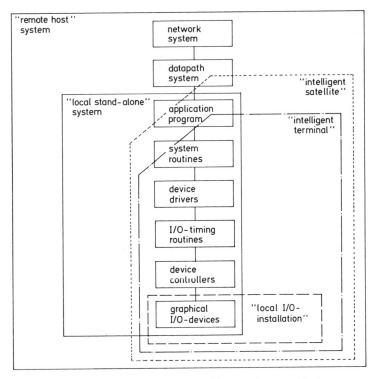

Fig. 5.11. Architectural differences between various types of interactive graphical systems

of the local I/0 system and ending with the intelligent satellite system. Fig. 5.11 shows how the different systems are distinguished.

Local I/0 systems provide locally just the input and output devices, not even containing their controllers. Of course, an interface for the line to the remote host is required. With many terminals attached to a host (which is generally already busy processing batch programs) and with a high degree of interaction (as is typical for CAD applications), the host is likely to be overloaded and unable to provide acceptable response time. Data concentration processors with buffer capability on the host side are seldom efficient enough to remove this obstacle.

Intelligent terminal systems provide the controllers for input and output by themselves. They contain (hardware or micro-programmed) I/0 processing facilities for performing the I/0 timing. They also contain a processor for executing the device driver routines (low-level software), most of the systems routines, and possibly a small section of the application program (medium-level software), e.g. for syntactic analysis of the input and prompting. In any case, intelligent terminal systems are able to do some stand-alone low-level picture editing and to buffer the user's actions locally for a later updating of the remote host's data base. The application program proper and the application data base are held and controlled by the remote host to which the intelligent terminal is connected.

Intelligent satellites can be viewed as very well equipped intelligent terminals. They will hold locally all systems routines and nearly the whole application program. Access to the host will be used for taking advantage of its more powerful hardware facilities (especially memory and special hardware processors) and peripherals, and for accessing external data and software. Control over the execution of the application program may be local. Some functions of the data path system (the organizing facility of the network system) may be local as well. Intelligent satellite systems usually have a local mini-computer with storage media such as drums, disks, or tapes. Medium-size application programs may be executed totally on the satellite without any back-up from the host.

Local stand-alone systems may be intelligent satellites or even intelligent terminals, if they are sufficiently well equipped (including, for instance, secondary storage like floppy disks and also a hard-copy device). It is generally good practice in CAD to provide some stand-alone capabilities to the local installations of remote host systems in any case. As mentioned in Chapter 3.2.3.3, in a fully established CAD environment we will usually find local processing power, storage, and hard-copy capability *plus* a back-up connection to a larger central host computer or computer network. Again, the boundaries between the different types of interactive systems tend to blur in practice.

5.2.3 Graphical I/O Devices

5.2.3.1 Input Devices

The data flow from input devices is limited by the user's maximum data output rate, which is much lower than his maximum data input rate. Therefore, graphical input devices are relatively simple [17].

Light-pen

The light-pen allows direct working on the screen and is fairly necessary for highly interactive work (Fig. 5.12, page 341, courtesy of Lundy). There are two principally different ways in which light-pens are handled, depending on the type of output device used. They may take the picture element directly from the display file (as done with random writing refresh vector displays, which have a timing correspondence between reading the elements from the display file and writing them on the screen), or they may take the position picked on the screen (as done with refresh raster displays) and find the picture element by scanning the display file and checking for correspondence. Hence, no searching is required; the identification of the graphical element pointed at with the light-pen is immediate. Storage-type devices do not have this capability. They require the direct identification to be simulated by the input of a pair of coordinates on the display surface with a subsequent search for the nearest graphical element. Direct input devices based upon other physical effects (ultrasonic waves, for instance) are being developed. Whether these attempts will be successful is yet to be seen. In the context of GKS, the light-pen may be the source of pick input and locator input. It can also provide valuator input (e.g., only one component of the locator input), or a choice input, if a menu is simulated on the screen.

Tablet

The data tablet is another direct graphical input device, as far as the input of point coordinates is concerned. Most often a one-to-one mapping from the tablet to a display screen provides an immediate echo. However, the tablet cannot provide the immediate identification of graphical information, as the light-pen does. Tablets have found their widest application for digitizing purposes. The tablet provides locator-type input to GKS immediately. Together with appropriate software, it can easily be used to simulate other logical input devices, such as choice or text input, by means of menus. Pick input may also be obtained with a tablet, if the software of the driver performs the necessary searches for the nearest graphical primitive.

Other locator input devices

Other input devices perform a similar function to the tablet, but need to have a display for echoing under all circumstances. They are used to control the position of a cursor on the display surface, whose coordinates are used as input values upon some operator action which creates an interrupt. (Instead of a cursor, another graphical element may be moved around. The coordinates of a reference point in this element are then used for input.) The most common of these devices is the joy-stick or joy-switch, an upright handle which may be turned freely around two axes, controlling either the position of the cursor or the speed at which it moves. Another common device is the mouse, a small ball rolling on two orthogonal wheels, whose position is converted to point coordinates. The tracking ball operates in a similar way. Thumb wheels provide separate control of the x and y coordinates of a cross-hair on the display. These devices are equivalent to the tablet in terms of function.

Keyboard and function keys

An alphanumeric keyboard is a standard device for input of commands and numbers. It is required for communication with the operating system and with the utilities which set up the environment for using the CAD system itself. Keyboards are sometimes extended by function keys, some of which may be programmable with respect to their effect, while some may have a fixed meaning, such as controlling a cursor position. Keyboard and function keys are the common sources of text input and choice input to GKS.

5.2.3.2 Output Devices

There are two major classes of output devices:

— devices for hard-copy production;
— interactive graphical devices.

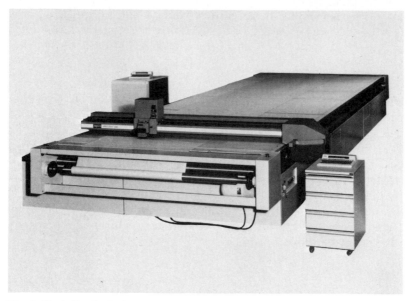

Fig. 5.13. A flat-bed plotter (courtesy of Aristo Graphic Systeme, Hamburg)

Graphics is not only an excellent means of man-machine communication, but also (for thousands of years) of communication between humans. Hence, as a product of design activities we expect to have a hard-copy of the results available, which can be carried along as a basis for discussing the pros and cons of the particular design with other people. Hard-copy devices (in the widest sense) are indispensable components of CAD systems. More recently, increased attention is being given to color output devices [18].

Drum Plotters

Drum plotters compose two-dimensional lines on paper by performing one one-dimensional motion with the pen, the other one by transport of the underlying paper. The lines are actually sequences of small straight lines in (between 8 and 24) predefined directions. The line increment is on the order of a few tenths of a millimeter. Drum plotters are among the cheapest plotter devices. They are well suited for the production of large series of pictures with medium quality. Drum plotters with color capability are available.

Flat Bed Plotters

Flat bed plotters (Fig. 5.13, courtesy of Aristo Graphic Systeme) generally provide higher resolution quality. The movement of the pen in both directions may be controlled at up to 1/1000mm accuracy (which is more than most applications require). Pens of different colors may be permanently installed in the moving pen holder or brought from a fixed storage place when needed. Common ways of holding the paper in place are by electrostatic attraction, by creating a vacuum under the paper, or by mechanical means (clips). Frequently a micro-processor is integrated with the plotter, giving the operator additional control (scaling, speed control, special character fonts, etc.). Table plotters, which represent top-quality plotter devices, are also in the top range with respect to installation cost.

Electrostatic Plotters

Electrostatic plotters produce a picture by "printing" small points in a predefined raster line by line. This principle of operation requires an intermediate step between the output of line drawing primitives from a program and their actual representation on paper. All the information constituting one picture must be buffered and processed into a sequence of rows of dots. Thus, with electrostatic plotters, one never sees part of a picture before its definition is complete. Despite the additional processing required, electrostatic plotters are fast compared to the line drawing plotters (drum or flat bed plotters). The time needed to output a complete picture does *not* depend on the complexity of the picture. Picture production time is constant, regardless of whether there are only a few lines or whether the paper is almost completely covered with them. The line quality has improved significantly due to recent developments, but — on the average — it is below that of the line drawing devices. Color cannot be reproduced on electrostatic plotters, but area shading is possible. Prices are in a medium range.

Laser Printer/Plotters

Laser printer/plotters write the picture line by line similarly to the electrostatic plotters. (Writing is done by a laser rather than by an electron beam.) They are very fast, and best suited for combining alphanumeric and graphic output. Laser printer/plotters are expensive machines, and not typical for CAD applications.

Inkjet Plotters

Inkjet plotters have been developed particularly for graphics output of colored areas rather than colored lines. They are not yet very popular in CAD environments. The production of colored pictures with these machines is oriented more toward the presentation of results to management or customers, rather than toward communication on a technical level (see Chapter 6.3). The prices of these devices are rapidly decreasing.

Other Printer/Plotters

Other printer/plotters operate on a mechanical basis and produce pictures comparable to those of the inkjet plotters. Needles or flexible hammers are hit against ribbons of (potentially) different colors while being moved along a line to be printed (Fig. 5.14, courtesy of EPSON).

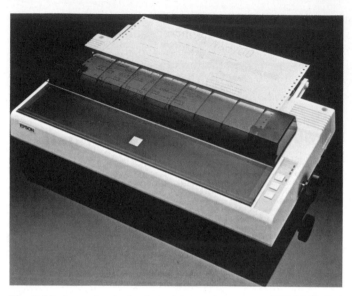

Fig. 5.14. A mechanical printer/plotter (courtesy of EPSON, Düsseldorf)

Microfilm Plotters

Microfilm plotters are the domain of COM (computer output on microfilm
or microfiche). Output may be on 105mm microfiches, 16mm or 35mm movie
film, 24x36mm or 40x40mm slides. The picture lines are either drawn directly
on the film by electron or laser beam, or are projected onto the film from
a tiny screen. For black-and-white output high resolution may be achieved.
Combined alphanumeric and graphic output on one picture is possible. Color
resolution is approximately equivalent to black-and-white quality (equal to or
better than television). Microfilm output is particularly suited for archival purposes without loss of picture quality for later reproduction. Prices range from
medium to very high, depending upon the technical quality and capabilities
wanted.

Other Hard-copy Devices

Hard-copy devices operating on a photographic or electrical basis are generally
directly coupled to interactive display devices. For black-and-white applications
various techniques derived from standard reproduction technology are available.
For color applications, the most common technique involves photography with
instantly developing films.

Output devices for interactive graphics have more variety, and may constitute a more important bottleneck for CAD introduction than the input devices
or plotters. Thus, we will discuss them in more detail here. We distinguish
between

- storage-type devices;
- refresh devices;
- compound devices.

Other classification schemes may distinguish between *vector-oriented* and *raster-oriented* displays, or between *cathode ray tube (CRT) type* and *non-CRT type* displays [19].

Storage Tube

The classical *storage-type device* is the storage tube display (Fig. 5.15, page 341, courtesy of Tektronix). Modern storage tubes store the picture information on a special storage grid closely facing the display screen. The information is stored in regions that are less negatively charged, due to the emission of secondary electrons as a result of writing with high-energy electrons (write function). An electrostatic field directs a low-energy electron stream toward the display screen; it can pass the storage screen only at locations of reduced negative charge (those regions which have been written on). The electrons that pass the storage screen lightup the display screen (read-out function). As the storage screen is negatively charged everywhere, no electrons are caught, and the stored information remains unaffected by the low-energy electrons. The information is destroyed by a flash of medium-energy electrons (erase function). Between the energy levels of the read-out electrons and the medium energy level of the erase electrons, there is a small gap in which electrons may pass the storage screen everywhere without affecting its charge state (write-through function). This gap has been made accessible by recent technological development to provide some refresh capability on storage tube displays. This capability is essential in many applications. Apart from the limited refresh capability, storage tubes cannot erase parts of a picture selectively (only the whole screen); they cannot produce grey scales or colors, and it is not possible to underlay images of existing hard-copy pictures (slides, etc.) onto computer-generated graphical information. Their main advantage is the relatively low cost, and the possibility of displaying extremely complicated pictures with many lines on one screen. With the extension of the write-through capability, storage tubes may be considered compound devices: a compromise between storage and refresh.

Plasma Panel Displays

Plasma panel displays use a panel with a raster of gas discharge channels, one for each representable point. Two orthogonal grids — one on each side of the panel — provide the electrodes and allow writing and erasing of each point selectively, as well as writing and erasing whole rectangular arrays of points. Writing and erasing are performed by controlling the voltage of one line of each grid. Plasma panels are raster-oriented, and provide neither grey scale nor color display. Underlaying existing pictures is easy, as the flat screen is transparent. Plasma panels are of medium speed and not very expensive. However, it is not yet certain that they will evolve into a large-scale technology which would be able to take over a considerable share of the storage tube market.

Vector Refresh Display

The classical *refresh-type device* for computer graphics output is the vector refresh display (Fig. 5.12, page 341). Vector displays are based upon the CRT (cathode ray tube), and represent a picture by repeatedly writing lines on the screen at a refresh rate of 25 cycles per second or more. As the rate at which the electron beam can be deflected is limited by the hardware, and yet the refresh cycle rate has a stringent lower limit to avoid flickering, there is built-in upper limit on the number of vectors that a refresh display can show on one picture (the actual number depends of course on the technological level, and on the amount of money one is willing to spend). Vector displays write the picture in a random way;, they may provide grey scales and color to some extent. Underlaying pictures is not easily achieved. Vector displays range from moderate cost to very expensive devices, depending upon the performance required. The range from about $10,000 to over $100,000 demonstrates this wide variety in technology [19].

TV Raster Scan Displays

Raster scan displays, which have evolved from television technology, are also based on the cathode ray tube principle. However, the electron beam scans the whole screen systematically and continuously, which makes the task of beam deflection much easier. Their bottleneck is the very high rate at which the beam intensity has to be controlled. Another limitation is the TV picture format. These disadvantages, however, are more than compensated in many applications by the ability to present areas (instead of lines) in grey scale or color and by the compatibility with standard television technology. Underlaying picture via video technique is relatively simple. Raster scan displays range in cost from low to medium levels.

Other Raster Scan Displays

Non-TV raster scan devices are based on the same technology; however, they lack the compatibility with television. They lead into higher and very high resolution displays (Fig. 5.16, page 341, courtesy of Tektronix). They require special electronics hardware that cannot be drawn from the television market and, hence, it is not certain whether they will become cheap enough to play a significant role, or whether they will be restricted to some special applications such as high-performance real-time simulation.

Other Compound Types

Compound-type devices combine storage and refresh capabilities in a single device. The storage tube with write-through capacity is one of these devices. Another one is the *laser display* combined with a fast serial memory (shift register or perhaps a video disk). Laser displays are now under development, or in the early phase of production. The present day technology in laser displays already achieves a rather high resolution in storage mode (7k by 5k points for a hard-copy with 5k by 3.5k points on the screen), and adequate resolution in refresh mode. No grey scale or color is provided. Underlaying pictures could be added easily. Laser displays will certainly be developed further in the near future. The very high intensity combined with the very small light-spot size gives them the potential for very high resolution on large-screen real-time systems.

Some other physical effects may be used for developing displays, though these developments are still in a very early stage. *Liquid crystals, light-emitting diodes*, and *electro-luminiscent powder layers* will all be of a storage type with random access to the raster points. Liquid crystals have the advantages of reflecting light and consuming only a little power, but they lack color. Light-emitting diodes may easily be incorporated into integrated circuits which may be useful in some special applications. Electro-luminiscent powder layers have the potential to be very inexpensive. All these types would provide a flat screen, and can be expected to be rugged. As soon as inexpensive chips can be produced, containing read-only memory and a dot matrix display of about 16 by 16 points which totally covers the face of the chip (for instance, by means of fiber optics), there might be a revolutionary break-through of production of such devices for interactive computer graphics. It would be possible to build up screens in any desired size and format. Microprocessors would easily provide a writing speed fast enough to handle such compound-type systems in interactive mode.

Magneto-optical bubble panels have only a serial write and erase access, and thus are very slow but quite simple to handle as well. Perhaps there will eventually be applications for this tool.

5.2.3.3 CAD Workstations

The term "workstation" was introduced in Chapter 2.3.1 in the context of the graphical kernel system GKS, as a means to describe the capabilities of graphics hardware in a generalized way. In GKS, a workstation is an abstract concept. However, the term "workstation" also has another meaning strictly related to hardware. It is used for a set of graphics hardware components, enhanced by some local computing power, and arranged with special attention to ergonomic aspects [20]. Common parts of workstations are: a large work table with digitizing tablet, two screens with different characteristics, off-screen hard-copy, plotter, etc. The two screens are frequently either an alphanumeric screen for command echoing and system messages plus a graphics screen for the graphic interaction, or a black-and-white vector refresh display for fast interaction plus a color raster display for the presentation of several more slowly changing views of the objects being worked on. Several commercially available workstations are shown in Figs. 5.17 through 5.21 on pages 172, 341 and 342. These figures have been made available by courtesy of Calma Ltd., Applicon (2), Ferranti Cetec Graphics Ltd., and Siemens.

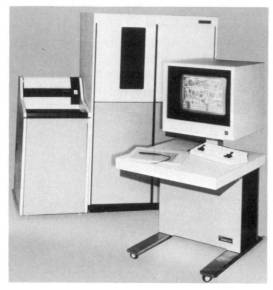

Fig. 5.19. Example of workstation design (courtesy of Applicon, Burlington, USA)

Fig. 5.21. Example of workstation design (courtesy of Siemens, München)

5.2.4 The Graphical Kernel System (GKS)

5.2.4.1 System Description

The reasons for describing GKS as a representative sample of graphics software were discussed earlier (see Chapter 2.3.1).

GKS has had a long and intensive technical review which benefited from the earlier work of GSPC [21, 22, 23] and the meeting at Seillac [24]. The

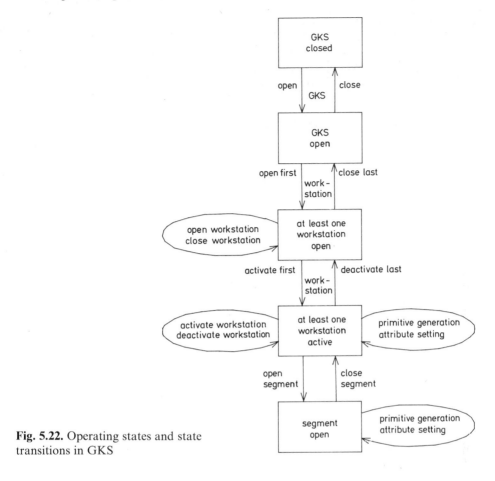

Fig. 5.22. Operating states and state transitions in GKS

final form of GKS can truly be called an international standard, in the sense that it evolved from intensive international cooperation. It differs quite dramatically from the earlier versions (see, for instance, [25]). Yet their main concepts are still very evident and, if anything, have been clarified and strengthened over the period. One concept that has significantly helped in structuring GKS is the strict classification of a number of operating states. In each of these states, only certain actions are allowed (Fig. 5.22).

We will describe GKS here based on [26], and taking examples from [27]. In particular, we will discuss some essential design decisions, which are typical for the process of developing a full functional specification of a software tool. Note: GKS can also be taken as an example of the overwhelming amount of effort that has to be put into a specification when one really labors to achieve completeness, consistency, orthogonality and other worthwhile goals. In the development of CAD systems, a comparable amount of time and manpower can be allotted to the specification task only in very rare cases. In general, CAD system development will have to cope with specifications that are much less complete, partially inconsistent, or otherwise flawed.

Right from the start of the standardization activities in 1974, the main objective was to allow easy portability of graphics systems between different installations. Although GKS should be capable of being used in small stand-alone graphics programs, it was also essential that large suites of CAD programs could be written and moved from one installation to another, possibly with quite different hardware, without the need for significant reprogramming that might involve changes not only to the syntax, but also to the program structure.

One of the major problems of GKS design was that the characteristics of graphics hardware exhibit significant differences, and will continue to do so in the future. It is obviously difficult to represent a wide range of facilities by a single abstraction which would satisfactorily approximate a flat bed plotter, a storage tube, a high-performance vector display and a color raster display. It was felt that the provision of implementation dependent defaults for unavailable facilities (say, color on a black-and-white storage tube) would not always be appropriate. There was a need for the application programmer to have some control over the mapping of graphics primitives to a particular device. Hence, a rather sophisticated parametric abstraction was conceived: the workstation concept. A *graphics workstation* is equipped with a single display area and a number of input devices. It may have a certain amount of intelligence, either locally connected to the display itself or in form of a workstation driver running under GKS control as part of the application program. A workstation is described as belonging to a standard type (one of a set of types) available at a given installation (plotter, storage tube, refresh display, etc.). The application programmer has the ability to modify its overall behavior so as to make optimal use of its features in that environment.

An operator can have a number of GKS workstations under his control at the same time. For example, he may output a large CAD drawing on a plotter while getting a quick-look view on a separate storage tube. Or he may be interactively changing his model on a refresh display, while taking occasional hardcopies on a plotter.

The application programmer has considerable flexibility in how he uses each workstation. Different workstations may be set to view different parts of the whole graphics picture. The frequency of update may be different on different devices.

The CAD application programmer may insert statements into his program inquiring which capabilities are implemented in the graphics hardware of its run-time environment. He may design and implement the program so that it will adjust its behavior to the available facilities. For example, with a refresh display one program will show any modification of the display information immediately, while with a storage tube, it will collect a number of changes until the whole picture is redrawn. The lack of a tablet may necessitate a different method of entering locator positions. The type of echoing may depend on the line speed between display and computer. Such adaptive behavior may be programmed into the CAD system to improve its portability in terms of the range of graphics hardware installations on which it can run.

Besides the workstation concept, the treatment of the visual appearance of graphical information on the display surface is peculiar to GKS. Graphics primitives such as line drawings can have *attributes* associated with them, such as color, thickness, linestyle, etc. There are basically two approaches to specifying such attributes. The first is to have a set of "modal" attributes. This term indicates that the state of the process being addressed can have an attribute value stored, which remains in effect until it is redefined. The property defined by this attribute value (the color red, for instance) is added to all subsequently generated objects (lines and others). This approach is used in many graphics packages, and has been adopted for the GSPC core proposal as well [23]. For example, the sequence

```
COLOR(RED)
THICKNESS(THICK)
STYLE(SOLID)
DRAW LINE
COLOR(GREEN)
STYLE(DASHED)
DRAW LINE
```

would draw a thick, red, solid line followed by a thick, green, dashed line. Each modal attribute remains in effect until it is reset. Thus "thick" is an attribute applicable to both lines.

The advantage of this method is that it guarantees a certain appearance of the lines on whatever hardware is installed — provided that the hardware is at all capable of doing what is requested. However, there is a wide variety of hardware that simply cannot follow such rigid requests. The programmer of the device driver might decide to map red lines onto dashed green lines onto solid lines if the device cannot reproduce color. But this choice will often fail to agree with the choice that the application programmer would make. The GKS designers had to pose and settle the question of whether they considered it more important to specify a certain visual appearance rigidly associated with the geometrical properties of graphical information, or just to distinguish one graphical item (called a primitive in GKS) from another with respect to its appearance, leaving it to a second and less rigid step to specify how this distinction should be realized. A design decision of this kind will have a significant influence on the structure of the application programs that use the graphics kernel system.

The solution adopted in GKS is to provide one major attribute per primitive, called the primitive index, running from 1 up to an implementation maximum. The GKS program equivalent to the one above would look like this:

```
SET POLYLINE INDEX(1)
POLYLINE
SET POLYLINE INDEX(2)
POLYLINE
```

plus the definition of how indices 1 and 2 should be represented on one device or another. Upon display, the indices are used to look up corresponding entries in a table associated with the workstation, and the table defines a whole "bundle" of appearance attributes for each bundle index. These entries may be preset by calls from the application program to GKS. They are modal attributes in the sense defined above, but associated with one workstation each rather than with GKS as a whole. The application programmer may set the representation of index 1 as red, thick, and solid, while index 2 could mean green, thick, and dashed (effectively achieving the same result as the above GSPC-like program). The advantage of making the pen specification workstation-dependent is that the representation may be quite different on another workstation. For example, a designer using a flat bed plotter for his final drawing output and a storage tube during his interactive work could recognize different colors as indicating different linestyles on his display (red = solid, green = dashed, for instance) — provided that the application programmer has decided to distinguish the different bundle attributes in this way.

The elementary graphical items treated in GKS are called primitives. GKS has defined six *output primitives:*

– POLYLINE;
– POLYMARKER;
– TEXT;
– FILL AREA;
– CELL ARRAY;
– GENERALIZED DRAWING PRIMITIVE (GDP).

For line drawing, a polyline — which generates a sequence of lines connecting an ordered set of points (given as a parameter) — is the fundamental line-drawing primitive. The motivation for having a polyline as a primitive, rather than a single line, is that in most applications a set of lines is needed to form some shape. Since a polyline rather than a line is the basic primitive, attributes such as linestyle apply to the complete polyline instead of a single line segment. Thus, a red dotted or green dashed curve is drawn as a single entity.

The polymarker is an obvious primitive, once polyline has been defined. Text similarly produces a string of characters, rather than a single character so that there is some similarity of level among the three main output primitives.

The three remaining primitives demonstrate the spreading influence of raster graphics and the need to allow access to the hardware features of certain output devices. For example, raster displays support cell arrays on the hardware level. Consequently, this primitive has been made available in GKS in a generalized way. The GKS primitive "fill area" defines a boundary whose interior can be filled in some pattern and color, — or simply hatched if the hardware can only produce lines. Some plotters provide such features as circles, arcs, or interpolation curves. The "generalized drawing primitive" (GDP) provides a standard way of addressing such non-standard capabilities (circles, arcs, etc.).

Polyline and polymarker have a single attribute, the index; at a given workstation this index determines a bundle containing

for POLYLINE: LINETYPE, LINEWIDTH SCALE FACTOR, COLOR, and for POLYMARKER: MARKERTYPE, MARKERSIZE SCALE FACTOR, COLOR.

Text on the other hand has two sets of attributes, some of which are set by the text bundle table:

TEXT: FONT, PRECISION, COLOR

while the remaining attributes are set modally on GKS level; that is, they are bound directly to a primitive when it is generated. The motivation for this split is that the overall form and shape of the text is considered more as a geometric property which should remain invariant on whatever output device is used, while the appearance (form and quality) of the individual characters may vary.

The *geometric text attributes* are:

- *HEIGHT:* defines the required height of the character in the user's coordinate system.
- *EXPANSION FACTOR:* defines the actual width on the basis of the nominal width expressed in the height/width ratio of a given font.
- *CHARUP VECTOR:* defines the degree of rotation for every character in the text line. Characters can therefore be drawn at any orientation.
- *PATH:* defines the direction in which characters are drawn. The normal setting is RIGHT while LEFT draws them from right to left. Similarly, UP and DOWN have their obvious meanings.
- *SPACING:* controls the amount of space between characters, beyond that nominally provided by the font.

It is recognized that some devices may have difficulty specifying characters with this degree of sophistication. Consequently, the PRECISION attribute (with values STRING, CHARACTER, STROKE) in the text bundle table defines the closeness of the output to the specified requirements:

- *STRING:* the position of the first character is all that is guaranteed to be correct. Thus, a device's hardware character generator can be used. If a different orientation or size is requested, it can be ignored.
- *CHARACTER:* the position of each individual character box must be correct. The form of the character within each box is workstation-dependent. Again, hardware characters could be used but, in that case, they would probably have to be output one at a time.
- *STROKE:* all the text attributes have to be implemented correctly. This will almost certainly require the hardware to have a very flexible character generator, or else the text output must be simulated in software using polylines or fill area primitives.

This method of defining text in GKS permits the use of sophisticated hardware character generators if available. Otherwise, the high-precision text has to be produced by software. In order to avoid the processing required for such a software simulation, the application programmer may choose a simple and cheap text representation of precision STRING or CHARACTER for all but the final drawing.

Similar to text, the fill area primitive also has two sets of attributes: the first one regarded as part of the geometry, independent from the workstation, the other one selected by index and defined in a workstation table. The geometric properties are relevant when the interior is filled with a certain pattern:

- *PATTERN SIZE:* defines what size will be assigned to the pattern. The pattern is replicated in both x and y directions, until the complete area is covered.
- *PATTERN REFERENCE POINT:* specifies the origin for the replicating process.

These attributes are mainly oriented towards raster devices, but simulations for vector devices are also defined. The following attributes are associated with each workstation individually:

- *INTERIOR STYLE:* defines the mode of filling as hollow (not filled), solid, patterned, or hatched.
- *STYLE INDEX:* specifies for pattern an entry in a pattern table, to be used for filling. If the interior style is hatched, the index is used to determine which of a number of predefined hatch styles is used.
- *COLOR INDEX:* is used for both hollow and solid, and refers to the color table.

The next essential topic to discuss is the segment facility in GKS. A single graphical primitive will not generally correspond to an information chunk in the communication between the designer and the CAD system (see Chapter 3.3.5.2). GKS provides means to group a number of primitives together into a meaningful information package called a segment, which may be handled as a whole. Segments can be individually deleted as a unit, or highlighted to stand out from other information. They may be moved around, scaled, or rotated. This is achieved by having a transformation matrix associated with each segment, which may be altered after the segment is defined.

On workstations which provided their own storage capability, segments may be stored and made visible or invisible by appropriate requests from the application program to GKS. Sometimes the need arises to display a segment on a workstation that was not active when the segment was created. A typical example is a plotter which is not activated until a complete and correct picture has been composed on an interactive display. For such purposes, GKS provides a *device-independent segment storage* which can keep copies of segments as they are formed. All transformations performed on the segment will also apply to its device-independent copy. From the device-independent storage, the segments can be copied to other workstations. Facilities are also provided for inserting a segment into another segment. The difference is that a copy operation — as the name suggests — produces a duplicate of the segment, while insertion copies all the primitives contained in the segment into a newly created segment. These facilities are supported only in higher levels of GKS implementations.

For archiving graphical information, and for transport to and from other installations or systems, GKS provides the GKS metafile facility (GKSM). The application program may direct graphical output to a GKS metafile workstation, which will write it onto a sequential file. The application program can also transmit its own records (containing non-graphical information) to the

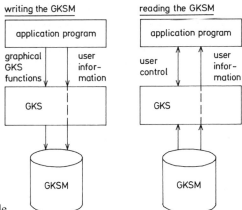

Fig. 5.23. Communication between an
application program and the GKS Metafile

metafile via GKS. In a subsequent job, the same or another application program
may have GKS read and interpret the metafile, effectively regenerating whatever
graphics information is on the file. User records may either be ignored or passed
to the application program for further interpretation (Fig. 5.23).

Obviously, the segmentation decision made for GKS is by no means the
only one possible. One could envisage systems that treat individual primitives
as whole units for handling purposes. One might also consider higher levels
of structuring, such as segments containing references to other segments. The
decision made for GKS in this respect — as in all others — is a compromise,
based on the maximum international agreement that could be achieved as to
what is required by the application community and could be provided without
overloading the implementation with requirements that might be shifted to
another layer in the application program.

A common need of interactive graphics user is the ability to switch between
overall views of their model and some kind of detail view. The window/viewport
concept involves a standard computer graphics technique of mapping some
rectangle of the application space (called the window) onto a rectangle of the
display surface (the viewport). In GKS, where several workstations may be
active at the same time, it makes sense to allow different views of the same
picture to be seen on different workstations. This flexibility is achieved by having
three different coordinate systems and two distinct window/viewport mappings
(see Chapter 2.3.1). The applications programmer defines his output in terms
of a world coordinate (WC) system, which is mapped onto some part of the
normalized device coordinate (NDC) plane. The active workstations can then
present separate views of the NDC space when the application program chooses
a separate mapping from that space to the device coordinates for each workstation.

Multiple windows are a useful facility in GKS. It is quite common that
the application programmer wants to display several distinct parts which are

most appropriately defined in different coordinate systems. A conventional way to do this would be to redefine the window each time as required. For example:

```
SET WINDOW(XMIN,XMAX,YMIN,YMAX)
DRAW PICTURE A
SET WINDOW(X2MIN,X2MAX,Y2MIN,Y2MAX)
DRAW PICTURE B
```

Here PICTURE A is drawn when the first coordinate system is defined, while PICTURE B is drawn with the second coordinate system. The user effectively sees a display made up of two parts with different coordinate systems. The application program would have to memorize the corresponding windows associated with pictures A and B, and reset them whenever required. However, on input the problem becomes more severe, since both pictures coexist on the same surface and it is not immediately obvious whether a point on the surface refers to the space of picture A or B. Hence, it is not possible for GKS to transform the coordinates of a point on the device back into the user world in a unique manner. The problem has been solved by giving the different world coordinate systems disytinct names (in fact, numbers), and by making them known to the GKS process. Thus, the application program and GKS can inform each other which mapping is to be applied in each instance. The equivalent form of the above program in GKS would look like:

```
DEF WINDOW (1,XMIN,XMAX,YMIN,YMAX)
DEF WINDOW (2,X2MIN,X2MAX,Y2MIN,Y2MAX)
SELECT (1)
DRAW PICTURE A
SELECT (2)
DRAW PICTURE B
```

Note that due to this technique, the application programmer will have a tendency to define all the potentially needed coordinate systems collectively at the start of execution and then select a particular transformation whenever required. The more conventional technique would have transformation definitions scattered throughout the program. This is another example of how strongly the layout of a software machine influences the structure of the programs that are built on top of it.

Input in GKS is defined in terms of a set of logical devices which may be implemented on a workstation in a number of ways. The different types of input are:

– *LOCATOR:* provides a position in world coordinates. The position indicated on the display will be within one of the window/viewport transformations defined. This will be used to give the correct world-coordinate position.
– *VALUATOR:* provides a real number.
– *CHOICE:* provides an integer defining one of a set of possible choices.
– *PICK:* provides a segment name and a pick identifier associated with a particular primitive.
– *STRING:* provides a character string.

Fig. 5.25. GKS example 2 output

The implementation of the logical device on a workstation may be done in a variety of ways. For example, while it may be natural to input a STRING using a keyboard, it could also be done by free-hand drawing on a tablet, or by hitting a set of light buttons indicating particular characters on a display. The exact form of the implementation dependes on the individual workstation in terms of hardware and software.

Input can be obtained in three distinct ways:

– *REQUEST:* this is like a FORTRAN READ. The system waits until the input event has taken place, and then returns the appropriate value. Only one input request is valid at a time.
– *SAMPLE:* the current value of a GKS input device is examined. This is most frequently used for devices which provide a continuous read-out of their value. For example, the current position of a potentiometer or of the stylus on a digitizer can be sampled.
– *EVENT:* this mode is used for devices which would normally cause interrupts on the workstation. For example, a light pen hit or a touch of the tip switch on a tablet would normally generate an event. Upon occurrence of the interrupt, a record containing the input information and indicating its source is stored in a queue. The queue is ordered according to the time when the interrupt occurred. Functions are available to retrieve these records from the list for interpretation by the application program.

Earlier versions of GKS had a much more complex input system, with non-sequential listing of input events. It was decided that such functions should be built on top of GKS, rather than being a part of the kernel system.

5.2.4.2 GKS Examples

In this section, some important features of GKS are demonstrated using sample programs taken from [27].

In the first example (Sample Listing 5.1), we demonstrate the window/viewport transformation and the attendant clipping behavior. The result is shown in Fig. 5.24.

Sample Listing 5.1. The GKS program for Fig. 5.24.

```
          REAL      WLINEX(5), WLINEY(5), BX(5), BY(5)
          REAL      TRIAX(4), TRIAY(4)
          INTEGER   NOCLIP/0/,CLIP/1/
          DATA      BX /0.,1.,1.,0.,0./
          DATA      BY /0.,0.,1.,0.,0./
          DATA      TRIAX /-7.,2.,14.,-7./
          DATA      TRIAY /-7.,11.,-7.,-7./
          DATA      WLINEX /-10.,-10.,10.,10.,-10./
          DATA      WLINEY /-10.,10.,10.,-10.,-10./
C   OPEN GKS (ERROR FILE IS ON DEVICE 22)
          CALL GOPKS (22)
          CALL GOPWK (1,1,6)
C    DEFINE NORMALIZATION TRANSFORMATION
          CALL GSW( 1, -10., 10.,-10., 10.)
          CALL GSW( 2, -10., 10.,-10., 10.)
          CALL GSW( 3, -10., 10.,-10., 10.)
          CALL GSVW( 1,0.05,0.45,0.55,0.95)
          CALL GSVW( 2,0.5 ,0.9 ,0.55,0.95)
          CALL GSVW( 3,0.55,0.95,0.05,0.45)
          CALL GACWK (1)
C    SET AND DRAW WINDOW BOUNDARIES
C    IT SHOWS THE BOUNDARIES OF THE (0,1)-NDC COORDINATE SPACE
          CALL GSELNT (0)
          CALL GPL (5,BX,BY)
C    SELECT MARKER TYPE 3
          CALL GSPMI(3)
C    1. IMAGE
C    SET NEW VIEWPORT AND DRAW THE WINDOW BOUNDARIES
          CALL GSELNT (1)
          CALL GPL (5,WLINEX,WLINEY)
C    PICTURE NUMBER IN THE UPPER LEFT CORNER
          CALL GTX (-8.,8.,1,1H1)
C    FIRST IMAGE IS TO BE CLIPPED AT THE WINDOW
          CALL GSCLIN (CLIP)
C    POLYMARKER AT TRIANGLE CORNER POINTS
          CALL GPM (3,TRIAX,TRIAY)
C    POLYLINE (TRIANGLE)
          CALL GPL (4,TRIAX,TRIAY)
C    2. IMAGE
C    SET NEW VIEWPORT AND DRAW WINDOW BOUNDARIES
          CALL GSELNT (2)
          CALL GPL (5,WLINEX,WLINEY)
          CALL GTX (-8.,8.,1,1H2)
C    SECOND IMAGE IS NOT CLIPPED AT THE WINDOW
          CALL GSCLIN (NOCLIP)
C    POLYMARKER AT TRIANGLE CORNER POINTS
          CALL GPM (3,TRIAX,TRIAY)
C    POLYLINE (TRIANGLE)
          CALL GPL (4,TRIAX,TRIAY)
C    3. IMAGE
C    SET NEW VIEWPORT AND DRAW THE LIMITATION OF THE WINDOW
          CALL GSELNT (3)
          CALL GPL (5,WLINEX,WLINEY)
          CALL GTX (-8.,8.,1,1H3)
C    THIRD IMAGE IS NOT CLIPPED AT THE WINDOW (BUT AT THE NDC-SPACE)
          CALL GSCLIN (NOCLIP)
          CALL GPM (3,TRIAX,TRIAY)
          CALL GPL (4,TRIAX,TRIAY)
          CALL GDAWK (1)
          CALL GCLWK (1)
          CALL GCLKS
```

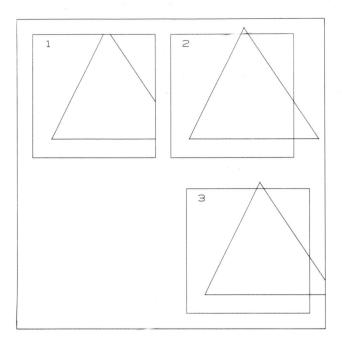

Fig. 5.24.
GKS example 1 output

Sample Listing 5.2. The GKS program for Fig. 5.25.

```
C    REAL TIME CLOCK
      REAL     X(3),Y(3),PHI,MHX(6),MHY(6),SHX(5),SHY(5),HHX(10)
     1         ,HHY(10),MH(6),MM(6),MS(6),PI
      INTEGER  I,DIGIT(24),J,K,ICH
      DATA     DIGIT /24H3 2 1 1211109 8 7 6 5 4 /,PI/3.14159/
C    DEFINITION OF THE HANDS
      DATA     SHX/-0.02,0.,0.02,0.,-0.02/
      DATA     SHY/0.,-0.04,0.,0.7,0./
      DATA     MHX/-0.06,-0.02,0.02,0.06,0.,-0.06/
      DATA     MHY/0.,-0.1,-0.1,0.,0.65,0./
      DATA     HHX/-0.015,-0.1,-0.02,0.02, 0.1,0.015,0.1,0. ,-0.1,-0.015/
      DATA     HHY/0.    ,-0.1,-0.2 ,-0.2,-0.1,0.    ,0.2,0.5, 0.2,0.    /
      DATA     MH/1.,0.,0.,0.,1.,0./,MM/1.,0.,0.,0.,1.,0./
      DATA     MS/1.,0.,0.,0.,1.,0./
      INTEGER WORLDC/0/
C     INTEGER EMPTI/??????/  IS IMPLEMENTATION DEPENDENT
      CALL GOPKS(22)
      CALL GOPWK (1,2,6)
      CALL GACWK (1)
      CALL GSW ( 1,-1.,1.,-1.,1.)
      CALL GSELNT (1)
      CALL GCRSG(10)
C    DRAW FRAME AND HANDS AXES BY THREE CIRCLES
      X(1) = 0.
      Y(1) = 0.
```

```
        X(2) = 1.
        Y(2) = 0.
        CALL GGDP (2,X,Y,1,1,EMPTI)
        X(2) = 0.95
        CALL GGDP (2,X,Y,1,1,EMPTI)
        X(2) = 0.01
        CALL GGDP (2,X,Y,1,1,EMPTI)
C   DRAW MARKERS AND DIGITS
C   SET CHARACTER HEIGHT
        CALL GSCHH (0.08)
        CALL GSCHSP (-0.1)
        DO 50 I=1,48,4
        X(1) = COS ((I-1)*PI/24.)*0.9
        Y(1) = SIN((I-1)*PI/24.)*0.9
        X(2) = X(1) * 0.9
        Y(2) = Y(1) * 0.9
        CALL GPL (2,X,Y)
        X(3) = X(2) * 0.8
        Y(3) = Y(2) * 0.8 - 0.05
        IF (I.GT.9.AND.I.LT.22) X(3) = X(3) - 0.07
        ICH = (I+3)/2-1
        CALL GTX (X(3),Y(3),2,DIGIT(ICH))
   50   CONTINUE
        CALL GCLSG
C   DRAW HANDS
        CALL GCRSG (1)
        CALL GPL (5,SHX,SHY)
        CALL GCLSG
        CALL GCRSG(2)
        CALL GPL (6,MHX,MHY)
        CALL GCLSG
        CALL GCRSG(3)
        CALL GPL(10,HHX,HHY)
        CALL GCLSG
C   MOVE HANDS FOR 10000 MINUTES
C   FOR CLOCK TERMINITION BY AN OPERATOR SAMPLE OR EVENT INPUT IS NEEDED
        PHI = -PI/30.
        DO 100 J=1,10000
        DO 200 K=1,60
        CALL GACTM (MS,0.,0.,0.,0.,PHI,1.,1.,WORLDC,MS)
        CALL GSSGT (-1,MS)
C   DELAY FOR A VECTOR DEVICE WITH SEGMENTATION FACILITY BUT WITHOUT
C   HARDWARE TRANSFORMATION
        CALL DELAY (985)
  200   CONTINUE
        CALL GACTM (MM,0.,0.,0.,0.,PHI,1.,1.,WORLDC,MM)
        CALL GACTM (MH,0.,0.,0.,0.,PHI/12.,1.,1.,WORLDC,MH)
        CALL GSSGT (2,MM)
        CALL GSSGT (3,MH)
        CALL GUPDWK (1,1)
  100   CONTINUE
        CALL GDAWK (1)
        CALL GCLWK (1)
        CALL GCLKS
```

Sample Listing 5.3. The GKS program for Fig. 5.26 (see page 341).

```
C   STATIC PRIMITIVE ATTRIBUTES
         INTEGER   STRIN(8), RIND, GIND, BIND, BLAIND, WK
         INTEGER   SOLI, DASHED, DOTTED, DASHDT
         INTEGER   STROKE/2/
         REAL      PX(2),PY(2), PX1, PY1, CUPX,CUPY, IUP
         REAL      ANGLE, PI, RADIUS, CIRCX(2), CIRCY(2)
         DATA      RADIUS/30./,CIRCX, CIRCY /50.,50.,50.,80./
         DATA      RIND/1/,GIND/2/,BIND/3/,BLAIND/4/,WK/1/
         DATA      PI /3.1415927/
         DATA      IUP /3.5/
         DATA      STRIN/1HA,1HB,1HC,1HD,1HE,1HF,1HG,1HH/
         DATA      SOLI/1/,DASHED/2/,DOTTED/3/,DASHDT/4/
C        INTEGER EMPTI/??????/  IS IMPLEMENTATION DEPENDENT
         CALL GOPKS (22)
         CALL GOPWK (WK,1,3)
         CALL GACWK (WK)
         CALL GSW  (1,0.,100.,0.,100.)
         CALL GSELNT (1)
C   DEFINE PENS
C   PEN NO 1, LINETYPE = SOLID, COLOUR = RED
         CALL GSPLR (WK,1,SOLI,1.,RIND)
         CALL GSTXR (WK,1,1,STROKE,1.,0.,RIND)
C   PEN 2, LINETYPE = DASHED, COLOUR = GREEN
         CALL GSPLR (WK,2,DASHED,,1.,GIND)
         CALL GSTXR (WK,2,1,STROKE,1.,0.,GIND)
C   PEN 3, LINETYPE = DOTTED, COLOUR = BLUE
         CALL GSPLR (WK,3,DOTTED,1.,BIND)
         CALL GSTXR (WK,3,1,STROKE,1.,0.,BIND)
C   PEN 4, LINETYPE = DASHDOTTED, COLOUR = BLACK
         CALL GSPLR (WK,4,DASHDT,1.,BLAIND)
         CALL GSTXR (WK,4,1,STROKE,1.,0.,BLAIND)
C   DRAW A CIRCLE USING PEN 1 (SOLID LINETYPE,BLACK)
         CALL GGDP (2,CIRCX,CIRCY,1,1,EMPTI)
         ANGLE = PI/2.
         PX(1) = CIRCX(1)
         PY(1) = CIRCY(1)
C   SET CHARACTER HEIGHT
         CALL GSCHH (IUP)
         DO 300 I = 1,8
         CUPX = SIN (ANGLE)
         CUPY = COS (ANGLE)
         CALL GSCHUP (CUPX,CUPY)
C   USER-DEFINED PENS 1...4
         CALL GSPLI (MOD(I-1,4)+1)
         CALL GSTXI (MOD(I-1,4)+1)
         PX1 = CIRCX(1) + (RADIUS + 4.) * CUPX
         PY1 = CIRCY(1) + (RADIUS + 4.) * CUPY
         CALL GTX (PX1,PY1,1,STRIN(I))
         PX(2) = PX(1) + RADIUS * CUPX
         PY(2) = PY(1) + RADIUS * CUPY
         CALL GPL (2,PX,PY)
         ANGLE = ANGLE - PI/4.
     300 CONTINUE
         CALL GUPDWK (WK,1)
C    SHORT VERSION FOR DEACTIVATE AND CLOSE ALL WORKSTATIONS AND GKS
         CALL GECLKS
```

The second example (Sample Listing 5.2) demonstrates the transform segment function when moving the hands of a clock. Depending on the particular device capabilities connected to GKS, different actions are performed within the system so that the visual effect will remain nearly the same. Either the segment transformation is performed by hardware functions of the device; or a device-dependent segment mechanism is used allowing for the deletion of a selected segment and a redisplay of just the transformed segment; or the display surface has to be erased completely and all segments have to be redrawn. In the last case, no real-time movement of the second hand is normally possible. The result is shown in Fig. 5.25.

The third example (Sample Listing 5.3) is a simple example of using text and pen attributes in a static way; that is, each time a new pen and text representation is set, the subsequent output is drawn using the new attributes, without changing output already created. Within this program, a circle and eight surrounding letters are drawn. Application-defined pens are used to generate lines. Characters of different color are drawn at different angles around a circle. Precision "STROKE" is defined for all characters. The result of this GKS example is shown in Fig. 5.26 (on page 341).

5.3 CAD System Use of Interactive Graphics Functions

One of the most important basic applications of interactive computer graphics in CAD systems is the input and manipulation of complexly structured objects via their graphical representation on a display. The concepts of command interpreters and graphical core systems, as discussed in Chapter 2.3, are the methodological basis for implementating the communication aspect of CAD systems [28].

We will discuss two different approaches for integrating a communication module with application modules. With respect to the concepts developed in Chapter 3, these two approaches have the following different views of the system:

– one might consider the monitor and the application modules as integral parts, utilizing the communication module as a software machine. In this case, the application process will have to set up the proper environment in which the communication process can be executed;
– or (because the tasks of monitoring and communicating are fairly independent from the application) one might see the monitor and the communication module as the principle system constituents, which call upon a library of application modules for solving specific problems. In this case, the application process will run in an environment provided by the general-purpose monitor and communication system.

As representatives of these two approaches we will present the two systems KI [29, 30] and GRADAS [31].

Certain problems have to be dealt with in every implementation of an interactive graphics dialogue monitor:

- how do we attract the operator's attention to some piece of information on the screen? How can we prevent him from overlooking something important?
- how can we hold his attention and avoid tiring him unnecessarily?
- how can we associate different meanings and different levels of importance with different pieces of the displayed picture?

Various means are available to deal with these problems: different line styles or line widths, high-lighting, blinking, shading and coloring. But what is best suited to a particular environment often has to be discovered after some time of actual use.

5.3.1 The KI System

The KI system has the following structure (see also Chapter 2.3.2):

- the innermost part is the graphical kernel system GKS;
- the next part of the KI system is the set of the KI kernel functions (KI kernel system);
- the outermost part of the KI system composed of two sets of functions: the command sequences and the programmer defined KI commands. Both sets of commands can be extended.

The kernel functions of KI are built on top of the GKS interface. They provide the user with a set of the most common commands for solving graphical problems. This level establishes a symmetry between input and output, in the sense that an operator input generates an output (echo) which has a semantic relation to the input data. For example, for an input list of points, a polyline could be output as a command echo.

The operator issues commands by typing them in or by hitting the button that was previously assigned to each command. The commands activate KI functions which request missing data from the operator in a dialogue. The data is checked and eventually corrected. Then GKS functions are called upon to make the result visible.

In an interactive dialogue-process, the operator can define macros (command sequences for frequently-used series of KI commands) and store them for later reference. A name can be associated with each macro; this can later be used as if it were an original KI command name. Macros can be assigned to menu buttons on a choice device which will execute the corresponding macros when hit. The definition of a macro is a simple task, and may be done even by the "ad hoc" user of the KI system; for this purpose, the desired commands are bracketed by the commands "begin command sequence" and "end command sequence". The commands sequence of a macro is executed sequentially when the macro is invoked, except in the case of a loop definition through the two control statements "REPEAT(last n,m times)" and "REPEAT(last n)". The first instance causes the interpreter to repeat the last n commands in the sequence (prior to the REPEAT) m times, while in the second case, the repetition continues until an interrupt is generated by hitting the "escape" button. Afterwards, execution is resumed with the next command following the REPEAT.

Problems in data handling arise in connection with the command sequences. There are the options

- to execute commands inside macros with data which are predetermined at the time of macro definition. These data should not be entered in an interactive mode when the macro is invoked;
- to transfer data from one command to the next within command sequences, without operator action for each command.

In KI, a compromise was made between the expected use of macros and the required expense of implementation. Hence, only the following features were implemented, which provide useful macro capabilities without requiring to much sophistication:

- macros do not have local data, but there is the possibility to transfer data from one command to the next;
- nesting of macros is not possible; this means that one macro cannot be an element of another macro;
- loops cannot be nested;
- storage management is performed under user control; macros are stored in primary memory only temporarily, while they are being created. There are functions for storing them on files, for reading them from files into the main storage (as is necessary before executing), and for deleting them from files or from primary storage;
- functions for editing already-defined sequences are provided.

A much more powerful capability, which makes KI more readily adaptable to new applications, is the extensibility of the set of KI commands. The extension is done either by an experienced operator or by a programmer. Such extensions have been found necessary for solving more complex problems. The basic elements for defining new KI commands are the functions of GKS, other already-existing commands and the command set of the implementation language. The newly-defined commands are compiled and linked to the KI system. The facilities are available in KI to assign names to new commands and/or to associate each with a button, and to declare them to the system in order to make them usable in the interactive mode.

The programmer-defined KI commands are more efficient in execution and more powerful in functionality than the macros, as they are not restricted to the predefined command set of the interpreter. When generating new commands, the programmer has to respect a set of rules which guarantee that the new commands will fit smoothly into the overall dialogue.

Disadvantages of extended KI commands compared with macros are:

- new commands cannot be generated dynamically in a dialogue process right at the time when the need for them arises. Instead, a separate step of compilation and linkage to the system is necessary;
- the programmer has to have a thorough knowledge of the KI system in order to define correct commands.

The programmer of KI commands does not have any direct access to the GKS functions and data structures. He must use the modules of KI — which completely envelop the GKS, although it is actually GKS that drives the interactive graphical communication. KI consists of the following modules:

- supervisor, data input, parsing, semantical data checking, generation of echo, editing, passive command execution, and storage functions.

Input functions enable the operator to enter commands and data. They transport the input data to the parser.

The task of the supervisor is to control the system. It determines the present state, the path through the states, and the functions to be performed in each state. There are five states in KI: definition of menus, definition of macros, execution of commands, execution of macros, and waiting for command input.

When waiting for command input, KI will accept input of "command" type only. All other input data is ignored. When the command switches to the state "definition of menus", all the following commands until "end of definition" are used for constructing a menu. When the command switches to the state "definition of macros", the following commands are not executed but stored in their defined sequence. All other commands are interpreted and executed directly. Input, echo, checking, and editing are done under control of the command and supported by auxiliary functions. If a macro is activated, the predefined and stored sequence of commands is executed; each command is performed in the same way as a single KI command.

For maximal efficiency of communication, and to give the user an immediate control of data, KI provides the following echoes:

- The graphical kernel system is preset by KI in such a way that it generates a (low-level) system echo for all activated input devices. This system echo makes the actual device state visible, or indicates the acceptance of an event input. Thus, the operator is given immediate feedback when handling the input tools and entering data.
  In a very fast loop, he can adjust a value at an input device, and immediately receive a system echo which enables him to correct his adjustment. When he wants to enter the value, he performs a special action (creating a trigger or an interrupt) which causes GKS to accept the actual data and to add the corresponding record to the input queue, from which it may be taken by KI. The acceptance of input is immediately confirmed by a special system echo.
- Data entered into GKS can only be corrected in the KI state "editing". KI takes the data from GKS and converts them into KI data, which it can check and eventually correct in the context of previously-input data. Checking and correction can be done by default or through programmer-defined functions.
  With the KI data, another echo is produced (either by default or programmer-defined function). This echo is now on a higher level, and already has some semantic meaning to the operator. The operator can now correct the new or previously-entered data, or proceed with the input process.

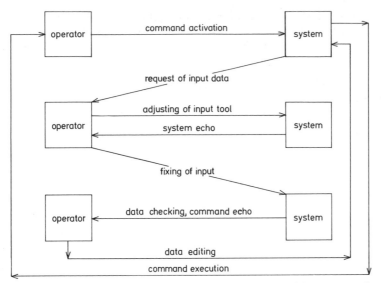

Fig. 5.27. The dialogue process of interactive man-machine communication

This concept can be realized in a man-machine dialogue (Fig. 5.27).

In the dialogue process, control switches back and forth between the operator and the system. The human has control over the dialogue in the following states: command activation, adjusting the input tool, entering data with optical feedback and editing data after the output of command echoes. The system controls the dialogue in these states: request of input data, semantic data checking inside the commands, and passive command execution.

There are three nested loops of interaction involved between human and machine:

– the command loop, consisting of command activation, data loop, and passive command execution;
– the data loop, composed of data request, input loop, data checking, command echo, and data editing;
– the input loop, in which a system echo indicates the current user input as optical feedback.

In principle, data can be entered at all input devices which are activated by the operator. Data and commands have to be entered in a fixed order. At any given time, only the current command can be activated.

KI communicates with GKS through the input functions REQUEST, SAMPLE, AWAIT, GET, and CLEAR. At the beginning of a command, all possibly existing data in GKS are deleted by "CLEAR". Waiting for event data to be entered into the GKS input queue occurs when the function "AWAIT" is requested. Data can be brought to KI by the GKS function "REQUEST". "SAMPLE" reads the current data of activated devices (such as the current position of a trackball) without any user action. Finally, the input function "GET" ascertains the existence of event data in the GKS input queue.

The application program communicates with KI via a single entry, which calls for the next input. Information is exchanged between the application program and KI according to four parameters:

- the type of input requested;
- the type of echo used to reflect the input actions to the operator;
- the type of prompting to be used for requesting data missing in the input;
- a data record, in which KI returns the complete set of input data for interpretation by the application program.

5.3.2 The GRADAS System

The GRADAS system [31] is an approach that concentrates as many functions as possible in an application-independent system, while attempting to minimize the programming work required for implementing a new application. Besides implementing from scratch, GRADAS allows the user to extend existing implementations to new applications. GRADAS provides not only a *dialogue* module based on a *graphics* module, but a *data base* and a *logics* module as well. The graphics module is not GKS, but one could easily see GKS being used in its place. The logics module knows as much about the semantics of the application as can be specified in an application-independent way; it may be regarded as a subsystem which checks the input against a conceptual schema and context-sensitive semantic restrictions. With GRADAS, the implementation of each new application calls for a separate step of system definition and generation. The application programmer defines the objects to be dealt with, their graphical representation, the syntax of the communication about these objects, and the context in which these objects may exist. He also defines the semantics by implementing application methods and binding them into the system. In GRADAS, the whole set of methods (whether or not they depend on the application) is called the methods base. Fig. 5.28 illustrates the principle streams of information flow among system methods during generation (left part of the figure) and during application (right part).

Adaptation of the GRADAS system to a new application area starts with the definition of new primitive objects, called the user primitives. Formally, these primitives are each represented by the following (see Fig. 5.29):

- an object number, expressing an internal identification number plus some internal system characteristics of the object;
- the total length of the subsequent information;
- a name to be used as the identifier of this object in the data base;
- pointers to the graphics information and the so-called "text", which is syntactically a character string, and semantically contains information to be interpreted, checked for plausibility, and used for building the logic information structure using context-sensitive methods of the GRADAS methods base.

The user primitives are application-dependent. Therefore, GRADAS gives the user the possibility for providing the definition of "his" primitives, and

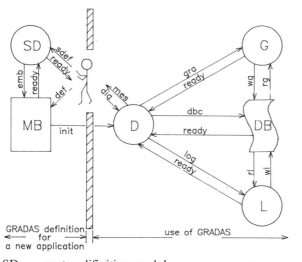

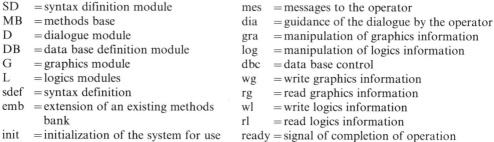

SD	= syntax difinition module	mes	= messages to the operator
MB	= methods base	dia	= guidance of the dialogue by the operator
D	= dialogue module	gra	= manipulation of graphics information
DB	= data base definition module	log	= manipulation of logics information
G	= graphics module	dbc	= data base control
L	= logics modules	wg	= write graphics information
sdef	= syntax definition	rg	= read graphics information
emb	= extension of an existing methods bank	wl	= write logics information
		rl	= read logics information
init	= initialization of the system for use	ready	= signal of completion of operation

Fig. 5.28. Principle streams of information in the GRADAS system

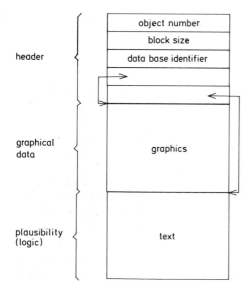

Fig. 5.29. The content of GRADAS user primitives

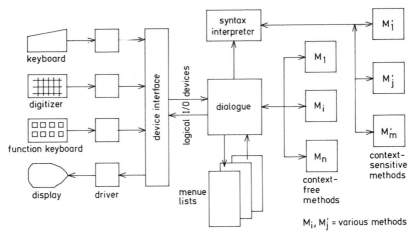

Fig. 5.30. The GRADAS dialogue module controls the operation of context-free and context-sensitive methods

must then have an automatic mechanism for mapping between user primitives and the primitives of the underlying graphics kernel system. User primitives that have a relevance on the semantic level are called master objects, and each one is marked as such in its object number. Underlying primitives, that are not to be used individually but are simply constituents of user primitives, are marked as slave objects.

The GRADAS system architecture is shown in Fig. 5.30, with emphasis on its interactive dialogue. The dialogue monitor interprets the menu lists, and uses the graphics kernel as one of the context-free methods to address the various graphics hardware components via their device interface. It builds a user primitive from the following information:

- commands;
- specifications;
- attributes;
- data.

The commands control the communication between user and system (examples: load a drawing from the data base, define a menu, define a drawing area, etc.) and implement the picture editing (examples: input data, delete data, insert data). The specifications select the user primitives to which each command should apply; these are elements of the user data structure (examples: house, street, cable, text, switchbox). The data are the parameters for the methods to be activated. Attributes give additional information about the objects which are selected using the specifications (line type, etc.). Each user primitive is passed to the syntax interpreter, to be handed over to one of the context-sensitive methods. This method will analyze the "text" and enter the object into the data base. The same method (or other context-sensitive methods) will also construct all the semantic relations of the new primitive to those currently existing in the data base. If the new primitive cannot be inserted into the existing struc-

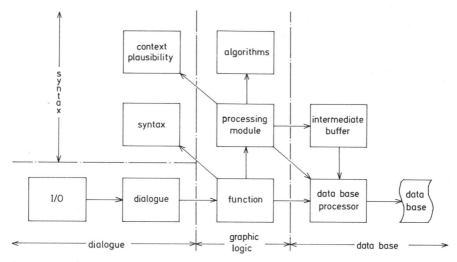

Fig. 5.31. Principal GRADAS components

ture in a legal way, an error is detected and a corresponding message is displayed to the operator. The control functions implemented in GRADAS for organizing the cooperation of both context-free and context-sensitive methods, are shown in Fig. 5.31. GRADAS provides context-free methods for:

– management of pictures (creation, deletion);
– editing pictures;
– editing the text portion of user primitives.

We will now discuss some implementation aspects of GRADAS. GRADAS stores the user primitives separately from the information structure constructed by the context-sensitive methods. The primitives are stored as a sequential set of storage blocks, each one containing both the graphics and the text information. Thus, access to this elementary information is simple and fast. The more complicated semantic information structures are stored in a structured data base. The main advantages of such an arrangement are

– clean separation of the data types (primitive data and semantic data structures);
– simplification of data management;
– fast system response during interaction.

5.4 Design of Efficient CAD Data Bases

5.4.1 Introduction

The storage of graphical and non-graphical data in a uniform way, as it is needed in most CAD systems, requires complex data base management systems.

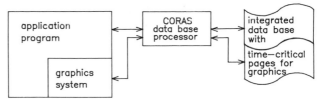

Fig. 5.32. Graphical information storage separate from the data base

This results from the conflicting requirements which the DBMS has to meet, in order to manage and store both the objects of the user world (or more precisely, their representations according to the user-defined schema) on one hand and the graphical representation of these objects (or parts of them) on the other. We have touched upon this problem already during the discussion of GRADAS in the previous section. The need for fast response during interactive CAD system applications calls for simple, preferably sequential storage structures. This need is emphasized by the large amount of data that is generally required to produce a display.

A storage structure that is generally well suited for storing graphical information is not generally suited for representing objects of the user world. Graphics blocks or graphics files are most often sequentially organized in order to speed up the display process. More complicated, say, hierarchical structures would slow down the interaction with the operator in an unacceptable way. User objects, however, require the handling of more complicated structures: A solid, for instance, may be represented by references to its surfaces, a surface by references to edges, and so on (see Fig. 2.7). But when the solid is to be displayed on a pen plotter or a vector display, it requires a representation as a list of vectors in a display file. As a consequence, CAD systems call for the redundant storage of information in both forms: in a structured way embedded in the semantic information structures, and in a sequentialized form suitably prepared for display.

This approach complicates the modification and deletion of objects, and shows all usual the consistency problems of a redundant data representation. Furthermore, retrieval according to graphical and non-graphical qualifications at the same time is complicated (for example, when searching for all objects of a certain type in a given region of the display). A further complication arises when the graphics files are kept separate from the conventional data base (Fig. 5.32). Therefore, the integration of the conventional data base and the graphics file (Fig. 5.33) is desirable, and is the proper way to implement a CAD system.

We will now describe an approach for DBMS design which appears to provide a solution to the problems stated above. The basic idea is to give the data base administrator the possibility of telling the DBMS which pieces of information are critical with respect to the interactive dialogue process. The concept is based on the general principle that the DBMS will store information on certain "pages" on direct-access peripheral devices, and that the retrieval process will be speeded up if the information to be retrieved is stored on the

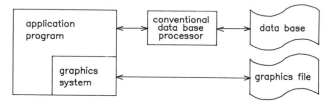

Fig. 5.33. Integrated information storage with special treatment of time-critical retrieval processes

same page, or at least on consecutive pages. In addition, the DBMS can provide better performance if it is told what other information is likely to be needed together with the piece that has just been retrieved. The proposed concept distinguishes between

– time-critical data structures;
   the DBMS will attempt to store all instances of this structure in the same internal page of the data base (or on consecutives pages);
– time-critical references.
   only one data structure is stored on each internal page, together with references to other elements of the data structure.

   Combinations of both are possible and useful, at least for a restricted number of instances. It is evident that difficulties arise as soon as a given data structure is addressed by the attribute 'time-critical' in two or more different ways; for instance, by combinations of time-critical data structures and time-critical references, or by two time-critical references.
   In this case, the DBMS can store all instances which are clustered by the 'time-critical' attribute on the same internal page, or on specific consecutive pages. An instance which is not bound by 'time-critical' can be moved to another page if a new instance allots to it the status of a time-critical reference. It is obvious that extensive use of the attribute 'time-critical' can reduce its benefits; if all parts of the data structure are made time-critical, nothing has been gained.
   The concepts described above have been implemented in the DBMS CORAS, which we will discuss in more detail in the next section. We will also present a tool (CSDL) for data base schema definition, which allows us to define internal and external data base schemas according to user needs and with efficiency considerations in mind.

5.4.2 CORAS — Core System for Associative Storage

CORAS (Core System for Associative Storage) evolved from the associative storage structures LEAP, SAM, and DATAS [32, 33].
   The interface where an application program and CORAS meet is best illustrated by the following level structure:

- real view of the user   = information level
- logical view of the user   = data structure level
- logical view of the system   = storage structure level
- real view of the system   = memory structure level

The information level and the data structure level (which is an abstraction and formalization of the information level) are where the user wants to perform some operations with the objects of his interest. The transition from the application program to CORAS occurs between the logical view of the user and the logical view of the system (which in this case is CORAS). CORAS provides a data definition language (DDL) and a data manipulation language (DML) to perform the joining of the two views. The tools that CORAS offers at this interface are independent of the structures on the data structure level. The system routines of CORAS organize and administrate the representation of these data structures in storage.

The real world is represented in CORAS in the form of *entities*, which are the basic elements of CORAS data structures. There exist four entity classes:

- simple entities;
- list entities;
- relation entities;
- set entities.

Each entity can be accessed by one or several names (synonyms). Each entity (not only the simple entities) can have attributes that describe it in more detail. Relation entities, set entities, and list entities may contain entities of any class as elements. A relation entity R establishes a binary relation R(A,B) between two entities A and B. A list entity contains an ordered collection of entities of the form $L = ((1,A),(2,B),(3,A),..)$, where an entity can appear as a list element several times. The set entity represents an unordered set of other entities.

CORAS has functions (procedures) for the generation, production, manipulation, and deletion of logical system structures on a basic level. Above the management of physical storage, CORAS is divided into modules:

- the name storage, containing the names of entities with reference to the entity data in
- the data storage;
- the relation storage, which contains tables expressing the relations between the entities in the form of triads (triad = a three-part expression indicating "relation, entity 1, entity 2").

The storage administration system manages the external and internal storage areas (virtual storage addressing). It contains a paging system for the page transport to and from the external storage and provides for system integrity. Name storage, data storage, and relation storage are divided into pages of variable quantity, and are expandable. Each page of the name storage is implemented as a hash table. The entity class is attached to the entity name, along with the page number and the address in the data storage (these two are called an ID pair) The structural and elementary data information comprising the entities is stored in the data storage. Each entity is accessed by the corresponding ID pair. An entity consists of a structure description (composed of a head with four subheads) along with four lists. With this internal organization, each list can be extended independently. The first list contains the synonyms of the entity name. User-specific data is stored in the second list. The third and fourth lists contain ID-pair references to lists and sets. The relations between entities are stored as triads in the relation storage; the representation of entities by ID pairs allows direct access to the triads.

5.4.3 A CORAS Extension for CAD Applications

CORAS offers to the user the required data base functions for conventional (non-graphical) application (functions for storage, retrieval, and modification of data). It has been extended to incorporate the handling of graphical information efficiently. The main idea is to offer to the user the possibility of a direct and compact description of graphical information in a way other than by long lists of vector coordinates. A circle, for example, is suitably described and stored by its center C and radius R, a curve by a few control points and the approximation function. This means that they are represented in a procedural form with only a few parameters stored explicitly; all other information may be derived by calculation. This is a practical example of the principles of algorithmic modelling described in Chapter 4.2.4. As a consequence, the DBMS must be able to deal with procedures as elements, in just the same way as with data. It should know the procedure for expanding the (C,R)-representation of a circle into all the points required for display. Of course, one could leave this expansion to the application program, but this would imply a considerable additional burden on the application programmer, and reduced efficiency during execution. In order to support such needs, CORAS allows us to define new sets of graphical primitives in procedural form, in addition to the inherent data base primitives. Such extensions have been implemented for many frequently-used graphical elements such as conical sections, surfaces, polylines, etc. With such primitives, and combinations of them, the user may define the necessary graphical shapes for his particular application.

   Following this approach, it is evident that CORAS has to support two kinds of data retrieval mechanisms:

a) a normal retrieval where entities, for instances, are retrieved using information that is stored in the form of data (example: give all circles with radius greater than a given value);
b) a retrieval that calls for the application of an expansion procedure (in our example: give the circle that is closest to some point on the display).

   Retrieval questions of this latter type are typical for graphics, but are also characteristic for other questions posed to CAD DBMS's. If the density and geometry of solids is stored in the data base and we ask for all solids above

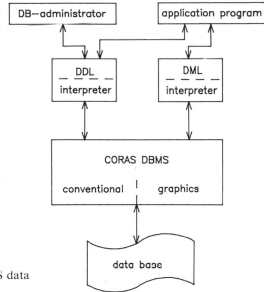

Fig. 5.34. An overview of the CORAS data base management system

a certain weight limit, the weights would have to be computed from geometrical and density data before they can be used in a comparison. The provision of algorithmic capabilities is just as essential as data storage capabilities for CAD systems. The methods base approach discussed in more detail in Chapter 5.5.3 is a generalized approach to this problem. In CORAS, a special solution — suitable to a wide range of applications — has been implemented by providing application-oriented extensions to the graphic kernel system primitives in the form of

a) problem-oriented primitives (such as circle, torus, etc.);
b) and problem-oriented primitive functions (such as intersection, nearest neighbor, etc.).

Corresponding extensions of the language interface for definition and manipulation of the data structures (DDL, DML) have been provided. Thus, CORAS users (both the human user and the application programs) can handle the extended graphical capabilities of the CORAS DBMS as efficiently as other, more conventional data base functions (Fig. 5.34).

In application, the performance of CORAS is basically determined by the degree of complexity of the retrieval operations, and by the amount of data to be handled. A performance evaluation which does not take into account the characteristics of the application is meaningless. However, the conversion of some of the DBMS functions from software to hardware could significantly improve the overall performance in any case.

5.4.4 CSDL as an Example of a Language for Designing
Conceptual Schemata of Data Bases

Contemporary data base technology leaves the task of designing the conceptual schema to the data base administrator (DBA). Without computer assistence, the DBA must manually make the translation of the unstructured knowledge about the data first into logical and then into physical structures. In many cases, the DBA will be confronted with incomplete requirements about the data and their semantics, because the users who formulated them either were inexperienced or had only a limited understanding of the data. Even if we disregard this problem, the DBA will still have difficulties in grasping the totality of the data and the complex relations among them. Manually translating unstructured knowledge into the formalism of DBMS's is time-consuming and increases the likelihood of making errors, if no suitable methodology is strictly enforced [34].

CSDL (conceptual schema definition language) [34] is an interactive language for expressing information about the data involved in an application. It combines powerful abstraction mechanisms for expressing the semantics of the data and transactions performed upon them.

The basic constructs of CSDL are:

– entities representing concepts of the physical or abstract objects in an application domain;
– simple frames which group one or more concepts to form a meaningful relationship.

There are three basic classes of semantic operators: selection, linking and naming. All of these classes can be identified in most application domains, and they appear in one form or another in most of the data models.

Selection corresponds to specialization: the means for deriving a specialized concept from a general one. Linking is the grouping together of several concepts or frames to form a new concept or another relationship. Naming is one of the most important operations, despite its neglect in most data models. For the symbol names and the naming conventions help the user of a data base to understand the correspondence between the symbols and the real-world entities or relationships they represent. In many cases this correspondence needs to be made explicit in the conceptual schema and this is done in CSDL through definitions.

Every concept must have a definition. Concepts are divided into primary and derived ones. Primary concepts are those whose identity can be recognized independent of the defining properties of other concepts.

CSDL frees the designer from having to know the details of the underlying data structure that stores the conceptual schema, and from the tedious task of making it consistent. Thus, the designer can concentrate on the semantics of the application.

The first step in any data base design is the extraction of all the characteristics of that part of the real world which is to be represented in the data base. The representation of the object system's properties and their integration into

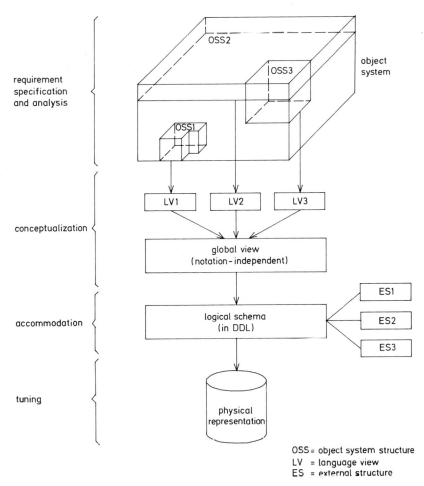

Fig. 5.35. The different steps in mapping objects from the real world onto a data base

one conceptual model is the next portion of the logical data base design. The model obtained by this process is an abstract one which represents the inherent properties of the object system and is independent of any model or notation supported by the DBMS. For communication to a DBMS, however, the conceptual model has to be expressed in the terms of this particular DBMS. This is the "data base accommodation" step. Since local views were integrated at a high level of abstraction to yield a binding model common to all applications, it is now necessary to represent the user's views in terms of the data description language (DDL) supported by the particular DBMS. The whole process, from the determination of user requirements through conceptual model and final accommodation in terms of the selected DBMS, is the logical data base design process [35].

Figure 5.35 shows schematically the definition of a data base schema using the notations of CSDL. The various objects of the real world (object system

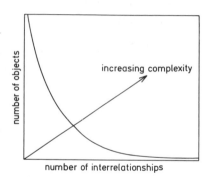

Fig. 5.36. Increasing complexity in the data base

structures) are each mapped via the corresponding language level into a single and notation-independent global view. This global view is formalized by means of the data definition language (1) into the various external views (for humans and programs) and (2) into the storage structure on the physical storage devices. The internal organization of the data (representing the object system and its models) on storage devices constitutes the "physical" design of the data base.

In the conceptual model, any misconception of the object system or misrepresentation of its characteristics has a strong effect on the ability of a data base to satisfy the users' information needs. This problem has centered attention on the logical data base design state. The systematic process by which one traverses the different stages of logical data base design and performs the mappings from one level of abstraction to the next is commonly called a logical data base design methodology.

Two parameters have a strong influence on the complexity of data base design:

- the number of objects to be represented;
- the number of relations among objects.

The area above the curve in Fig. 5.36 represents the area in which intuitive design becomes most difficult. To model an object system in which many objects and activities are interrelated a systematic and well-structured approach is necessary.

Two basically different trends can be observed. One approach first generates a global schema and then derives local views from it; the other approach first models the local views of different users and then integrates them to form a global view. Examples for these methodologies are presented in [36, 37, 38].

5.5 Integrated Systems and Methods Bases

5.5.1 The Concept of Integrated Systems

The software environment in which CAD systems are being developed is usually characterized by:

- FORTRAN, or — more precisely — the FORTRAN dialect of the available computer;
- several subroutine packages for access to non-standard features of the computer installation such as graphic devices, data bases, etc.;
- the job control language of the particular computer;
- the implicit assumption of the availability of certain hardware resources (a certain amount of memory capacity, for instance).

Transfer of a CAD system from one installation to another requires — assuming that the two environments are not identical — requires:

- modification of those FORTRAN statements that are not common to both dialects;
- adaptation of those parts in the system that have been influenced by the computer architecture (such as the word length).
- adaptation of the package calls to other packages (at least some of them);
- adaptation of the job control language;
- adjustment to more stringent hardware resources.

In the 1970s, a number of so-called "integrated systems" were developed [39, 40]. An integrated system consists of a set of subsystems for solving problems from various engineering disciplines, and of a "system nucleus" whose facilities are shared by all the subsystems. Its primary purpose is

- to provide a user-oriented environment for formulating and solving application problems from various disciplines in specialized subsystems;
- to support the development of such subsystems (in particular CAD systems), and to minimize the work necessary for adapting a given system to a new computer environment.

This goal is achieved by localizing all the environment dependency within the system nucleus. In addition, the system nuclei support the development of application systems by providing higher-than-FORTRAN-level capabilities that are often needed. Examples of such capabilities are: data structuring, language processing, program and data management, documentation management and user guidance. The idea of concentrating basic software for all applications in a nucleus has also been adopted for IPAD [41]

CAD system nuclei envelop the basic computer (hardware and manufacturer-supplied software) and hide it behind a software machine, which provides facilities for constructing higher-level software machines:

- the facilities of the *nucleus* may be used by the CAD system developer for providing new CAD capabilities (such as three-dimensional modelling). The term "subsystem" is used for these new CAD capabilities. If the subsystem is useful for solving problems related to a large class of objects (a finite element or a line-drawing subsystem, for example), it is called a *problem oriented subsystem*;
- the capabilities of one or more *problem-oriented subsystems* may be combined by an application programmer to formulate the design tasks for specific objects of design (such as welding machines). Due to the fact that all subsystems belong to the same family (being based on the same nucleus), they may

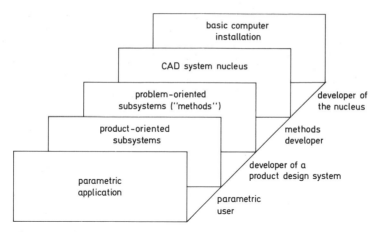

Fig. 5.37. The level concept in an integrated system

be combined freely without the danger of conflicts. Subsystems on this level are generally *product-oriented*;
– a product-oriented subsystem may still leave some parameters open. The *parametric user* may specify such parameters and perform variations on a basically fixed design.

Fig. 5.37 illustrates the various levels of the nucleus concept. The existence of distinct levels of applications has also been recognized in the area of CAD turn-key systems [42 ,43]. Pioneering work on system nuclei was done at MIT starting in the mid-'60s. The "Integrated Civil Engineering System" or ICES [44] is still the most widely-used CAD system nucleus. (The term "Integrated System" is generally used synonymously to indicate what we prefer to call the "nucleus".) Other systems followed the same philosophy, placing emphasis on different aspects (portability, efficiency, ease of subsystem development, interactivity). The systems

– DINAS [45, 46],
– GENESYS [47],
– IST [48] and
– REGENT [49, 50]

belong to this class of CAD system nuclei. We will discuss REGENT in more detail as a representative of this class.
   Every implementation of the REGENT system consists of

– the nucleus;
– a number of subsystems for general-purpose use, such as
   * DABAL [51] for easy access to the REGENT file management system;
   * GIPSY [52, 53, 54] for graphic data processing;
– any number of application-oriented subsystems;

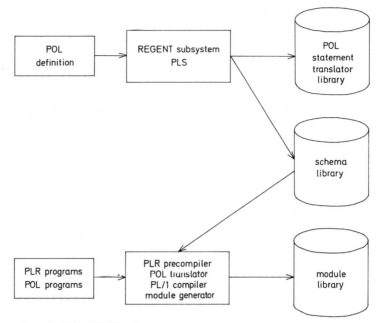

Fig. 5.38. The generation of a REGENT subsystem

The nucleus itself consists of software machines for the support of

− subsystem development (see Fig. 5.38)
   * definition of a schema for the subsystem data structure. This data structure
     is global with respect to the subsystem, and hence accessible from every
     where within it (but not from other subsystems);
   * generation of modules. A module may be considered as a subprogram
     on a logical level. However, modules are not bound into the application
     program before they are actually needed. They reside in a module library,
     and are loaded into primary memory when requested. Thus they differ
     from normal subprograms not in functional respect, but in their resource
     aspect only;
   * definition of a subsystem language (POL = "problem-oriented language"
     or "product-oriented language"). The REGENT subsystem PLS [55] gener-
     ates statement drivers for compilation of the POL statements in the new
     subsystem language;
− subsystem execution:
   * generation of an executable application program. The application program
     that is written in one or more subsystem languages is first translated into
     PL/1, and then into machine code by the standard PL/1 compiler. RE-
     GENT subprograms that are used in this application are statically bound
     into the program (see Fig. 5.39);
   * at execution time, the REGENT nucleus performs the function of an execu-
     tive system for the application program. Run-time facilities for support

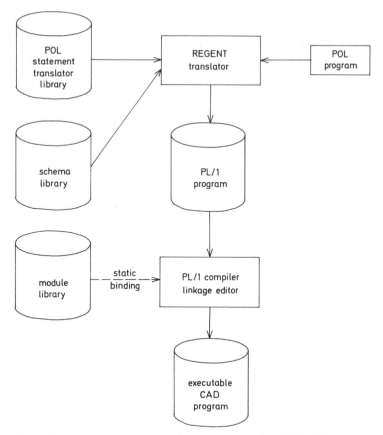

Fig. 5.39. The generation of a CAD program with REGENT

of the special REGENT capabilities are provided. Resource management, program flow control, and message management are performed. The application program may be executed in batch or interactive mode (see Fig. 5.40).

The components of a subsystem —

— subsystem language,
— schema for the subsystem data structure,
— the modules,
— the messages (as part of the modules)

— are stored in three libraries: a schema library, a library for the POL statement drivers, and a module library. Subsystem data are stored in

— a data base and/or files (Fig. 5.40).

The subsystem is completed by

— the documentation.

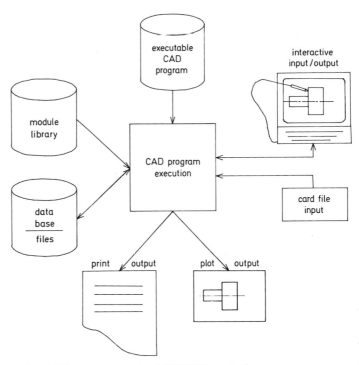

Fig. 5.40. The execution of a CAD program under REGENT control

None of the system nuclei mentioned above provides computer-based tools for documentation support and user guidance. The reason for this is historical. When the system nuclei were developed, computer power was not yet so readily available as it is today. The system nuclei, though oriented towards interactive data processing, found their dominant application in batch processing. Furthermore, they developed and operated mostly in a batch environment, and with typical batch subsystems such as the finite-element ICES subsystem STRUDL II [56] or the graphical REGENT subsystem GIPSY [53, 54].

5.5.2 REGENT as an Example of a CAD System Nucleus

In the REGENT system, every subsystem language provides PL/1 as a subset. Thus the familiar constructs of conventional high-level languages are available in all subsystem languages. Besides this, the language provides "problem-oriented" or "product-oriented" statements (POL-statements). The application program containing PL/1 and various POL statements is compiled into plain PL/1 by the REGENT translator. Subsequently, it is treated (compiled, link-edited, executed) as a normal PL/1 program. Fig. 5.39 illustrates this aspect of REGENT. For processing POL statements, the REGENT translator dynamically calls statement drivers that were each generated by PLS on the basis

Sample Listing 5.4. Definition of a PLOT statement with the REGENT subsystem PLS.

```
ENTER PLS;          /* Now we are in PLS                        */
SUBSYSTEM GIPSY; /* We define a statement for GIPSY             */
STATEMENT 'PLOT';
   SKIP '(';        /* The opening bracket is ignored           */
   EXECUTE;
      /* All statements between EXECUTE and END EXECUTE         */
      /* will be generated at translation time and replace      */
      /* the original POL statement. At the same time           */
      /* substitutions will be performed in order to replace    */
      /* variables in the EXECUTE clause by corresponding       */
      /* expressions derived from the actual POL statement      */
   CALL GIPLOT( QQ , NEXT_EXPRESSION ) ;
      /* The statement CALL GIPLOT( next_expression ) ;         */
      /* replaces the original POL-statement in the generated*/
      /* PL/1 program, with next_expression being substituted*/
      /* by whatever expression is found between the brackets*/
   SKIP ')';        /* The closing bracket is ignored           */
 END STATEMENT;
 END PLS;
```

of a POL-statement definition. As an example, the subsystem GIPSY allows a statement of the form

PLOT(< any–graphical–object >);

The definition of the syntax and semantics of this statement using the PLS language in REGENT is shown in Sample Listing 5.4. According to this translation definition, the POL statement

PLOT(ABC);
would be replaced by the PL/1 statement

CALL GIPLOT(QQ , ABC) ;

The variable QQ appearing in this statement is implicitly declared as pointer, and represents the name of the REGENT environment. Access to the REGENT facilities is performed through this variable, which is inserted into all procedures in the REGENT translation process. Hence, this name QQ must be considered as a resource reserved for unique use by the REGENT system alone, and forbidden for any other use. This is spelled out in the REGENT user manual, in line with rule (R5) in Chapter 4.3.2.3

The compactness and readability of a problem-oriented language is illustrated by the following example of a complete GIPSY program (see Sample Listing 5.5), which computes the difference of a cube and a sphere to produce Fig. 5.41.

Sample Listing 5.6 will produce the same picture, but illustrates how the concept of processes is implemented in the REGENT environment. Subsystems may be considered as software machines in the sense of Chapter 4.3.1. Their execution corresponds to a process (in the sense of Chapter 3) which is created and initiated by the ENTER statement and terminated and deleted by the END statement. However, a process may by suspended and put into a dormant state

Sample Listing 5.5. A program in the problem-oriented graphics programming language GIPSY. This program will produce Fig. 5.41.

```
ENTER GIPSY;
 DECLARE SURFACE(6) PLANE;
/* SPACE(n) means: a SPACE element with up to n surfaces    */
/* SPACE elements are convex                                 */
 DECLARE INNER_SPHERE SPACE(1);
 DECLARE CUBE SPACE(6);
/* BODY means: it is a general, not necessarily convex body */
 DECLARE OBJECT BODY;
/* length units are CM, unless specified otherwise          */
  CHANGE UNITS LENGTH CM;
/* a PLANE is defined by a point in the plane and by
   the vector pointing to the material side                 */
 SET SURFACE(1)=PLANE(POINT( 0, 0, 0),POINT(-3, 0, 0));
 SET SURFACE(2)=PLANE(POINT(-3, 0, 0),POINT( 0, 0, 0));
 SET SURFACE(3)=PLANE(POINT( 0, 0, 0),POINT( 0, 0, 3));
 SET SURFACE(4)=PLANE(POINT( 0, 0,-3),POINT( 0, 0, 0));
 SET SURFACE(5)=PLANE(POINT( 0, 0, 0),POINT( 0, 3, 0));
 SET SURFACE(6)=PLANE(POINT( 0, 3, 0),POINT( 0, 0, 0));
/* Both cube and sphere are centered at (-1.5, 1.5, 1.5)     */
 SET CUBE=SPACE(SURFACE(1)+SURFACE(2)+SURFACE(3)
               +SURFACE(4)+SURFACE(5)+SURFACE(6) );
 SET INNER_SPHERE=SPACE( BALL(POINT(-1.5,1.5,1.5),1.8) );
/* we now subtract the inner sphere from the cube           */
 SET OBJECT=BODY(SPACE(CUBE-INNER_SPHERE));
/* we specify the direction of projection,
             the projection plane by its normal vector,
             and the location of the projected origin of the
             3D-coordinated system in the projection plane   */
CHANGE PROJECTION PARALLEL (-100.,-95. ,+130.),
       PROJECTION PI_NORMAL(-100.,-95. ,+130.),
       PROJECTION ORIGIN ( 60. MM , 40. MM );
/* we specify the representation of lines, pen 4 is thick    */
CHANGE STANDARD PEN(4),
       INVISIBLE LINETYPE DASHED;
OPEN PLOT DIN A(6) BROAD;
PLOT(OBJECT);
/* we now wish to plot the shifted object, but suppress
                                invisible lines             */
CHANGE INVISIBLE LINETYPE OMITTED;
PLOT(SHIFT(OBJECT,  5. CM, -5. CM , 0. ) );
END GIPSY;
```

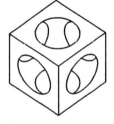

Fig. 5.41. The result of a sample program written in the problem-oriented language of the REGENT subsystem GIPSY

Sample Listing 5.6. A GIPSY program that produces the same picture as Sample Listing 5.5, but with intermediate suspension of the GIPSY process.

```
/* the names of the GIPSY process and of the object, which are
      to be passed from one activation of the process to the
      next one, are represented as POINTERs                         */
DECLARE (PROCESS_NAME, OBJECT_NAME) POINTER;
/* for explanations see Sample Listing 5.2                          */
ENTER GIPSY;
  DECLARE SURFACE(6) PLANE;
  DECLARE INNER_SPHERE SPACE(1);
  DECLARE CUBE SPACE(6);
/* the object is allocated explicitly; otherwise it
      would disappear at the end of this program block.
      See Chapter  4.2.3                                            */
  DECLARE OBJECT BODY BASED(OBJECT_NAME);
  ALLOCATE BODY OBJECT;
  CHANGE UNITS LENGTH CM;
  SET SURFACE(1)=PLANE(POINT( 0, 0, 0),POINT(-3, 0, 0));
  SET SURFACE(2)=PLANE(POINT(-3, 0, 0),POINT( 0, 0, 0));
  SET SURFACE(3)=PLANE(POINT( 0, 0, 0),POINT( 0, 0, 3));
  SET SURFACE(4)=PLANE(POINT( 0, 0,-3),POINT( 0, 0, 0));
  SET SURFACE(5)=PLANE(POINT( 0, 0, 0),POINT( 0, 3, 0));
  SET SURFACE(6)=PLANE(POINT( 0, 3, 0),POINT( 0, 0, 0));
  SET CUBE=SPACE(SURFACE(1)+SURFACE(2)+SURFACE(3)
                 +SURFACE(4)+SURFACE(5)+SURFACE(6) );
  SET INNER_SPHERE=SPACE( BALL(POINT(-1.5,1.5,1.5),1.8) );
  SET OBJECT=BODY(SPACE(CUBE-INNER_SPHERE));
  CHANGE STANDARD PEN(4),
         INVISIBLE LINETYPE DASHED;
  CHANGE PROJECTION PARALLEL (-100.,-95. ,+130.),
         PROJECTION PI_NORMAL(-100.,-95. ,+130.),
         PROJECTION ORIGIN ( 60. MM , 40. MM );
  OPEN PLOT DIN A(6) BROAD;
  PLOT(OBJECT);
END GIPSY LEAVE(PROCESS_NAME);
/* at this point the GIPSY process becomes suspended
      (dormant, idle), but it still exists and may be referred
      to as PROCESS_NAME. It may be reactivated at any place
      where this name is known; and the object BODY, which was
      created, may be reused wherever its name OBJECT is known
ENTER GIPSY REENTER(PROCESS_NAME);
  DECLARE OBJECT BODY BASED(OBJECT_NAME);
  CHANGE INVISIBLE LINETYPE OMITTED;
  PLOT(SHIFT(OBJECT,  5. CM, -5. CM , 0. ) );
  FREE BODY OBJECT;
END GIPSY;
```

by the LEAVE option of the END statement, thus associating a name with this particular subsystem process. The same process may then be reactivated at a later time. In the meantime, any other subsystem may be active. Hence, REGENT subsystem processes may not only be created one within another, but they may also operate in an alternating way.

One particular feature of REGENT not available in other system nuclei is the recursive extension capability. Any subsystem language may itself be used to write modules of another subsystem. This capability was achieved by using PL/1 as the basis for all subsystem languages and for the normal module programming language. All nuclei provide extensions of a conventional programming language for module production; the base language is FORTRAN in most cases, except for REGENT. The language extensions are dialects called ICETRAN in ICES, ISTRAN in IST, GENTRAN in GENESYS, or PLR in REGENT. These dialects of the base language generally provide all the features of the base language itself, plus some additional capabilities that have been found beneficial in a CAD environment. The common features of the nuclei are

– dynamic program management;
– data structure management;
– file management.

We will briefly describe these features for REGENT.

5.5.2.1 Dynamic Program Management

In a PL/1 program an external entry (corresponding to a subroutine in FORTRAN) is declared and called as follows:

DECLARE EXPROG ENTRY(< parameter description >) EXTERNAL;
CALL EXPROG(< actual parameters >);

In order to make the program executable, the compiled version of the subprogram EXPROG must be available at module binding time (see Chapter 5.2.2). The binder program will then produce a single piece of code from both the calling program and the subprogram. If a modification in either the calling program or the called program is needed, the binding process must be repeated (and accompanied by recompilation of the modified program). For large CAD systems with hundreds of subprograms, this is a time-consuming procedure. It can be avoided by delaying the binding until execution time. In REGENT all that is needed in the calling program is to replace the attribute EXTERNAL by DYNAMIC in the above declaration. The module management will then retrieve the desired program from the library and pass control to it. With this method, only those programs that are actually needed will ever be loaded into primary memory. Thus dynamic program management provides the advantages of overlay loading, but with much more convenience to the user.

5.5.2.2 Data Structure Management

"Dynamic arrays" are hierarchical data structures in a virtual memory. The elements of dynamic arrays are each identified by the name of a basis, a sequence of indices defining the access path in the data structure tree, and the schema of the element to be retrieved. An example is given below.

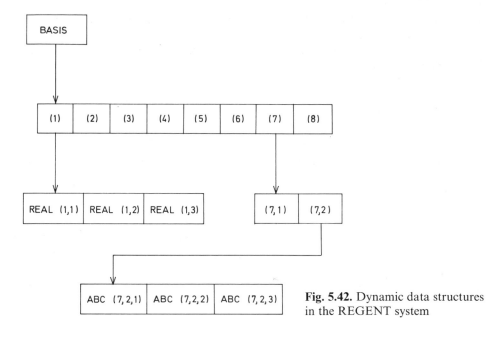

Fig. 5.42. Dynamic data structures in the REGENT system

DECLARE BASIS DESCRIPTOR;
DECLARE 1 ABC DYNAMIC(BASIS),
        2 < description of the data aggregate ABC > ;
DECLARE REAL DYNAMIC(BASIS) DECIMAL FLOAT(6);

With these declarations and a few special statements of the PLR language, the data structure shown in Fig. 5.42 could be built. The REAL data and the data aggregates ABC may be used in any PLR statement, just like any other PL/1 data. The expression REAL(1,3) is a shorthand writing of BASIS(1,3)->REAL. PLR provides statements for creating, expanding, combining, reducing, and deleting these data structures. They are often used to store arrays of data when the number of data elements is not known in advance. This situation arises, for instance, when a curve is digitized and the number of data points is not known before the end this operation. Dynamic arrays can grow automatically with each new data item added to them. In addition to these functional capabilities, they provide the user with control of the storage resource. A virtual memory is simulated by software automatically. However, the user may override this automatic behavior to improve the efficiency.

An interesting aspect of the dynamic data structures is the fact that some of their features turn up in modern computer architectures, where they find hardware support instead of only being software-supported. First of all, the virtual memory concept has now become a widespread capability of operating systems. But also, the abstract data structure of the dynamic arrays turns up in recent computer architectures. The STARLET computer [57] has a generic data structure that is very similar to what we find in system nuclei from ICES through REGENT: a hierarchy of vectors which are self-descriptive due to some descriptors, and whose elements may contain either elementary data or identifiers of other such vectors.

5.5.2.3 File Management

Long-term data storage is a common need in CAD. Data bases are used for this purpose, as are the file systems provided by the computer installation. In many cases, however, neither one of these is ideally suited. The use of a data base may cost too much because of the overhead produced by the data transformation and data security features. This is particularly true for large files of data that are passed from one program to another without any intermediate operations on them (as when the results of finite-element programs are passed to a post-processor). One the other hand, the filing systems of the computer's operating system often provide insufficient support on the level of the programming language. Files must be managed (created, manipulated, grouped into files of files, etc.) from within the application program. For this reason, the CAD system nuclei provide their own file management systems.

The REGENT file management system supports both sequential and direct access files. All PL/1 data structures and dynamic arrays may be stored in these files. The files may be grouped together into a tree structure (files of files). Every level in the tree has its own catalogue and password protection. A whole tree of files appears to the operating system like a single file. The subsystem DABAL provides a user-language interface for manipulation in both batch and interactive modes.

5.5.3 Methods Bases

More recently, similar system architectures have become better known as "methods bases" or "banks of methods" [58]. In a sense, the "integrated systems" idea is a predecessor of the methods base concept [59]. However, for methods bases, documentation support and interactive user guidance have been included in the concept right from the beginning. See, for instance, [60, 61, 62, 63, 64]. The experienced user would employ a methods base in much the same sense as he would use an integrated system: he would state and solve his problem by formulating it in a problem-oriented language. The inexperienced user, however, will be guided from a first and perhaps imprecise statement of his problem (maybe even in ordinary language) to the formalism required for the application of the appropriate method. The methods base will try to recognize in the initial problem statement patterns that are characteristic for the range of methods that it can propose; it will ask for further data about the problem until the appropriate method has been identified; it will then continue to ask for additional information as is needed for applying the method. Keywords and/or a hierarchical structure will be used to navigate in the problem domain.

Whether or not a significant amount of design knowledge can be preprocessed into the formalism and structure required for this approach is yet to be seen. It is perhaps not a question of whether this approach is principally feasible but simply a matter of time and man-power required to create this formalization, which may cause the failure of this concept if attempted on an overly broad scale. In limited areas, however, methods bases will not only help users to obtain solutions for isolated problems, but will also provide a means for computer-aided education in the corresponding problem domain.

5.6 Summary

This chapter described several basic aspects of implementation methodology. The first part was concerned with the specification and the definition of requirements, presenting SADT as an example of a high-level specification tool. After this introduction, the different phases of a system development were described.

The second part of this chapter gave a short introduction to interactive computer graphics and the usual graphical I/O-devices. Here a knowledge of the concepts presented in Chapter 2 (device-independent graphics software; general purpose command interpreters) was assumed. As an example of a possible CAD system use of interactive graphics functions, the GRADAS system was presented and discussed in some detail.

The next part of this chapter was concerned data base design, especially with the design of conceptual schemata of data bases (using SCDL as an example) and with the data base design process.

For aiding the implementation of CAD systems, "system nuclei" have been developed. These nuclei provide a software environment that supports the development of CAD systems better than the conventional environment of computer operating systems. Most system nuclei make the following facilities available: management of programs and data, definition of new user languages, standardization of system messages, and file management. The programming languages of the system nuclei are extensions of FORTRAN or PL/1. In these systems, the problem- or product-oriented languages for the user of a subsytem may be interpreted or compiled. In the latter case, the user languages may themselves be used for implementing higher-level subsystems.

5.7 Bibliography

[1] P. Schnupp, Chr. Floyd: Software-Programmentwicklung und Projektorganisation. 2. Aufl. Berlin (1979) de Gruyter.
[2] J. Encarnação: Logical Design Techniques and Tools. Siemens Forsch.- u. Entwickl. Berichte, Bd. 7 Nr. 6. Heidelberg (1978) Springer-Verlag, pp. 332–335.
[3] D.T. Ross, K.E. Schoman: Structured Analysis for Requirements Definition. IEEE Trans. SE 3 (1977), pp. 6–15.
[4] SofTech: Prospectus: An Introduction to SADT. SofTech, Inc., Waltham, Mass., Doc. No. 9022-78, Feb. 1976.
[5] E.G. Schlechtendahl: CAD Process and System Design. In: J. Encarnação (ed.):

Computer-Aided Design: Modelling, Systems Engineering, CAD-Systems. Lecture Notes in Computer Science, Vol. 89. Heidelberg (1980) Springer-Verlag.

[6] M. Jackson: Software Development as an Engineering Problem. Angewandte Informatik (1982) 2, pp. 96–103.

[7] E.B. Daly: Management of Software Development. IEEE Trans. SE 3 (1977), pp. 229–242.

[8] A. Altmann, G. Weber: Programmiermethodik. Arbeitsberichte des IMMD, Erlangen, 10 (1977) Nr. 3.

[9] H. Hanusa, H. Kuhlmann, G. Pfaff: On Constructing Interactive Graphics Systems. Proc. EUROGRAPHICS '82, Manchester. Amsterdam (1982) North-Holland Publ. Co.

[10] J. Encarnação, H. Hanusa, W. Straßer: Tools and Techniques for the Description, Implementation, and Monitoring of Interactive Man-Machine-Dialogues. Proceedings of the 1982 International Zurich Seminar on Digital Communications. IEEE Catalog No. 82CH1735-0.

[11] Informationsverarbeitung; Programmdokumentation; DIN 66230, Ausg. 1.81. In: DIN Taschenbuch 166, Informationsverarbeitung 4. Berlin (1981) Beuth.

[12] C. Machover: A Guide to Sources of Information about Computer Graphics. IEEE Computer Graphics 1 (1981) 1, pp. 73–85.

[13] C. Machover: A Guide to Sources of Information about Computer Graphics. IEEE Computer Graphics 1 (1981) 3, pp. 63–65.

[14] J. Encarnação, W. Straßer (eds.): Geräteunabhängige graphische Systeme. München (1981) Oldenbourg.

[15] R. Lindner: Aspects of Interactive Computer Graphics, Applications and Systems. Proc. 3rd European Electro-Optics Conference, Geneva, 1976. Soc. Photo-Optical Instrumentation Engineers, Bellingham, Wash. (1976), pp. 274–288.

[16] R. Lindner: Rasterdisplay-Prozessoren — ihre Bedeutung, Konzepte und Verfahren. Dissertation. Techn. Hochschule Darmstadt (1979).

[17] V.L. Wallace: The Semantics of Graphics Input Devices. Computer Graphics 10 (1976) 1, pp. 62–65.

[18] R. Ganz, H.-J. Dohrmann: Farbgraphische Ausgabesysteme. ZwF 76 (1981) 5, pp. 223–239.

[19] L.C. Hobbs: Computer Graphics Display Hardware. IEEE Computer Graphics and Applications 1 (1981) 1, pp. 25–39.

[20] F.M. Lillehagen: CAD/CAM Work Stations for Man-Model Communication. IEEE Computer Graphics and Applications 1 (1981) 3, pp. 17–27.

[21] ACM/SIGGRAPH: Status Report of the Graphics Standards Planning Committee of ACM/SIGGGRAPH. Computer Graphics 11 (1977) 3.

[22] ACM: Special Issue: Graphics Standards. ACM Computing Surveys 10 (1978) 4.

[23] ACM/SIGGRAPH: Status Report of the Graphics Standards Planning Committee of ACM/ SIGGRAPH. Computer Graphics 13 (1979) 3.

[24] R.A. Guedj, H.A. Tucker: Methodology in Computer Graphics. Amsterdam (1979) North-Holland Publ. Co.

[25] R. Eckert, G. Enderle, K. Kansy, F.J. Prester: GKS '79 — Proposal of a Standard for a Graphical Kernel System. Eurographics 79 — Conference Proceedings Bologna (1979), pp. 2–17.

[26] ISO TC97/SC5/WG2 N117; Draft International Standard ISO/DP 7942; Information Processing, Graphical Kernel System (GKS), 1982.

[27] W. Straßer: Hardware and System Aspects of Computer Graphics : A Tutorial. In: J. Encarnação, O. Torres, E. Warman (eds.): CAD/CAM as a Basis for the Development of Technology in Developing Nations. Amsterdam (1981) North-Holland Publ. Co., p. 285.

[28] J. Encarnação: The Input and the Manipulation of Complex, Structured Graphical Objects. Position paper for the SEILLAC II Workshop, May 1979, France. Report of the Mathematisch Centrum, Amsterdam, Jan. 1979.

[29] H.G. Borufka, G. Pfaff: Konzept eines Kommandointerpretierers. Report GRIS 79-8. Techn. Hochschule Darmstadt, Fachgebiet Graphisch-Interaktive Systeme (1979).

[30] H.G. Borufka, H. Kuhlmann, P. ten Hagen: Dialogue Cells, a Method for Defining Interactions. IEEE Computer Graphics and Applications 2 (1982) 4.

[31] R. Konkart, E. Alff, C. Hornung: Graphisches Informationssystem auf der Grundlage einer relationalen Datenbank. In: R. Gnatz, K. Samelson (eds.): Informatik Fachberichte, Bd. 11. Heidelberg (1977) Springer-Verlag, pp. 261–276.

[32] V. Glatzer, J. Encarnação: DATAS — Datenstrukturen in assoziativer Speicherung. Angewandte Informatik (1972), pp. 417–424.

[33] G. Weck: SAD — Ein Modell einer strukturabhängigen assoziativen Datenstruktur. Dissertation. Saarbrücken (1974) Universität des Saarlandes.

[34] N. Roussopoulos: Tools for Designing Conceptual Schemata of Databases. Computer Aided Design 11 (1979) 3, pp. 119–120.

[35] A.P. Buchmann, A.G. Dale: Evaluation Criteria for Logical Database Design Methodologies. Computer Aided Design 11 (1979) 3, pp. 120–121.

[36] J.A. Bubenko: IAM — An Inferential Abstract Modelling Approach to Design of Conceptual Schema. ACM/SIGMOD Int. Conf. on Management of Data. Toronto, August 1977.

[37] B.K. Kahn: A Structured Logical Database Design Methodology. NYU Symposium on Database Design. New York City, May 1978.

[38] J.M. Smith, D. Smith: Principles of Database Conceptual Design. NYU Symposium of Database Design. New York City, May 1978.

[39] E.G. Schlechtendahl: Comparison of Integrated Systems for CAD., Int. Conf. Computer Aided Design, IEE Conf. Publ. 111, Southampton (1974), pp. 111–116.

[40] — : Integrierte Programmsysteme. Report KfK-CAD 2. Kernforschungszentrum Karlsruhe (1975).

[41] R.E. Fulton: Using CAD/CAM to Improve Productivity. Mechanical Engineering 103 (1981) 11, pp. 64–69.

[42] H. Grabowski: Veränderte Arbeitsstrukturen durch CAD-Systeme. ZwF 74 (1979) 6, pp. 294–300.

[43] H. Grabowski, H. Maier: Der Konstrukteur als Programmierer. NC-Report 1-81 (1981), pp. 125–130.

[44] D.T. Ross: ICES System Design. Cambridge (1976) MIT Press.

[45] K.P. Beier: Systemsoftware für ein integriertes schiffbautechnisches Programmsystem. Dissertation. Berlin (1976) Techn. Univ.

[46] K.P. Beier, W. Jonas: DINAS — A Transportable Executive System for Interactive Computer Aided Design. Proc. Int. Conf. Interactive Techniques in Computer Aided Design Bologna (1978), pp. 393–403.

[47] Alcock, Shearing and Partners: GENESYS Reference Manual. Loughborough (1971) The GENESYS Centre.

[48] P.J. Pahl, L. Beilschmidt: Informationssystem Technik. Programmierhandbuch. Report KfK CAD-81. Kernforschungszentrum Karlsruhe (1978).

[49] E.G. Schlechtendahl: Grundzüge des integrierten Programmsystems REGENT. Angewandte Informatik (1976) 11, pp. 490–496.

[50] E.G. Schlechtendahl, K.H. Bechler, G. Enderle, K. Leinemann, W. Olbrich: REGENT-Handbuch. Report KfK 2666 (KfK-CAD 71). Kernforschungszentrum Karlsruhe (1981).

[51] K. Leinemann: Dynamische Datenstrukturen des integrierten CAD-Systems REGENT. Angewandte Informatik (1977) 1, pp. 26–31.

[52] R. Schuster: System und Sprache zur Behandlung graphischer Information im rech-nergestützten Entwurf. Report KfK 2305. Kernforschungszentrum Karlsruhe (1976).

[53] G. Enderle, K.H. Bechler, F. Katz, K. Leinemann, W. Olbrich, E.G. Schlechtendahl, K. Stölting: GIPSY-Handbuch., Report KfK 2878. Kernforschungszentrum Karls-ruhe (1980).

[54] G. Enderle, K.-H. Bechler, H. Grimme, W. Hieber, F. Katz: GIPSY-Handbuch Band II. Report KfK 3216. Kernforschungszentrum Karlsruhe (1981).

[55] G. Enderle: Problemorientierte Sprachen im REGENT-System. Angewandte Infor-matik (1976) 12, pp. 543–549.

[56] M.F. Nelson: ICES STRUDL II. In: Three-Dimensional Continuum Computer Pro-grams for Structural Analysis. New York (1972) ASME, pp. 23–24.

[57] W.K. Giloi, R. Güth: Das Prinzip der Datenstruktur-Architekturen und seine Reali-sierung im STARLET-Rechner. Informatik-Spektrum 5 (1982) 1, pp. 21–37.

[58] K.R. Dittrich, R. Hüber, P.C. Lockemann: Methodenbanksysteme: Ein Werkzeug zum Maßschneidern von Anwendersystemen. Informatik-Spektrum (1979) 2, pp. 194–203.

[59] E.G. Schlechtendahl, G. Enderle: Ansätze zu Methodenbanken im technisch-wissen-schaftlichen Bereich. Angewandte Informatik 8 (1982), pp. 399–409.

[60] H. Barth: Grundlegende Konzepte von Methoden- und Modellbanksystemen. Ange-wandte Informatik 8 (1980), pp. 301–309.

[61] R. Eggensberger: Design eines interaktiven didaktisch orientierten Methodenbank-systems. Angewandte Informatik 9 (1981), pp. 394–399.

[62] H. Noltemeier: Modelle — Methoden — Daten. In: H. Noltemeier (ed.): Computer-gestützte Planungssysteme. Würzburg (1976) Physica-Verlag, pp. 247–253.

[63] B. Schips: Ein Beitrag zum Thema "Methodenbanken". Angewandte Informatik 11 (1977), pp. 465–470.

[64] E.G. Schlechtendahl: Der Systemkern REGENT als Basis zur Entwicklung tech-nisch-wissenschaftlicher Programmsysteme. 9. Int. Kongress über die Anwendungen der Mathematik in den Ingenieurwissenschaften, Weimar, 28.6.-4.7.1981, Hochschule für Architektur und Bauwesen, Heft 1 (1981), pp. 89–92.

6 Engineering Methods of CAD

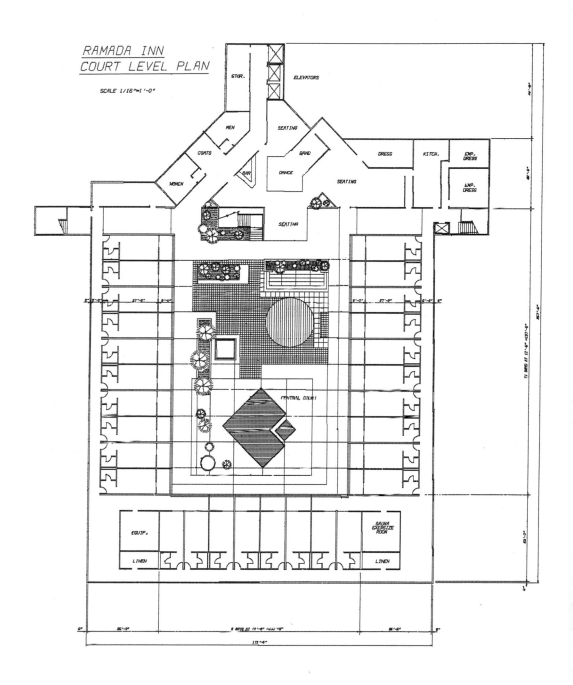

Architectural CAD application
(courtesy of Versatec, Santa Clara, USA)

6.1 Geometry Handling

According to Voelcker and Requicha [1] "Geometry plays a crucial role in nearly all design and production activities in the discrete goods industries. Curiously, the industries' primary means for specifying geometry — two-dimensional graphics — has not changed significantly for more than a century. Dramatic changes are likely to occur in the next decade, however, because the deficiencies of current methods are retarding the progress of automation and are stimulating the development of new, computationally oriented schemes for handling mechanical geometry."

They consider three different kinds of problems:

- Development of modelling schemes for representing as data the assemblies, stock (raw materials), and the capabilities of particular tools that affect manufacturing, assembly, and inspection processes.
- Development of algorithms that will automatically produce (from the data models of parts, assemblies, stock and tools) manufacturing, assembly inspection plans, and command data for numerically controlled tools.
- Design, implementation, and testing of integrated computer systems which embody such representation and planning systems.

We will deal here with the first kind of problem. First we will very briefly present some fundamentals in geometry: in particular perspective transformation and rotation in 3-D space; then we will discuss the problem of hidden-line and hidden-surface detection, and finally the geometric specification of parts and assemblies.

6.1.1 Introduction: Points in 3-D Space

Linear transformations of points in 2-D space and 3-D space play a fundamental role in all geometric problems. The basic operations are:

- translation;
- rotation;
- scaling;
- perspective view or projection.

Matrix algebra is the appropriate tool for performing these functions. Here we will discuss only the 3-D case. For 2-D, we would simply have to omit one dimension.

Points are usually represented as 3x1 column matrices or 1x3 row matrices. The operations of rotation and scaling can be represented as multiplication of the point vectors by appropriate square matrices. If row matrices are chosen for representing points (as we will do here), the multiplication is from the left-hand side: point·matrix. If one operation is to be followed by a second one, the second matrix is simply multiplied from the left-hand side again: point· matrix$_1$·matrix$_2$.

Translation

Translation of a point is represented by adding the row matrix of the endpoint of the displacement vector. Thus, when a large number of points is undergoing the same sequence of transformations (for example, when they are all to be rotated, then translated and finally scaled in the same way), the three operations cannot be combined into a single one, as would be possible for a sequence of three rotations (by multiplying the matrices in proper sequence). However, there is a way to convert the translation operation into a multiplication: the introduction of "homogeneous coordinates" [2]:

– The point [x y z] has the homogeneous coordinates [x y z 1]
  or, even more generally, [ax ay az a],
  where a is an arbitrary scalar.

   Now, instead of translating [x y z] by adding, say, $[d_x \ d_y \ d_z]$, we write:

$$[ax \ ay \ az \ a] \cdot \begin{bmatrix} 1 & 0 & 0 & 0 \\ 0 & 1 & 0 & 0 \\ 0 & 0 & 1 & 0 \\ d_x & d_y & d_z & 1 \end{bmatrix}$$

   Homogeneous coordinates allow us even to handle points at infinity properly: the homogeneous coordinate [x y z 0] identify a point at an infinite distance on the line directed from the origin of the 3-D coordinate system towards the point [x y z].
   Whether a system operates with natural coordinates or with homogeneous coordinates is an essential design decision. Systems that perform a large number of identical linear transformations will benefit significantly from homogeneous coordinates (interactive systems without hidden-line removal, for example). This statement applies particularly when special hardware is provided for performing the 4x4 matrix multiplication. Some high-performance graphics workstations offer this feature for the real-time 3-D manipulation of wire-frame graphics (wire-frame model = a 3-D model consisting of points and straight lines connecting them). For systems in which other functions dominate (such as hidden-line determination or non-geometrical applications), the natural coordinates may be the better choice.

Rotation

The rotation of a point in the x−y plane is shown in Fig. 6.1. Returning to natural coordinates, the rotation matrix R_z is given by Eq. (6.1).

$$\begin{bmatrix} \cos \alpha_z & \sin \alpha_z & 0 \\ -\sin \alpha_z & \cos \alpha_z & 0 \\ 0 & 0 & 1 \end{bmatrix} \qquad (6.1)$$

   A rotation about an arbitrary axis may always be defined in terms of a sequence of three rotations by α_x, α_y, α_z around the three axes (x, y ,z), respec-

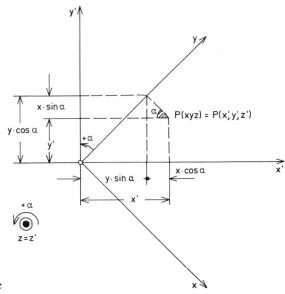

Fig. 6.1. Rotation in the x-y-plane

tively. As each of the rotations is defined by a rotation matrix like Eq. (6.1), the complete 3-D rotation is defined by the overall rotation matrix R where

$$R = R_x \cdot R_y \cdot R_z \qquad (6.2)$$

with

R_x = rotation in the yz-plane about the x axis followed by
R_y = rotation in the xz-plane about the y axis followed by
R_z = rotation in the xy-plane about the z axis.

The rotated point has the new natural coordinates

$$[x\ y\ z] \cdot R \qquad (6.3)$$

where

$$R = \begin{bmatrix} A & B & C \\ D & E & F \\ G & H & I \end{bmatrix} \qquad (6.4)$$

and

$A = \cos \alpha_y * \cos \alpha_z$
$B = \cos \alpha_y * \sin \alpha_z$
$C = -\sin \alpha_y$
$D = \sin \alpha_y * \sin \alpha_x * \cos \alpha_z - \cos \alpha_x * \sin \alpha_z$
$E = \sin \alpha_y * \sin \alpha_x * \sin \alpha_z + \cos \alpha_x * \cos \alpha_z$
$F = \cos \alpha_y * \sin \alpha_x$
$G = \sin \alpha_y * \cos \alpha_x * \cos \alpha_z + \sin \alpha_x * \sin \alpha_z$
$H = \sin \alpha_y * \cos \alpha_x * \sin \alpha_z - \sin \alpha_x * \cos \alpha_z$
$I = \cos \alpha_y * \cos \alpha_x$

Eqs. (6.3) and (6.4) describe a rotation around the origin of the coordinate system. The rotation around some arbitrary rotation center $[x_c \ y_c \ x_c]$ can be achieved by first translating the point by $-[x_c \ y_c \ x_c]$ (which would bring the rotation center into the origin), then rotating and finally translating back by $+[x_c \ y_c \ x_c]$. The advantage of using homogeneous coordinates is that these three operations can very easily be combined into a single matrix multiplication.

Scaling

Scaling of a point also fits into the matrix multiplication scheme. A point whose coordinates should be scaled by factors s_x, s_y, s_z in the x, y, and z directions will have the new natural coordinates given as:

$$[x y z] \cdot \begin{bmatrix} s_x & 0 & 0 \\ 0 & s_y & 0 \\ 0 & 0 & s_z \end{bmatrix} \tag{6.5}$$

Scaling with respect to an arbitrary point is best done in homogeneous coordinates in a similar way as rotating around an arbitrary point.

Projection

For perspective view or projection, we restrict our discussion first to the central projection from an origin that is located on the z-axis at $[0 \ 0 \ c_z]$ onto a plane parallel to the $x-y$-plane at an elevation c_z. The coordinates $[X \ Y]$ of the projected point are then given by:

$$X = \frac{c_z - q_z}{c_z - z} \cdot x$$

$$Y = \frac{c_z - q_z}{c_z - z} \cdot y \tag{6.6}$$

For the special case where $q_z = 0$, we obtain

$$X = \frac{c_z}{c_z - z} \cdot x = \frac{1}{1 - \frac{z}{c_z}} \cdot x$$

$$Y = \frac{c_z}{c_z - z} \cdot y = \frac{1}{1 - \frac{z}{c_z}} \cdot y \tag{6.7}$$

Using homogeneous coordinates, we obtain a rather simple 4x4 matrix for this projection. The projected point has the coordinates

$$[ax \ ay \ az \ a] \cdot \begin{bmatrix} 1 & 0 & 0 & 0 \\ 0 & 1 & 0 & 0 \\ 0 & 0 & 0 & -1/c_z \\ 0 & 0 & 0 & 1 \end{bmatrix} \tag{6.8}$$

A general central projection from an arbitrary point onto an arbitrary projection plane may be obtained by combining rotation and translation operations so as to achieve the standard situation described here. With homogeneous coordinates, these operations may be combined into a single matrix. For further details on transformations in 3-D space see [3], for example.

In CAD, parallel normal projection plays a central role, as standard design drawings represent their objects in this way. For a top view of an object, we have to project its points onto the $x-y$-plane from a point at infinity on the z-axis. Using Eq. (6.7), we obtain for this standard case:

$$\lim_{c_z \to \infty} \frac{c_z}{c_z - z} = 1 \tag{6.9}$$

or, as we would expect:

$$\begin{aligned} X &= x \\ Y &= y \end{aligned} \tag{6.10}$$

This projection has several advantages. It clearly avoids a tangential intersection of line-of-sight and the projection plane, thus eliminating the problem of having to handle points at infinity. It avoids strange distortions of the projected picture, which sometimes make it difficult to recognize an object from a central projection. It requires a minimum of computation, as the projection simply implies dropping one of the coordinates of a 3-D point. For top view, the z-coordinate has no influence on the representation: it is only used for visibility testing. Parallel normal projection minimizes the program run-time and simplifies the visibility-test procedures.

The most general projection implies that we specify independently:

– the projection origin;
– the projection plane;
– origin and directions of the 2-D coordinate system in the projection plane.

Schuster [4] has treated the general projection problem using vector algebra in natural coordinates instead of homogeneous coordinates. Here, we briefly outline his approach. Underscored letters in the subsequent paragraphs indicate vectors. A point p is to be projected onto plane B. B is defined by a point $r \varepsilon$ B and the normal vector n (see Fig. 6.2):

– 3-D space: coordinates (x, y, z) with base vectors e_x, e_y, e_z;
– 2-D space: coordinates (X, Y) with base vectors e_X, e_Y;
  these unit vectors will be chosen such that the origin of the (X,Y) coordinate system coincides with the projection of the origin of the 3-D space; the directions of the 2-D coordinate will be defined later;
– plane B: point r and normal n;
– 3-D point: p;
– projection origin: q;
– projected point: x in 3-D space, X in 2-D space.

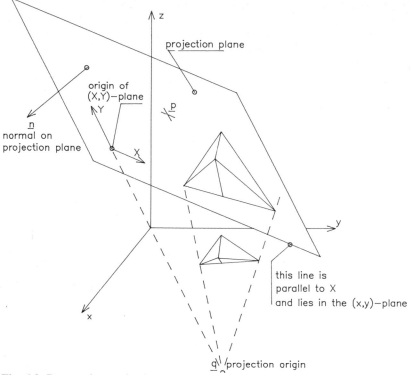

origin of
(X,Y)–plane

n
normal on
projection plane

projection plane

this line is
parallel to X
and lies in the (x,y)–plane

q / projection origin

Fig. 6.2. Perspective projection

The plane is given by equation

$$(x-r)\cdot n=0 \tag{6.11}$$

The projection beam through p and its projection q is given in vector notation as:

$$x=p+t(q-p) \tag{6.12}$$

with t as a scalar parameter. From these two equations we obtain immediately:

$$(p+t(q-p)-r)\cdot n=0 \tag{6.13}$$

We can solve this equation for the parameter t, which can then be inserted into (6.12) to obtain the equation for the projected point in 3-D space:

$$x=\frac{((q\cdot n)-(r\cdot n))\,p+((r\cdot n)-(p\cdot n))\,q}{(q-p)\cdot n} \tag{6.14}$$

X in the 2-D space must coincide with x in the 3-D space:

$$X=X\,e_X+Y\,e_Y=x \tag{6.15}$$

So far, the base vectors e_X and e_Y in the 2-D space are arbitrary. The x-direction e_X may, for instance, be chosen to coincide with the line of intersection of the projection plane B with the $x-y$-plane in the 3-D space, in such a way that the 3-D space origin is projected onto the 2-D space origin. The equations of these planes in 3-D space are as follows (with subscripts 1, 2 and 3 indicating the vector components in the 3-D space):

$$B: n_1 x + n_2 y + n_3 z = 0$$
$$x-y\text{-plane}: z = 0$$

Thus, after normalization, we obtain:

$$e_x = \frac{1}{(n_1^2 + n_2^2)^{\frac{1}{2}}} (-n_2, n_1, 0) \tag{6.16}$$

The Y-component must be orthogonal to both e_x and n. Hence:

$$e_y = n \times e_x$$

$$e_y = \frac{1}{(n_1^2 + n_2^2)^{\frac{1}{2}}} (-n_1 n_3, -n_2 n_3, n_1^2 + n_2^2) \tag{6.17}$$

With Eqs. (6.14), (6.15), (6.16) and (6.17), we can now determine the components X und Y of the 2-D vector X. Eqs. (6.14) and (6.15) are used, together with e_x and e_y as expressed by Eqs. (6.16) and (6.17). Multiplication by e_X makes the e_Y-component disappear. We obtain:

$$X = \frac{(q \cdot n - p \cdot n)(p \cdot e_X) + (r \cdot n - p \cdot n)(q \cdot e_X)}{(q-p) \cdot n} \tag{6.18}$$

Similarly, multiplying Eq. (6.15) with e_Y results in:

$$Y = \frac{(q \cdot n - p \cdot n)(p \cdot e_Y) + (r \cdot n - p \cdot n)(q \cdot e_Y)}{(q-p) \cdot n} \tag{6.19}$$

After performing the vector multiplication and introducing the abbreviations:

$$|n| = (n_1^2 + n_2^2 + n_3^2)^{\frac{1}{2}} = 1$$
$$L_i^2 = 1 - n_i^2, \quad i = 1, 2, 3$$
$$d = q \cdot n$$
$$s = r \cdot n,$$

we obtain finally:

$$X = \frac{s(q_2 n_1 - q_1 n_2) + p_1(sn_2 - q_2 L_3^2 - q_3 n_2 n_3) + p_2(-sn_1 + q_1 L_3^2 + q_3 n_1 n_3) + p_3 n_3(q_1 n_2 - q_2 n_1)}{L_3 d - p_1 n_1 L_3 - p_2 n_2 L_3 - p_3 n_3 L_3}$$

$$Y = \frac{s(q_2 n_2 n_3 - q_1 n_1 n_3 + q_3 L_3^2) + p_1 n_1(sn_2 - q_3) + p_2 n_2(sn_3 - q_3) + p_3(q_1 n_1 + q_2 n_2 - sL_3^2)}{L_3 d - p_1 n_1 L_3 - p_2 n_2 L_3 - p_3 n_3 L_3} \tag{6.20}$$

6.1.2 The Hidden-Line/Hidden-Surface Problem

6.1.2.1 General Considerations

The problem of eliminating the hidden planes and edges of non-transparent 3-D solids, the so-called visibility problem, has been tackled since the middle of the '60s. Various algorithms have been designed by Appel, Encarnação, Galimberti & Montanari, Loutrel, Newell, Roberts, Schumacker, Warnock, Watkins, Weiss. For surveys see [5, 6, 7, 3].

Visibility algorithms may be classified as hidden-surface algorithms and hidden-line algorithms. Hidden line algorithms are designed for edge-oriented output tools, such as vector displays and plotters; hidden-surface algorithms are oriented towards raster output devices.

The basic procedural kernel of all these algorithms usually follows one of three distinct strategies, which may be classified as:

– surface test;
– point test;
– combined surface/point test.

Surface test: Here, as the name implies, a surface element is the basic entity tested. (A surface element is a portion of the whole surface. Its interior is described by some mathematical form, and it is connected to adjacent surface elements along its edges.) In its elementary form, this test deals with planar faces only. Its basic idea is that faces whose outward normal vector points towards the projection point, are visible, while all others are invisible. This test does not take into consideration that a surface element of a solid may be hidden by another surface element of the same body, or of another body. Thus it can be applied to single convex solids only. Furthermore, the surface test assumes that all edges of a visible face are entirely visible. Fig. 6.3 shows an example where a surface test would fail to determine the visibility properly. It could not determine that part of the front surface of solid 2 is hidden by solid 1. Formally, in the surface test the angle σ between the line of sight (from the projection origin to a face) and the normal vector N of the face (pointing outward from the solid) is determined from the inner product of these vectors according to Eq. (6.21). If the inner product is negative (or $\sigma < 90°$), then the face and of all its edges are visible as a whole:

$$N \cdot CQ = |N| \cdot |CQ| \cdot \cos(180° - \sigma) \leqq 0 \qquad (6.21)$$

N = external surface normal
CQ = line of sight

Hence, in Fig. 6.4 face F_1 is visible, while face F_2 is invisible. Since the surface test considers whole surfaces rather than single points, it is very fast but has limited applicability. A pure surface test can only be applied to *convex solids*, and this is often too strong a limitation.

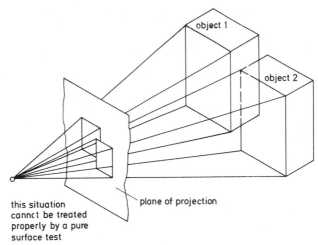

this situation
canne t be treated
properly by a pure
surface test

plane of projection

Fig. 6.3. The surface test cannot handle all situations properly

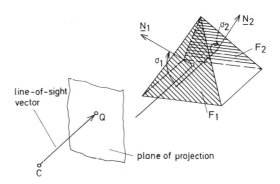

Fig. 6.4. Principle of the surface test

Point test: In this method, a line or curve is broken up into very small segments, each of which is drawn only if a testpoint on the segment is not hidden by any surface in space. In Fig. 6.5, the line from P_1 to P_2 consists of two parts $P_1 - P_g$ and $P_g - P_2$. With a pure point test, many test points on $P_1 - P_2$ would have to be considered in order to locate P_g properly. This approach requires large amounts of storage space and computer time. In principle, these tests have the advantage of being universally applicable, notably even for curved edges resulting from sculptured surfaces. However, because of the computer resources required, the pure point tests are not practical.

Combined point/surface test: In this category we place all procedures that attempt to combine the two tests. The manner in which this combination is implemented distinguishes the visibility test procedures that have been published.

We will now present two procedures of the combined point/surface test type.

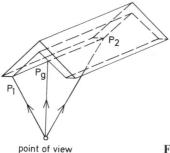

point of view   **Fig. 6.5.** Example illustrating the point test

6.1.2.2 The Priority Procedure

This procedure was developed for the solution of the hidden-line problem for solids bounded by *planar faces*. The priority procedure is very general. It can treat more than a single solid and is not restricted to convex shapes. Hence, holes, gaps, even individual surfaces (without thickness) can be treated. As a preparation for the priority procedure, the surface of the solid must be broken up into triangles (regardless of what its original representation was). For planar faces, this is a straightforward operation; but curved surfaces must be approximated by joining triangles. This segmentation into triangles will not be described further here (see [8], for example). From now on, we will consider the solid's surface as an unordered set of triangles. It is now possible to devise the visibility strategy in a way that will highly optimize running time and storage requirements.

The priority procedure consists of two main steps:

1. assignment of priority;
2. determination of coverings.

Without loss of generality, we can assume that the projection is onto the xy-plane with the projection origin on the positive z-axis. This standard situation can always be achieved by rotating and shifting the projection plane, the projection origin, and the solid accordingly. We start by collecting all surface elements F_i in a list, which we are now going to order according to their priority.

1. ASSIGNMENT OF PRIORITY
This step of the algorithm determines the order of processing of the triangles due to mutual hidings (involving the hiding of one surface by another on the same solid).

Given a set of triangles, let:

g, h = surface points, defined by their coordinates x, y, z;
i, j = running indices for surfaces;
F   = set of all surfaces

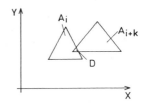

Fig. 6.6a. Determination of intersections in the
projection for the priority procedure

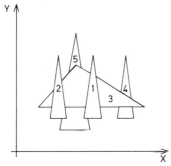

Fig. 6.6b. Assignment of priority

We investigate points g and h of surfaces F_i and F_j:

$$g \varepsilon F_i$$
$$h \varepsilon F_j$$

The triangles to be processed are projected by the projection operator f
onto the xy-plane:

$$f : F_i \rightarrow A_i$$
$$f : F_j \rightarrow A_j$$

where

A = projection of F.

The elements of the sets A_i and A_j (the projected points) are defined by
the x and y coordinates of their corners. A point c is now computed, such
that (Fig. 6.6a):

$c \varepsilon D$ where
D = intersection (A_i, A_j)

Hence, c is within the overlapping part of two projected triangles. From
the inverse mapping of this point c to F_i and F_j, one obtains the two corresponding z-coordinates on faces F_i and F_j. The highest z-coordinate of c among
these sets determines the highest priority. The list of all elements F_i is continuously reordered according to this priority.

If the intersection is the empty set, no priority assignment is possible. In
this case, the surface F_i is exchanged with the last element of the surface list,

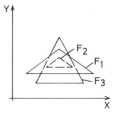

Fig. 6.6c. Removal of completely hidden boundaries

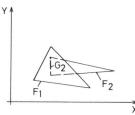

Fig. 6.6d. Removal of boundary lines (line G_2)

the list length is shortened by one, and the sorting process to determine priority starts anew. After completion of the algorithm, the result is a list of triangles, which can be processed from top to bottom to determine mutual coverings. Fig. 6.6b shows an example. In this case the priority list would be as follows: 1, 2, 3, 5, 4.

In the case of a raster display, we have now almost completed the whole task: we simply output all elements in the inverse order of their priority. Any surfaces elements, that would have to be hidden by others, would thus first be displayed, but would be covered later either partially or entirely by elements of higher priority. In the cae of vector oriented output devices, however, we have to continue the hidden-line removal by software.

2. DETERMINATION OF COVERINGS

After determination of priorities, we must investigate which parts of the triangles are to be drawn and which are not. For this purpose, all three boundary lines of a triangle are compared with all other surface edges of higher priority. We maintain a list of all (straight) line segments that will have to be drawn as visible. If a face is declared fully invisible, its boundary lines are removed from the line list, like those of F_2 in Fig. 6.6c. The next covering surface is then immediately examined.

If a surface is partially visible, then only the completely hidden lines are removed from the line list (line G_2 in Fig. 6.6d). Maintaining the line list raises the storage capacity requirements of this method, but saves substantial amounts of processing time.

The algorithms that determine coverings must distinguish between the following four situations, which are illustrated in Fig. 6.7:

a) the end-point of a partially hidden line is hidden;
b) the starting point of a partially hidden line is hidden;
c) both starting point and end-point are not hidden;
d) both starting point and end-point are hidden.

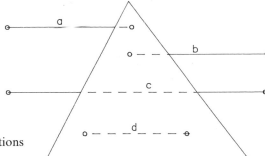

Fig. 6.7. Different line-covering situations encountered in the priority method

The formal treatment of these situations and their algorithmic implementation are described in [6].

6.1.2.3 The Overlay Procedure

The overlay procedure is applicable to solids whose surfaces are each defined by a so-called $u-v$ grid. Each surface element is defined by a function with two parameters u and v:

$$face_j = \{f_j(u,v), u_{j1} \leq u \leq u_{j2}, v_{j1} \leq v \leq v_{j2}\}$$

Thus, each surface element may be considered as being spanned by a $u-v$ line grid. The procedure uses the overlaying of an imagined Cartesian grid (on the projection plane) uponover the projection of the $u-v$ grid of the surfaces.

This procedure consists of the following steps:

a) calculation of the $u-v$ line grid;
b) construction of the Cartesian grid;
c) assignment of $u-v$ elements to the Cartesian grid;
d) calculation of the visibility of the nodes;
e) determination of the visible $u-v$ line elements.

a) *Calculation of the $u-v$ line grid:*

Using the corresponding surface equations, the individual nodes of all the $u-v$ line intersections are determined. Each node belongs to exactly one u-line and one v-line (see Fig. 6.8) and is determined by its x, y, and z coordinates.

b) *Construction of the Cartesian grid:*

Imagine an n by n Cartesian grid drawn on the projection plane. The grid lines form rectangles which will be used as a basis in the subsequent tests. The size of the grid can be chosen arbitrarily. In Fig. 6.9 a value of n=11 was selected. The surface element defined by the $u-v$ lines is overlaid on this grid. If a node is to be tested for visibility, we first determine which rectangle

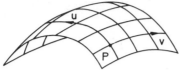

Fig. **6.8.** Coordinates of the nodes of a surface element

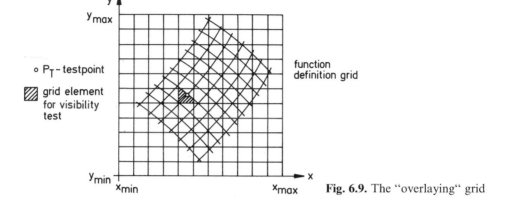

Fig. **6.9.** The "overlaying" grid

contains its projection. The visibility test now concerns itself only with this rectangle, and not with the whole surface. All the surface elements having sets of points in this rectangle must now be determined.

c) *Assignment of the u−v elements to the Cartesian grid:*

In this step, the individual surface elements are in this step approximated by rectangles, as shown in Fig. 6.10. The rectangles are constructed such that, after projection, their sides run parallel to the x and y axes. This is done to simplify the programming and to minimize computer running time. In the following steps d) and e), however, the true u−v elements will be considered instead of the approximation. Since the individual u−v elements are completely enveloped by their linear approximation, no information needed for determining the visibility is lost.

d) *Calculation of the visibility of the nodes:*

First the Cartesian grid lines which envelop the test point are determined (see Fig. 6.9):

$$X_n \leq X \leq X_{n+1}$$
$$Y_m \leq Y \leq Y_{m+1}$$

x, y = coordinates of the projection of the node to be tested.

Then we determine the surface elements whose projections have a non-empty intersection with the rectangle. For this purpose, we have to determine all elements which contain a point that will coincide with the test point after projec-

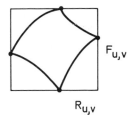

Fig. 6.10. The approximating rectangle $R_{u,v}$ $R_{u,v}$

no.	case	comment	meaning
1	⊘——⊛– – –○	1st end-point is visible	⊘ ... visible node
2	○– – –⊛——⊘	2nd end-point is visible	○ ... invisible node
3	⊘————⊘	both points are visible	⊛ ... visible intermediate point
4	○– – – – – –○	both points are invisible	—— ... visible line element
5	⊘–⊛–⊛–⊘	a test point on the u-v line not visible	– – – ... invisible line element
6	○–⊛–⊛–○	a test point on the u-v line is visible	

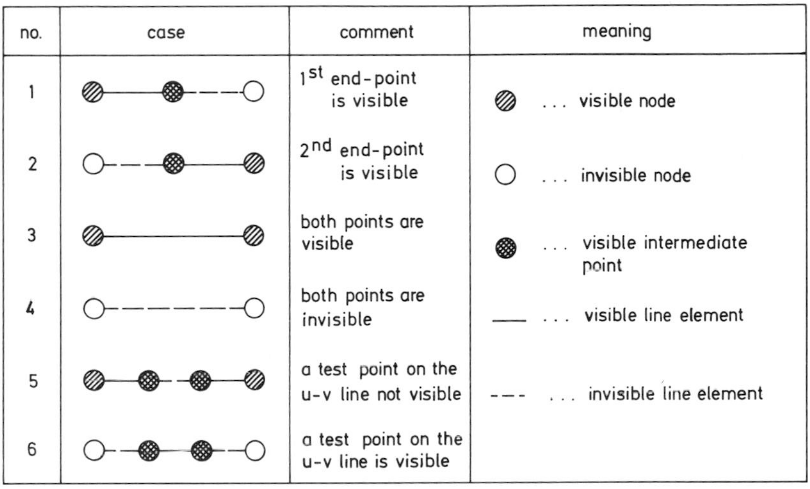

Fig. 6.11. Possibilities for the connection of nodes

tion. The $u-v$ elements are broken into two triangles and approximated by a plane. Now the triangles containing the test point are determined, and all corresponding z-coordinates z_D are computed using the planar approximation. Now we compare all values of z_D and consider all nodes with

$$z_D > z_M$$

as being invisible, where z_M is either a predefined value or the minimum value of all z_D's corresponding to the same test point.

e) *Determination of visible $u-v$ line elements:*

After having determined the visibility of the $u-v$ nodes on all surfaces, the next task is to test the visibility of the connecting $u-v$ grid lines. Visibility of two adjacent points does not necessarily imply that the whole connecting line is visible. Parts of the connection may be hidden by other surface elements. This is particularly important for coarse grids. Six different situations may be encountered, as listed in Fig. 6.11.

When only one end-point of a $u-v$ grid node connection is visible, we have to examine the connecting projection by means of test points in order to determine where the visibility ends. This testing proceeds in discrete steps, which have to be chosen as a compromise between accuracy (small steps) and running

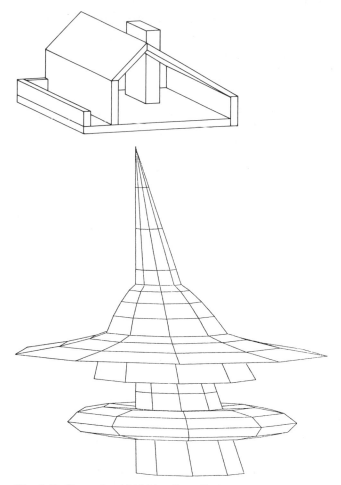

Fig. 6.12. Examples of hidden-line elimination with the priority procedure

time (large steps). The same procedure is required for testing the connection between two visible or two invisible nodes in order to detect any section of the connecting line that may be invisible (or visible).

Fig. 6.12 shows two examples, which were projected using the two visibility test procedures described above.

6.1.2.4 Generalization of the Visibility Problem

A visibility algorithm consists of several major steps. Each step provides a particular mapping, and the total algorithm is a concatenation of such mappings. Consequently, interposed between the domain of a visibility transformation (the set of 3-D objects) and its range (the set of visible segments), there may exist a sequence of intermediate representations. A formal definition of a visibility algorithm is possible.

Definition: A visibility algorithm is a quintuple

$$VA = (O, S, I, \Sigma, \Phi)$$

where

O is a set of 3-D objects. A 3-D object is defined as a set of coordinates plus a set of relations specifying the 3-D object topology. In general, a topology may be represented as a tree. "3-dimensional scene" is the root; the nodes are 3-D objects, faces, edges, and start/end-points of edges;

S is a set of visible segments in 2-D (the result of the hidden-surface transformations). These segments are the visible parts of the elements of O;

I is a set of "intermediate representations";

Σ is a set of strategy functions which control the sequence of application of all other functions of the algorithm;

Φ is a set of "transition functions" = {PM, IS, CT, DT, VT}

where

PM is a function that produces the perspective views ("projective mapping"). Hence, the domain of PM is 3-D, and its range is 2-D;

IS is a function that calculates the intersection of two graphical items. In 2-D the items are two line segments, in 3-D they are a polygon and a line segment;

CT is a function that performs a "containment test" in 2-D. CT checks whether a point is inside a given bounded surface. The result of CT is Boolean. It is "true" if the point is contained, and "false" otherwise;

DT is a function that performs a "depth test". DT compares two points and finds out which one has the greater depth, depending on the point of observation;

VT is a function that performs a "visibility test" for a given surface. VT yields a Boolean value, "true" if the surface is potentially visible and "false" if the surface is totally invisible.

Using this definition, visibility algorithms can now be formalized and represented graphically by "strategy diagrams" [3]. However, it is not a trivial task to convert the different algorithmic formulations of visibility-test procedures into a form that allows them to be mapped onto the generalized scheme. For seven visibility-test procedures — namely

– the "priority" method (Chapter 6.1.2.2);
– the "overlay" procedure (Chapter 6.1.2.3);
– Appel's "quantitative invisibility" method;
– Galimberti & Montanari's "nature" method;
– Warnock's "scan grid" method;
– Watkins' "scan line" method;
– Weiss' "analytical" method;

– this generalization was done by Klos [9]. Without going into further detail, let us note that such a generalization is required if one attempts to design and build a special-purpose computer for hidden-line and hidden-surface removal, which is not to be restricted to a single algorithm [10].

6.1.3 3-D Modelling

6.1.3.1 Introduction

During the design of a product, many aspects have to be considered, such as:

– function;
– shape;
– manufacturability;
– maintenance;
– economics.

The design of the shape is a central part of all the activities, as all other aspects have a significant influence on the shape. Some branches of industry are concerned mainly with 2-D shapes: electronic circuit layout, plant layout, and others. But even in these applications, the 3-D aspect will have to be considered to some extent. For many applications the "$2\frac{1}{2}$-D" approach is sufficient. The term $2\frac{1}{2}$-D does not have a precise definition; it merely indicates that not all aspects of three-dimensional geometry have to be fully considered. Geometrical arrangements that can be described as layers of 2-D layouts are called $2\frac{1}{2}$-D problems. Electronic circuit boards are a typical example. The third dimension is often indicated merely by an integer indicating the sequence number of the respective layer. In $2\frac{1}{2}$-D problems, we know automatically that the individual objects cannot cross each other, nor can they be folded. Hence, the algorithms can be much simpler and faster than in the fully 3-D case. A different case of "$2\frac{1}{2}$-D" geometry is the design of objects with rotational symmetry in mechanical engineering; even the design of gearings does not yet involve full 3-D problems, as long it is merely concerned with bodies of revolution with parallel axes. CAD methods for dealing with 2-D and $2\frac{1}{2}$-D objects were fairly well established by the end of the '70s. The same is true for many types of objects in 3-D space, particularly for objects with a single dominant dimension (networks of trusses, frames, or pipes). Surfaces in space (flat and sculptured) also have a deep and sufficiently broad theoretical foundation, upon which systems have been built. The theory of 3-D objects with unrestricted complexity, however, is not yet fully developed. All systems that have been developed have certain restrictions with respect to their applicability, even when they are able to model almost everything by means of approximations.

For computer-aided design of three-dimensional objects, the geometric aspect of part and assembly specifications is critically important [1]. Standard drafting practice suggests that geometric specification should be viewed as two- or three-phase process. Initially, a nominal or ideal 3-D object — a "shape" — is defined, typically by a drawing that does not account for tolerances. In the second phase, tolerances are introduced; at this point one no longer defines a single 3-D object, but rather a class of 3-D objects which are functionally equivalent and interchangeable in assembly processes. Attributes that would be conveyed by notes in engineering drawings are specified in the final phase, or in conjunction with tolerancing.

Engineering drawings are an imperfect medium for the specification of parts. Because engineers and technicians possess vast stores of pertinent "world knowledge" (the purpose of the device, general mechanical principles, etc.), they usually can extract from drawings the information needed to make and assemble parts correctly. Machines — or programs for interpreting drawings — usually cannot. Thus, new approaches are needed for the difficult problem of precisely specifying (to automatic manufacturing systems) what is to be made.

It is not hard to devise ad hoc schemes for manipulating geometry in computers, but these systems lack some basic properties that are essential for fully automatic production. For example: a reliable representation scheme should be complete and consistent; every part in a given class should have a representation, and every representation should specify exactly one part. None of the industrial graphics systems popular today exhibits these properties.

But there is more to geometric specification than nominal shape description. Any industrially viable medium must provide means for specifying tolerances, surface finishes, and similar geometric attributes in a complete and consistent manner. Further, a viable system must be convenient for others to use and it must be reasonably efficient.

6.1.3.2 Wire-Frame Models

Wire-frame models already have a long tradition in modelling 3-D objects. Stress and strain analysis of truss and frame structures was among the first large-scale computer applications for design analysis. The geometric model for these analyses is immediately suited for graphic representation. The (usually straight) elements of the structure may be plotted directly after perspective projection of the corresponding nodes. The elementary geometrical analysis tools indicated in Chapter 6.1.1 are sufficient for this task. Curved structural elements do not pose any serious additional problems.

The same technique has been applied successfully for plant layout. In many respects, pipes may be represented as straight or curved lines. Components (vessels, pumps etc.) can be approximated by a wire frame to some extent for visualization purposes. A cylindrical vessel, for instance, needs only two circles and four straight connecting lines in a coarse wire-frame model. However, this approach has its limitations, where the number of lines in a model becomes more abundant. The perspective view will then produce a mere mess of lines, from which the observer can no longer reconstruct a mental model of the three-dimensional situation. The two principal limitations with respect to visualization are:

- the impossibility of removing lines that ought to be considered as hidden;
- the lack of contour lines, which result from viewing sculptured surfaces.

Wire-frame models are suited for performing certain geometrical analyses with a design: for example, the distance of points can easily be retrieved. However, the wire-frame model can produce no information about surfaces and volumes. Questions of surface area, volume, weight, or possible interference of some body with another will remained unanswered. In fact, there is no way besides visual inspection of a number of perspectives by humans to tell whether the model represents a feasible 3-D body or assembly of bodies.

Despite these limitations, we should not forget that many existing CAD systems are based on wire-frame models, and also that there are many useful applications for these models in the early phases of design. The simplicity of the geometrical algorithms (based on points and their connections) lends itself to hardware implementations, so that the model or the viewing point may be changed in real time under the control of the operator at a workstation. Many design variants can thus be constructed and inspected with a minimum of delay.

6.1.3.3 Surfaces in Space

The next step toward increased complexity is the treatment of surfaces in space. Depending on the type of surfaces, we distinguish systems for

– flat surfaces;
– sculptured surfaces based on flat surface approximations;
– sculptured surfaces based on patches or (u,v)-grid lines;
– analytic surfaces;
– combinations of these types.

The approximation of surfaces in space by flat elements has become common practice in finite-element analysis of membrane, shell, or plate structures. Accuracy of analysis requires that the surface be broken down into a large number of elements anyway. The degree of approximation required for the analysis is generally sufficient for all visualization purposes. For complicated shapes, hidden-line removal is mandatory; but, as only flat surfaces are involved, a large number of visibility-test procedures are at the disposal of the application programmer. Quite often, a pure surface test (see Chapter 6.1.2) is sufficient, at least for some suitably chosen projections.

Many applications, however, call for the modelling of smooth surfaces. Typical such areas may be found in the design of aircrafts, ships, and cars. The design task is generally the smoothing (or fairing) of a previously rough surface approximation. Various optimization criteria may have to be applied (steady change in curvature, elimination of changes in sign of curvature, minimization of some weighted function of curvature). Only in rare cases can we describe the whole surface by a single analytical function. In general, the surface has to be composed from patches that join at their edges. The representation of sculptured surfaces as joining patches in parametric form —

$x = x(u, v, \{p\})$; $y = y(u, v, \{p\})$; $z = z(u, v, \{p\})$
with $u_1 < u < u_2$; $v_1 < v < v_2$
and $\{p\}$ = patch parameters

Table 6.1. Surface definition systems

System	Operations	Curve functions	Surface types
AUTOKON	fairing	cubic spline	—
EUKLID	interpolation	cubic spline	—
SYSTRID1	fairing, interpolation	polynomials	Bézier surfaces
VIKING	interpolation	polynomials	lofting
UNISURF	interpolation	Bézier curves	Bézier surfaces

— has proven to be a most powerful method. The patch parameters {p} are best defined on the basis of values associated with the nodes of the patch (coordinates, derivatives, curvature). Different methods for representing these patches can guarantee various degrees of continuity along the edge (as when continuous curvature is required). Coons's representation of patches was the pioneering work in this field [11]). Coons's patches belong to the *local* type of surface representation: if some change is made to one point, which forms the basis of some adjacent patches, then only the immediate environment of the surface is influenced. Other methods (such as Gordon's blending function interpolation [12]) are more global: a local change will influence the surface everywhere. More recently, one can notice an increasing trend towards the use of B-splines [13, 14].

The elementary operations which ought to be provided by a system that deals with sculptured surfaces are:

- definition and modification of surfaces;
- *interpolation*; that is, the evaluation of points that lie on the surface between the nodes of the defining (u,v)-grid;
- computation of the lines of intersection of the surface with an arbitrary plane;
- computation of the lines of intersection of two surfaces;
- *fairing*; that is, the determination of a surface that approaches a given rough approximation according to a specified smoothing criterion.

Table 6.1 lists a number of systems for surface treatment from [15].

For sculptured surfaces, as well as for non-convex 3-D objects, we have the very general problem that the edges of faces may be partially visible (parts of the edges may be hidden by faces of the same or other 3-D objects). Hence, for a complete and and accurate visibility test, we have to follow *all* the edges of all potentially visible faces and test (almost) *all* points on them to see whether they are hidden by any other face. The complexity of this task rises dramatically as the number of 3-D objects (or the number of faces of each 3-D object) is increased. The performance of 3-D-object-modelling programs depends strongly upon their strategies to eliminate as quickly as possible many of the faces against which a point has to be tested. It is the old principle of "divide and conquer" that has to be used to cut the immense problem into a number of smaller ones. How the subdivision is accomplished is a matter of strategy, and represents a characteristic feature of the different visibility-test procedures. In any case, computer science techniques for sorting and searching are an indispensable ingredient of all these methods. The two combined point/surface test procedures described in Chapter 6.1.2 are typical examples of the subdivision principle. More recently, the principle has been investigated in greater detail in [16, 17, 18].

6.1.3.4 3-D Solid Modelling

Representation schemes for 3-D objects (often called "solids") should satisfy the following criteria [19]:

- validity;
  We require that there exists a real 3-D object corresponding to any given representation. A single line dangling in space, or M.C. Escher's famous drawings of impossible objects, may illustrate the notion of validity by counterexample.
- completeness;
  We require that all the operations we provide in a system are applicable to all possible representations of solids within the schema used. For instance, if hidden-line removal could be applied to convex solids but not to non-convex ones, we would consider the scheme as incomplete.
- uniqueness;
  We require that there exists *only one* 3-D object corresponding to any given representation. Wire-frame representations may be ambiguous, and hence are not unique.
- conciseness;
  The schema for representation of solids should not contain redundant information.
- ease of creation and modification;
  In order to minimize the computational effort during interactions with the 3-D model, the internal representation should be as close as possible to the mental schema that the operator prefers when building or modifying a solid or an assembly of solids.
- efficiency;
  The efficiency of the algorithms operating on the internal representation of solids depends significantly on that internal representation. Different representations may be better suited for different algorithms. Hence, it may be advantageous to jeopardize the principle of conciseness for the sake of greater efficiency, and to maintain some redundancy in the data model.

The elementary operations which we expect to be available for 3-D models are:

- to build a model;
- to modify a model;
- to generate a projective display for line-drawing hardware;

Table 6.2. Origin of selected 3-D modelling systems

System	Country	Organization	Implementation language(s)	Reference
SHAPES	USA	Draper Lab.	BAL/360	[20,21]
TIPS	Japan	Hokkaido Univ.	FORTRAN	[22,23]
GDP/GRIN	USA	IBM	FORTRAN	[24,25]
PADL-1	USA	Univ. Rochester	FLECS + FORTRAN	[26,27]
PADL-2	USA	Univ. Rochester + industries	FLECS + FORTRAN	[28]
SYNTHAVISION	USA	MAG-I	FORTRAN	[29,30]
GMSOLID	USA	General Motors	PL/1	[31,32]
U.M./BORKIN	USA	Univ. Michigan	FORTRAN	[33]
BUILD-2	UK	Cambridge Univ.	Algol 68	[34,35]
CADD	USA	McAuto	FORTRAN + BAL	
COMPAC	FRG	T.U. Berlin	FORTRAN	[36,37]
DESIGN	USA	MDSI	Pascal	[38,35]
EUCLID	France	Matra/Datavision	FORTRAN	[39]
GLIDE	USA	Carnegie-Mellon Univ.	Bliss + Pascal	[40,41]
MEDUSA	UK	CIS Ltd.	FORTRAN	
PROREN-2	FRG	Ruhr Univ.	FORTRAN	[42]
ROMULUS	UK	Shapedata Ltd.	FORTRAN	[43]
GIPSY	FRG	KfK	REGENT + PL/1	[4,44]

- to generate a projective display for area-drawing hardware (gray-scale or color) with hidden surfaces removed;
- to identify objects (points, edges, faces, volume elements) in the 3-D model by pointing to their 2-D representations within a display;
- to evaluate collisions between separate solids;
- to compute geometrical and inertial properties (surface area, volume, mass, center of mass, moments of inertia).

Other operations are desired in various applications:

- generation of manufacturing information;
- treatment of imprecise dimensions (tolerances);
- generation of shadows produced by various light sources; representation of light reflections on the surfaces;
- treatment of translucent solids.

A number of solid modelling systems are listed in Tables 6.2 and 6.3. (These tables are based on [45].) 3-D modelling systems may be distinguished in various ways. Their fundamental characteristics are:

- the representation schema for solids;
- the user functions for building solid models;
- the types of surfaces allowed;
- the language facilities provided for the user to formulate the modelling operations.

Table 6.3. Basic facilities of 3-D modelling systems

System	Primary representation scheme	Domain defined by half-spaces	Input based on	Input modalities
SHAPES	⎡ CSG based on	QS	CSG	SC; T/I; (IG)
TIPS	⎣ half-spaces ⎤	"arbitrary"	CSG	T/B
GDP/GRIN	⎡ CSG	QS	CSG	SC; IG
PADL-1	based on	pl + cyl(⊥)	CSG	T/I
PADL-2	bounded	QS	CSG	SC; IG
SYNTHAVISION	⎣ primitives ⎦	QS + SS	CSG	T/B
GMSOLID	hybrid CSG + B-rep.	QS	CSG + sweep	IG
U.M./BORKIN	B-rep.	pl	CSG + sweep	T/I; (IG)
BUILD-2	B-rep.	QS	CSG + EOP	SC; IG
CADD	B-rep.	QS + SS	sweep	IG
COMPAC	B-rep.	QS	CSG + sweep	T/B?
DESIGN	B-rep.	QS	CSG	IG
EUCLID	B-rep.	≃ QS	CSG + sweep	T/I; IG?
GLIDE	B-rep.	pl	CSG + sweep + EOP	SC; T/I
MEDUSA	B-rep.	≃ QS + SS	CSG + sweep	IG
PROREN-2	B-rep.	QS	CSG + sweep	T/I
ROMULUS	B-rep.	QS	CSG + sweep	SC; T/I
GIPSY	half-spaces	QS	CSG	T/B

CSG = constructive solid geometry	pl = plane
B-rep = boundary representation	⊥ = orthogonal positioning
QS = quadric surfaces	≃ = approximate
SS = sculptured surfaces	SC = subroutine call
sweep = translational and/or rotational sweep	T/I = text/interactive
	T/B = text/batch-oriented
EOP = Euler operations	IG = interactive graphics
cyl = cylinders	(IG) = simple interactive graphics

Two representation schemes are commonly used in 3-D systems:

– the boundary representation (B-rep) scheme;
– the constructive solid geometry (CSG) model.

The boundary representation scheme is more familiar to the user who has previous experience with wire-frame models. Each solid is defined by its boundaries. Each boundary is a (planar or sculptured) surface bounded by edges of an adjacent boundary. Three or more edges join at nodes. The boundary representation is best suited for generating projective views, as the important elements for this operation (edges and faces) are readily available in the solid representation. Geometric and inertial properties may be computed from a boundary representation by means of Gaussian integration.

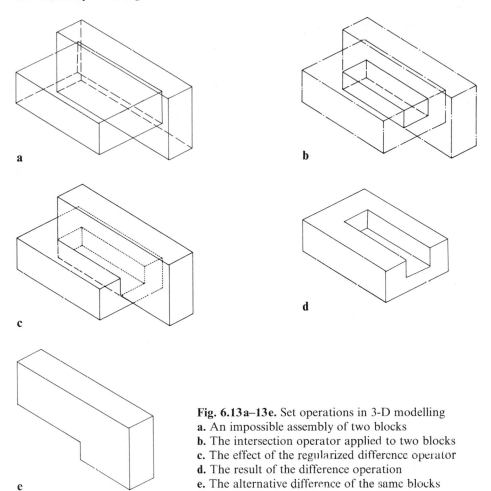

Fig. 6.13a–13e. Set operations in 3-D modelling
a. An impossible assembly of two blocks
b. The intersection operator applied to two blocks
c. The effect of the regularized difference operator
d. The result of the difference operation
e. The alternative difference of the same blocks

The constructive solid geometry representation is based on a two-level scheme. On the lower level, bounded volume primitives are defined on the basis of half-spaces (one half-space for a sphere, three for a circular cylinder, six for a square block). In simple cases, as when only rectangular blocks are used, the half-spaces may be defined by parameters (like position, orientation, and size) associated with the volume primitive, rather than being represented explicitly in the schema. On the second level, these primitives are combined by Boolean set operators (union, intersection, difference). More precisely, we have to use the regularized form of these set operators [46]. Figs. 6.13a through 6.13e illustrate the effects of particular operators. The principle advantage of CSG is that it guarantees the validity and uniqueness of the model: a boundary representation can always be derived in a unique way.

The boundary representation is not suited for input. Most systems (see Table 6.3) offer volume elements or half-spaces together with the above-mentioned set operations for formulating the model, in a way that is consistent with the internal CSG representation.

Another important technique for defining a solid is the sweeping operation. In the most general case, a bounded surface element is moved along an arbitrary trajectory in space. In most practical cases, the sweeping operation corresponds to a translation along a straight line, or to a rotation. These sweeping operations are particularly useful for modelling manufacturing processes.

Solid modelling systems generally allow one of the following classes of surfaces:

– planes;
  Although most industrial products have curved surfaces, solid modelling based on planar surfaces has a wide range of possible applications. Finite element analysis of a 3-D object is generally based on a model, which represents the 3-D object by a large number of small blocks (pyramids, for instance), thus approximating the surface in terms of numerous planes. The same principle of approximation may be generalized to other applications: display with hidden-line or hidden-surface removal, geometric and inertial analysis. Such approximations may require hundreds or thousands of flat patches to be treated. However, the algorithms for treating planar surfaces are simple, well-known, and fast. Some care must be taken not to show those lines between patches that result from the method of approximation without existing in reality.
– quadric surfaces;
  Quadric surfaces are defined by a second-order polynomial in the three spatial coordinates. Quadric surfaces are very popular in solid modelling systems. Most systems, however, do not treat the general quadric surface, but are restricted in some way. Spheres, cylinders, and cones (and planes of course) are the common quadrics. Some systems provide the facility to handle toroidal surfaces as well. The need for treating the torus arises from the many practical occurrences of this shape.
– sculptured surfaces defined on a (u,v)-grid;
  Sculptured surfaces, as the kind popular in surface-handling systems (B-spline patches, for instances), play an "outsider" role in solid modelling. The algorithms for performing the required operations in 3-D modelling have not yet been developed to a state of satisfactory completeness and efficiency. In particular, the combination of solids defined by different types of surfaces (some by quadrics, others by patches) is a yet unresolved problem.
– super-quadric surfaces;
  Recently, the theory of super-quadrics has made some progress [47]. Super-quadrics are generalizations of quadrics. For simplicity, we can use a two-dimensional space to illustrate this generalization. While

$$x = a \cos \vartheta; \; y = b \sin \vartheta$$

is the parametric representation of an ellipse, the super-ellipse

$$x = a \cos^\varepsilon \vartheta; \; y = b \sin^\varepsilon \vartheta$$

represents a wide range of two-dimensional shapes, from a slightly rounded rectangle (with sides a and b) to an image which looks like an "X" (or two thin sticks of lengths a and b crossing each other perpendicularly at their mid-points). Super-quadrics can describe solids of relatively complicated shape by means of very few surfaces, at least in an approximate way. They also have the potential to describe slightly rounded edges on an otherwise rather square body. Whether super-quadrics will find their way into practice is yet to be seen.

– fillets and chamfers;
Most technical objects have edges that deviate only slightly from the ideal mathematical shape. Fillets and chamfers are typical examples of such deviations. Two approaches may be taken to handle these features: the "correct" representation based on the same techniques as the overall solid model (boundary representation or constructive solid geometry) or the approximate representation as an attribute associated with the edges of a boundary representation. In the latter case, these deviations from ideal geometry cannot be treated by the same overall algorithms. They can be used to modify the displayed picture locally in a manner suitable for perception by a human. But their treatment in hidden-line or hidden-surface algorithms, as well as in geometric or inertial computations, is incomplete. Efficiency considerations nevertheless call for such a simplified special treatment of minor local modifications of the geometry.

Historically, solid modelling systems were first oriented towards batch data processing. This was due to the large amount of storage and computer time required for analyzing 3-D models. Consequently, the original language interface for the user was either a package of subroutines or a command or programming language (see Table 6.3). Even today, 3-D model analysis is typically a batch job requiring several of minutes of fast processor time for non-trivial problems. For building the model, however, graphic interaction is becoming attractive. Hidden-line removal is generally suppressed during model-building. The resulting picture in the building phase very much resembles a wire-frame model, showing all (hidden and non-hidden) lines; but the data structure being built represents the correct 3-D model.

The computer graphics literature gives examples of computer generated pictures of three-dimensional objects, that approach the quality of color photographs. Light source reflections on the surfaces, translucency and shadows significantly contribute to this effect. Such pictures may be generated on color raster display devices using the "ray-casting" technique. With this technique, an area of the projection plane is divided into a number of pixels (picture elements); lines of sight are followed from the anticipated position of the eye to each one of these pixels; the point of intersection of this line of sight with the first surface is then analysed by continuing along the lines to all light sources;

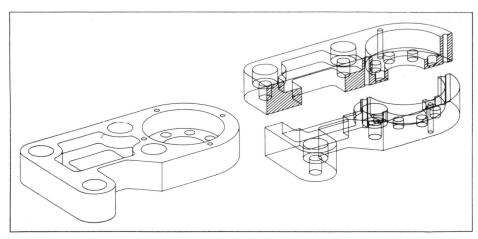

Fig. 6.14. A perspective view of a 3-D solid model (line drawing) (courtesy of Ferranti Cetec Graphics Ltd., Edinburgh, UK)

any light source that is not hidden by interfering other surfaces will contribute to the intensity and color of this visible point. Similarly, lines of sight are followed through translucent material. For high resolution images (for example, 1024 by 1024 pixels) the computational effort is generally beyond what can be justified in a CAD environment.

Figs. 6.14 (courtesy of Ferranti Cetec Graphics, Ltd.) and 6.15 (page 343, courtesy of Applicon) show two examples of projective representations of solid models. Other examples will be given in Chapter 7.

6.2 Numerical Methods

6.2.1 Introduction

In the late 1960s and especially in the early 1970s, a tremendous development of numerical methods for design applications took place. This rapid development resulted from a feedback process involving both computer technology and engineering sciences:

– computers became increasingly powerful, and cheaper as well. Thus methods which required many computations and a large memory could now be applied at moderate expense, while in previous decades hundreds of man-years would have been required to do the same computations manually;
– the successful application of numerical methods led to intensive research with the goal of making more and bigger problems tractable by these methods.

Numerical methods have had their greatest impact on the analysis part of the design process. The most widely known group of methods are the *finite element methods*; they are primarily used to determine stresses and deformations in structural components for prescribed load cases. *Finite difference methods* play a dominant role in determining the forces which are exerted by fluids (gases or liquids) upon structures. Many methods have been developed for the *simulation* of dynamic processes (both continuous and discontinuous). *Optimization methods* may to some extent replace human judgment in the analysis-synthesis-evaluation loop of the design process. So far, however, their applicability is restricted mainly to variational design (see Fig. 3.13). Whether deterministic optimization methods (as opposed to artificial intelligence methods) are suited to play a major role in the synthesis process (contributing to the design of a schema rather than determining optimal values of attributes in the schema) is still an open question.

The progress achieved in many industries (such as aerospace, nuclear, electronics, and armaments) would not have been possible without the integration of numerical methods into the design process. However, the problems increased along with the computing power. For many problems, even today's computers are too small and too slow.

6.2.2 Finite Element Methods

Finite element methods (FEM) are most widely applied in structural analysis, although applications in fluid flow and thermal analysis are also quite successful. A tremendous literature on finite element methods is available. One of the fundamental sources is [48]. It is not our intention to provide a thorough introduction to the numerical method of finite elements. In this respect, the reader should study the relevant literature, such as [49, 50, 51]; instead, we will concentrate on the question of embedding finite element analysis methods into the CAD process. The importance of finite element methods for CAD stems from the fact that a number of general-purpose finite element programs has become commercially available, and a large community of engineers has obtained the necessary expertise to apply these programs to their problems. Detailed knowledge of the finite element theory and the associated mathematical methods is not required for most practical applications.

In order to imbed finite element programs properly into the design process, the availability of such a program alone is not sufficient. Fig. 6.16 shows a family of programs, which is a prerequisite for successful applications.

- As a first step, based upon the geometrical definition of the object to be analysed, a finite element mesh must be generated. For small problems this mesh may be prepared manually; but for problems with more than a hundred elements or so, automatic mesh generation by a (usually batch) program is advised.
- In most cases, inspection of the generated mesh by experienced users will indicate that the first mesh is not completely satisfactory. The user may want to refine the mesh in certain areas to improve the resolution and accuracy of the analysis; he may want to make the mesh coarser in irrelevant areas for reduction of the computer costs, or he may want to add geometrical

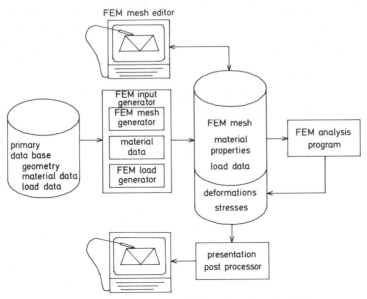

Fig. 6.16. Program structure for FEM applications in CAD

details which are significant for the structural analysis but could not be derived automatically from the geometrical data in the primary data base. This modification of the finite element mesh is best done at an interactive graphics terminal.

– Material data and data describing the load cases must then be added to the finite element program data base.

– Finite element programs usually require significantly more computer resources than their input generators and post-processors. They are typically large batch programs which may consume hours of computer time, depending upon problem size and complexity. It is common practice to have the input generators and the post-processor near the design engineer and to submit the finite element analysis job to a large remote computer (see Chapter 4.3.4).

– Presentation of the results for complex structures is in itself a nontrivial task. For interpretation and evaluation of the results, the user may want to see certain parts of the structure from various view points, with the resulting deformations and stress representations superimposed. Here again, interactive graphics has become a fruitful tool.

Quite often, the interpretation of the result leads to the need for further analysis of the same structure with a modified mesh and/or modified load case, in a repeated application of the above steps until the results are considered reliable. If the results are unsatisfactory in the light of the specification, another design iteration will be required, which is likely to produce changes in the geometrical data or material data of the primary data base. The finite element analysis will have to be redone, starting either from a new input generation or perhaps from a modification of the obsolete finite element data base. The latter procedure may be cheaper, but it introduces the risk of inconsistencies, along with the problems of data validity which were described in Chapter 3.3.5.1.

Programs for generation of the primary input are usually closely related to the objects to be analized. They are tailored to the particular application and to the schemas used to represent geometry, loads, and material information in the primary data base. They are generally not portable to other design objects or companies. Programs for interactive mesh modification (which in medium-size problems may also be used for mesh generation from scratch) and presentation post-processors are commercially available for a number of finite element programs. Quite a few of them provide interfaces for more than one such program.

Many finite element programs were developed for application in a limited environment only. The flexibilty of the finite element method, however, led to the development of a market which has been well established since the early '70s. Some of the finite element programs which have found international distribution are summarized in [52]. Some of them are well known in the CAD community: these include ANSYS [53], ASKA [54], NASTRAN [55], MARC [56], SAP [57], STRUDL-II [58]. The summary of 43 general-purpose structural mechanics programs shown in Table 6.4 is taken from [59] and demonstrates the predominance of the finite element method for general-purpose structural mechanics.

In the 1960s and until early in the '70s, the development of finite element programs was at least partly concentrated around specialized research institutes. Comparative reviews and conferences about recent developments were quite common. Since then, many of the better-known programs are supported by and commercially available from various software houses or computer manufacturers. For instance, several versions of STRUDL exist which provide quite different capabilities. The proliferation of dialects which is typical of the FORTRAN world finds its parallel in the finite element program versions. Reliable and up-to-date information about the actual power of particular finite element programs should be obtained from the organizations that maintain these programs for sale, rent, or remote use (software houses, computer manufacturers, computer networks). Most valuable information is collected in the meetings and newsletters of the user communities that have been established for many of the better-known finite element programs. One of the largest user groups of this kind is the ICES USER'S GROUP gathered around ICES-STRUDL.

Flexibility is the advantage of the finite element method. Thus, expertise obtained through the analysis of one type of structure is immediately helpful for other structures. The most widely used type of analysis is static analysis, based on the linear theory of elasticity. Problems with several times ten thousand degrees of freedom are not unusual in static analysis. Dynamic analyses are also quite common. Because these require more computer power, the structural model is generally condensed to a smaller number of degrees of freedom (up to several thousands). Many programs support the analysis of free vibrations, transient response to time-varying loads, and power spectrum analysis for random excitations (earthquake loads, for instance). Because the individual finite element programs do not overlap completely in their capacities and requirements

Table 6.4. Comparison of general-purpose structural mechanics programs

KEY:
+ = YES
− = NO
U = undefined

Column groups:
- **DISCRETIZATION METHOD** (1–8): 1 DISPLACEMENT, 2 HYBRID, 3 MIXED, 4 FE-FOURIER SERIES, 5 FINITE DIFFERENCE, 6 POINT MATCHING, 7 FORWARD INTEGRATION, 8 OTHER
- **TYPES OF GEOMETRY** (9–12): 9 1 DIMENSIONAL, 10 2 DIMENSIONAL, 11 2 DIM. CURVED, 12 3 DIMENSIONAL
- **LOADING CASES** (13–18): 13 STATIC, 14 FREE MODES, 15 FORCED MOTION, 16 TRANSIENT (GENERAL), 17 STATIONARY TEMP.-FIELDS, 18 INSTAT. TEMP.-FIELDS
- **TYPES OF MATERIALS** (19–28): LINEAR ELASTIC [19 ISOTROPIC, 20 ANISOTROPIC, 21 LAYERED, 22 SANDWICH, 23 TEMP.-DEPENDENT], 24 NONLIN. ELASTIC, 25 RIGID-PLASTIC, 26 ELAST.-STRAIN HARD., 27 OTHER TYPES, 28 LARGE DEFLECTIONS
- **COMPUTER REQUIREM.** (29–33): 29 IN-CORE PROGRAM, 30 MIN. MEMORY SIZE (K WORDS), 31 NO. OF DISK-FILES, 32 NO. OF TAPES, 33 RANDOM ACCESS
- **SOFTWARE ASPECTS** (34–43): 34 PROGRAM LANGUAGE, 35 PREPROCESSOR, 36 POSTPROCESSOR, 37 PLOT ROUTINES, 38 INTERACTIVE MODES, 39 RESTART CAPABILITY, 40 ERROR DIAGNOSTIC, 41 SUBSTRUCTURING, 42 DISTR. BY DEVELOPER, 43 DISTR. BY SOFTWARE CENTER

PROGRAM NAME	1	2	3	4	5	6	7	8	9	10	11	12	13	14	15	16	17	18	19	20	21	22	23	24	25	26	27	28	29	30	31	32	33	34	35	36	37	38	39	40	41	42	43
1 AC50-A	U	U	U	U	U	U	U	U	−	+	−	−	+	−	−	−	+	−	+	+	+	+	−	−	−	−	−	−	+	20	−	−	−	F4	−	−	−	−	−	−	−	+	−
2 ADEPT	−	−	−	−	−	+	−	−	+	−	−	−	+	−	−	−	−	−	+	U	−	−	−	+	−	−	−	−	−	76	−	−	−	AT	−	−	−	−	+	+	+	U	U
3 AMSA 20	+	−	−	−	−	−	−	−	+	+	−	+	+	−	−	−	−	−	+	−	−	−	−	−	−	−	−	−	−	35	U	U	U	F5	−	−	−	−	−	−	+	U	−
4 ANSYS	+	−	−	+	−	−	+	−	+	+	+	+	+	+	+	+	+	U	+	+	+	+	+	−	−	+	+	+	−	50	1	−	+	F	+	+	+	+	+	+	+	+	−
5 ASAS	+	−	−	−	−	−	−	−	+	+	−	+	+	+	+	+	−	−	+	+	−	−	−	+	−	+	+	+	−	32	U	U	U	F	−	−	−	−	−	+	−	+	−
6 ASKA	+	−	−	+	−	−	−	−	+	+	+	+	+	+	+	+	+	−	+	+	+	−	−	+	+	+	+	−	−	32	1	U	+	F4	+	+	+	−	+	+	+	+	+
7 BASY	+	+	−	−	−	−	−	−	+	+	+	+	+	+	+	+	−	−	+	−	−	−	−	−	−	−	−	−	−	16	U	U	U	F	−	−	−	−	+	+	−	+	−
8 BERSAFE	+	−	−	−	−	−	−	−	+	+	−	+	+	+	−	−	−	−	+	−	−	−	−	−	+	−	+	+	−	~90	9	−	+	F4	+	+	+	−	+	−	+	−	−
9 BOSOR 4	−	−	−	+	−	−	−	−	−	−	+	+	+	+	+	+	−	−	+	+	+	+	−	+	+	+	+	−	−	64	1	−	+	F4	−	−	−	−	+	−	+	+	+
10 COSA	+	−	−	−	−	−	+	−	+	+	−	+	+	+	−	−	−	−	+	−	−	−	−	+	−	+	−	−	−	64	1	−	+	F	−	−	−	−	+	+	+	+	−
11 DYNAS	U	U	U	U	U	U	U	+	+	+	−	−	+	+	+	+	+	+	+	−	−	−	−	−	−	−	−	U	−	80	8	−	+	F	−	−	+	−	+	+	+	+	−
12 EASE 2	+	−	−	−	−	−	−	−	+	+	+	+	+	−	−	−	−	+	+	−	−	−	−	−	−	−	−	−	+	30	1	−	+	F/A	+	−	+	−	+	+	+	−	+
13 ELAS 75	+	−	−	−	−	−	−	−	+	+	+	+	+	−	−	−	−	−	+	+	+	+	−	+	−	−	−	−	+	20	−	−	U	F4	−	+	+	−	+	−	−	+	−
14 FARSS	+	−	−	−	+	−	−	−	−	−	+	+	+	+	+	+	−	−	+	+	−	−	+	−	−	−	−	−	−	20	1	−	+	F4	+	+	+	+	−	+	−	−	+
15 FESAP	+	−	−	−	−	−	−	−	+	+	+	+	+	+	+	+	−	−	+	−	−	−	+	−	−	−	−	−	−	20	8	−	1	F4	+	+	+	−	+	−	+	−	−
16 FLHE	+	−	−	−	−	−	−	−	+	+	−	+	−	−	−	−	+	+	+	−	−	−	−	−	−	−	−	−	−	60	U	U	U	F	−	−	−	−	−	+	U	+	−
17 ISOPAR SHL	+	−	−	−	+	+	+	−	−	+	+	+	+	−	−	−	−	−	+	−	+	+	+	−	−	−	−	−	−	65	9	−	+	F	−	−	−	−	+	−	+	−	−
18 ISTRAN/S	+	−	−	−	+	−	−	−	+	+	−	+	+	+	−	−	−	−	+	−	−	−	+	−	+	−	−	+	−	64	20	−	+	F/A	+	−	+	−	+	+	−	+	−
19 KSHEL	−	−	−	−	−	+	−	−	−	−	+	−	+	+	+	+	−	−	+	−	−	−	−	+	−	−	−	+	+	33	−	+	−	F	−	−	−	−	−	+	−	+	−
20 MARC	+	−	−	−	−	−	−	−	+	+	+	+	+	−	−	−	−	−	+	+	+	+	+	−	−	+	−	+	−	60	U	U	U	F	+	−	−	−	+	U	−	−	+
21 MINIELAS	+	−	−	−	−	−	−	−	+	+	+	+	+	+	+	+	−	−	+	+	+	+	−	−	−	−	−	−	+	32	−	−	−	F4	−	−	−	−	−	−	−	+	−
22 NASTRAN	+	−	−	−	−	−	−	−	+	+	+	+	+	+	+	+	−	−	+	+	+	+	−	−	−	+	−	+	−	50	U	−	+	F	+	+	+	+	+	+	+	−	+
23 NEPSAP	+	−	−	−	−	−	−	−	+	+	+	+	+	+	+	+	−	−	+	+	+	+	−	−	−	+	−	+	−	45	12	+	+	F	+	+	+	−	+	+	−	+	−
24 NONLIN 2	+	−	−	−	−	−	−	−	+	+	+	+	+	−	−	−	−	−	+	+	+	+	−	−	−	+	−	+	−	57	1	−	+	U	−	−	−	−	+	−	−	−	−
25 NONSAP	+	−	−	−	−	−	−	−	+	+	+	+	+	+	+	+	−	−	+	+	+	+	+	−	−	+	+	+	−	120	−	−	−	F	−	−	−	−	+	−	+	−	−
26 NOSTRA	+	−	−	−	−	−	−	−	+	+	+	+	+	+	+	+	−	−	+	−	−	−	−	−	−	−	−	+	−	28	6	−	+	F	+	+	+	+	+	+	−	−	U	U
27 PAFEC 70	+	+	−	−	−	−	−	−	+	+	+	+	+	+	+	+	−	−	+	+	−	−	−	−	−	−	−	−	+	10	1	−	+	F	+	+	+	−	+	+	+	+	−
28 FRAKSI	+	+	−	−	−	−	−	−	+	+	+	+	+	+	−	−	−	−	+	−	−	−	−	−	−	−	−	+	−	33	4	−	+	F4	−	+	−	−	+	+	+	−	−
29 REXBAT	+	−	−	−	−	−	−	−	+	+	+	+	+	+	−	−	−	−	+	+	+	+	−	+	−	−	−	+	−	65	10	−	+	F	+	+	+	+	+	+	+	+	−
30 SABOR/DRASTIC6	+	−	−	+	−	−	−	−	−	−	+	+	+	+	+	+	−	−	+	−	−	−	−	+	+	+	+	+	+	45	13	1	+	F	−	+	+	−	+	+	+	+	+
31 SAMBA	+	−	+	−	−	−	−	−	+	+	+	+	+	+	−	−	−	−	+	−	−	−	−	−	−	−	−	−	−	24	1	−	+	AL	−	−	−	−	+	+	+	+	+
32 SAP IV	+	−	−	−	−	−	−	−	+	+	+	+	+	+	+	+	−	−	+	+	+	+	−	−	−	−	−	+	−	18	10	−	+	F4	−	−	−	−	+	+	−	−	+
33 SATANS	−	−	−	+	−	−	−	−	−	−	+	−	+	+	+	+	−	−	+	−	−	−	−	−	−	−	−	+	+	36	−	−	−	F4	−	−	−	−	−	+	−	−	+
34 SESAM 69	+	−	−	−	−	−	−	−	+	+	+	+	+	−	−	−	−	−	+	−	−	−	−	−	−	−	−	−	−	40	+	+	+	F4	−	−	−	−	−	−	+	+	−
35 SHORE	−	−	−	+	−	−	−	−	−	+	−	−	+	+	+	+	−	−	+	−	−	+	−	−	−	+	−	−	−	62	1	+	U	F5	−	−	+	+	+	+	+	−	+
36 STARDYNE	+	−	−	−	−	−	−	−	+	+	−	+	+	+	+	+	−	−	+	−	−	−	−	−	−	+	−	−	−	32	4	+	+	F	+	+	+	−	+	+	+	+	+
37 STARS	−	−	−	−	+	−	−	−	+	−	+	−	+	+	+	+	−	−	+	+	+	+	+	+	−	+	−	+	U	U	U	U	U	F	+	−	+	−	+	+	−	U	U
38 STRIP	−	+	−	−	−	−	−	−	+	+	+	−	+	−	−	−	−	−	+	−	−	−	−	−	−	+	−	+	−	64	+	U	+	F4	+	+	−	−	+	+	+	+	−
39 TEXGAP	+	+	+	−	−	−	−	−	−	−	+	+	+	−	−	−	+	−	+	−	−	−	−	−	−	−	−	−	−	25	9	−	+	F4	−	+	+	−	+	+	−	+	−
40 TIRE	−	+	−	−	−	−	−	−	+	−	−	+	+	−	−	−	−	−	+	−	−	−	−	−	−	−	−	+	−	105	U	U	+	F/A	−	−	−	−	−	−	−	+	−
41 TITUS	+	−	−	−	−	−	−	−	+	+	+	+	+	−	−	−	+	+	+	−	−	−	−	−	−	+	−	−	−	27	U	U	U	F	−	+	+	−	+	+	+	−	+
42 VISCEL	+	−	−	−	−	−	−	−	+	+	+	+	+	−	−	−	+	−	+	−	−	−	−	−	−	−	−	−	−	20	15	−	+	F	−	+	+	−	+	−	−	−	+
43 ZP 26	+	−	−	−	−	−	−	−	−	+	−	+	+	−	−	−	−	−	+	+	−	+	−	−	−	+	−	+	+	98	−	−	−	F4	+	+	+	−	−	+	−	+	−

(in terms of analysis capabilities, library of finite element types, users' convenience, computer resource requirements), many organizations apply more than one finite element program (for example: MARC for nonlinear analysis, NASTRAN for dynamic analysis).

Examples of structures analized with the finite element method are given in Chapter 7.1.

6.2.3 Finite Difference Methods and Other Methods

As with finite element methods, this book does not intend to initiate the reader into the numerical aspects of finite difference methods. The reader is referred to the extensive and easily accessible literature on this subject. Finite difference methods are generally based on approximate representations of partial differential equations, while finite element methods are commonly derived from integral representations of the problem. Finite difference methods are presently used in more domains than finite elements. They are often related to the determination of loads. Examples of domains of application are:

– fluid dynamics (determination of pressure fields);
– thermodynamics (determination of temperature fields);
– neutron physics (determination of radiation fields in nuclear reactors).

More recently, however, finite element methods begin to spread into these domains, too (see, for instance, [60]).

The variety of finite difference methods is larger than that of finite element methods. This stems from several reasons. One is the variety in the type of the underlying differential equation (the Navier-Stokes equation, the Poisson equation, and the Stefan-Boltzmann equation are used in the above mentioned domains). Another reason is the greater dependency of finite difference formulations on geometry. Finite difference programs which are suited to solve fluid dynamics problems in rectangular boxes are not in general applicable to the same problems in cylindrical geometry or in networks of pipes. As a consequence, programs based upon finite difference methods are closely associated with particular objects, and not easily transferrable. Thus, no large market has developed like the one for finite element programs. On the other hand, the source code of each finite difference program generally exhibits more similarity to the underlying physical (differential) equation, and is hence more easily understood, modified, and adjusted to other problems. The finite difference approach tends to lead to a relatively large library of small and clearly structured separate programs which are adjusted to actual needs, rather than one big and powerful (finite element) program which should suit many purposes. This approach calls for an environment which provides the necessary software know-how, and adequate tools for software development and modification (see Chapter 4.1.3.2). "Black box" finite element programs are less demanding in this respect.

The same arguments apply to other methods which have undergone significant progress within the last few years: spectral methods and boundary integral equation methods. The breakthrough in spectral methods came with the invention of the Fast Fourier Transform algorithm [61]. Conventional Fourier transformation requires a number of significant operations (multiplications, for instance) which grows by a factor of n-squared, where n is a figure characterizing the desired resolution. The fast Fourier transformation reduces this to an n*log(n)-dependence. As an example, for doubling the resolution in all directions of a three-dimensional problem, the conventional transformation would require 64 times the number of operations, while fast Fourier transformation increases the number of operations only by a factor of about 8. For higher resolutions, the difference may easily reach several orders of magnitude [62].

Boundary integral equation methods [63, 64] significantly reduce the size of a problem: a three-dimensional problem of fluid flow in a three-dimensional control volume is reduced to a merely two-dimensional problem related to the two-dimensional surface of the control volume. This advantage is offset to a certain extent by the fact that the resulting system of linear equations has a fully populated and irregularly structured matrix of coefficients. For this reason, the boundary integral equation method generally cannot take advantage of the efficient algorithms which have been developed for sparse and cleanly structured (banded) matrices as they arise in conventional finite difference or finite element schemes. Combinations of the two methods with the goal of benefiting from the merits of bothhave been developed recently [65].

These new methods provide very high computational efficiency, but their range of applicability is sometimes restricted by assumptions regarding the geometry (symmetry assumptions, for instance) or the class of solutions (potential fields). Nevertheless, such advanced methods have made problems tractable at moderate cost which would have been too expensive to solve with more conventional finite element or finite difference schemes [66]. As an example, consider the analysis of a large cylindrical component (diameter: 4.3 m; height: 8.2 m; wall thickness: 80 mm) in a power reactor pressure vessel after the rupture of a large coolant pipe. In this case, the feedback regarding the influence of the structural deformation upon the pressure field must be analized concurrently, and superimposed on the pressure field as it results from the primary cause. 44000 degrees of freedom describing the pressure field and the flow field in the water plus 1000 degrees of freedom describing the structural behavior during the affected time period can be analized in a couple of hours. The pressure field and the structural deformation as viewed in such an analysis are shown in Fig. 6.17.

This example indicates a trend which has become more and more important in design analysis. For the first screening investigations in a preliminary design phase, individual aspects — such as static stress considerations — may be considered separately. In detail design, however, functional aspects, structural aspects, economics, manufacturing, and many other aspects will have to be investigated concurrently and with respect to their interactions. In this phase of design analysis, it becomes essential to reduce the amount of overhead required for switching between various analysis programs. Data base systems (Chapter 2 and 5) and system nuclei (Chapter 5.1.2.4) are particularly useful for this purpose.

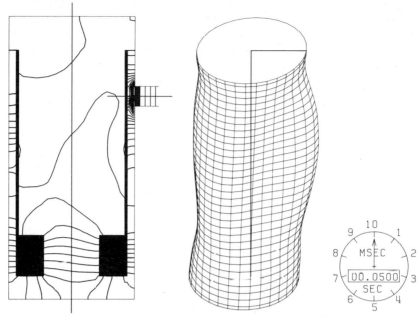

Fig. 6.17. Pressure field in a reactor pressure vessel (left) and deformation of vessel internals after a postulated pipe break (right, displacement amplified): the results of a combination of finite difference and spectral techniques

6.2.4 Simulation

6.2.4.1 Survey

"Simulation is a very wide-open and somewhat ill-defined subject of great importance to those responsible for the design of systems as well as those responsible for their operation" [67]. A similar broad definition is given in [68]: "We therefore define system simulation as the technique of solving problems by observation of the performance, over time, of a dynamic model of the system". Simulation methods are applied in many areas [69]: social, ecological, and agricultural systems; military and business applications; health care; manufacturing, marketing, production planning and control; financial systems; computers and computer networks; energy forecasting; and many others. It is surprising that the recent literature on simulation methods does not reflect the importance of simulation in design. In fact, a large portion of the analysis aspect of the design process is devoted to simulation.

In general, simulation methods are divided into two groups:

– discrete simulation;
– continuous simulation.

In addition, combinations of the two in one system have been developed, but are less widely known. The major differences among the various simulation systems are:

- the organization of time and activities;
- the naming and structure of entities;
- the testing conditions for activities;
- the type of statistical tests possible on data;
- the ease of changing the model structure.

In any case, a "model" of the real system is established, and the changes of the state of this model are observed. Such a model consists of

- a *system*, which is constituted by
- *entities*. Each entity is characterized by a set of
- *attributes*, which describe the state of the entities.
- *Activities, events* or *processes* may create and delete entities or change their state.

If we combine the terms "system", "entities", and "attributes" into "schema" and replace "activities, events, or processes" by "operation", we note a similarity between the concepts used for simulation and those described in Chapter 3 for data bases and design processes. The difference between continuous and discrete simulation lies in the assumptions regarding the continuity of changes of state. Discrete simulation deals with discrete changes of state (creation and deletion of entities, individual and finite changes of attribute values). Typical applications may be found in the simulation of digital systems (computers). Continuous simulation approximates continuous changes of state, as described by a set of ordinary differential equations, by appropriate numerical integration. (A typical example is the behavior of a motor vehicle on a bumpy road). Many simulation problems may be considered as deterministic: in this case the dynamic behavior is fully defined by the model and its initial state. Quite often, however, the system behavior is influenced by stochastic processes. This applies to both technical applications (roughness of a road, failure rate of mechanical components, work load in a computer network) and non-technical ones (such as those encountered marketing). Thus, a significant part of the development of simulation methods was devoted to the treatment of stochastic processes.

Simulation can be done completely on a computer, or may integrate real components and people as part of the process. As an example, the dynamic behavior of a car or an aircraft may be simulated with a human driver or pilot involved in a real-time simulation.

The principal difference between simulation as part of the design process and many other simulation applications is that the systems or objects which are simulated for design analysis do not yet exist in reality. They exist only as conceptual models in human brains, and partly as data representations in data bases.

6.2.4.2 Simulation Languages

The schematic overview of simulation languages shown in Fig. 6.18 is based on [67]. Continuous system simulation was originally the domain of analog

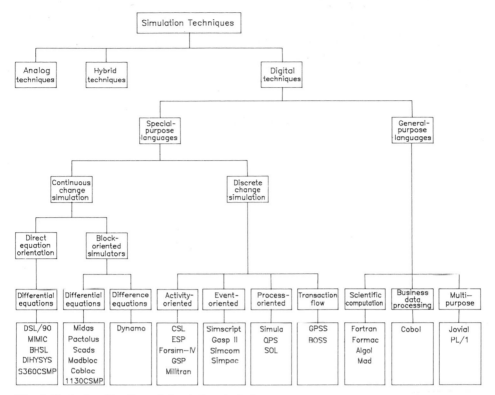

Fig. 6.18. A classification of simulation techniques

computers. Their basic functions (integration, multiplication by a constant, sum-
mation, and — to some extent — multiplication of variables and generation
of functions of a single variable) satisfied many needs. They were easy to handle,
and faster than digital computers. The situation, however, has changed with
time. The need to include more functions (multiplication and division, functions
of several variables, logical decisions) led to combinations of analog and digital
techniques in hybrid computers. Because of the growing speed of digital computing and the development and spreading of programming languages for continuous simulation, digital simulation techniques became more and more dominant.
Special-purpose languages for continuous simulation are based on two different
representations of dynamic problems:

– block diagram representation;
– differential equation representation.

The first simulation languages were block oriented (such as DYNAMO
[70], the original version of CSMP and others). The step from analog to digital
was easy with these languages because of their common (block-oriented) way
of representing models. Large and complex problems, however, would require
huge block diagrams to be drawn. Such large problems may be formulated

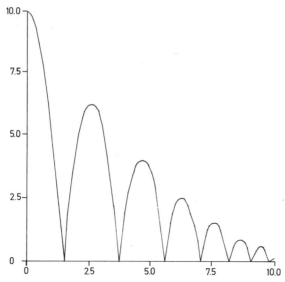

Fig. 6.19. The "bouncing ball" problem calls for combined continuous and discrete simulation

more concisely by a set of differential equations in mathematical notation. The differential-equation-oriented languages basically aim at a formal rewriting of these equations in machine-readable form, without intermediate graphic representation as block diagrams. Examples of these languages are DSL/90 [71] and CSMP III [72].

Quite often, dynamic problems which are described by partial differential equations may be treated by continuous simulation languages. For this purpose, the partial differential equation is approximated by finite differences in the space domain. Thus the continuous field is discretized in space. The resulting set of ordinary differential equations — with time as the only independent variable — makes problems tractable by conventional simulation programs, which otherwise would require the application of more sophisticated numerical methods, like finite elements or finite differences in more dimensions.

A similar separation may be found in early discrete simulation languages. Flow-chart-oriented languages based on GPSS [73, 74] are particularly easy to learn, while statement-oriented languages like SIMULA [75] provide more flexibility.

In activity-oriented languages, the components of the simulated system (the entities) are either idle (do not change their state) or else perform activities in time which — if certain conditions are met — lead to instantaneous changes of the system state. By the cyclic scanning of all activities from time step to time step and modification of the system state accordingly, the simulation proceeds through small intervals in time.

Many problems may be formulated more effectively in an event-oriented language. With languages of this type, time proceeds in jumps from one event to the next one, each resulting in a discrete change in the system state. Upon each event, the system components are scanned to see whether they will give rise to one or more events in the future under the new system conditions (for instance, sending a message will cause a future event: the arrival of the message at some other place). All future events are sequenced in time, and the event which will occur soonest determines the next time step.

Process-oriented languages attempt to combine the compact notation of activity-oriented languages with the efficiency of event-oriented languages. An example of such a language is SIMULA [75]. A single subprogram in SIMULA may represent many processes of a similar type, each of them in a different state. Each process will cause the corresponding program to resume execution at the appropriate reactivation point.

In addition to these special-purpose languages, simulation programs may be written in general-purpose languages like FORTRAN, PL/1, or PASCAL. In the case where a digital computer is combined with real components (simulated aircraft and real cockpit), process control languages like PEARL [76] would be advisable. In the CAD environment, the use of general-purpose languages appears to be more widespread than the use of specialized languages, at least for the simulation of continuous processes. This is because

- the simulation programs must interface with other programs and data bases used in this environment. This interfacing is most easily achieved when only a single language (generally FORTRAN) is used for all purposes;
- many organizations use a home-made simulation package — usually based on FORTRAN — which suits their own needs better than the so-called special-purpose simulation languages, which may be too "general purpose" in the particular case.

Many practical problems call for both discrete and continuous simulation. Pritsker and Young use the example of pilot ejection from an aircraft to illustrate such needs [77]. In the first phase of this process, the pilot's seat is guided by its mounting rails and moves under the forces of the ejection system. When the seat disengages from the rails, the equations of motion for the aircraft and the pilot become suddenly decoupled from each other. Atmospheric drag forces start to act on the pilot. Thus, a discrete change in system state separates two phases of continuous simulation. Another example has been treated in [78]: the bouncing ball. The falling ball changes height and velocity continuously under gravitational forces. A discrete change in state occurs when the ball is reflected from the ground (see Fig. 6.19). Simulation systems for problems of this type must be able to detect situations which call for a discrete change in system state. In addition to such features, the simulation system DYSYS provides for the exact simulation of transport processes at variable speed (such as material transport through a piping system with varying pumping power). Another system capable of combined continuous and discrete simulation is GSL [79].

6.2.5 Optimization

6.2.5.1 Problem Formulation

In a sense, design may be considered an optimization task. Even if the specification does not explicitly call for an "optimum" design, the designer will always try to optimize in one or more respects:

- production cost and time;
- ease of assembly and maintenance;
- ease of use;
- time and resources required for the design.

Instead of posing an optimization criterion, the same aspects may set forth constraints which have to be met by the design. However, there are significant differences between optimization and design:

- Design, while aiming at an optimal solution within the limits of certain constraints, does not generally start from an explicit formulation of the optimization criteria and all the constraints. Even worse, in many cases design is confronted with an uncertain and moving target (see Chapter 3.1.2). The definition of what is "optimum" is commonly left to human judgment. While some constraints may be formally given (a maximum allowable stress value, for instance), the distance from such a limit is often associated with a certain value and included in the judgment. Often, this judgment must also take into account uncertainties in the specification. Thus the designer may decide not to select the solution which appears to be "optimal" based on the presently available information. He may rather prefer a "second choice" if it provides more flexibility for adaptation to changing requirements. What is meant by flexibility (or maintainability, manufacturability, etc.) is certainly not easily expressed in terms of formal parameters and a formal measure of merit function.
- Optimization assumes that a single measure of merit function (often called "objective function") and the complete set of constraints can be expressed formally in terms of the design parameters. The optimization task may be given as in [80]:

$$\text{minimize } f(x)$$
$$\text{subject to } x \, \varepsilon \, S$$
$$h_i(x) = 0; \, i = 1 \ldots r$$
$$g_j(x) \leq 0; \, j = 1 \ldots c$$

In this formulation, x is the n-dimensional vector of the design parameters that have been identified as the ones which may adjusted to obtain an optimum. S is an allowable domain in the corresponding n-dimensional space; and $f(x)$ is a single function of these parameters. Functions in the form $h_i(x)$ represent implicit restrictions (equality constraints). Each of them effectively subtracts one dimensionality from the design parameter space by defining a hyper-surface on which the solution must lie. The (inequality) constraints $g_j(x)$ further reduce the allowable domain; they define other hyper-surfaces in the parameter space which constitute boundaries for allowable solutions. Note that the above formulation is general enough to cover the maximization task

maximize $f'(x)$

as well. We simply substitute

$f(x) = \text{arbitrary\_constant} - f'(x)$.

Hence it does not matter whether we formulate optimization as finding the minimum or the maximum of a measure of merit. A special case is the problem of finding a feasible solution without imposing an optimum criterion. This case may be represented by an optimization task with a measure of merit

$f(x) = \text{arbitrary\_constant}$.

Other constraint formulations are included in the above scheme as well:

$g'_j(x) \leq C'$ or
$g''_j(x) \geq C''$

may reduced to the above formulation by substituting

$g_j(x) = g'_j(x) - C'$ or
$g_j(x) = g''_j(x) - 1/C''$,

respectively.

Many textbooks on optimization describe methods for various classes of optimization problems [80, 81, 82, 83, 84]. The different classes may be characterized by

– the continuity aspect;
– the dimensionality of the parameter space;
– the type of functions allowed for f, h_i, g_j.

The methods for finding the optimum solution may be classified as

– techniques based on analytical approximations, using the functions themselves and their derivatives, or
– search techniques (often called "hill climbers").

Which one of the many different techniques is best suited for a given problem depends very much on the problem characteristics.

6.2.5.2 Optimization Problem Characteristics

Continuity

The overwhelming majority of optimization methods deal with continuous functions as well as continuous allowable domains in the parameter space. Application examples which may be found in the literature usually exhibit continuous behavior of the measure of merit, and of the constraint functions. With respect to the parameter space, discrete subsets are typical for many design applications.

The discretization is often a consequence of standardization: diameter values, for instance, or screw sizes can not be chosen from a continuous domain, but rather from a set of standard values. Two approaches may be used to solve such problems:

- We perform discrete optimization in a strict sense by selecting allowable parameter values only. Many optimization techniques will fail in this case because they are based on the assumption of continuity.
- We disregard the discreteness problem while solving the optimization problem. Once the optimum is found in the continuous parameter space, we select from the allowable set of discrete parameters those values which appear to be "closest" to the optimum without violating the constraints. Since, in most practical cases, the measure of merit is flat near the optimum — that is, a small deviation from the optimum usually has only an insignificant effect on the measure of merit — ,this approach will produce a solution which is at least close to the real optimum. The advantage of this approach is that it leaves us a greater choice of optimization techniques.

Dimensionality

A wide class of optimization problems is of dimensionality one. The problem may then be considered as the task of finding the minimum (or maximum) of a curve in a certain interval. Search methods for solving this problem include the Fibonacci Search and the Golden Section Search [84]. These methods differ in their strategies for selecting the inspection points within the interval. If the interval is not limited, the Reversed Fibonacci Search may be used. Other methods apply curve-fitting techniques to the function: Newton's Method or the Method of the False Position [80]. These (direct) methods require the evaluation of the derivative of the measure of merit, or its approximation by a difference quotient.

Problems with a parameter space of higher order may be classified as "small" (up to order five), "intermediate" (from order five to a hundred), and "large" scale (up to a thousand), according to Luenberger. Today's theoretical and computational capabilities permit direct solution techniques for many small problems, while the intermediate scale is the domain of a large number of general-purpose search techniques (except for linear problems, which are more easily tractable by direct techniques since their derivative evaluation is trivial). Large problems call for special methods that account for specific structures in the problems themselves. Optimization for design, however, is far from ready for appliocation on this large scale.

Function Type

The following classification according to function types is generally used:

- linear problems;
- nonlinear unconstrained problems;
- nonlinear constrained problems.

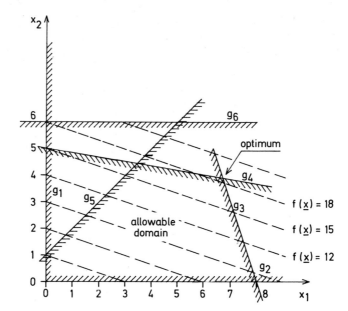

Fig. 6.20. A linear
programming example
in two dimensions

Linear Problems

A linear optimization (or "linear programming") problem is defined by [82]:

maximize $f(x) = \Sigma\, a_{0i}{}^{*}x_i$
subject to
$g_j(x) \geq \Sigma\, (\, a_{ji}{}^{*}x_i - a_{j0})$
with $i = 1 \ldots n; j = 1 \ldots m$.

A different formulation introduces auxiliary variables x_{n+j} for expressing
the constraints

$\Sigma\, a_{ji}{}^{*}x_{n+j} - a_{j0} - 0$
$x_{n+j} \geq 0$

A graphical representation of the optimization task is possible only for two
parameters. Fig. 6.20 illustrates the problem

maximize $f(x) = x_1 + 3{}^{*}x_2$
subject to
$g_1:$ $\qquad\qquad x_1 \geq 0$
$g_2:$ $\qquad\qquad x_2 \geq 0$
$g_3:$ $\qquad 3{}^{*}x_1 + x_2 \leq 24$
$g_4:$ $\qquad x_1 + 4{}^{*}x_2 \leq 20$
$g_5:$ $\qquad\quad x_1 - x_2 \leq -1$
$g_6:$ $\qquad\qquad x_2 \leq 6$

The allowable domain of parameter values is indicated for each of the constraints by lines hatched on their allowable side. Note that the last of the con-

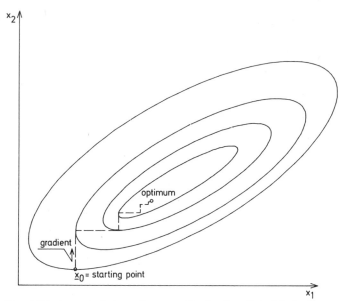

Fig. 6.21. Approach to optimum with the Gradient Method

straints is irrelevant, since the combination of the remaining constraints is more restrictive. The isolines of the measure of merit

$$f(x) = \text{const}$$

indicate the optimum location on the boundary of the allowable domain.

The basic approach for solving linear programming problems is the SIM-PLEX method. This algorithm, and others which are based on it but modified for higher efficiency, are extensively covered in textbooks (such as [80]). For FORTRAN and Algol listings of linear programming algorithms, see [82].

Nonlinear Unconstrained Problems

One of the oldest and most widely used methods for minimizing a function of several variables is the Method of Steepest Descent. An equivalent name is the Gradient Method. At a starting point x_0 in the parameter space, the gradient $g(x)$ is determined and a new position

$$x_1 = x_0 - a^* g(x_0)$$

is chosen such that

$$f(x_1) < f(x_0)$$

is minimal for all $a > 0$.

x_1 is then used as a new starting point. Fig. 6.21 shows the successive steps of this method for a two-dimensional case. The method will converge to a local optimum. But in the general case the optimum which is thus found may not be the "best" one. It may be better then all other points in a certain neighborhood, but there may exist a better global optimum. When there are

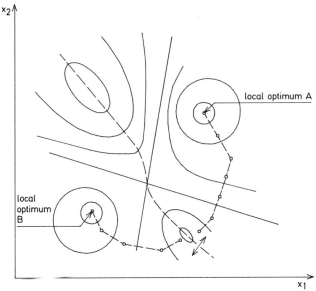

Fig. 6.22. The starting point of the Gradient Method determines which local optimum is found

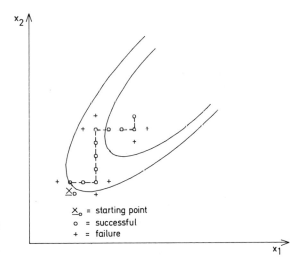

Fig. 6.23. Approach to optimum with the Unidirectional Method

several local optima, the one found will depend on the starting position x_0, as illustrated in Fig. 6.22.

A particular case of a nonlinear measure of merit is the quadratic problem

$$f(x) = 1/2* \Sigma a_{ij}*x_i*x_j + \Sigma b_i*x_i$$

For this problem deep mathematical foundations are available [82]. More general measures of merit are often approximated locally by such a quadratic

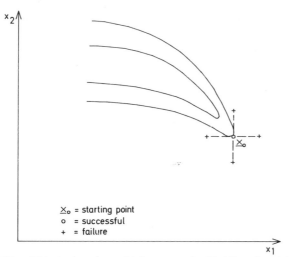

x_2

$\underline{x}_o$ = starting point
o   = successful
+   = failure

x_1

Fig. 6.24. A situation which causes the Unidirectional Method to fail

function and treated accordingly with the Gradient Method. A similar approach is the use of Newton's Method. Combinations and modifications of these two basic direct methods have been developed for improved efficiency [81]. For FORTRAN and Algol listings, see [82]. The common feature of these methods is the use of the derivatives of the measure of merit with respect to the design parameters.

Techniques which make use of the function values only are called Search Techniques. A primitive method of this type is Unidirectional Search (see Fig. 6.23). From a starting point x_0 we move a certain step into one of various directions, holding all but one parameter constant. If the measure of merit is improved, we continue to move into this promising direction (possibly with increasing step size). Upon failure (no further improvement in this direction), we try other directions in the same way. If none of the directions indicates an improvement, we have found an optimum within the range of the step sizes. The accuracy may be improved as far as desired by continuing this process with a reduced step size. The Unidirectional Method may fail, however, in extreme situations, as shown in Fig. 6.24. The problem of sometimes finding a local optimum — but perhaps not the global oone — is the same with this method as for the Gradient Method.

A completely different type of search technique is the Random Search. Several procedures of this type have been developed, including the Evolution Strategy which is claimed to simulate biological evolution [85, 86]. The Random Search techniques proceed by evaluating the measure of merit at points selected at random in the parameter space, using allowed values of x. They are not necessarily located close to previous inspection points, as with the other (deterministic) methods. The benefit of Random Search is that it depends much less upon the starting point and thus has the potential of finding the global optimum, even if the measure of merit and the constraints are very complex functions

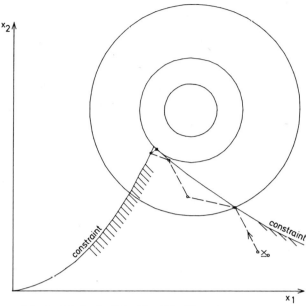

Fig. 6.25. Approach to optimum with the Method of the Feasible Direction

in a parameter space of high dimensionality. Furthermore, Random Search can deal with discrete design parameters without any problem. Since a totally random search would likely produce a prohibitively large number of inspections, the various Random Search techniques all utilize strategies for modifying the probability distribution of the inspection points in accordance with past evaluations of the measure of merit.

Nonlinear Constrained Problems

The methods which are available for solving unconstrained optimization problems require modifications when constraints are introduced. Methods utilizing the derivatives of the measure of merit may be adapted to constrained problems by using the concept of the Feasible Direction [87]: When the optimization algorithm reaches a boundary, it can no longer proceed in the direction of the gradient into the forbidden domain. A feasible way to proceed is the projection of the gradient onto the tangent plane of the constraints. For nonlinear convex constraints, this direction may need further correction to assure that the next inspection point will fall inside the allowable domain. The result is a zigzagging path formed by the sequence of inspection points (indicated in Fig. 6.25), which follows the boundary closely. It is worth noting that finding a feasible and usable direction (feasible = does not violate constraints; usable = improves the measure of merit) is in itself a linear optimization problem [81].

A different approach is the modification of the measure of merit by a suitably chosen penalty function $P(x)$ or a barrier function $B(x)$, as described, for instance, in [88]. We minimize $f(x)+P(x)$ or $f(x)+B(x)$, respectively, instead

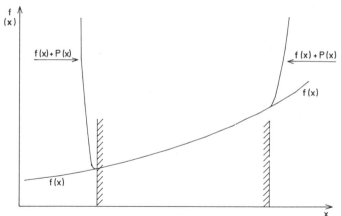

Fig. 6.26. A measure of merit modified with a penalty function

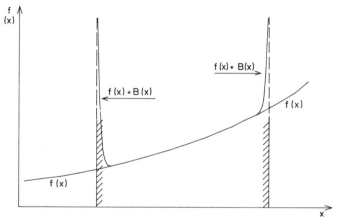

Fig. 6.27. A measure of merit modified with a barrier function

of $f(x)$ proper. The penalty function is null in the allowable domain but rises steeply as we move across a boundary into the forbidden region (see Fig. 6.26). The barrier function, however, modifies the measure of merit *inside* the allowable domain, as shown in Fig. 6.27. Thus, while with the penalty function approach we might slightly violate a constraint with our final solution, the barrier function approach may stop us slightly before reaching the actual feasible optimum. Both methods effectively push the solution to as close to the boundary as is needed, provided that their respective functions (barrier or penalty) are sufficiently steep.

Similar corrections must be applied to direct search techniques. The unidirectional search, for instance, would fail in a situation like the one shown in Fig. 6.28, if applied without further consideration. Random search techniques are readily applicable to constrained problems; due to their versatility they will succeed whether there is a boundary or not. However, the convergence rate may be improved if recognition of a boundary is used to modify the proba-

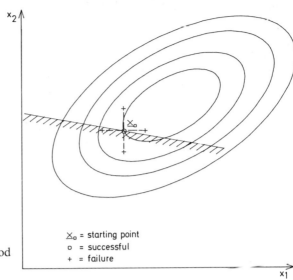

Fig. 6.28. A constraint which causes the Unidirectional Method to fail

$\underline{x}_o$ = starting point
o = successful
+ = failure

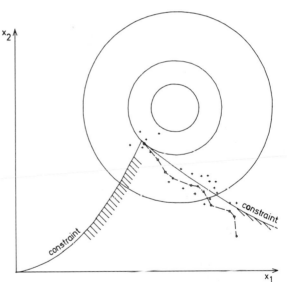

Fig. 6.29. Approach to optimum with Random Search

bility distribution of the next inspection points (as compared to blind random searching). Fig. 6.29 shows the approach to optimum for a random search in the same case as for Fig. 6.25. Both figures are taken from [89].

6.2.5.3 Applications

The application of optimization techniques to design requires first of all a formal statement of the problem. The design task has to be properly prepared before optimization techniques may be applied. The main steps to be taken by way of preparation are (see Fig. 6.30):

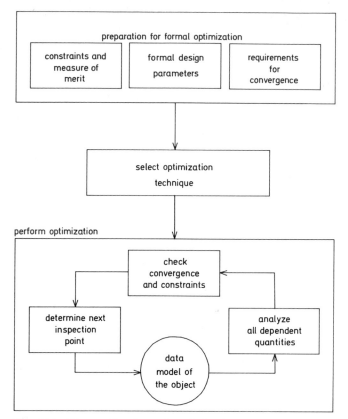

Fig. 6.30. The application of optimization methods in CAD requires a formal model and a formal measure of merit

– Formalization of the design parameters and all dependent quantities used in the evaluation of the constraints and of the function of merit. This task corresponds to the definition of a schema for an object of design, and is thus a familiar task to the computer-aided design specialist.
– Formulation of the algorithms for computing the constraints and the measure of merit. In practical cases these functions are often not expressed directly in terms of the design parameters, but rather as functions of dependent variables (such as stress levels). Numerical analysis and simulation problems are generated as subtasks of the optimization.
– Definition of convergence criteria. Optimization is an iterative process in most practical cases. Criteria must be set forth to define when the solution should be accepted as final.

After these preparations, an optimization technique can be selected and the optimization may proceed. The individual steps of the optimization process are very similar to variational design (see Chapter 3.2.2). The values of certain attributes of the design object have to be determined. The correspondence is as follows:

optimization	↔	*variational design*
determine next inspection point		synthesis
compute dependent quantities, including measure of merit and constraint functions		analysis
check violation of constraints and convergence to optimum		evaluation

Considerable resources (computer time, money, manpower) may be required for the actual performance of the necessary analyses for a single inspection point. If we assume that many evaluations (say 50 to several hundred) are needed to approach the optimum, the resource requirements are likely to become unacceptable. A possible remedy is the use of the "response surface" technique [90]. With this method, we consider each quantity $y_k(x)$ as a hyper-surface in the $(n+1)$-dimensional space spanned by the n design parameters and by y_k. Before actually performing the optimization, we compute a sufficiently large number of points on these hyper-surfaces, using the complete model of the design object and the most refined analysis techniques. Based on these points we try to represent the real hyper-surface by an approximate one, which should be accurate enough but much easier (and hence less costly) to evaluate. This approximation is the "response surface". In the most simple case it would be a linear function of the design parameters. In many practical cases it turns out that the approximations have to account for dependence on only a small number of design parameters, if the quantity y_k is dominated by the influence of only a few parameters. This can drastically reduce the computational effort, and may make automatic optimization feasible in cases which otherwise would have had prohibitive resource requirements. It is interesting to note that the determination of a "good" approximative response surface is in itself an optimization task.

Despite the similarity between "design" and "optimization", the number of successful applications of optimization techniques to design problems appears to be surprisingly small. In 1979, a special issue of *Computers and Structures* on "Trends in Computerized Structural Analysis and Synthesis" contained only a single paper on optimization techniques for the synthesis of structures [91]. The reason for this lack of application examples is probably twofold:

– the difficulty in formulating a quantitative measure of merit or constraint function involving aspects like "manufacturability" and "maintainability", or even aesthetic aspects;
– the very high dimensionality of the design parameter space in practical applications.

In structural design, the area of weight minimization for truss structures appears to be fairly well covered [92]. Examples of optimization applications

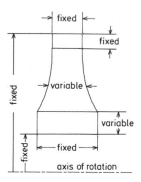

Fig. 6.31. Rotating disk; optimization example by de Silva [95]

in pre-contract ship design are given in [93]. Aoki also gives a number of optimization examples [81]. One of the problems involves optimization not only of a product, but of the whole project, including development, production, and use of the product. It is based on an empirical model for the total project costs of a three-stage launch vehicle. The model was developed by Lockheed Missiles and Space Company and was solved by Rush [94] in a parameter space of dimension 25 with 26 constraints. This is an interesting example indicating the value of optimization in a very early design stage. Optimization techniques have also been applied in the early development phase of the German fast breeder project. Heusener used a combination of random search (while far from the optimum) and the feasible gradient method (when approaching the optimum) which gave an improved convergence rate over the use of either of these methods alone [89]; the problem involved 9 parameters and 11 constraints. Typically, 40 to 50 evaluations of the measure of merit were needed for finding an optimum. Since the analysis of each point in the parameter space would have required very costly thermal-hydraulic and neutron physics calculations, the response surface technique was used. De Silva [95] illustrates a minimum-weight design for a rotating disk subject to geometrical and stress constraints (see Fig. 6.31). The problem is quadratic in the variables which define the disk shape. Polygons with 4 to 11 corners were used to approximate the curved shape. Typically, 50 to a few hundred evaluations of the measure of merit were needed for the approach to optimum.

Although we may expect the number of automated design optimizations to increase in the future, in all likelihood they will be restricted to relatively simple subproblems (such as optimum weight design of not-too-complicated parts), or to very early stages of design in which the product or perhaps even the whole project may be described with sufficient accuracy by a model of small-to-medium complexity (say up to dimensionality 20 or 30). A possibly new approach would be an interactive optimum design, with man included in the system. The optimization algorithm (probably based on random search) would be guided by an operator who

– monitors certain design constraints (such as unacceptable style) while others (such as gross dimensions) are monitored by algorithms;

- adds his personal judgment of the present design to the measure of merit;
- guides the direction of search by influencing the probability distribution for the next inspection point.

A system called OSW (Optimization Software), which provides a bank of methods for various optimization problems, was developed at the Technical University of Berlin [96]. OSW has been implemented under the CAD system nuclei IST and DINAS (see Chapter 5.1.2.4).

6.3 Computer Graphics for Data Presentation

6.3.1 Introduction

The application of powerful numerical methods to the analysis of design objects generally produces huge amounts of data. In order to make these results useful for interpretation and evaluation, they need to be presented in a readily understandable form. Long lists of printed data are totally unsuited for comprehension by a person. Graphic representations are the appropriate solution [97]. The subject of computer graphics is closely related to numerical methods and, hence, has been included in this chapter. The superiority of graphic data presentation stems from two facts:

- Information contained in graphical representations can be perceived by a person in an immediate and integrated way (in parallel), while lists of printed data must be parsed more or less sequentially. "One picture is worth a thousand words."
- The graphic representation can produce evidence of features like "peaks" or "waves" or "shock fronts". Such features are often essential for the evaluation. Note that finite difference or finite element techniques do not intrinsically treat such features, but the results may be expressed most effectively in these terms.

To a great extent, graphic representations are used for the following purposes:

- immediate presentation of results to the engineer who is responsible for the analysis;
- reporting results to a customer or supervising authority;
- publications, presentations;
- long-term documentation.

The requirements regarding turn-around time and visual appeal of the representations vary considerably. For the analyst, fast response has the highest priority: thus either graphic displays or fast plotters (such as electrostatic plotters) are appropriate. For reports and publications, aesthetic aspects become more important, which makes line plotters (particularly table plotters) more attractive.

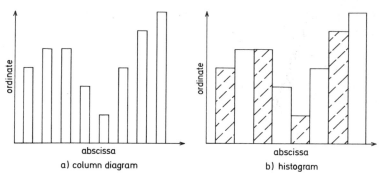

Fig. 6.32. Representation of a discontinuous function of one variable

For presentations and long-term documentation, the space requirements for the display medium can be minimized by utilizing graphic output on microfilm, microfiche, or videotape. Representation of analysis results on a display or plotter medium is only part of the task. In most cases (except for the immediate presentation of results to the analyst himself) the representation of the data must be edited. Coordinate axes must be added to diagrams; annotations, sketches or scaled-down drawings of the design object must be included with the data representation. This is a typical task for interactive graphics.

6.3.2 Functions of One Variable

6.3.2.1 Diagrams

The standard technique for representing a function of one variable is by means of a diagram. Various forms of diagrams (for single functions) are shown in Fig. 6.32 through Fig. 6.34. They are based on the same data points and are placed in order with an increasing degree of continuity. Column diagrams (Fig. 6.32a) or histograms (Fig. 6.32b) should be used to display discontinuous functions. Such functions occur quite often when the abscissa does not represent a continuous coordinate but rather a number of discrete values (such as different design options, or discrete power levels, for instance). Continuous diagrams (Figs. 6.33, 6.34) usually result from one-dimensional analyses (temperature, pressure, stress level distributions), time response simulations, or frequency response analyses. Here the abscissa represents a space coordinate, time, or frequency respectively. Or else the function may continuously depend on a design parameter (such as maximum allowable temperature). Fig. 6.33 shows a linear interpolation of such a continuous function between computed data points. Fig. 6.34 is a smooth representation of the same function. Both approximations and interpolations (piecewise as with spline functions or over the whole range with a single polynomial) are common techniques for smoothing. The difference between the linear interpolation and a smoothed representation is of an aesthetic nature. The smooth curve looks better, but the linear interpolation is more

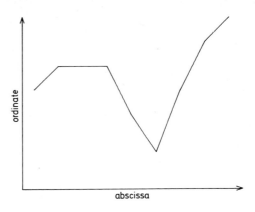

Fig. 6.33. Representation of a continuous function of one variable by linear interpolation

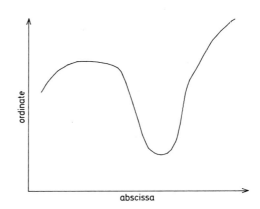

Fig. 6.34. Smooth curve representation of a function of one variable

truthful. It does not suggest a more accurate analysis than was actually achieved. Furthermore, when cost and turn-around time are of great concern, the linear interpolation is cheaper and faster than smoothing. Thus, for technical communication Fig. 6.33 would be preferable, while for commercial presentations or advertisements the smooth curve will probably be the better choice.

6.3.2.2 Representations of Several Functions in One Diagram

The representation of more than one function of only one variable does not pose great problems. We may distinguish between the different curves by using different linestyles or colors, by adding markers, or by shading, hatching, or coloring the area below a curve. Fig. 6.35 shows a histogram. In this instance, three quantities (with different hatching) are shown added together to form each total. This possibility applies only to quantities having the same measure (for example, production costs of different components of an object, adding

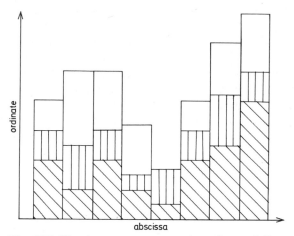

Fig. 6.35. Simultaneous representation of several discontinuous functions having the same measure

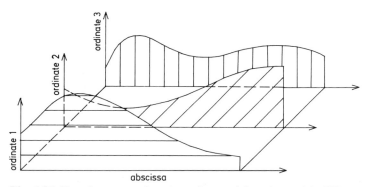

Fig. 6.36. Pseudo-perspective view of several functions with different measures

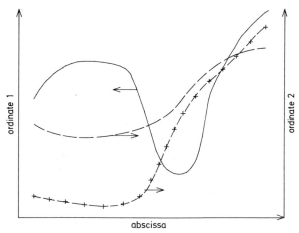

Fig. 6.37. A diagram with two ordinates for functions of different measures

up to the total production costs). Pseudo-perspective representations (as shown in Fig. 6.36) may be used for quantities without a common measure, such as cost, weight, efficiency, and manufacturing time. While hatching (or shading, or coloring) is not necessary in this case, it certainly improves the readability of such diagrams. Continuous functions of one variable are often distinguished by different line styles (line widths, line colors) or by adding markers to the curves. More than one ordinate axis may be added to the diagram but to use more than two (or possibly three) is not recommended (see Fig. 6.37).

6.3.3 Functions of Two Variables

With the growing capability of the numerical computer programs, the detail analysis of design objects has shifted from one-dimensional to two-dimensional or even three-dimensional problems. Graphical representations, however, are at first glance limited to the two dimensions of a display screen or a plotter. Thus, while the representation of a function of one variable is a simple task, representations of functions of more variables may require rather sophisticated methods.

6.3.3.1 Marker Clouds

In order to present a single *scalar* function of two variables one may map the value of this function onto the reciprocal distance of markers. Thus the apparent density of the displayed markers indicates the variations of the function. As an example, the function

sin(x)*sin(y)

over a 2π range in either direction is shown in Fig. 6.38. In this instance, the markers are distributed regularly within small rectangles for which some representative value was computed. Another option is to use a pseudo-random number generator to make the representation look smoother. This type of representation is often chosen to represent densities of physical quantities (such as densities of a certain material in a mixture). If color is available, the random marker cloud technique may be used successfully to represent several densities in one diagram, with the corresponding markers displayed in different colors. In principle, black and white markers of different shape could also do the same job. But different colors make the perception of the separate functions much easier. In many fluid dynamics programs, markers are used to depict the movement of material through time. At the start of the computation, the material densities are mapped onto marker populations. These markers are then viewed as "marked particles" which move according to the computed velocity field. Markers of different size (Fig. 6.39) or shape or color can each be associated with a function value.

The applicability of the marker cloud technique depends upon the hardware which is used for visualization. The technique is unsuited for drum or table

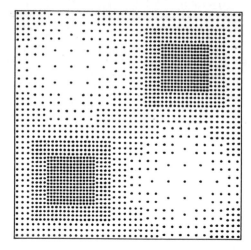

Fig. 6.38. Representation of a function of two variables by regular marker clouds

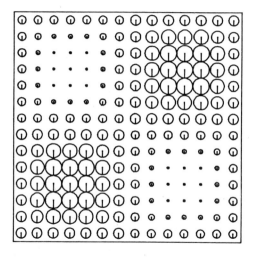

Fig. 6.39. Representation of a function of two variables by markers of different size

plotters because it may require many hours to draw so many markers. The technique is useful for electronic displays (particularly storage tube and raster displays) as well as raster plotters (electrostatic or ink jet) and microfilm plotters.

6.3.3.2 Hatching, Shading and Coloring

A different technique for representing a single scalar function of two variables is based on hatching, shading, or coloring areas. The hatching technique can be used on vector-oriented hardware (line plotters and storage tubes). For refresh displays, hatching may soon exceed the refresh capacity and lead to flicker. On raster-oriented hardware (plotters as well as displays), shading is preferred

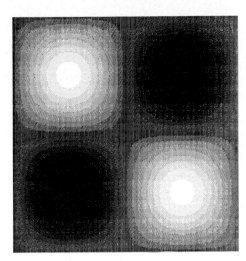

Fig. 6.40. Representation of a function
of two variables by shading

because it can produce a smooth-looking picture (as opposed to hatching which is always restricted to discontinuous steps in a representation). Fig. 6.40 shows the same function as Fig. 6.38 with finer raster and 16 levels of shading. Color is even better suited for showing both discontinuous and smooth variations of a function.

The shading technique can even be used with the most primitive plotting device — the line printer. Appropriate choice of characters (from blank to M overprinted with W) can produce the impression of a coarse black-and-white raster display. However, in a CAD environment suitable plotters and displays are commonly available so that the use of a printer as a plotter is less important.

Hatching, shading, and coloring are less well suited to representing more than one function in a single picture. A combination of coloring, marker clouds, and contour plots, however, could be used to display a small number of functions in a single picture. But care should be taken not to overload one picture with too much information.

Colored images for the representation of computerized results of structural mechanics programs were already being published in the early '70s [98]. But the breakthrough of color is yet to come, although the color graphics market is developing rapidly [99]. Considering the advantages of color data presentations, this is surprising. A major problem with color is the cost of reproduction, which is significantly higher than for black-and-white line drawings or gray-shaded pictures. In any case, colored pictures require a more delicate treatment (in this book, for instance, they are collected on a few special pages to save cost). Fig. 6.41, page 343, uses color to visualize the same two-dimensional function which appears in Fig. 6.38 through 6.42. Even though color pictures can now be *produced* more cheaply and much more easily than years ago (due to progress in color display and the use of instant color photography), the *reproduction* problem is likely to persist for a relatively long time.

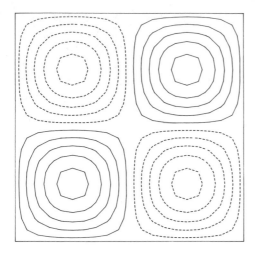

Fig. 6.42. Representation of a function of two variables by contour lines

6.3.3.3 Contour Plotting

A wide-spread technique for representing a scalar function of two variables is the contour plot (or isoline plot). Fig. 6.42 is a contour plot of the same function as in Fig. 6.38. The advantage of the contour plot is that it is suited for vector-oriented hardware (line plotters, vector tubes), which is as yet more common than area-oriented graphic hardware. The hardware may even have an influence upon the algorithm that is used to produce contour plots. Let us assume that the function is defined as a two-dimensional array $Z(I, J)$ on a raster of points identified by indices $0 < I < M, 0 < J < N$. The most simple algorithm scans one rectangle (formed by four adjacent points) after another, and determines whether a section on the contour line passes through each rectangle. The sections of the contour line are then plotted piecewise as they are found. As a consequence, a vector-oriented plotter may spend an unacceptable amount of time to produce the lines (no problem on raster-oriented hardware). Thus, for vector-oriented plotters, an algorithm should be used that follows a contour line throughout the whole data field in order to plot it without interruption. Contour following is also required if the line is to be smoothed. Care must be taken to assure that adjacent isolines will not cross each other after smoothing. Because of this problem, simple linear interpolations (as in Fig. 6.42) are often preferred to smoothed curves.

The example used above is particularly easy because the data which represent the surface are arranged in a regular rectangular pattern. A slightly more general problem has the same degree of complexity: if the positions x and y of the data points do not form a rectangle but may be arranged in two-dimensional arrays $X(I, J)$ and $Y(I, J)$, then very simple algorithms may be used. The same is true for data resulting from finite element analyses as long as information about the topology of the finite element net is available (which nodes form an element? which elements are based on each node?). In all of these cases the "neighborhood" of the data points is either explicitly or implicitly known. The problem becomes more difficult when only a vector of data $X(I)$, $Y(I)$, $Z(I)$ is given. The problem now resembles the task of constructing a solid body based on information about the vertices alone, without any knowledge about the topology of faces and edges. Nevertheless, contour-following algorithms have been developed for this task (as in [100]). Such algorithms are often based on implicit assumptions of the following type:

- the surface does not overlap itself;
- the projection of the surface onto the $x-y$-plane is convex or has a predefined boundary;
- the surface is spanned by triangles between the data points, the edges of the triangles representing shortest connections between the projections of the data points in the $x-y$-plane.

Whether or not isolines are helpful for our perception of the behavior of a function of two variables depends very much on the function itself. Isolines are well suited to indicate a small number of pronounced structures like

- peaks or
- wave fronts.

They become less suitable if the function shows no such pronounced structures, or too many of them. It is impossible to perceive hills and valleys from isolines alone. They give no indication of the direction of slope (see, for instance, Fig. 6.17). The missing information should be supplied by additional aids to visualization, such as:

- annotations;
- different line-styles at different levels (in Fig. 6.42, lines corresponding to positive or negative values are solid or dashed, respectively);
- different markers added to the lines;
- area-oriented techniques (marker clouds, shading, coloring).

6.3.3.4 Pseudo-Perspective View

Another way to represent two-dimensional functions applies techniques which are known from the representation of curved surfaces. The function values are mapped onto a third spatial coordinate and the resulting surface in space can be treated in just the same way as a real curved surface in space. The same techniques for hidden-line removal or smoothing are applicable. Fig. 6.43 shows the same function used previously in pseudo-perspective view. Pseudo-perspective views are very helpful for data presentation because

- they are equally applicable for line oriented and area oriented hardware;
- they provide an excellent means of perceiving the general shape of the function, even providing gross quantitative information.

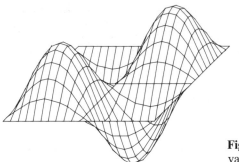

Fig. 6.43. Representation of a function of two variables by a pseudo-perspective view

Problems arise when the function values pass through several decades, or when hills in the front part of the view hide relevant information (as in Fig. 6.43, where a hill in the background is hidden). Showing the logarithm of the function instead of the function itself may help in the first case; viewing from different vantage points may help in the latter.

An excellent method for visualizing a two-dimensional function is to produce detailed three-dimensional representation, as by milling the surface on a NC-machine. Other techniques for generating a three-dimensional visualization are as yet in an experimental stage. Numerically generated holograms (to be viewed under laser light) and the use of two displays, with light polarization by means of filters (for viewing through polarized glasses and a half-transparent mirror) have not yet reached a stage that would make them attractive to the CAD community.

6.3.3.5 Vector Plots

The above-mentioned techniques are applicable to the representation of scalar functions. Vector functions (such as velocity field) may be represented as vector plots (see Fig. 6.44). The vectors are represented as starting at the points of interest and pointing in the vector direction. The arrow length is given in proportion to the vector length (or in the case of extreme variations, in proportion to its logarithm). Care must be taken to avoid overlapping of the vectors, which would obscure the information. Two vector fields may be represented in the same plot by using different arrow heads or different colors.

6.3.3.6 Two-Dimensional Functions on Curved Surfaces

Often the need arises to represent a two-dimensional function on the curved surface of a body. A typical example is the distribution of temperature or stress on the surface of a technical component. Pseudo-perspective views are not applicable in this case; hatching is not advisable (hatching lines would

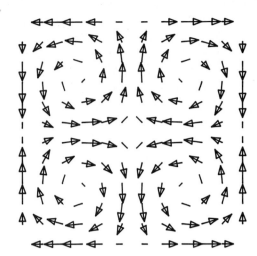

Fig. 6.44. Two-dimensional vector plot

have to be curved); but other techniques (marker clouds, shading, coloring, isolines, and vector plots) are applicable. Obviously, different techniques should be used to represent the three-dimensional shape of the surface and the behavior of the function. If curved lines are used to represent the surface, shading or coloring is well suited for function representation. If the surface is represented by different shades (or colors), isolines are best suited to depict the function.

In summary, none of the techniques described here is the best in all cases. The available hardware has a significant influence upon the best choice; but for rapid and successful design analysis, there is no substitute for providing several of these techniques in an interactive graphics environment, so that the user can select among the various options according to his needs.

6.3.4 Functions of More than Two Variables

Three-dimensional functions (stresses, temperatures, etc.) result from static three-dimensional analysis or two-dimensional transient analysis (where time is the third dimension). When we represent a three-dimensional function on a two-dimensional display surface, we actually lose two dimensions (the dimension of the function value itself and one space or time dimension). Thus, we must look for techniques to simulate these two missing dimensions. Three methods can be used to overcome this problem:

– Clouds of markers in 3-D space with varying size or color (according to the function value) can be projected from different view points (possibly with some scissoring applied). Human perception must reconstruct the full three-dimensional information from these views. As an alternative to several static projections, interactive display techniques might be provided to let the domain of interest be rotated under user control. As a compromise, the image may rotate or wobble in a predefined way; this technique is applicable for

computer-generated movies and videotapes. 3-D vector fields can be represented in this manner.
– Stereoscopic projection of marker clouds requires the overlay of two projections from appropriate viewpoints. Because of the problems associated with
the separation of the two images (each one must be seen with one eye only)
the technique has not become very popular. Wearing special glasses to separate light according to color or polarization is too much of a burden for
the user.
– The most successful way to represent three-dimensional functions is the use
of techniques for two-dimensional functions (see above), allowing time to
simulate the third dimension. Computer generated movies or video tapes
are an excellent tool for representing three-dimensional behavior.

6.3.5 Graphic Editing

The editing operations for data presentation usually comprise the following
functions:

– Generation of coordinate axes:
Care must be taken to assure the consistency of the displayed axes with
the corresponding data display. In particular, when linear transformations
(shift, rotate, scale) are applied to an already generated data display, the
associated axes must be submitted to the same transformations.

– Annotations:
Descriptive text must be added to most data displays.

– Viewing transformations and picture combinations:
It quite often happens that data curves from different sources must be combined into a single diagram: analysis data have to be shown together with
scaled drawings or sketches of the objects to which they relate. Thus, graphics
for data presentation and graphics for geometric modelling need to be interfaced in an appropriate way. A suitable method is a the use of a standardized
data schema for both applications.

Fig. 6.45 shows the concept of an editing system which has been developed
and used successfully at Karlsruhe [101, 102]. It is based on two data formats:

– the PLOTCP format for data vectors and matrices [103];
– the AGF-plotfile format for graphic information [44, 104, 105].

Graphic information can be produced from

– the geometrical description of objects (3-D or 2-D) in the graphical programming language GIPSY [44, 104] or from interactive display terminals;
– the results of various simulations;
– the results taken from corresponding experiments. Both data sources (experiments and simulation) can either generate standard (PLOTCP) data files or
else generate graphic data without utilizing the intermediate interface.

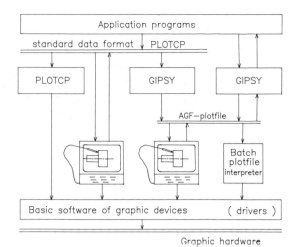

Fig. 6.45. Data format interfaces
in a data presentation system

Batch and interactive processors are available to combine information from these sources, to edit it, and to display it on various hardware. Since the output format of the graphic editors is again the standard AGF-plotfile, the edited pictures can sometimes be used in editing other pictures, for instance, by insertion into them.

6.4 Summary

Numerical methods play an important role in CAD. Finite element methods are most widely used for structural analyses. For some time during the 1970s, computer aided design was almost synonymous with finite element analysis. Today, finite element programs with various degrees of sophistication are commercially available. Computer centers offer their facilities to organizations which have less frequent need for such analyses. Static analysis based on linear theory of elasticity is most common. It can be mastered by the design engineer after a moderate amount of training. Dynamic analyses and non-linear analyses require a high degree of expertise, and are preferably performed by small groups of specialists in cooperation with the designer.

Finite element analysis is spreading in other domains: thermal analysis and fluid mechanics. The fundamental advantage of finite element methods is their flexibility with respect to geometry. But the conversion of the geometrical description of the object into the form required by the analysis programs — and the presentation of the results — produce considerable pre- and post-processing costs. Finite difference methods exhibit other advantages. They are easier to implement, and are often more efficient for regular geometries. But they lack the geometrical flexibility. Boundary integral equation methods and spectral methods, though rapidly developing, remain specialized and very efficient tools for particular cases; so far, they do not appear to have become widespread in the design environment.

Simulation methods have been developed for many classes of problems in the past. The most pronounced basis for distinction among these methods is whether they deal with continuous or discontinuous changes of state. Queueing problems are typically treated with discontinuous simulation. Continuous simulation problems always have a mathematical representation as a set of ordinary differential equations. For applications that call for both continuous and discontinuous simulation, combined methods have been developed. A number of simulation systems are commercially available, or may be employed at computer service centers by a remote user.

Optimization methods can help to support the synthesis part of design. In most cases, design optimization requires the solution of a non-linear constrained problem. A practical difficulty is the need for the *formal* statement of a measure-of-merit function and of the constraints. Many design requirements cannot be formally stated; or it might simply consume too much time or manpower to achieve a formal statement. Another problem is the large number of parameters influencing a design. For this reason, the application of optimization methods is more promising in an early design stage — on the basis of a crude model with only a few design parameters — than in final design, where the number of parameters becomes prohibitive because of the many details to be considered.

Numerical analysis methods inherently produce huge amounts of numerical data, which must be brought into a comprehensible form. Graphical representation techniques are well suited for this purpose. Functions of one variable are generally represented as diagrams. For functions of two variables, various techniques are possible; the usefulness of these techniques depends both on the behavior of the function and on the available graphical hardware. Computer-generated movies or videofilm, combined with color-coding of the displayed information, is best suited for the visualization of complicated multi-dimensional results.

6.5 Bibliography

[1] H.B. Voelcker, A.A.G. Requicha: Boundary Evaluation Procedures for Objects Defined via Constructive Solid Geometry. Tech. Memo No. 26. Production Automation Project, University of Rochester (1978).

[2] R.F. Riesenfeld: Homogeneous Coordinates and Projective Planes in Computer Graphics. IEEE Computer Graphics and Aplications 1 (1981) 1, pp. 50–55.

[3] W.K. Giloi: Interactive Computer Graphics. New Jersey (1978) Prentice-Hall.

[4] R. Schuster: System und Sprache zur Behandlung graphischer Information im rechnergestützten Entwurf. Report KfK 2305, Kernforschungszentrum Karlsruhe (1976).

[5] I.E. Sutherland et al.: A Characterization of Ten Hidden-Surface Algorithms. ACM-Computing Surveys 8 (1974), pp. 1–55.

[6] J. Encarnação: Computer Graphics. München (1975) Oldenbourg.

[7] W.M. Newmann, R.F. Sproull: Principles of Interactive Computer Graphics. London (1979) McGraw-Hill.

[8] H. Meschowski: Grundlagen der euklidischen Geometrie. BI-Hochschultaschenbuch 105/105a. Mannheim (1966).

[9] W.F. Klos: Einheitliche formale Beschreibung, qualitative und quantitative Untersuchung von Visibilitätsverfahren Diplomarbeit. Universität des Saarlandes, Fachbereich Informatik (1975).

[10] C. Hornung: An Approach to a Calculation Minimized Hidden-Line Algorithm. In: J. Encarnação (ed.): EUROGRAPHICS '81. Amsterdam (1981) North-Holland, pp. 31–42.

[11] A.A.G. Requicha, N.M. Samuel, H.B. Voelcker: Part and Assembly Description Languages II: Proposed Specifications for Definitional Facilities in PADL-1 and Tentative Specifications for Command Facilities. Tech. Memo No. 20a, Production Automation Project, University of Rochester (1974).

[12] S.A. Coons: Surfaces for Computer-Aided Design of Space Forms. Report Project MAC TR-41, Massachusetts Institute of Technology (1967).

[13] W.J. Gordon: Blending-Function Methods for Bivariate and Multivariate Interpolation and Approximation. SIAM Journ. Numer. Anal. 8 (1971) 1, pp. 158–177.

[14] A.R. Forrest: On Coons' and Other Methods for the Representation of Curved Surfaces. Computer Graphics and Image Processing 1 (1972) 4, pp. 341–359.

[15] W.J. Gordon, R.F. Riesenfeld: B-Spline Curves and Surfaces. In: R. Barnhill, R.F. Riesenfeld (eds.): Computer Aided Geometric Design. New York (1974) Academic Press, pp. 95–126.

[16] H. Nowacki: Curve and Surface Generation and Fairing. In: J. Encarnação (ed.): Computer Aided Design: Modelling, Systems Engineering, CAD-Systems. Lecture Notes in Computer Science, Vol. 89. Heidelberg (1980) Springer-Verlag, pp. 137–176.

[17] E. Catmull, J. Clark: Recursively Generated B-Spline Surfaces on Arbitrary Topological Meshes. Computer Aided Design 10 (1978) 6, pp. 350–355.

[18] E. Cohen, T. Lyche, R.F. Riesenfeld: Discrete B-Splines and Subdivision Techniques in Computer Aided Design and Computer Graphics. Computer Aided Graphics and Image Processing 14 (1980) 2, pp. 87–111.

[19] D. Doo, M. Sabin: Behaviour of Recursive Division Surfaces Near Extraordinary Points. Computer Aided Design 10 (1978) 6, pp. 356–360.

[20] J.H. Laning, D.A. Lynde, V. Morregia: SHAPES User's Manual. Charles Stark Draper Lab., Inc., Cambridge, Mass. (1973).

[21] J.H. Laning, S.J. Madden: Capabilities of the SHAPES System for Computer Aided Mechanical Design. Proc. First Ann. Conf. Computer Graphics in CAD/CAM Systems, Cambridge, Mass., April 9-11, 1979, pp. 223–231.

[22] N. Okino, Y. Kakazu, H. Kubo: TIPS-1: Technical Information Processing System for Computer Aided Design and Manufacturing. In: J. Hatvany (ed.): Computer Languages for Numerical Control. Amsterdam (1973) North-Holland, pp. 141–150.

[23] N. Okino et al.: TIPS-1. Report Institute of Precision Engineering, Hokkoido University, Sapporo, Japan (1978).

[24] W. Fitzgerald, F. Gracer, R. Wolfe: GRIN: Interactive Graphics for Modelling Solids. IBM J. Research and Development 25 (1981) 4, pp. 281–294.

[25] M.A. Wesley: Construction and Use of Geometric Models. In: J. Encarnação (ed.): Computer Aided Design: Modelling, Systems Engineering, CAD Systems. Lecture Notes in Computer Science, Vol. 89. Heidelberg (1980) Springer-Verlag, pp. 79–136.

[26] H.B. Voelcker, A.A.G. Requicha, E.E. Hartquist, W.B. Fisher, J.E. Shopiro, N.K. Birell: An Introduction to PADL: Characteristics, Status, and Rationale. Tech. Memo No. 22, Production Automation Project, University of Rochester (1974).

[27] H.B. Voelcker, A.A.G. Requicha, E.E. Hartquist, W.B. Fisher, J. Metzger, R.B. Tilove, N.K. Birell, W.A. Hunt, G.T. Armstrong, T.F. Check, R. Moote, J. McSweeney: The PADL-1.0/2 System for Defining and Displaying Solid Objects. Computer Graphics (Proc. SIGGRAPH '78) 12 (1978) 3, pp. 257–263.

[28] C.M. Brown: PADL-2: A Technical Summary. IEEE Computer Graphics and Applications 2 (1982) 2, pp. 69–84.

[29] R.A. Goldstein, R. Nagel: 3-D Visual Simulation. Simulation 16 (1971) 1, pp. 25–31.

[30] R.A. Goldstein, L. Malin: 3-D Modelling in the Synthavision System. Proc. First Ann. Conf. Computer Graphics in CAD/CAM Systems, Cambridge, Mass., April 9–11,1979, pp. 244–247.

[31] J.W. Boyse: Preliminary Design for a Geometric Modeller. Report Research Pub. GMR-2768, Computer Science Dept., General Motors Research Labs., Warren, Mich., July 1978.

[32] J.W. Boyse, J.E. Gilchrist: GMSolid:Interactive Modeling for Design and Analysis of Solids. IEEE Computer Graphics and Applications 2 (1982) 2, pp. 27–40.

[33] H.J. Borkin, J.F. McIntosh, J.A. Turner: The Development of Three-Dimensional Spatial Modelling Techniques for the Construction Planning of Nuclear Power Plants. Proc. SIGGRAPH '78, Computer Graphics 12 (1978) 3, pp. 341–347.

[34] I.C. Braid: New Generations in Geometric Modelling. Proc. of Geometric Modelling Project Meeting, P-78-GM-01, CAM-I, Inc., St. Louis, Mo., March 14–16, 1978.

[35] R.C. Hillyard: The Build Group of Solid Modelers. IEEE Computer Graphics and Applications 2 (1982) 2, pp. 43–52.

[36] G. Spur, J. Gausemeier: Processing of Workpiece Information for Producing Engineering Drawings. Proc. 16th Int. Machine Tool Design and Research Conf., Manchester, UK (1975), pp. 17–21.

[37] G. Spur: Status and Further Development of the Geometric Modelling System COMPAC. Proc. of Geometric Modelling Project Meeting, P-78-GM-01, CAM-I, Inc., St. Louis, Mo., March 14-16, 1978, pp. 1–35.

[38] D.R. Hakala, R.C. Hillyard, P.J. Malraison, B.E. Nourse: Natural Quadrics in Machine Design. Proc. Autofact West, Vol 1, CAD/CAM VIII, Nov. 1980, Anaheim, Calif., pp. 363–378.

[39] Y.J. Bernascon, J.M. Brun: Automated Aids for the Design of Mechanical Parts. Report Techn. Paper MS75-508, Society of Manufacturing Engineers (1975).

[40] C. Eastman, M. Henrion: GLIDE: A Language for Design Information Systems. Proc. SIGGRAPH '77, Computer Graphics 11 (1977) 2, pp. 24–33.

[41] C.M. Eastman, K. Weiler: Geometric Modelling Using the Euler Operators. Proc. First Ann. Conf. Computer Graphics in CAD/CAM Systems, Cambridge, Mass., April 9–11, 1979, pp. 248–259.

[42] H. Seifert, N. Bargele, B. Fritsche: Different Ways to Design Three-Dimensional Representations of Engineering Parts with PROREN2. Proc. Conf. Interactive Techniques In Computer Aided Design, Bologna, September 21–23, 1978, pp. 335–343.

[43] P. Veenman: ROMULUS — The Design of a Geometric Modeller. In: W.A. Carter (ed.): Geometric Modelling Seminar. P-8--GM-01, CAM-I, Inc., Bournemouth, UK, Nov. 1979., pp. 127–152.

[44] G. Enderle, K.H. Bechler, F. Katz, K. Leinemann, W. Olbrich, E.G. Schlechtendahl, K. Stölting: GIPSY-Handbuch. Report KfK 2878, Kernforschungszentrum Karlsruhe (1980).

[45] A.A.G. Requicha, H.B. Voelcker: Solid Modeling: A Historical Summary and Contemporary Assessment. Computer Graphics and Applications 2 (1982) 2, pp. 9–24.

[46] R.B. Tilove: Set Membership Classification: A Unified Approach to Geometric

Intersection Problems. IEEE Transactions on Computers, Vol. C-29 (1980) 10, pp. 874–883.

[47] A.H. Barr: Superquadrics and Angle-Preserving Transformations. IEEE Computer Graphics and Applications 1 (1981) 1, pp. 11–23.

[48] O.C. Zienkiewicz: The Finite Element Method. 3rd edition. London (1977) McGraw-Hill.

[49] R. Glowinski, E.Y. Rodin, O.C. Zienkiewicz: Energy Methods in Finite Element Analysis. Chichester (1979) J. Wiley & Sons.

[50] R.H. Gallagher, O.C. Zienkiewicz, M. Morandi-Cecchi, C. Taylor: Finite Elements in Fluids, Vol. 1, 2 and 3. Chichester (1975/1975/1978) J. Wiley & Sons.

[51] W. Pilkey, K. Saczalski, H. Schaeffer: Structural Mechanics Computer Programs, Surveys, Assessments, and Availibility. Charlottesville (1974) Univ. Virginia Press.

[52] St.J. Fenves, N. Perrone, A.R. Robinson, W.C. Schnobrich: Numerical and Computer Methods in Structural Mechanics. New York (1973) Academic Press.

[53] J.A. Swanson: ANSYS — Engineering ANalysis SYStem Users' Manual. Elizabeth, Swanson Analysis Systems, Inc.

[54] E. Schrem: ASKA. In: Three-Dimensional Continuum Computer Programs for Structural Analysis. New York (1972) ASME, pp. 31–34.

[55] R.H. MacNeal: NASTRAN. In: Three-Dimensional Continuum Computer Programs for Structural Analysis. New York (1972) ASME, pp. 21–22.

[56] D.J. Ayres: Elastic-Plastic and Creep Analysis Via the MARC Finite-Element Computer Program. In: Fenves et al.: Numerical and Computer Methods in Structural Mechanics. New York (1973) Academic Press, pp. 247–263.

[57] K.J. Bathe, E.L. Wilson, E. Peterson: SAP IV: A Structural Analysis Program for Static and Dynamic Response of Linear Systems. Report No. EERC-73-11, Berkeley (1973) Univ. California Press.

[58] M.F. Nelson: ICES STRUDL II. In: Three-Dimensional Continuum Computer Programs for Structural Analysis. New York (1972) ASME, pp. 23–24.

[59] G. Ruoff, E. Stein: The Development of General Purpose Programs and Systems. In: W. Pilkey, K. Saczalski, H. Schaeffer: Structural Mechanics Computer Programs. Charlottesville (1974) Univ. Virginia Press, pp. 703–719.

[60] T.J.R. Hughes: Finite Element Methods for Fluids and Fluid-Structure Interaction. Preprints 1st Int. Seminar on Fluid Structure Interaction in LWR Systems. Report ISSN 0172-0465. Berlin (1979) Bundesanstalt für Materialprüfung, pp. 19–28.

[61] J.W. Cooley, J.W. Tukey: An Algorithm for the Machine Computation of Complex Fourier Series. Math. Comput. 19 (1965), pp. 297–301.

[62] D. Gottlieb, St.A. Orszag: Numerical Analysis of Spectral Methods: Theory and Applications. Philadelphia (1977) Soc. for Industrial and Applied Mathematics.

[63] J.L. Hess, A.M.O. Smith: Calculation of Potential Flow about Arbitrary Bodies. Progr. Areonautical Sciences 8 (1967), pp. 1–138.

[64] R. Krieg, B. Göller, G. Hailfinger: Transient, Three-Dimensional Potential Flow Problems and Dynamic Response of Surrounding Structures. Journal of Computational Physics 34 (1980) 2, pp. 164–183.

[65] O.C. Zienkiewicz, D.W. Kelly, P. Bettes: Marriage 139' la Mode — The Best of Both Worlds (Finite Elements and Boundary Integrals). In: R. Glowinski, E.Y. Rodin, O.C. Zienkiewicz: Energy Methods in Finite Element Analysis. Chichester (1979) John Wiley & Sons, pp. 81–107.

[66] U. Schumann (ed.): Computers, Fast Elliptic Solvers, and Applications. London (1978) Advance Publ.

[67] R.E. Shannon: Systems Simulation: The Art and Science. Englewood Cliffs (1975) Prentice-Hall.

[68] G. Gordon: System Simulation. Englewood Cliffs (1978) Prentice-Hall.

[69] H.J. Highland, N.R. Nielson, L.R. Hull (eds.): 1978 Winter Simulation Conference. IEEE 78CH1415-9. New York (1979) Institute of Electrical and Electronic Engineers.

[70] A.L. Pugh III: DYNAMO User's Manual. Cambridge, Mass. (1961) MIT Press.

[71] W.M. Syn, R.N. Linebarger: DSL/90 — A Digital Simulation Program for Continuous System Modeling. 1966 Spring Joint Computer Conference (1966).

[72] "CSMP-III": Continuous System Modelling Program III (CSMP-III) Program Reference Manual. IBM Form SH19-7001-2, Don Mills (1972) IBM Canada Ltd.

[73] P.A. Bobllier, B.C. Kahan, A.R. Probst: Simulations with GPSS and GPSS V. Englewood Cliffs (1976) Prentice-Hall.

[74] G. Gordon: The Application of GPSS V to Discrete System Simulation. Englewood Cliffs (1975) Prentice-Hall.

[75] O.-J. Dahl, B. Myhrhaug, K. Nygaard: SIMULA 67 Common Base Language. Report S22, Oslo-Bergen-Tromso (1970) NORSK Norwegian Computer Center.

[76] "PEARL": Full PEARL Language Description. Report KfK-CAD 130, Kernforschungszentrum Karlsruhe (1977).

[77] A.A.B. Pritsker, R.E. Young: Simulation with GASP-PL/1. New York (1975) John Wiley & Sons.

[78] E.G. Schlechtendahl: DYSYS, A Dynamic System Simulator for Continuous and Discrete Changes of State. Report KFK 1209, Kernforschungszentrum Karlsruhe (1970).

[79] D.G. Golden, J.D. Schoffler: GSL — A Combined Continuous and Discrete Simulation Language. SIMULATION 20 (1973), pp. 1–8.

[80] D.G. Luenberger: Introduction to Linear and Nonlinear Programing. Reading (1973) Addison-Wesley.

[81] M. Aoki: Introduction to Optimization Techniques. New York (1971) Macmillan.

[82] H.P. Künzi, H.G. Tzschach, C.A. Zehnder: Numerische Methoden der mathematischen Optimierung. Stuttgart (1967) Teubner.

[83] R. Fletcher (ed.): Optimization. London (1969) Academic Press.

[84] D.J. Wilde, C.S. Beightler: Foundations of Optimization. Englewood Cliffs (1967) Prentice-Hall.

[85] H.P. Schwefel: Numerische Optimierung von Computer-Modellen mittels Evolutionsstrategie. Basel (1977) Birkhäuser.

[86] R. Heckler, H.P. Schwefel: Superimposing Direct Search Methods for Parameter Optimization onto Dynamic Simulation Models. In: H.J. Highland, N.R. Nielson, L.R. Hull: 1978 Winter Simulation Conference. IEEE 78CH1415-9. New York (1978) Institute of Electrical and Electronic Engineers, pp. 173–181.

[87] G. Zoutendijk: Methods of Feasible Directions. Amsterdam (1960) Elsevier Publ. Co.

[88] H. Czap: Nichtlineare Optimierungsmethoden. In: H. Noltemeier (ed.): Computergestützte Planungssysteme. Würzburg (1976) Physica-Verlag, pp. 93–110.

[89] G. Heusener: Optimierung natriumgekühlter schneller Brutreaktoren mit Methoden der nichtlinearen Programmierung. Report KFK 1238, Kernforschungszentrum Karlsruhe (1970).

[90] R.H. Myers: Response Surface Methodology. Boston (1971) Ally and Bacon, Inc.

[91] A.K. Noor, H.G. McComb Jr. (eds.): Trends in Computerized Structural Analysis and Synthesis. Computers and Structures 10 (1979), pp. 1–430.

[92] K. Svanberg: Optimization of Geometry in Truss Design. Computer Methods in Appl. Mechanics and Engineering (1981), pp. 63–80.

[93] H. Nowacki: Optimization in Pre-Contract Ship Design. Conf. Computer Applications in the Automation of Shipyard Operation and Ship Design. Tokyo (1973), pp. 327–338.

[94] B.C. Rush, J. Bracken, G.P. McCormick: A Nonlinear Programming Model for Launch Vehicle Design and Costing. Oper. Res. 15 (1967), pp. 185–210.

[95] B.M.E. de Silva: The Application of Nonlinear Programming to the Automated Minimum Weight Design of Rotating Disks. In: R. Fletcher (ed.): Optimization. London (1969) Academic Press, pp. 115–150.

[96] H. Nowacki: Modelling of Design Decisions for CAD. In: J. Encarnação: Computer Aided Design: Modelling, Systems Engineering, CAD-Systems. Lecture Notes in Computer Science, Vol. 89, Heidelberg (1980) Springer-Verlag, pp. 177–223.

[97] E.G. Schlechtendahl: Graphische Datenverarbeitung in der Kerntechnik. In: J. Encarnação, W. Straßer (eds.): Geräteunabhängige graphische Systeme. München (1981) Oldenbourg.

[98] H.N. Christiansen: Application of Continuous Tone Computer Generated Images in Structural Mechanics. In: W. Pilkey, K. Saczalski, H. Schaeffer: Structural Mechanics Computer Programs. Charlottesville (1974) Univ. Virginia Press, pp. 1003–1015.

[99] R. Ganz, H.-J. Dohrmann: Farbgraphische Ausgabesysteme. Zeitschrift für wirtschaftliche Fertigung 76 (1981) 5, pp. 223–239.

[100] M.R. Patterson: CONTUR: A Subroutine to Draw Contour Lines for Randomly Located Data. Report ORNL/CSD/TM-59, Oak Ridge (1978) Union Carbide Corp., Nuclear Division.

[101] D. Kühl, K. Leinemann: Erfahrungen mit dem Einsatz des AGF-PLOTFILE-Formats. Angewandte Informatik 9 (1979), pp. 401–405.

[102] K. Leinemann, P. Royl, W. Zimmerer: Integration graphischer Systeme für Darstellungszwecke. KfK-Nachrichten 1-2, Kernforschungszentrum Karlsruhe (1980), pp. 75–80.

[103] W. Zimmerer: PLOTCP — Ein FORTRAN IV-Programm zur Erzeugung von Calcomp Plot-Zeichnungen. Report KFK 2081, Kernforschungszentrum Karlsruhe (1975).

[104] G. Enderle, K.-H. Bechler, H. Grimme, W. Hieber, F. Katz: GIPSY-Handbuch Band II. Report KfK 3216, Kernforschungszentrum Karlsruhe (1981).

[105] G. Enderle, I. Giese, M. Krause, H.-P. Meinzer: The AGF-Plotfile — Towards a Standardization for Storage and Transportation of Graphics Information. Computer Graphics 12 (1978) 4, pp. 92–113.

7 CAD Application Examples

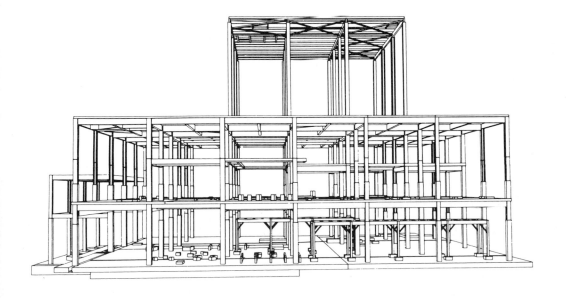

3-D building layout
(courtesy of Compeda Ltd., London, UK)

A selection of CAD application examples will always contain some element of arbitrariness. The examples given in this chapter are taken from industrial practice, and represent some of the most common CAD application types. More application examples may be found in the proceedings of the relevant conferences (such as [1, 2, 3, 4, 5]) and journals (such as [6]). An even wider spectrum of applications is published not in the computer-oriented literature, but rather in the journals and conference proceedings of the various branches of industry.

7.1 Typical Classes of Applications

7.1.1 Numerical Analysis and Presentation

Finite element analysis, as the best-known application, is represented by Figs. 7.1 through 7.3. Figs. 7.1 and 7.2 (courtesy of Messerschmitt-Bölkow-Blohm,

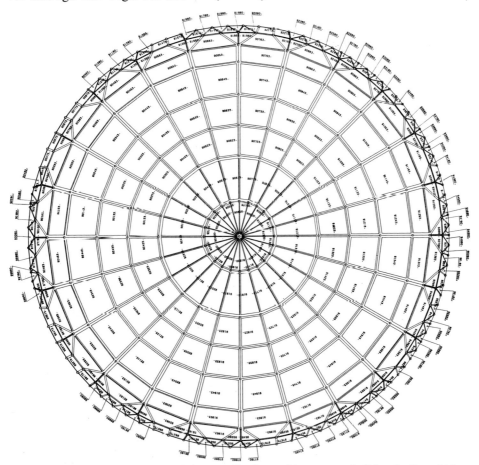

Fig. 7.1. Finite element model of the rear fuselage with pressure bulkhead of an Airbus A310, front view (courtesy of Messerschmitt-Bölkow-Blohm, Hamburg)

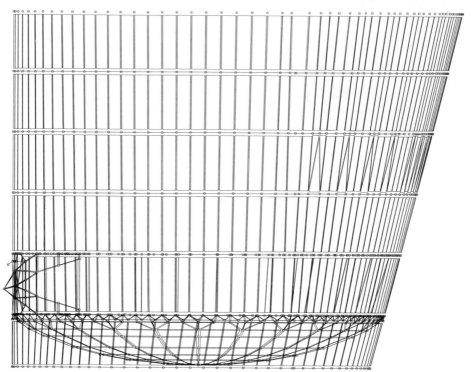

Fig. 7.2. Finite element model of the rear fuselage with pressure bulkhead of an Airbus A310, side view (courtesy of Messerschmitt-Bölkow-Blohm, Hamburg)

Hamburg) show the finite element discretization of part of the rear fuselage with pressure bulkhead for an Airbus A310, in front view and side view respectively. The gross dimensions are 3550 mm length and 3400 mm in diameter. The model contains 4709 finite elements and a total of 6577 degrees of freedom. Representations of this type are useful for checking the correctness of the topology and geometry of the model. In this case, each finite element is drawn as a polygon, slightly smaller than its actual size; this makes checking for missing elements easier than it would be with elements drawn as full size polygons. The same representation technique is chosen for Fig. 7.3 (courtesy of IKO Software Service, Stuttgart), which shows the finite element model of a destroyer with 22000 degrees of freedom. Checking a model of this complexity requires projections from different viewing points, and is best done in interactive mode at a display terminal.

Figs. 7.4 and 7.5 (courtesy of IKO Software Service, Stuttgart) are *presentations of results* from finite element analyses. Fig. 7.4 shows the radial stresses in the flange of a nuclear reactor pressure vessel. The isolines are obviously linear interpolations between computed nodal points. They give a clear indication of the degree of detailing used for the model. The isolines of Fig. 7.5 show stresses in a tube plate of a heat exchanger. From the curves one cannot decide whether the smoothness is a consequence of fine modelling or the result

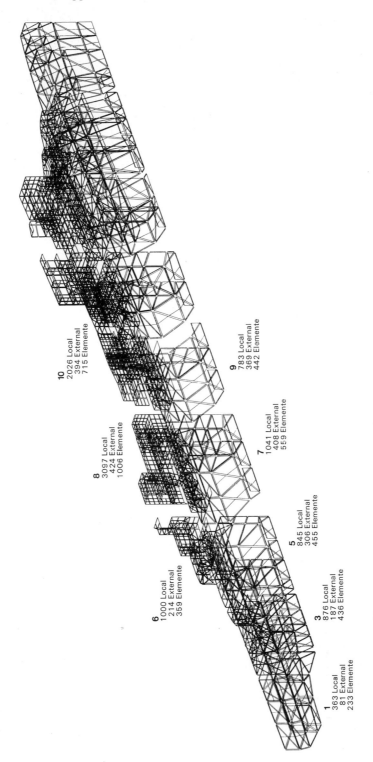

Fig. 7.3. Finite element model of a ship (courtesy of IKO Software Service, Stuttgart)

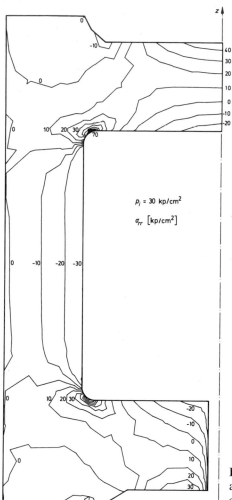

$p_i = 30$ kp/cm^2

σ_{rr} [kp/cm^2]

Fig. 7.4. Presentation of finite element analysis results (stresses) for a pre-stressed concrete pressure vessel of a nuclear reactor (courtesy of IKO Software Service, Stuttgart)

of an *a posteriori* smoothing (see Chapter 4.3). In either case, stress concentrations are made evident by the isolines alone; but for evaluation the annotations (levels of stress) are definitely needed.

7.1.2 Three-Dimensional Applications

Smooth *surface design* is illustrated by Figs. 7.6 and 7.7 (courtesy of Bayerische Motoren Werke, München). The figures demonstrate that even a few lines can give a good impression of the three-dimensional shape. However, the lines only

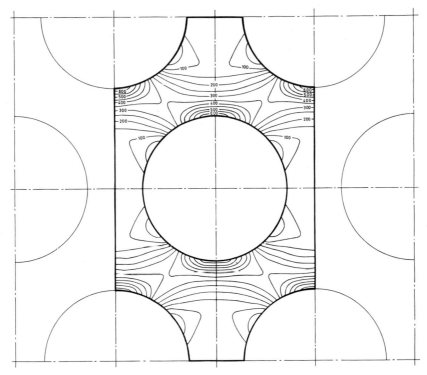

Fig. 7.5. Presentation of finite element analysis results (stresses) for a heat exchanger tube plate (courtesy of IKO Software Service, Stuttgart)

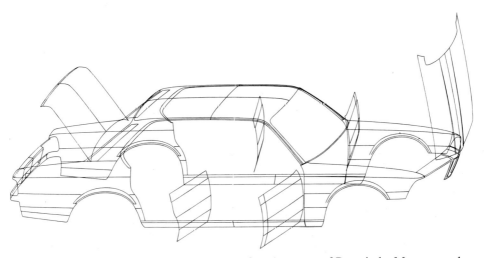

Fig. 7.6. Section lines representing a car's surface (courtesy of Bayerische Motorenwerke, München)

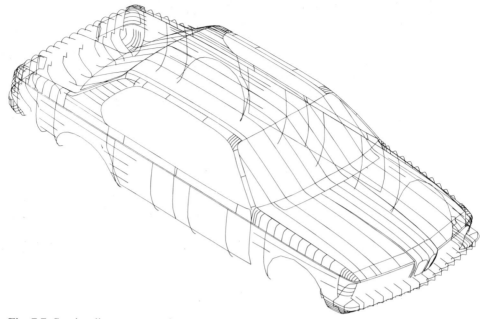

Fig. 7.7. Section lines representing a car's surface (courtesy of Bayerische Motorenwerke, München)

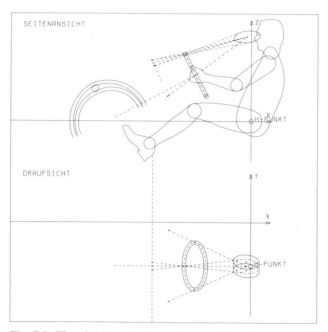

Fig. 7.9. The viewing situation of a car driver (courtesy of Volkswagenwerk, Wolfsburg)

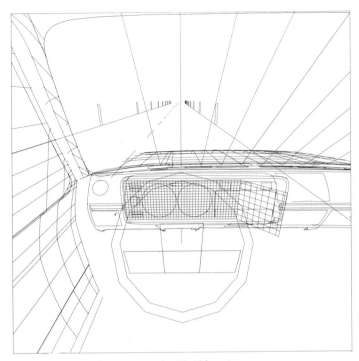

Fig. 7.10. Driver's view (courtesy of Volkswagenwerk, Wolfsburg)

outline the boundaries of the surface patches, which are used to represent the car's surface with high accuracy. Simulation and presentation of the *kinematics* of moving parts is a traditional CAD application area. Fig. 7.8 (page 344, courtesy of Bayerische Motoren Werke, München) shows various positions of a car's front wheel support. Without the color, which definitely improves the perceptibility of the different positions, the picture would simply be a mess of lines. Overlaying the positions in three orthogonal, colored projections on one drawing gives a vivid impression of the movements of the part. Another three-dimensional projection example is shown in Figs. 7.9 and 7.10 (courtesy of Volkswagenwerk, Wolfsburg). Fig. 7.9 indicates the viewing situation of a driver in his normal position; Fig. 7.10 shows what the driver would see, and what part of the environment or the instrumentation might be hidden by components of the car (by the steering wheel, for instance).

7.1.3 Functional and Geometrical Layout

Two-dimensional functional layout is demonstrated by Fig. 7.11 (courtesy of Volkswagenwerk, Wolfsburg). This figure shows part of a car's electric circuitry.

Examples of *geometric layout* are given in Figs. 7.12, 7.13, and 7.14 (courtesy of Siemens, Erlangen). Fig. 7.12 represents part of a building layout. Figs.

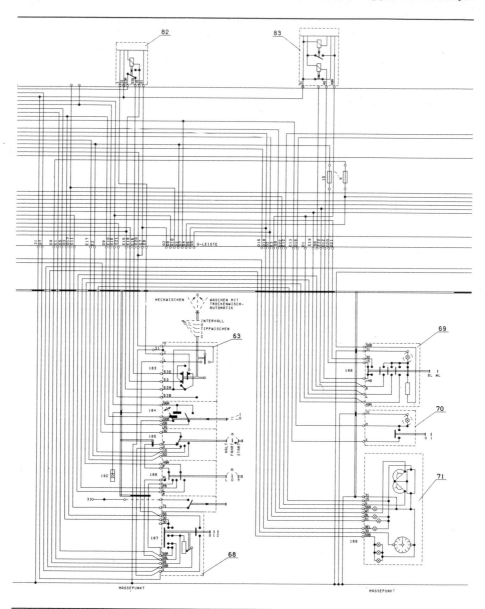

Fig. 7.11. Electrical circuit layout for a car (courtesy of Volkswagenwerk, Wolfsburg)

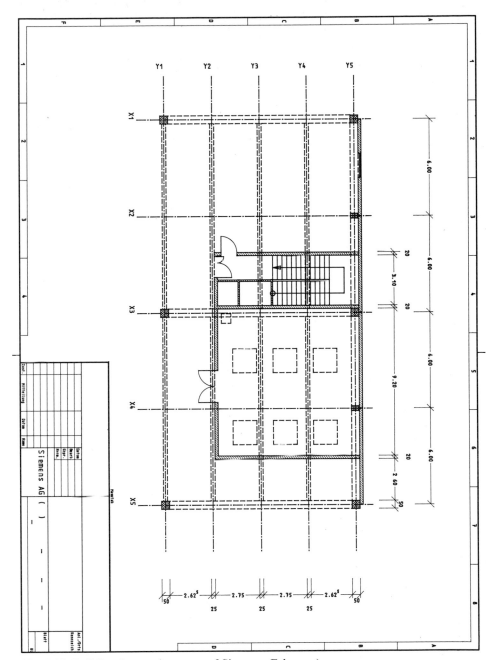

Fig. 7.12. Building layout (courtesy of Siemens, Erlangen)

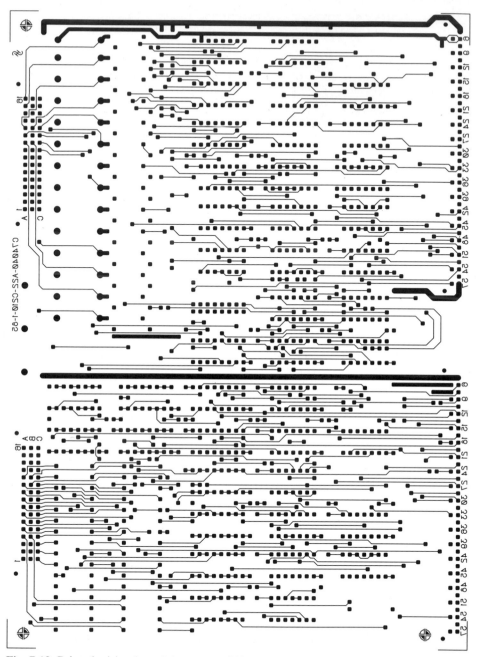

Fig. 7.13. Printed wiring board (courtesy of Siemens, Erlangen)

Fig. 7.15. Architectural CAD application (courtesy of GMW Computers, Hertshoreshire, UK)

7.13 and 7.14 (page 345) show the layout of a printed wiring board (Fig. 7.13 shows one layer only; the colored picture illustrates how the three layers fit together).

7.2. CAD Application in some Specific Examples of Industry

Figs. 7.15 and 7.16 (page 346), as well as the illustrations on pages 1, 7, 35, 89, 149, 219, 293, 307, 321, and 333) show CAD applications from various branches of industry. The figures were made available by purveyors of CAD systems.

7.3 Bibliography

[1] Proceedings of the International Conference on Interactive Techniques in Computer Aided Design, Bologna, September 1978. Bologna (1978) ACM Italian Chapter.

[2] Proceedings International Conference Computer Aided Design. IEE Conference Publication Number 111. Southampton, (1974) Institution of Electrical Engineers.

[3] Proceedings of the Biannual International Conference on Computer Aided Design. Guildford (1974, 1976, 1978, 1980, 1982) Butterworth & Co., formerly IPC Science and Technology Press.

[4] Proceedings of the Annual Design Automation Conferences (e.g. Number 15 in 1978) Long Beach, Institute of the Electrical Engineers, New York, Association of Computing Machinery.

[5] Proceedings of the IFIP Congress 77, Toronto, August 1977. New York (1977) North-Holland.

[6] Computer Aided Design, published six times a year.

8 Trends

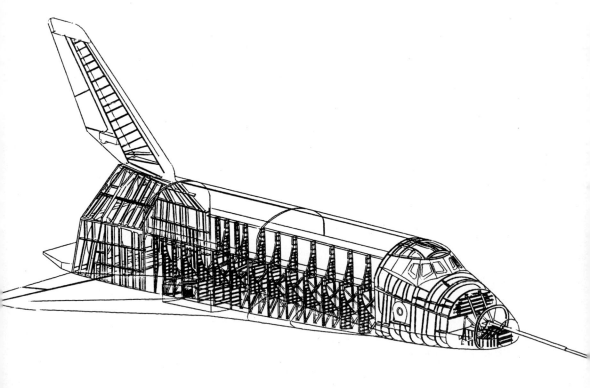

Space shuttle
(courtesy of Nicolet Instruments Ltd., Warwick, UK)

It is easy to make predictions about future developments, but it is extremely difficult to make such predictions accurately on a sound scientific basis. Fortunately, when the time comes for which the forecast was made, the forecast itself has often been forgotten or become irrelevant. Here, we do not claim to predict the future; we rather state a few present trends which appear to be having a significant impact on CAD in the later 1980s.

8.1 Availability of Computer Power

8.1.1 Configuration

The breakthrough of CAD, which began in the mid-'70s for medium- and small-size companies, arrived with the availability of moderate-cost mini-computers. These minis could be installed in the design environment under full control of the design office or department. The designer now had a computer of his own [1]. He no longer had to share computer power with administrative departments (financial, commercial, personnel), which generally had higher priority on the central computer. The attitude towards the "design computer" is different from from the traditional requirements for large central computers: in design, availability on demand has much higher priority than maximum utilization of the processor.

Starting from one or more design office computers, the trend can go in two directions:

- steady replacement of the design computers by more powerful ones, as the number of applications and their resource requirements increase;
- back-up by connection to a more powerful host computer or computer network.

The second approach appears more promising, since it does not burden the design office with all the organizational problems of running a multi-user computer center. Standardization of the hardware interface is a prerequisite for connecting computers into a network; it is necessary to standardize the concepts upon which software interfaces between computers are to be built, in order to make such networks more widely usable. This process is presently underway (see Chapter 4.3.4).

8.1.2 Hardware

For some time during the '70s, the mini-computers which were readily available to the designer seemed to be restricted to a (say) 32k primary memory of 16-bit words. This was a serious limitation. While processing speed was satisfactory in most cases (at least when floating-point arithmetic was supported by the hardware), the restriction on primary memory made many design applications impossible. CAD system implementers had to master the art of squeezing programs and data into a small memory. With the continuing significant decrease in memory cost [2], the present trend towards larger memory on minis will continue, associated with a continuing conversion from 16-bit words to 32-bit words. This trend has a double effect. First of all, user programs requiring, say, 60k or 120k words of memory now become executable on the "bigger minis". But in addition, more versatile operating systems are now feasible: virtual memory concepts can be implemented on small computers, making the minis fully competitive with much larger and more expensive computer systems in this respect. We expect this development to make three-dimensional design applications feasible on a broad scale [3].

As soon as primary memory is no longer the hardware bottleneck, secondary storage becomes more and more the restrictive component. Online direct access storage devices will play an increasingly important role as data bases on design computers grow. We expect here a replication of a development that has occurred in commercial data processing and in engineering applications on large main-frame computers: in the beginning, the user is happy with the processing capabilities of the computer; but soon he wants the computer to perform more and more memory functions, including the organization of the memory in a form that allows fast and ready access to specific information. A particular need for voluminous, efficient peripheral storage arises when the handling of geometric information about bodies and surfaces in three-dimensional space is associated with raster graphic display techniques. With luck, new storage techniques presently under development will make large picture libraries feasible at a justifiable cost.

8.1.3 Graphics Terminals

Interactive graphic display is the standard medium for man/machine communication and presentation in CAD. Storage tubes (sometimes with limited refresh capabilities added) have become most widely accepted, and this trend is expected to continue for practically all two-dimensional applications (such as functional and geometric layout), and most three-dimensional presentation tasks. Some applications call for more rapid changes of the picture (as when checking for geometrical interferences of three-dimensional bodies during assembly). These applications continue to advance the development of cheaper refresh displays.

We expect to see a competition between raster graphics and the already-established vector graphics techniques in this field. Raster technology has a significant economic potential, because it can draw from the mass production of television components. One of the main problems with raster displays is the refreshing process. In order to make raster display attractive for real-time graphics and high interaction rates, this problem needs to be resolved. So far, map and direct cell processors are used, but they do not provide sufficient refresh rates [4]. Lindner proposes to perform real-time scanning of a *vector* display file, containing vector information rather than raster point information [5]. His concept is based on hardware that performs very fast arithmetic, along with a strategy which avoids the computation of vectors that do not influence the actual scan line. With this concept, the dominant limitation would no longer be the real time and interaction capability, but rather the picture complexity (not to exceed about 250 vectors and 5000 points). Another possible solution is the use of many parallel special-purpose vector generators (chips that implement the conversion from vector to raster representation), one generator for each vector or small group of vectors. With such concepts, real-time graphics with more than 1000 vectors is conceivable. The bottleneck of this approach is the overhead and the complexity of the hardware needed for the parallel multi-vector generator.

Raster graphics has a significant potential, since it is more flexible than vector displays. But many of its capabilities (area-oriented graphic representations, possibly with color) are uncommon in the basically line-oriented design world. Hence, a breakthrough of raster graphics in CAD should not be expected on the basis of this additional power, but only if it succeeds in the economic competition with the vector-oriented refresh displays or even storage tube displays. Other areas of computer graphics application (like cartography) have a stronger incentive for raster display development. CAD will probably benefit from this development. For applications that are not dominated by graphics, but rather require a mixture of graphics communication with line commands or the entry of alpha-numerical data in tabular form, we expect a spreading of the double screen concept: an alphanumeric display with full screen support combined with a graphic display, in a single graphics terminal.

8.2 System Architecture and Software

8.2.1 Special-Purpose Systems

Two strategies for introducing CAD can be observed in the past and present time. They are associated with the installation of either a special-purpose turn-key system [6] or the utilization of a freely programmable general-purpose computer (mini or large). In the first case, a special design task that occurs frequently in the environment can be performed more efficiently soon after the turn-key system has been installed. Many turn-key systems are intended only for drafting, simply replacing the drawing board. But systems for more specific applications (such as plant layout) have become available, providing better support of the design through built-in technological information (design rules, etc.). We expect further specializations and enhancements of these turn-key systems with more built-in intelligence. This is the domain where microprocessors are likely to have the most significant impact on CAD: they will be hidden in the turn-key system, providing it with adaptable processing power. Such systems can be more easily adapted to the specific requirements of a company (company standards) or even the wishes of individual designers in ergonomic respects (the syntax of man/machine communication, for instance).

8.2.2 General Purpose Systems

The second approach does not try to offer a system for solving a design task directly. It rather provides a suitably structured set of software machines for building design systems (see Chapters 3.2.5.3 and 4.3). CAD system nuclei (see Chapter 5.1.2.4) belong to this category; their orientation is very general with respect to the range of CAD applications. More specialized sets of tools have been developed for various branches of industry [3]. Portable CAD systems have begun to compete with turn-key systems on a rapidly growing market. A recent survey lists 49 commercially available CAD systems [7]. Freely programmable CAD systems provide better potential for integration of non-CAD activities, while requiring a higher level of software know-how [8]. The technology of building such systems is now fairly well established. We quote from [1]:

- It is possible to design, assemble and routinely operate such large systems;
- The introduction of these systems requires a complete and radical revision of all earlier procedures, the thorough retraining of personnel, and probably considerable organizational, personnel and management changes;
- It is much harder than one would at first think to design a truly modular, truly open-ended software system;
- The return from undertaking these difficult tasks justifies doing them. Nobody subsequently suggests going back to the old methods.

"Design integration" — that is, the support of *all* design activities by building design systems which are tailored to the company and its products — is the explicit goal of these systems. We do not expect to see a trend toward the wide distribution of a few of these "integrated" systems. We rather expect a proliferation of their basic ideas in implementations of CAD systems that are adapted to their environment. The fundamental architecture is likely to converge.

8.2.3 Distribution of Processing Power

The decrease of hardware cost and the fast development of microprocessor technology are revolutionizing the whole field of CAD, and opening new dimensions of use. Future systems will probably be influenced by associative and parallel processors. This trend is strongly supported by the cost decrease of large and fast secondary storage.

Developments of this kind make us confident to expect solutions with acceptable processing time and justifiable costs for many problems that are as yet expensive to treat: hidden-line and hidden-surface detection, picture processing and picture analysis. The graphic input tends to develop from fixed turn-key systems toward user-programmed dialogue systems, using application-dependent high-level constructs for the definition and execution of dialogue. Several research projects are underway, aiming at the sound ergonomic design and

efficient implementation of systems that can be adapted to user skills and personal ergonomic wishes.

More and more graphic systems are designed and implemented in a distributed architecture. In any case, more intelligence will be installed in the display
itself, relieving the main computer from the routine work that is related to
viewing only: translation, scaling, etc. This development is supported by technological progress (microprocessors, multiprocessors, large-scale integration) and
the awareness of the increasing need for more efficient communication (office
automation, home computing). But a distributed system architecture also calls
for the flexible rearrangement of functions. This requirement is fulfilled neither
by satellite graphics systems with a rigidly assigned function distribution, nor
by programmable satellites that require preplanning and predetermination of
the division of labor. In both cases, changes in the application spectrum or
in the relative limitations of resources (time versus money, for instance) call
for redesign — or at least reprogramming — of the whole system. In [9] a
solution is proposed which does not require a predefinition of the functional
distribution. The proposal integrates into the system a data collector and ana-
lyzer, an optimizer, and an automatic interprocess communication. Thus, with
the knowledge about the application programs that have to be executed for
each actual task, the optimizer should be able to find an optimal assignment
of functions to the individual distributed processors. The concept aims at a
dynamic redistribution of functions as the system workload changes.

8.2.4 Languages

We must distinguish between various language levels:

- CAD system specification;
- CAD system implementation;
- formulation of design algorithms;
- CAD user language;
- parameter setting.

So far, we do not see any formal specification languages spreading in the
CAD world. System specifications should describe the abstract function of the
system, make statements about the operational environment, specify the available resources and their relative value, and list performance requirements. Verbal
formulations will continue to dominate this domain.

CAD system implementation requires the treatment of resource management
tasks (see Chapter 4). The implementation language should be suitable to deal
with such tasks. FORTRAN is definitely unsatisfactory. A common way out
of the problem is the use of FORTRAN-callable assembler subroutine packages.
Other implementation languages, such as PL/1, PEARL or ADA, are much
better suited in this respect and would allow the implementation of more readable systems which are easier to maintain. But we expect them to remain in
the minority.

Design algorithms generally comprise a considerable amount of arithmetical data processing. It is this domain where the use of FORTRAN has the greatest justification, although most other languages can do the same job as well. As design applications tend to shift from computational to organizational tasks (management of information and information structures) we expect a growing acceptance of languages like PL/1, Pascal, ADA, etc. Recent statistics on programming languages in Germany list 798 installations of PL/1, 557 of FORTRAN, 44 of Algol, and none of PEARL or Pascal [10]. But these statistics are dominated by business applications, which are not representative of CAD, as becomes evident from the total of 2893 COBOL and 2223 Assembler installations. The enormous investment in already-existing CAD programs will make a significant shift away from FORTRAN impossible. What is actually needed is an interface between programs implemented in different languages. The interface should allow binding and execution of mixed language modules. However, only a few attempts in this direction have been made in methods base systems [11] or in the versions of PL/1 (available on IBM and SIEMENS computers), which provides an interface between PL/1, FORTRAN, COBOL and ASSEMBLER).

Finally, we should not forget that FORTRAN 77, according to DIN 66027, 1980, is already a significant step over the previous FORTRAN standards, whose deficiencies led to the proliferation of FORTRAN dialects. At present, standardization efforts are underway in order to improve FORTRAN and while maintaining its popularity and upward compatibility. The programming language in the year 2000 for CAD applications (and many others) is still very likely to be called FORTRAN, but it may have become a much better language.

With the growing use of interactive graphic terminals, man/machine communication has shifted from the character string languages (command languages and programming languages) to visual (display screen), tactile (function keys, light-pen, tablet) and — in a few cases — acoustic communication. This trend will continue. The standardization of concepts now beginning [12, 13] will avoid an unnecessary proliferation of methods. It is hoped that formal notations for the specification of conversational languages based on these new means will develop. Such notations (like the Backus-Naur form for convential programming languages) would have a significant advantage in CAD.

8.2.5 CAD Systems in Research and Development (R&D)

One characteristic of recent technological development is the growing complexity of the systems, the requirement for more ingenuity and more refinement. Therefore, there is an increased need for more powerful tools in R&D. The problem-solving process in R&D is not a deductive process that can be automated by formulating and implementing algorithms. It requires the creativity of a person or even a large group of people integrated in the R&D process. In this respect, R&D has requirements similar to design, but on a larger scale. The division of work between persons and computers in R&D is based on

Table 8.1. The characteristics of persons and computers for problem solving

Man	Computer
Abstraction	Processing and filtering of bulk and complex data
Creativity	Fast processing
Deduction	Good information management capabilities, memory
Adaptability	Graphical I/O capabilities
Identification of trends	Reliable handling of lengthy, monotonous work
Formulation of hypotheses	

their particular capabilities (see Table 8.1). Interactive graphic systems developed for CAD applications have a great potential to be used beneficially in R&D.

Today, the use of CAD is in many areas the only way to obtain feasible solutions of R&D problems (micro-electronics, space and aircraft industries, nuclear and chemical industries). In other areas, the problem complexity, the amount of data to be handled and the need for better user control over the problem-solving process call for system architectures like those that have been developed for CAD. Modularity, man-machine communication, communication with other systems, reliability, high availability and — a matter of increasing importance — data security are required. Computer aided R&D is faced with a similar problem as CAD: the users of the system cannot be expected to be computer specialists. They need to have access to a bank of methods (containing the application programs, the operations, and the interaction methods) and to a data base (containing the data representation of the knowledge, of the problem itself, and of the various forms for representing the problem and its solutions). This means that computer-aided R&D systems should be designed and implemented along the same principles as CAD systems.

Interactive graphics systems are particularly suited for R&D support, because appropriate graphic symbols are the optimal means for communication, and because these systems allow a high rate of data exchange on output (for presentation) and on input (for interaction with the process). Graphic systems similar to those used in CAD have an increasing popularity in R&D, with the potential for improvement both in the quality and quantity of problem solutions, as well as for enhanced creativity and convenience of the user.

8.2.6 Problem-Solving Methods for CAD

Whether or not the development of problem-solving methods ("artificial intelligence") will be successful to the extent that the computer can not only relieve man from analytical work and memory tasks, but can take over some of the synthesis work, is still an open issue. This applies to both R&D and design applications. The development of artificial intelligence methods and their implementation in practice is still a research topic in itself [14, 15].

8.3 Social Aspects

8.3.1 Education

The social implications of introducing CAD have become equally as important as the technical and economical ones [16]. A significant difference exists among various organizations and even whole countries in this respect. Allan emphasizes the differences between the United States and European countries [17]. Among other differences, he states prevalent attitudes:

Europe	*United States*
* Make sure people are happy	Buy equipment and hire/fire people
* Don't change the way of working	Let the computer show a new way of working
* Don't degrade man	Achieve man/machine symbiosis
* Non-computer-oriented companies go to universities and government laboratories for help	Non-computer-oriented companies develop their own CAD systems

The last point in the above list reflects the differences between the CAD education of engineers in the United States and Europe. U.S. engineering education has a longer tradition in CAD. Allan states: "Fairly sophisticated computing training is a mandatory part of engineering and architecture programs. Engineering and computing are tied together in the U.S., while in Europe they seem to be separate specialties." This situation is changing steadily in Europe, and computer-oriented training is being integrated with engineering education.

In organizations which have not yet introduced CAD, a particular need for CAD education (from draftsmen through engineers to managers) exists. Probably the most promising approach is to hire one or more experienced CAD specialists. In the early phases of CAD introduction, the implications of the new technology and its effect upon the existing design process are often underestimated, while the potential benefits are overestimated and expected to pay off too soon. Vendors of turn-key systems do not always have the incentive to correct such false assessments of CAD introduction. Once CAD is established in an organization, the overwhelming part of the education task is done, and the training of growing community of users becomes a routine job.

8.3.2 Ergonomic Aspects

The ergonomic aspects of CAD systems are principally related to the man-machine interface; that is, to the interactive graphics terminal. In this context, three kinds of human factors have to be considered. They are associated with the physical environment, with man-machine communication, and with the operation of the system. Among others, the following factors are important:

- physical layout of the graphics terminal (keyboard, light-pen, comfortable chair, etc.);
- temperature level;
- noise;
- light;
- fast response time;
- work specialization;
- dependency on machine response;
- multishift operation;
- personnel training;
- equipment maintenance;
- reference documentation;
- user guidance.

Humcke and Kent [18] state "In defining a proper man-machine environment, utility is the directing force. Utmost considerations must be given to the operator, who must, as an individual, feel personally comfortable in an automated or production-oriented situation."

Once the technical problems are solved, CAD system design will be dominated by ergonomic aspects. Concentration on this aspect is a must if automated tools are to be accepted on a broad scale both by the anticipated users, the various organizations involved in setting up the relevant regulations, and by the public.

8.3.3 Acceptance

Acceptance of CAD is on the way to becoming less of a technical and economical issue. CAD has demonstrated that it can

- improve product quality;
- reduce lead times;
- relieve skilled designers from routine work;
- improve design and production economy by enforcing standards;
- make it easier to maintain accurate documentation.

But, at least in some European countries, CAD is faced with growing opposition because of social aspects [17]. CAD reduces the amount of routine work and, hence, eliminates jobs of the routine kind. Skilled personnel can move into more demanding positions; and such positions are created by CAD, too. But workers who are not flexible enough may indeed lose their jobs. A society which is shifting its emphasis from growth to security, will hesitate to accept these consequences of CAD. As a by-product of this trend, more attention is being directed toward the ergonomic design of CAD systems and terminals. Their appearance will be increasingly influenced by ergonomic considerations.

8.4 Standardization

An important task to be attacked in the next years is the standardization of operations, representation schemes, and data formats for CAD applications [19]. Some promising results have already been achieved in the area of two-dimensional graphics with GKS [12], and also for the definition of product data in mechanical engineering [20]. Even these two achievements have indicated that considerable efforts will be required to avoid incompatibilities between standards.

8.5 Summary

The present trends of CAD with respect to hardware, software, system configuration, and social aspects have been briefly summarized. Key issues that will have a significant influence on the future of CAD were identified.

Whatever the future of CAD will be, it is likely to provide another proof of "*Hofstadter's Law*: It always takes longer than you expect, even when you take into account Hofstadter's Law." [21]

8.6 Bibliography

[1] J. Hatvany: Trends and Developments in Computer-Aided Design. In: B. Gilchrist (ed.): Information Processing 1977. Amsterdam (1977) North-Holland, p. 267–271.

[2] C. Schuenemann: Speicherhierarchie-Aufbau und Betriebsweise. Informatik-Spektrum 1 (1978) 1, pp. 25–36.

[3] G. Spur, F.-L. Krause: Einordnung von CAD-Systemen. Markt und Technik 6 (12. Febr. 1982), pp. 41–50.

[4] R. Lindner: Aspects of Interactive Computer Graphics, Applications and Systems. Proc. 3rd European Electro-Optics Conference, Geneva (1976), pp. 274–288.

[5] R. Lindner: A Processor for Real-Time TV Raster Scan Conversion. Computers and Graphics 4 (1979) 1 pp. 23:28.

[6] J.J. Allan III, K. Bø: A Survey of Commercial Turnkey CAD/CAM Systems. Dallas (1978) Productivity Int.

[7] "CAD systems": Marktübersicht. Markt und Technik 6 (12. Febr. 1982), pp. 70–74.

[8] G. Spur, F.L. Krause: Stages of Integration for Computer Supported Design and Manufacturing Process Planning. Proc. Symp. Computer Aided Design in Mechanical Engineering (1976), pp. 67–82.

[9] N. Cullmann: Software Distribution in Satellite Graphics Systems. Angewandte Informatik 1 (1979), pp. 63–70.

[10] Programming Language Statistics: Die Computer Zeitung 12 (3. März 1982) 5, p. 14.

[11] K.R. Dittrich, R. Hüber, P.C. Lockemann: Methodenbanksysteme: Ein Werkzeug zum Maßschneidern von Anwendersystemen. Informatik-Spektrum 2 (1979) 2, pp. 194–203.

[12] "GKS": ISO TC97/SC5/WG2 N117; Draft International Standard ISO/DP 7942; Information Processing, Graphical Kernel System (GKS). 1982.

[13] ACM/SIGGRAPH: Status Report of the Graphics Standards Planning Committee of ACM/SIGGRAPH. Computer Graphics 13 (1979) 3.

[14] J.-C. Latombe: Artificial Intelligence and Pattern Recognition in Computer Aided Design. Amsterdam (1978) North-Holland.

[15] N.J. Nilsson: Principles of Artificial Intelligence. Heidelberg (1982) Springer-Verlag.

[16] G. Bechmann, K. Huxdorff, R. Vahrenkamp, R. Wehrle, B. Wingert: Auswirkungen des Einsatzes informationsverarbeitender Technologien untersucht am Beispiel von Verfahren des rechnerunterstützten Konstruierens und Fertigens (CAD/CAM). Eine sozialwissenschaftliche Begleituntersuchung. Ergebnisse einer Pilotuntersuchung. Report KfK-CAD 114, Kernforschungszentrum Karlsruhe (1978).

[17] J.J. Allan III: CAD in the U.S. and in Europe. In: J. Encarnação, W. Straßer (eds.): CAD-Fachgespräch (GI-Jahrestagung Berlin 1978) Report Fachgebiet Graphisch-Interaktive Systeme. Report GRIS 78-3. Techn. Hochschule Darmstadt (1978).

[18] D.J. Humcke, D.P. Kent: Ergonomics of a Large Interactive Graphics Operation. Computer Aided Design 9 (1977) 4, pp. 262–266.

[19] H. Nowacki: Notwendigkeit und Möglichkeiten der Standardisierung im CAD-Bereich. VDI-Berichte 413 (1981), pp. 107–118.

[20] IGES: Engineering Drawing and Related Documentation Practices — Digital Representation for Communication of Product Definition Data. Proposed American National Standard Y14.26M (Section 1, 2, 3, and 4). The American Society of Mechanical Engineers, New York, August 1980.

[21] D.R. Hofstadter: Gödel, Escher, Bach: An Eternal Golden Braid. New York (1980) Vintage Books, p. 152.

9 Subject Index

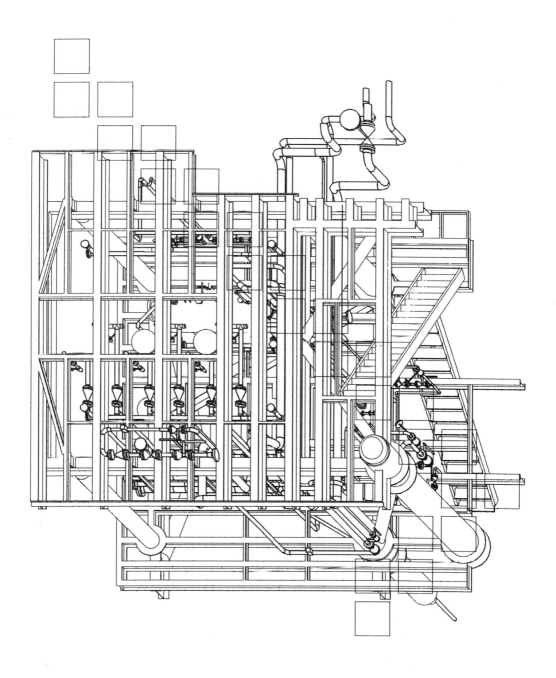

3-D plant layout
(courtesy of Compeda, London, UK)

10 Author Index

Page numbers in *italics* refer to the bibliography

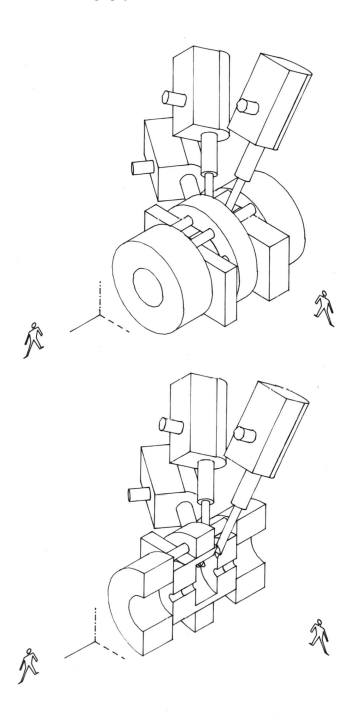

Schematic perspective (above) and section view (below) of the central cell of an mirror type fusion reactor experiment (courtesy of Kernforschungszentrum, Karlsruhe)

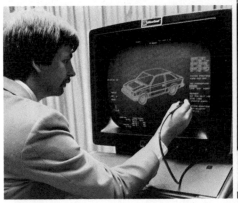

5.12

5.15

5.16

5.17

5.26

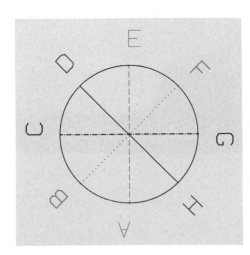

Fig. 5.12. A vector refresh display operated with a light-pen (courtesy of Lundy, Uxbridge, UK), see page 164

Fig. 5.15. A storage tube display (courtesy of Tektronix, Beaverton, USA), see page 169

Fig. 5.16. A raster color display (courtesy of Tektronix, Beaverton, USA), see page 170

Fig. 5.17. Example of workstation design (courtesy of CALMA, Sunnyvale, USA), see page 171

Fig. 5.26. GKS example 3 output, see page 185

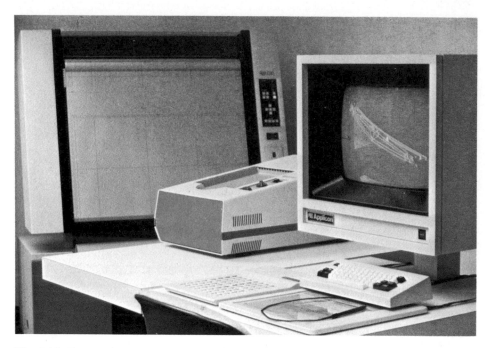

Fig. 5.18. Example of workstation design (courtesy of Applicon, Burlington, USA), see page 171

Fig. 5.20. Example of workstation design (courtesy of Ferranti Cetec Graphics Ltd., Edinburgh, UK), see page 171

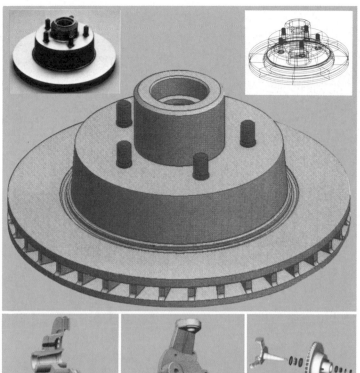

6.15

6.41

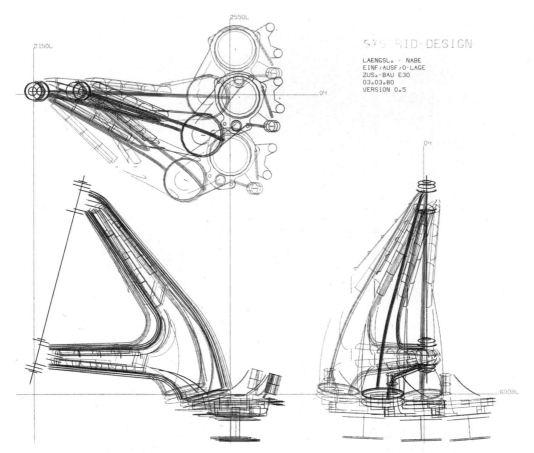

Fig. 7.8. Overlay representation of three positions of a car's front wheel support (courtesy of Bayerische Motorenwerke, München), see page 301

◀ **Fig. 6.15.** A perspective view of a 3D solid model (color raster graphics) (courtesy of Applicon, Burlington, USA), see page 248

Fig. 6.41. Representation of a function of two variables by pseudo-coloring, see page 279

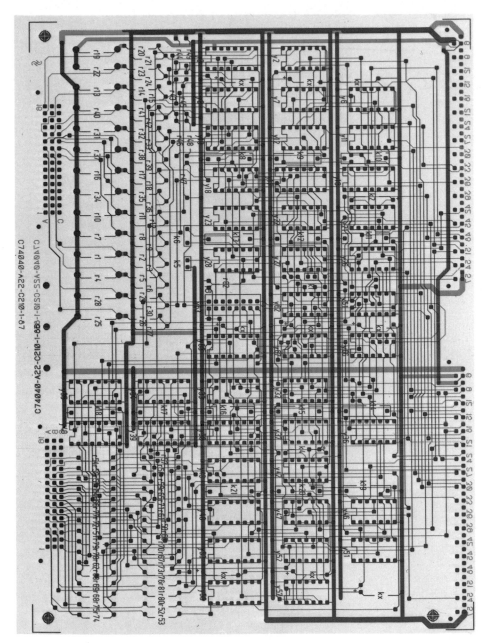

Fig. 7.14. Overlay picture of three layers of a printed wiring board (courtesy of Siemens, Erlangen), see page 301

Fig. 7.16. 3D solid modelling in mechanical engineering (courtesy of Applicon, Bur- ▶ lington, USA), see page 305

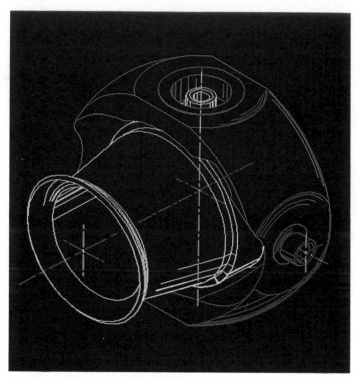

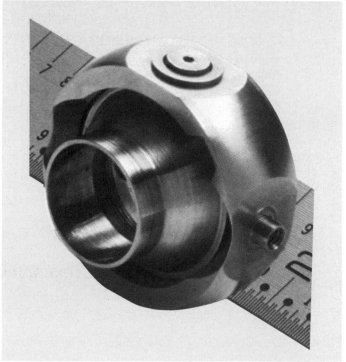

7.16

Symbolic Computation

Managing Editors:
J. L. Encarnação
(TH Darmstadt)
P. Hayes
(University of Rochester)

Devoted to topics in non-numeric computation, this new series currently embraces artificial intelligence and computer graphics, but will be open to fields ranging from simulation and modeling to information retrieval and text processing. The treatment of these topics will emphasize general computational concepts rather than concentrate on specific applications, but will also provide the necessary tools for solving practical problems.

As each speciality grows in importance – as is already the case with artificial intelligence and computer graphics – a subseries will be created to afford it adequate coverage.

The textbooks and monographs in **Symbolic Computation** will prove a reliable and up-to-date source of information for researchers, students and practitioners in all the fields served.

Springer-Verlag
Berlin
Heidelberg
New York
Tokyo

G. Enderle, K. Kansky, G. Pfaff

Computer Graphics Programming

GKS – The Graphics Standard

1983. ISBN 3-540-11525-0

The book covers computer graphics programming on the base of the Graphical Kernel System, GKS. GKS is the first international standard for the functions of a computer graphics system. It offers capabilities for creation and representation of two-dimensional pictures, handling input from graphical workstations, structuring and manipulating pictures, and for storing and retrieving them. It presents a methodological framework for the concepts of computer graphics and established a common understanding for computer graphics systems, methods and applications. This book gives an overview over the GKS concepts, the history of the GKS design and the various system interfaces. A significant part of the book is devoted to a detailed description of the application of GKS functions both in a Pascal and a Fortran-language environment.

Springer-Verlag
Berlin
Heidelberg
New York
Tokyo